ÉBOUÉ

Félix Eboué early in his career. Courtesy of Elie Gratien.

ÉBOUÉ

BRIAN WEINSTEIN

NEW YORK
OXFORD UNIVERSITY PRESS
1972

PREFACE

PROFESSOR RUPERT EMERSON of Harvard University suggested I write this book, and two other guides, Martin Kilson and Pierre Alexandre, insisted. Governor General Robert Delavignette gave me glimpses into and a feel for the Third Republic and its empire to whose evolution he contributed in important ways. Then, with the benefit of grants from the Joint Committee on African Studies of the American Council of Learned Societies and the Social Science Research Council and Howard University, I traveled intermittently from 1967 to 1970 in France, Africa, Guyane, and the West Indies to speak with those who knew Eboué, to consult their personal archives, and to examine official files when open.

The most important set of private papers were those belonging to Governor General Eboué himself, and I am profoundly grateful to his widow, Madame Eugénie Eboué-Tell, former Senator, and to his daughter, Madame Ginette Fontaine-Eboué, for having opened the family archives for the first time to a researcher and for having permitted me to study personal correspondence and diaries therein without restriction. They, like all other members of the family and over eighty more persons on four continents, granted me many hours of their time for interviews which form an important part of this book.

In spite of the importance of the Eboué archives and the insights provided by interviews, this study is not complete. At the time of my research French colonial archives were only partially available, and I was unable to examine British archives for 1940, a key year. Although I gleaned much information from telegrams, letters, and reports which the late General de Gaulle very kindly permitted me to study from World War II and which the American State Department provided for my perusal for the period 1940-1944, and from other documents found in private archives not mentioned here, many gaps remain. These gaps are perhaps more obvious to me and the scholar than to most interested readers, but they are important nonetheless.

Within the rules governing the use of official archival material, archivists in French archives in Paris and at Aix-en-Provence, in Guadeloupe, Africa, and the United States provided basic documentation. Mademoiselle Marie-Antoinette Ménier, who claims after ten years of association to be accustomed to my research habits, Madame Pouliquen, Jean-Claude Hervieux, Colonel Chapel, Oumar Bah, Mbenguia Marien, Dr. Arthur Kogan, Mrs. Dorothy Porter of Howard University, M. U. Agomuoh, and J. Winch helped me, and I am grateful to them. Pierre Kalck and Professor Eric de Dampierre helped me understand the rich history of the Central African Republic. Jean Cazenave de la Roche, Mayor Ulrich Sophie, and Albert Maurice, authors of earlier books in French, generously offered their assistance.

Professors Mercer Cook, Daniel Racine, and Pierre Alexandre read an earlier version of the manuscript and offered suggestions for improvement as did William Benjamin Cohen and David Gardinier, authors of important studies of French and African history. Jordan Ngubane, Leslie Rubin, and Marie Perinbaum offered suggestions on parts of the manuscript. Don Herdeck, of Georgetown University, looking at my work from a different point of view, insisted biography was more than social science, and Léon G. Damas, poet, provided unique insights.

Mrs. Patricia Falk Feeley and Mrs. Patricia Cristol guided this study through Oxford University Press from manuscript to book.

BRIAN WEINSTEIN

INTRODUCTION

A BIOGRAPHY of Governor General Félix Eboué seemed to me a strange project even though a fine scholar and wise friend suggested that I write it. I dismissed the idea at first, because the independence of African states, the challenge of racism around the world, and the affirmation of African identity impelled the writer to search for revolutionaries whose lives and accomplishments had earlier been suppressed in the interests of colonialism and racism. Like so many others, I felt the need to restore some balance: To study the deeds of black men or black women would mean to find the Frantz Fanons, the Dr. Kings, the Shakas, or the Malcolm Xs. How could one, in this age of general condemnation of colonializing, write about a black man who had served a European power so well that they buried him in the pantheon of their heroes?

Every French history book devotes a few lines to Félix Eboué, the black colonial administrator who began the rally to the Free French Forces of General de Gaulle in World War II and who thus helped keep France in the war on the side of the Allies. Four biographies written by men who knew him intimately or who admired him sincerely were published after the beginning of nationalist movements in Africa, and it seemed that one of the purposes of their publication was to discourage Africans who might ask for independence from France. The authors, two of whom were black Frenchmen, appeared eager to demonstrate that a black man could be completely assimilated and accepted as a Frenchman. Even more pervasive was Eboué's picture which appeared on colonial money and colonial publications; speakers invoked his memory in debates concerning the colonies from 1944, the year of his death, to 1960, the year of independence for France's African possessions.

While I was working on another project in the Bibliothèque Nationale in Paris, I was told that an essential book needed in connection with another project would take considerable time to locate. As I waited, it occurred to me to re-read two Eboué biographies, one by René Maran, his friend from school days, and one by Jean Cazenave de la Roche, his administrative collaborator for several years.

Maran and Cazenave de la Roche presented a glossy public image of their subject, I thought, and only hinted at a profounder complexity. They both implied that his life had at times been difficult, possibly for reasons of color, but that he had moved more or less cheerfully and inexorably toward the heroic role he was to play in World War II. They said enough to draw me emotionally to Eboué (even though I considered myself anti-colonialist) but not enough to convince me that the whole story had been told. I also thought they had not dealt very much with the context in which Eboué lived.

Two quite different references to Eboué by Frantz Fanon, whose anti-colonial writings are now read all over the world, surprised me. He wrote about his admiration for Eboué in an essay called "West Indians and Africans" and in his book *Black Skin White Masks*. In the first he said:

> . . . there had been Eboué, who though a West Indian, had spoken to the Africans at the Brazzaville conference and had called them "my dear brothers." And this brotherhood was not evangelical; it was based on color. The Africans had adopted Eboué.[1]

And in the second he wrote of a black man portrayed in a novel by René Maran who leaves Africa saying it is not his home and who wants to be done with Africa:

> When we read such passages we cannot help thinking of Félix Eboué, unquestionably a Negro, who saw his duty quite differently. . . .[2]

[1] "West Indians and Africans," in *Toward the African Revolution: Political Essays*, trans. Haakon Chevalier (New York: Grove Press, 1967), p. 25.
[2] *Black Skin White Masks: The Experiences of a Black Man in a White World*, trans. Charles Lam Markmann (New York: Grove Press, 1967), p. 71.

A French writer then suggested I base any final decision whether or not to attempt the book on the original materials, increasingly available as archives opened with the passage of time.

The widow of one of Eboué's best friends, René Maran, permitted me to study twenty letters written by the Governor General. References in the letters raised many questions in my mind, for he wrote about politics, colonial policy, art, and family affairs, and I was startled to find the name of a well-known black American philosopher, Alain Leroy Locke, who had taught at Howard. A rapid survey of other possible sources indicated that documents not previously exploited would be difficult to obtain. During the period of research—1967 to 1970—French archives were open only up to 1920, and some colonial documents written before that period had not yet been arranged for research. One of the members of the Eboué family graciously talked with me and showed me some family pictures but indicated that the family archives were not immediately available. Scholars familiar with the African countries where Eboué had worked gloomily reported that no one remembered him and that, moreover, Africans had destroyed archives from the colonial period. A white Frenchman whom many considered a close friend of Eboué showed himself jealous of his contemporary's fame and more interested in talking about himself than about any other subject. "Don't be discouraged," insisted Alfâ Ibrâhîm Sow, an African poet, "Go to Eboué's birthplace and begin at the beginning. Go to Guyane."

Guyane was indeed the beginning of my documentation both written and oral. Here lived Camille Lhuerre, one of Eboué's best friends, and here I found some of the future administrator's school records. More important than the occasional detail about Eboué's life was the context and milieu of Cayenne, his birthplace, and a city which has not very much changed since the nineteenth century. Seeing his mother's house did not mean I could hear his voice but it drew me closer to him. Participating even briefly in the rhythm of life in Cayenne did not mean that I could join him for an afternoon rum punch or that we could discuss problems of economic development, but it gave me a sense of the concerns of Guyanese.

After the visit to Cayenne other sources of information revealed themselves in the Caribbean, in France, and in Africa where the mention of Eboué's name opened doors that I feared might remain shut to me. There was personal correspondence, which Eboué kept meticulously and which his widow very generously permitted me to study, and other archives which opened. General de Gaulle allowed me to study some of his archives from World War II. I began to interview people who had known Eboué; more than eighty of his friends and associates listed below, received me and talked of their memories of him.

By hearing recounted a comment he made in a moment of discouragement, reading a letter to his father-in-law, discovering a cigarette burn on a document, I gradually acquired a sense of the man. By traveling to his homeland and then to every place he worked I began to get a sense of the context in which he was formed and which determined much of his life. I found that I was in the process of writing a biography of Governor General Félix Eboué without ever having made a conscious decision to do so. I realized I had never come to a conclusion about whether he was "good" or "bad," a conclusion which seemed irrelevant and presumptuous anyway. He was an interesting, complex man who made an impact on history, sufficient reason to write about him or about anyone else.

The following were interviewed: Madame Eugénie Eboué-Tell, Madame Ginette Fontaine-Eboué, Commandant Charles Eboué, Mr. Henry Eboué, Mr. Robert Eboué, Mr. Yves Gratien, Mr. Elie Gratien, Governor General Robert Delavignette, Madame Camille René-Maran, Mr. René Isambert, His Excellency Gabriel d'Arboussier, President Gaston Monnerville, Mayor Ulrich Sophie, Mr. A. Côme-Corneille, Madame E. Barat, Senator Marius Moutet, Governor General Henri Laurentie, Mr. Jean Cazenave de la Roche, His Excellency Mohammad Bechir Sow, President Othman Hanoun, Mr. Hetman, Mr. Sokambi Jean-Marie, Mr. Antoine Darlan, Mr. Louis Courbain, Chief Hadji, Chief Mbagolo François, Chief Wangaye, Mr. Herbert Pepper, Madame Roger Dévigne, Mr. Michel Lohier, Madame Frédériska Monlouis, Mr. Camille Lhuerre, Mr. Albert Darnal, Mr. Nafyn, Mlle. G. Archimède, Mr. Philippe Pain, Dr. Gabriel François-Julien, Mlle.

Paullette Nardal, Madame Antoine Wiltord, Mr. Marius Larcher, Mr. L.-C. Giles, Major G. Allen, Sir Robert Parr, Sir Charles Woolley, Mr. Jules Ninine, Mr. André Ninine, Mr. Roger Fortuné, Governor General R. Bargues, Mr. L. Boutin, Mr. Gaston-Joseph, Dr. Georges Boussenot, Madame Raoul Boniteau, Mr. André Haliar, Governor P.-O. Lapie, Mr. Georges Wormser, Count Joseph Reste de Roca, Mr. Henri Delmont, Colonel Chapel, Madame Béatrice Blacher, Mr. Ngao Pierre, Madame Clémentine Sokambi, Mr. Zinga Pirioua, Mayor Sokambi Achille, Reverend Gust Pearson, Mr. Sondjio Pierre, Mr. Naud, Mayor Fatrane, Mr. René Sadier, Chief Domatchi, Mr. Gaombali Abel, Mr. Georges Tourot, His Excellency Jean-Rémy Ayouné, Mr. Xavier Bellouard, Mr. Georges Céleste, Consul General Laurence Taylor, Mr. Ferdinand d'Alexis, Mr. Alexandre Buffon, Mr. Alexis Picut, President René Pleven, Mr. Jean Poupel, Mr. René Clap, Mr. Pierre Pélisson, Mr. H. Fourny, Governor Raphael Saller, Senator H. J. Lémery, Mr. Léon Damas, General Adolphe Diagne, Madame Villevieille.

CONTENTS

LIST OF ILLUSTRATIONS

LIST OF MAPS

Map design by David Lindroth

ÉBOUÉ

What is there to do if not to isolate one's self from a world that rejects you, and to analyze it? Such has been my conduct to this day. And such no doubt will continue to be my conduct until death arrives to deliver me from the complex that is suffocating me.

Jean Veneuse in René Maran, Un Homme pareil aux autres

Playing the game means liberating one's self from what the modern idiom calls the inferiority complex, by a total repudiation of prejudice . . . free of the prejudices which breed small and great human troubles I would be proud to bring about better understanding among different . . . groups . . . within a French context. . . . I shall pay particular attention to economic and social questions, as important to me as they must be to any Administrator worthy of the name.

Félix Eboué in speeches in letters

I

COLONIAL CHILDHOOD

ANY BLACK CHILD born and growing up in French Guyane in the last quarter of the nineteenth century would have felt the stagnation of the country, and if he had the brains and the means, would have tried to get out. This is not to say that Cayenne, the principal—the only—city, lacked potential for development. On the contrary, it had a port on the Atlantic; gold had been discovered in the hinterland; development projects had been started, but they failed, some quite disastrously. Underpopulation, difficult communications, hostile neighbors, the attractiveness of other areas, all contributed to Guyane's relative neglect although it had been a French colony for more than two hundred years.

The monarchy had, in the seventeenth century, gained control of Guyane, on the South American littoral between Brazil and Suriname, as well as the islands of Martinique and Guadeloupe in the Caribbean, and Réunion, off the East African coast. After the Napoleonic Wars of the nineteenth century these four possessions, subsequently called the "Old Colonies," plus scattered trading stations in Africa and in India were all that France had left of its first overseas empire that had once included Canada, the Louisiana Territory, part of India, and Santo Domingo.

White settlers, who could exert some pressure on Paris for development funds and protection, preferred Guadeloupe, Martinique, and Réunion to Guyane. In 1842, for example, Guade-

loupe had 126,000 inhabitants, including 26,000 whites; Martinique had 102,000 with 10,000 whites; Réunion had 93,000,
including about 20,000 whites; but Guyane, larger in territory
than the three islands combined, had a total population of only
22,500, including slightly more than 1000 Europeans.[1]

A reason for the small white-settler population, which gave advantages as well as disadvantages to the non-whites, was distance
and difficulty of communications with Europe. No ship traveled
directly the 9000 kilometers between France and Cayenne. Europeans went first to the fine natural port at Fort-de-France, Martinique, or to the island of Saint Thomas where they could wait for
a monthly ship, *"L'Annexe,"* which sailed down the South American coast to arrive finally in eight days at Cayenne. Another reason for the population differences between Guyane and the other
old colonies was that the forest and swamp region of Inini, the
interior of the colony, was inaccessible. The area could have been
opened for cultivation, settlement, and economic development if
the French government had been willing or able to spend the
money.

The economies of the old colonies depended almost entirely on
cane cultivation and its products, sugar and rum. African slave
labor planted, cut, and processed the cane, but not all European
settlers were plantation-, distillery-, or mill-owners; some were
quite poor, working as laborers. Not all Africans or men of at
least partial African descent were slaves; a few were plantation-
owners themselves, particularly after the French Revolution. Generally, however, rich people were white and poor people were
black, and on Martinique some whites were very rich.

In addition to sugar, Guyane produced spices, particularly in
the area of Roura, just east of Cayenne, where the Marquis de Lafayette owned the largest plantation, called La Gabrielle. Most
whites of Guyane, unlike absentee owner Lafayette, were certainly not of the French aristocracy, and their economic situation
was not so vastly different from that of the blacks. Those whites
who owned the generally small plantations, or *habitations,* were

[1] Alexandre Moreau de Jonnès, *Recherches statistiques sur l'esclavage colonial et sur les moyens de le supprimer* (Paris: Bourgogne et Martinet, 1842),
p. 29.

more often soldiers of fortune, drifters, and seamen who married local landholding women, black and white.

Absence of a group of rich whites in Guyane, its small population, racial mixing, inter-racial marriage, similarity of living styles lessened the possibilities of violence when slavery was finally abolished. When the French government, influenced by the great abolitionist Victor Schoelcher, freed the slaves in its colonies in 1848 and made all residents of the old colonies French citizens, Guyane remained peaceful while blacks and whites fought in Martinique.

After 1848 Guyane's weak economy deteriorated. In spite of pleas and threats, free men naturally drifted away from the old *habitations* to lead their own lives. Without a stable labor force, crops could not be planted or harvested; people turned to subsistence farming to satisfy their own needs. The discovery of gold in 1855 increased the flight from the land. Guyanese who might have wanted to go into business had difficulty raising the necessary capital because there was no bank, and the Ministry of the Navy, in charge of the colonies until 1894, refused to spend the money necessary for development. An official of the Ministry wrote, for example: "Unfortunately, France's position hardly permits her to do anything for this beautiful country at the moment. The country has no capital, no large *habitations,* little in the way of money."[2]

Deprived of their old sources of labor and unable to become businessmen, landholders contracted with former slavers to bring so-called free laborers from Africa and workers from China and India. These projects were unsuccessful but increased the heterogeneity in an already cosmopolitan community. By the end of the nineteenth century languages from all the continents of the world were spoken in Guyane.

The Guyanese of the coast, overwhelmingly of mixed white and black ancestry, preferred to call themselves "Creole" or "Colored," terms referring to any non-European born in the colony. The Creoles called the hinterland peoples—Indians and escaped slaves who had re-established tribal communities from their mem-

2 Archives Nationales de France, Section d'Outre-Mer (*Infra,* Arch. Nat. SOM), Guyane A 10 (14), Letter, Cayenne, 25 August 1848, from M. Mestro, Directeur des Colonies, to Ministère de la Marine.

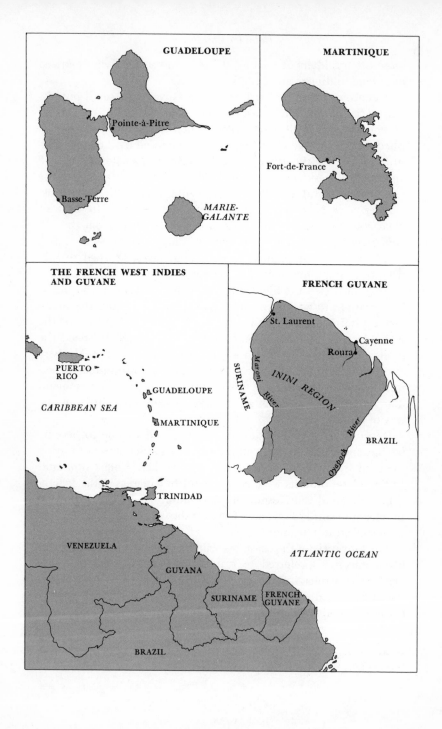

ories of Africa—the "Primitives." They referred to metropolitan Frenchmen as the "Metropolitains" or "Blancs" and locally born whites as "Blancs Créoles" or white Creoles. In Martinique and Guadeloupe the people, who called themselves "Antillais" or Antilleans, had derogatory terms for white Creoles, but this does not seem to have been the case in Guyane.

Because this small mixed population still could not supply an adequate labor force for development, the French government in the 1850's decided to turn Guyane into a prison colony, much to the horror and eternal shame of the Creoles. One of the *bagnes* or prisons off the Guyanese coast, became a synonym for Guyane. The name itself, Devil's Island, expressed best what the prison was. Even today, many years after the official closing of the prisons, it is the one thing that foreigners are likely to know about Guyane.

Metropolitan indifference, by the end of the nineteenth century, was climaxed when the Dutch in Suriname, west of Guyane, claimed a slice of French territory and got it without difficulty. In 1895 Brazilians to the south and east attacked Guyanese gold miners in a remote area presumed to be Guyanese; Creoles demanded action, but Paris hesitated to act militarily. It cared little for Guyane, and it was actively engaged elsewhere building a new overseas empire. French indifference caused consternation in Cayenne in 1896:

> France recoils before Cabral [of Brazil], but she pursues the shadow of Samory [the African]; she abandons the mouth of the Amazon, but she rushes to conquer "the loop" of the Niger . . . our grandchildren won't believe History.[3]

The Swiss arbitrated and in 1899 decided to grant Brazil the disputed area, 260,000 square kilometers of territory. Guyane was thus reduced to an area of about 92,000 square kilometers between the Oyapock and Maroni Rivers. Guyanese shouted betrayal but leading politicians of the day protested that they could do nothing.

After this experience, many people in Cayenne feared complete

3 *La Guyane* (Cayenne), 1 February 1896.

conquest by their neighbors or even by the English-speaking
North Americans. They fought to remain French. Becoming more
French was what the progressives of the time wanted; their conservative enemies in France were trying to deprive black men in
the colonies of the possibility of integration into the French nation. No one talked of independence.

Despite much French indifference and even hostility, the four
old colonies already had by the end of the nineteenth century a
political status similar to that of departments in metropolitan
France. They participated in the French political system. A law
of 3 May 1854 and subsequent decrees set up municipal government and a popularly elected General Council in each colony.
The Council voted the yearly budget proposed by the governor
whose role was similar to that of the prefects in France. Citizens,
black and white, voted for municipal councilors, members of the
General Council, and representatives to the French parliament.
The first generation of men born free voted for whites generally
before 1900, but the second generation began to vote for Creoles.

Despite the fact that elections were often fraudulent and controlled by the governor, they held out some hope. When a rumor
spread that someone in France had suggested that Guyanese be
deprived of their French citizenship and reduced to the level of
subjects in the new African colonies and deprived of their elected
councils, people showed their consternation, protesting that they
were not Africans, and hoped their elected officials would act.
There were riots in some places. In 1900 the Creoles successfully
fought the proposal of Governor Mouttet to transform the colony's poor secondary school into a vocational institute whose graduates, working as carpenters, would supposedly better "meet the
needs of the colony" than graduates who had followed the classical metropolitan curriculum.

Jobs as skilled laborers, civil servants in the local prison administration, and gold miners were always available in Guyane,
but many Creole families wanted more for their children; citizenship and the possibilities of education in France provided the
route. Youngsters with ambition and some means, therefore, left
for France to try to assimilate themselves socially and culturally
as individuals into the French nation, even though their country

View of Roura, 1967.

as a whole could not integrate itself administratively and politically as it wished. Lost for the most part to their own colony, these men and women often contributed in important ways to France and sometimes made an impact on French history.

ÉBOUÉ

Félix Eboué, born a free man and a French citizen in Cayenne 26 December 1884, grew up during the desperate Guyanese struggle for development and recognition, and it marked him for life. In his first seventeen years he saw the attempt to deprive Guyane of academic education; if successful, it would have condemned him to live in Cayenne working at some menial job. He felt the threats of revocation of citizenship, and of further territorial losses. Intensifying his sense of the position and history of Guyane were stories his grandmother, who lived with his family, told of slavery.

Eboué knew that his maternal and paternal great grandparents, the Léveillés and the Eboués, had been brought from Africa in the early nineteenth century to work on *habitations* at Roura. The fact that his great grandfather was called Eboué or Héboué or Eboé, an African name from Ivory Coast or Igbo-speaking areas of Nigeria, must have meant that he occupied a special position or that he had come to Guyane under special circumstances. Otherwise, the slave-owner would have given him a Christian or fanciful name. The family, which kept cowrie shells as a souvenir of Africa, believed that their ancestors came from a royal African lineage and that traders with whom they had been dealing kidnapped them from the river village where they lived. It is impossible to find the truth of the matter now.[4]

Héboué died before 1848, the year of liberation. His freed daughter moved from the *habitation* where she once thought she would spend her life to the area of Approuague. Here she farmed

---

[4] Professor Debien, French slave-trade scholar, has written that there are no lists of Guyanese slaves with their "nation" for the nineteenth century (Letter to Brian Weinstein, 2 December 1967). Yves Gratien told me about the family tradition (Interview, 3 May 1968). In the mid-nineteenth century the supposedly free African laborers were recruited in Gabon, according to Frédéric Bouyer, *L'Amour d'un monstre—D'Chimbo le Rongou: scènes de la vie créole* (Paris: Degorce-Cadot, 1866), pp. 18-19.

and in 1851 gave birth to a son, whom she names Yves Urbain Eboué. He moved, as a youth, to Cayenne.

The Léveillés had remained in the Roura area after 1848 and continued to work on the *habitation* where they had been slaves. In 1856 their daughter Palmyre gave birth to twin girls. One of them, Aurélie, moved to Cayenne, where she met and married Yves Eboué.

Yves and Aurélie Eboué had five children, four sons and one daughter.[5] Their youngest son's full name was Adolphe Félix Sylvestre Eboué. They chose the first name to honor his godfather, the local merchant Adolphe Bailly, the third to honor Madame Eboué's favorite brother, Sylvestre Léveillé, and they probably chose Félix because the name was popular that year. Almost everyone called him Félix or "Fé-Fé" for short.

Unlike some of his friends the young Félix Eboué appeared to have little or no European ancestry. Rich black in color, with full lips, broad nose, and tightly curled hair, "he was so black he was blue" some Guyanese said. In a society where whiteness and Caucasian features were the standard for beauty Eboué heard many jibes from fairer-colored schoolmates and whites about his striking Negro-ness.

If he had wanted to punish a mocking contemporary, he could easily have done so. He was a comparatively tall teenager with a strong chest and powerful arms, and he could outrun most. But, remembering local aphorisms often repeated by his mother extolling resignation and patience, like "Patience a maître malice" or "With patience we can thwart all the plats hatched against us by evil people," Eboué early in life began to practice maintaining his self-control. He therefore seemed placid in crowds or in the face of provocation even though he felt tense or angry. With intimate friends he exploded in laughter or complaint about an event that might have taken place some time before. He remembered and brooded about upsetting experiences, but instead of taking revenge or developing the self-hate described by Fanon in

---

5 Yves, Jr., born in 1874 or 1875, Maximilien in 1877, Edgar in 1880, Félix in 1884, and the daughter, Cornélie, in 1890 (all the above information comes from Arch. Nat. SOM, Guyane, Etat-Civil and Répertoires des Notaires de Cayenne).

Black Skin White Masks, he turned the experiences into anecdotes which, told to amuse his friends, covered over the bitterness that he may have felt.

Eboué could expect little comfort from his father, or from his brothers, who died young. His father spent many months of the year away from Cayenne searching for gold; eventually he became the assistant director of a gold placer called "Dieu-Merci." When he came home, however, visitors frequented his house for the traditional rum punch just before midday or in the late afternoon.

The Eboué house was in the middle of town, on a corner of the streets Christophe Colombe and Richelieu. A modest but typical traditional Guyanese structure it was built of wood, two stories high with slat windows and a courtyard where Madame Eboué kept chickens. Visitors sitting in the front room felt a good breeze, highly appreciated in the hot equatorial climate.

The children listened to visitors exchange stories with their father about their rather insecure business and the "primitives" or Africans, Bonis and Saramacas, and Indians who worked for them. Those who had been attacked by Brazilians talked about French indifference to Guyane and about the loss of income with the annexation by Brazil of the disputed land in 1899. They complained about the slow arrival of new equipment expected from Bordeaux. Adolphe Bailly, young Félix's godfather and supplier of goods and equipment to the gold men, would sigh that the monthly ship was delayed. "Maybe someday communications with the metropole will be better."

In the Eboué home as in many others a prime topic of conversation was white prisoners and themselves. Some of the prisoners allowed some freedom had robbed people in Cayenne. Creoles took a measure of amusement in seeing that friends working in the prison administration had whites as house servants.

The elder Eboué was neither a figure in local politics nor a Freemason like most of the male elite of the colony, but in a town of 8000 to 10,000—Cayenne's population at the end of the nineteenth century—people knew him. He was elected to the municipal council for a relatively short term, and he had some important relatives in the administration. His half-brother, Maximilien Liontel, was attorney general of Guyane for a few years; Liontel

south of France because they assumed the warmer climate would be better for their children, who were unaccustomed to European winters. Most attended the Lycée Montaigne.

The Lycée Montaigne de Bordeaux, Eboué's school from 1901 to 1905, consisted of one rather large building. Formerly a convent, it had three wings which educational authorities used to separate students into lower classes, intermediate classes, and terminal classes preparing for the baccalaureate. The third wing was also used for older students studying for entry into the Naval School.

In 1901 students in the lycée could choose modern or classical studies, modern languages being emphasized in the former. Eboué took his first school year in the modern section and won first prizes in French and in English. Teachers noted he did poorly in religious instruction, of little interest to him in spite of his mother's attachment to the Church. He wrote home about his grades, and Man-Lie sent all the money she could. She may, in fact, have mortgaged her house. Fortunately, the second year Guyane renewed his half-scholarship, and Eboué justified the confidence of his mother and the colony by making the honor roll and winning first prizes in geography and history of art. He continued to win several prizes each year, and not just in academic fields.

Friendship and extracurricular activities interested Eboué just as much as schoolwork, if not more. Creoles and Antilleans were not discriminated against in Bordeaux, although they were regarded sometimes as curiosities and had to learn to endure occasional cruel jokes. They made many friends among white schoolmates but tended to group together, sharing rooms in the city. On Sundays and holidays local families—Antilleans living in the area or a few whites—invited Creole students to their homes. Eboué went to these dinners with "Petit Camille" Lhuerre, a close friend from Guyane, occasionally with a new friend, René Maran, born in Martinique of Guyanese parents, and he was invited to the home of René Méneau, a white student whose family lived in the city. With these teenagers Eboué felt relaxed and spoke his mind. He expected loyalty from them and was himself intensely loyal to them.

The rugby team of the lycée at Bordeaux, 1902, with Eboué fourth from the left in the back row, and Camille Lheurre at the far right, hands in pockets. Courtesy of Camille Lheurre.

Eboué and Lhuerre loved the comradeship of team sports and joined a club, Les Muguets, that met regularly for rugby matches and racing. A fine sports field had been built in the suburbs, and Les Muguets played against other teams there. As a lycéen eighteen years old, Eboué was about five feet nine inches tall, thin, and had a grace of movement not easily forgotten. Sixty years later a former student at Bordeaux recalled seeing him on the playing field even though they had never met: "I remember a handsome deep black athlete. I was then just an enthusiastic beginner in rugby but I knew enough to admire his finesse."[11]

In the championship racing contest for southwestern France Eboué ran the hundred-meter event and came in second. He then went on to Paris for the nation-wide contest and came in third. Camille Lhuerre avidly followed his friend's exploits, and they exchanged pictures. Eboué gave "Petit Camille" a picture of him-

[11] Letter from H. Martin, Paris, 24 October 1967.

self taken in Paris with a humorous inscription referring to himself as Apollo.[12]

Eboué's relationship with René Maran was more intellectual; they studied philosophy together, and Maran, then beginning to write, showed his older friend poems which extolled stoic values. In one poem called "From a Dictation by Marcus Aurelius" Maran wrote that the truly wise person must master his own emotions and have a sense of Destiny in life. Master of himself, aware of his Destiny, the intelligent man will move directly and calmly through life to the inevitable end.[13] Eboué and Maran decided they were stoics.

It is seldom possible to determine satisfactorily why one is attracted to a particular philosophical system or another. Currents of thought articulated by Sorel, Barrès, Bergson and others in the early twentieth century in France encouraged nationalism, faith in intuition, and study of the role of the individual. Eboué studied the stoics and the pythagoreans. These ideas clearly comforted Eboué at various troubled times. In conversations and correspondence he often cited a phrase from a stoic or a pythagorean to help himself or René Maran bear a disappointment or a humiliating experience. The basic wisdom of many of these phrases resembled the *dolos* and stories Man-Lie had told back in Cayenne and reinforced his early attempts at great self-control.

Most of the people in the old colonies found that Roman Catholicism satisfied their needs for an ethical and moral system. Eboué's generation felt freer than their elders to reject the religion which had supported the monarchy and slavery; they supported the Republic which freed the slaves and extended suffrage and citizenship to the masses. They also were looking for a substitute religion. Stoic philosophy had little to say about the supernatural, but it did provide an ethical system which could appeal to people born in the old colonies who participated in the culture and politics of the empire. Possibly it appealed to them because

12 Camille Lhuerre, "10e anniversaire de la mort du Gouverneur Général Félix Eboué: souvenirs," *Parallèle 5* (Cayenne), 1 June 1954, and Interview with Camille Lhuerre, Cayenne, December 1967.

13 René Maran, "Sous la dictée de Marc Aurèle," *Le Livre du souvenir* (Paris: Présence Africaine, 1958), pp. 116-17.

it was originally elaborated by philosophers among peoples also absorbed within an empire, the Roman Empire, who sought a justification for and a meaning to their lives.

The philosophy consists of more than being able to "grin and bear" the misfortunes of life. It is true that some fatalism is part of the philosophy and Eboué was fond of citing Epictetus' "Some things depend on us and some things do not." On the other hand the Pythagorean *Golden Verses,* a list of precepts and duties toward other people which now sounds rather banal, warned against fatalism: "Note that men are the authors of their own troubles: unfortunate are those who, having happiness in their hands, close their eyes and ears!"[14]

Many other facets of stoic and pythagorean philosophy appealed to Eboué. Some of these ideas were, for example, that man may "overcome the world," an essentially evil world, by "overcoming . . . his own impulses" in the face of pain or pleasure. A person might thus be different from others, black rather than white, and he might come from a place people disdain or make fun of, but he still could become an independent being free from fear or shame: ". . . the withdrawal of the individual personality within itself remained ultimately an essential characteristic in the Stoic idea of life. . . ."[15]

Withdrawal of the personality and self-control, which Eboué had actually practiced before discovering the stoics, does not mean withdrawal from the real world. For the stoic, "life according to Nature and according to reason is a *duty* which the wise man has to fulfill. . . ."[16] Nature commands that man be a social animal, and an elite of virtuous men, friends even across political frontiers, can work together and to lead the world to a new order and harmony. Eboué underlined twice the following passage in the *Golden Verses:*

> Because deadly discord, which is for men an inseparable companion and second nature, harms them without their knowledge, don't let it approach you. Flee it with horror.[17]

---

[14] A. Siouville, *Les Vers d'or de Pythagore* (Paris: Collection du Symbolisme, 1913), p. 21. The phrase cited was underlined by Eboué in his own book.

[15] Wilhelm Windelband, *A History of Philosophy, Volume I: Greek, Roman, Medieval* (New York: Harper and Row, 1958), pp. 168, 170.

[16] *Ibid.,* p. 172.

[17] Siouville, *Les Vers d'or de Pythagore,* p. 21.

Order and harmony "could be grasped and expressed in conceptions" and could be studied through symbols, the pythagoreans said. He bought books on mathematics, music, and symbolism and studied them carefully. They influenced his thought.

In 1937, many years after his initiation to the stoic and pythagorean philosophers, Eboué gave a speech to a high school graduating class in Guadeloupe. The speech, called "Jouez le Jeu" ("Play Fairly" or "Play the Game"), reflected his stoic point of view, for playing is living life with its rules, goals, end. Life, Eboué said, can be likened to one of the games he played as a young man. There are rules, which some people know better than others. The rules, like the pythagorean golden verses, must be studied and followed. Study and education are the beginning of an effort on the part of a superior human being to develop his inner spirit and an independence of mind—"the only real independence"—meaning that one can be spiritually free from the outside world.

Playing means having an independent mind, Eboué said, even when the person is an integral and loyal part of a group; it means disinterestedness, and knowing "when to take the initiative even when circumstances are such that one is alone in taking it. . . ." An independent mind means self-control; it means respecting the values of people of other societies and being able to associate without fear with all members of one's own society, including those above and below oneself.[18]

Self-control, reflection about what an individual can or cannot do, involvement in public affairs to help bring about harmony among the nations, faith in friendship and team effort, respect for different values and civilizations, the unity of mankind, the sense of a particular role to be played by an educated elite were ideas central to the philosophy which Eboué began to formulate for himself in a systematic way in Bordeaux. Maran and Eboué became fast friends and often talked about their philosophy in the many years after they finished their schooling in Bordeaux.

At the beginning of 1905 Eboué was granted the baccalaureate diploma, thus completing his secondary education. Later in the

18 Félix Eboué, "Discours prononcé le 1er juillet 1937 à la distribution des prix du Lycée Carnot," in brochure published at Basse-Terre, 1937.

year he decided to move to Paris for he had chosen the colonial
service as a career and would need to prepare himself for it in the
French capital.

A CAREER

A black Creole with a baccalaureate could have chosen any
branch of the civil service, and Guyanese and Antilleans could
be found in respectable positions in almost every ministry with
the exception of the Ministry of Foreign Affairs.

Officials at the "rue Oudinot," or Ministry of Colonies, particularly encouraged young men from the old colonies to work in
France's new overseas empire in Africa, Madagascar, and Indochina; gentle encouragement to apply at Colonies also came from
other departments where Creoles applied for positions. There
were certainly racist notions in this encouragement—the hope
that blacks might work better with blacks perhaps, and the desire to keep more attractive positions for metropolitan or white
Frenchmen—but equally important was the fact that the colonies
did not attract as many whites as there were posts.

Men from the old colonies looking for secure positions were
therefore a rather high percentage of the colonial administrative
corps. In the history of the corps about 40 per cent of all administrators "did not originate on the mainland [of France]."[19] (This
figure includes Corsica.) In 1910-1911, for example, there were a
hundred and forty-five Guadeloupan, Martiniquan, and Guyanese
officials in the Ministry of Colonies out of a total force of 1394 or
slightly more than 10 per cent. After World War I the percentages
dropped because white veterans joined the service. Whites always
dominated, but the absolute numbers of Creoles and Antilleans
increased.[20]

That a black Creole might decide to become a colonial official
in Africa seems more strange today because of increased sensitivity to race and racial identity. But few Guyanese and Antilleans
associated their destiny with that of Africa; many of them were

[19] William Benjamin Cohen, *Rulers of Empire: The French Colonial Service in Africa: 1880-1960* (unpublished Ph.D. dissertation, Stanford University,
1968), p. 231.
[20] Calculations from the *Bulletin du Ministère des Colonies*.

not particularly African in physical appearance. More important was the fact they were not African in culture. They loved France, wanted French culture to be theirs, and believed that being French was the only way to have a successful career and lead a satisfactory life.

In their attitudes toward the African masses the first Senegalese, Dahomeyan, and Gabonese civil servants differed little from their Antillean colleagues. Those Senegalese with French citizenship who became colonial officials carefully distinguished themselves from peoples in colonies where they worked so that they would not be required to pay the same taxes or be subject to the same humiliating regulations.[21]

Some of these black Antilleans and Senegalese meticulously tried to enlarge the distance between themselves and African peasants through their mode of dress and behavior which might be highly formal. They did so not just for the purpose of enjoying certain rights but also because they feared being mistaken for African subjects by whites who would try to humiliate and degrade them in unbearable ways. On the other hand, some other black officials, writers, and lawyers from the Caribbean identified themselves very strongly with Africa and showed commitment to the struggle for change and even revolution. For most Antilleans and Creoles, however, a position in the colonial service was a position in the French system like any other.

Eboué had, however, given more thought than that to his career in the colonies. His interest in the "rue Oudinot" came from his colonial childhood and his sojourn in a colonial port. Conversations with his uncle, Maximilien Liontel, who had worked in the Ivory Coast, and with Camille Lhuerre's father and uncles who worked in the colonies encouraged him. He had some contact with René Maran's father, Herménégilde, a high-ranking official in Oubangui-Chari, a French colony in Africa. He thus had a good idea of an official's life in Africa, and his acquaintanceships provided him with an introduction to officials at the Ministry.

Eboué could, like a number of his colleagues, have gone to In-

---

[21] H. Oludare Idowu, "Assimilation in 19th Century Senegal," *Cahiers d'Etudes Africaines,* Vol. IX, No. 34, 1969, p. 217.

dochina, but something else attracted him to Africa and traveling as a colonial official was about the only way to get there. In Guyane he had known people born in Africa who were physically like himself, and had grown very conscious of the fact that, as he said to friends many years later, Africa was "the land of my ancestors." Oddly enough, what first excited his interest was the resistance of the Afrikaners against the British in South Africa; he and his schoolmates could not foresee that the blacks would be treated brutally by this supposedly heroic minority. Eboué grew a beard said to resemble that of the Afrikaner leader, Paul Kruger, whose picture he hung in his room. Friends even took to calling him "Kru-Kru."[22]

PARIS

Anyone interested in the colonial service could have applied for entry into the corps of clerks for native affairs, but Eboué decided to aim for the elite corps of administrators who held the most important posts and from whose ranks governors were to be chosen. The best way to enter the corps was through graduation from the Colonial School, "Colo," in Paris.

"Colo," the school at number 2, avenue de l'Observatoire, had been founded in 1889 mainly to train Southeast Asians as colonial officials and aides in their own countries. Concern about the quality of French administrators had soon transformed the institution into a training school for the corps of colonial administrators. After three years—one of preparation for entry and two of formal studies—graduates entered the corps and went to tropical Africa, the four old colonies, or Indochina. For a few years the school also trained colonial magistrates and prison officials; French clerks belonging to the corps of native or civil affairs could take a year of study in order to move up into the administrative corps.[23] Graduates were a minority in the administration until after World War I and tended, like the graduates of other

[22] According to Camille Lhuerre, Interview, Cayenne, December 1967, and in René Maran, *Félix Eboué: grand commis et loyal serviteur 1885-1944* (Paris: Les Editions Parisiennes, 1957), pp. 20-22.

[23] Most of my information about the school comes from Governor General Robert Delavignette, a former director (interviews, Paris, 1967, 1968).

French schools, to prefer each other's company in France and in Africa to that of non-graduates.[24]

In Paris to study, Eboué felt he was in the center of western civilization. He made contact with Antilleans and found a room in a small hotel on the rue Monsieur le Prince, in the heart of the Latin Quarter near the Colonial School. Here he studied a year for entrance to "Colo."

To prepare himself for the examination Eboué studied law, the history of French and European colonization, geography, and English; for the oral part of the exam he concentrated on questions about road construction, hygiene, and accounting like other students. In March 1906 he underwent routine medical tests to make sure his health was good, and he obtained the required police clearance. The school admitted him, and Guyane raised his scholarship to 1500 francs, almost double what he received in high school. Man-Lie continued to send her son as much money as she could.

Lecturers in those early days emphasized theory and legal studies; they came for the most part from the central offices of the Ministry of Colonies and had never been to Africa.[25] Although these men had begun to teach something about African cultures, based on articles written by early explorers, it was not until some years later that a new curriculum included a serious study of African languages and civilizations. A course syllabus for 1908 shows the biases and ignorance of the school, for a professor proposed to discuss the so-called "Inorganic Society-State of Blacks" and "Language—how languages are related to the value of races and the inferiority of black languages."[26]

There is no record that any black student protested against what was obviously a racist-oriented course. Eboué, like other Creoles, thus had to study about the so-called "inferiority" of his own race and dutifully recite back what he had learned. Placid in class, able to joke about the lectures with Camille Lhuerre, he was nonetheless unable to shake off the insults or to

24 Cohen, *Rulers of Empire* p. 43.
25 Interviews with Mr. Gaston-Joseph, July 1967, and with Count Joseph Reste de Roca, August 1968.
26 Assorted documents in Arch. Nat. SOM, Ecole Coloniale.

control his emotions. He became a very heavy cigarette smoker.

The only valuable courses about the colonies were probably the languages. Men in the Indochina section studied the languages of southeast Asia while men specializing in Africa did Arabic, Malagasy, and English. Eboué did well in Malagasy which he had chosen. The only course he appears to have failed was "military instruction"; he and other Creoles were not required to take their military service, like metropolitans, before entering "Colo," and he may have lacked the experience needed to pass. His first year's record was modest all the way around, however; he passed with a cumulative 592.30 points, quite close to the minimum, and ranked thirteenth out of eighteen in the African section.

One reason for the lackluster record was doubtless that Eboué, who celebrated his twenty-second birthday in December 1906, was caught up in enjoying Paris. He socialized, engaged in sports, and attended as many parades or official events as he could get into. Once, dressed in his colonial cadet uniform, he tried to get choice seats in the reviewing stand set up for an important parade. Stopped once or twice by guards Eboué pointed to a friend, probably his fellow student Roger Hellier, and said, "It's all right, all right. He is with me." Finally, when he had almost reached the desired seats, an official stopped him one last time. To Eboué's confident "He is with me," the official replied, "But who are you with?" and then forced him to leave the stand. Eboué told this story several times to friends although the picture he liked to paint of himself was more aggressive than his real character.

Eboué also enjoyed feminine company and seems to have had an Italian mistress. Maran, still in Bordeaux while Eboué was in Paris, corresponded with his friend during this period and later discreetly noted that Eboué knew a young lady who taught him Italian in his room.[27] He joined a sports club, SCUF (Sporting Club Universitaire de France) and played forward on one of its champion football teams. Members of SCUF met regularly in cafés and spent long hours over beer with each other. Camille Lhuerre and Eboué were inseparable, and a new friend, Yvon

[27] Maran, *Félix Eboué*, p. 20.

Delbos, a white student at the elite Ecole Normale Supérieure, joined them. Others were Roger Hellier and Louis Spas, who had the distinction of getting lower grades at "Colo" than Eboué, and Robert Hermine, another Guyanese. His comrades could always count on Eboué for a song, a well-played hand of bridge, or a good story. None seemed to take enough care of their limited funds, for relatives had to lend them money and a few restaurants complained directly to the Colonial School about unpaid bills. Eboué particularly was more generous with his funds than his situation merited.[28]

The second year Eboué moved from his little hotel to the rue de Vaugirard just around the corner and even more in the heart of the student Latin Quarter. Grades showed no improvement for in 1907-1908 he ranked fourteenth out of seventeen in the African section and twenty-third in a total graduating class (including the Indochina section) of twenty-seven. His two friends Roger Hellier and Louis Spas came in at the bottom of the class of 1908, but they all graduated.

AFRICA

After receiving a diploma from the Colonial School in July 1908 Eboué had a physical examination, obtained an official certificate of good "morality" to prove he had not been arrested, and then waited for an assignment.

The Ministry of Colonies personnel division informed the new administrator that he, like his fellow graduates, would have the rank of student-administrator, equivalent to an ensign in the navy, and would be on trial for a year in a colony. They assigned him to Madagascar at first, but a Martinquan classmate, Ferjus, named to the rather unpopular French Congo, asked him to exchange posts, a common occurrence. The Congo was no place for white women, people claimed, and because the man had recently married a Parisian, Eboué, a bachelor and wishing to please his classmate, acquiesced.

In the autumn of 1908 he outfitted himself in colonial shops with pith helmet, folding bed, gun, uniforms, and everything else

28 Lhuerre, Interview, Cayenne, December 1967.

Eboué, second from left in the first row, with his class at "Colo." Ferjus from Martinique, far right, second row. Courtesy of Elie Gratien.

necessary for life in Africa. Then he numbered each valise and listed the entire contents of all of them in a little notebook. He traveled back to Bordeaux to wait for his ship. There he saw Méneau, from high school days, and, of course, René Maran. They visited the lycée and drank in their favorite café. Christmas 1908, the day before his twenty-fourth birthday, Eboué left from Bordeaux to sail down the coast of Africa to Dakar, Freetown, Lagos, and Matadi in the Belgian Congo and then inland to his destination, Brazzaville, a city he would never like. Having left one colony to seek his career and to assimilate, he found himself in another where his Frenchness would eventually be proven.

II

EARLY DAYS IN
OUBANGUI-CHARI, 1909-1921

EBOUÉ found the view of empire from Brazzaville was quite different from the view of empire from a classroom. Beginning in the 1870's and 1880's a nationalist lobby had worked for the extension of French sovereignty into the French Congo, composed of what became Gabon, Moyen-Congo, Oubangui-Chari, and Tchad.[1] By 1909 colonialists in Paris were pointing to maps to show a huge bloc of seemingly rich possessions in Africa, but there were disappointments.

The claims looked good to Frenchmen sensitive about British expansion, angry about the loss of Alsace and Lorraine to the Germans thirty years previously, or worried about their country's low birthrate. Enthusiasts calculated that these colonies in equatorial Africa—added to those in west and north Africa, Indochina, and Madagascar—would send a flow of new resources to France, provide markets, permit an increase in French prestige, and bring France's population to beyond a hundred million, double that of Germany, even if the Africans were subjects and not citizens.[2]

In Brazzaville, the capital of the French Congo, called French

[1] Official spelling, used by the countries themselves, has been adopted here.
[2] Henri Brunschwig has discussed French colonialism in his *Mythes et réalités de l'impérialisme colonial français, 1871-1914* (Paris: Colin, 1960).

Equatorial Africa (Afrique Equatoriale Française) after 1910, the view was less optimistic. Administrators, sent to suppress resistance and organize the colonies, found that instead of the thirty or forty million inhabitants that some nineteenth-century explores "saw," vast regions were, in fact, uninhabited, and the total population did not exceed two or three million, much less than French possessions in west and north Africa. Compared with its immediate neighbors, German-controlled Kamerun and Belgian-controlled Congo, "A.E.F." came out very badly. Instead of rich land and important mineral resources ready for the taking, administrators found only natural rubber, ivory, and skins.

Energetic British, German, and Belgian traders made most of the profits, such as they were. The governors general, named to head the administration of the group, left frequently for Paris to beg subventions and loans from a government generally indifferent or incapable of providing all the funds when needed for the development of communication facilities, mineral exploration, and building construction. France's equatorial possessions in Africa quickly became and always remained the Cinderellas of the new overseas empire.

Lack of financial support from Paris—bitterly resented by the disappointed colonialist lobby—forced officials to depend on local taxes with some irregular subventions from Paris. Because there were few easily exploitable resources, and the small population was generally skeptical about the benefits of French rule, considerable force had to be exerted to collect these taxes. The early history of A.E.F. is marked by a cycle of exactions, revolts, and repressions.

What made matters even worse was the odious concessionary system. Following the example of the Belgians in the Congo, the French government granted huge tracts of land to private companies in 1899. These concessionary companies were, in fact, colonies within colonies; they had control over the resources and the peoples in the territory included in the grant in exchange for a commitment to begin the development programs the French government itself was unwilling to undertake. Although administrators were assigned to survey the activities of the enterprises, any official who objected strongly to what everyone knew were out-

right exploitation, pillage, and even torture and genocide by
agents of the companies would be quietly transferred by his governor to another area. Scandals concerning concessionary companies[3] brought back Pierre Savorgnan de Brazza, who had explored
and claimed the area for France in the 1870's and 1880's, on an
inspection mission in 1905. His report, considered too critical, was
never published, and he died on his way back to France.

In 1911 the government officially ended the concessionary system but a few companies in each colony reorganized and kept
some of their previous rights. They still had considerable power
because they purchased rubber and ivory and later the industrial
crops like cotton and coffee. Africans needed the money earned
from selling local products to these companies or they could not
pay their taxes to the colonial administration; without the taxes,
the administration would have collapsed.

Many colonial officials at the beginning of this century were
no better than the businessmen in their concern for development
or in their treatment of Africans. The first of them lacked not
only education or training, they were riffraff seeking their for-
tunes, ready to yield to the temptations of a situation in which
they had capricious control over the lives of other human beings.
They were, of course, under constant pressure to collect taxes by
whatever means; in addition, they had to recruit workers and
porters to carry goods to and from the hinterland.

Although there are several major rivers in this part of Africa
—the Congo, Oubangui, Ogooué, Chari, Mbomou—they are not
completely navigable. It took several weeks, if not months, to get
from Brazzaville to Tchad by river and by path. Administrators
provided canoers and porters for businesses and government missions; eventually they recruited workers for road construction and
the railroad built from Brazzaville to the sea. They raised black
armies for World War I and World War II and maintained a
local military force. The African men recruited left for areas far
from home. They ate poorly, slept in inadequate lodgings, worked

[3] Catherine Coquery-Vidrovitch has written extensively about the conces-
sions. See bibliography and see Renée Jaugeon, "Les Sociétés d'exploitation
au Congo et l'opinion française de 1890 à 1906," *Revue Française d'Histoire
d'Outre-Mer*, Vol. XLVIII, Nos. 172-73, 1961, pp. 353-437.

too long, and died in staggering numbers. The colony called Oubangui-Chari provided tens of thousands of these workers, porters, and soldiers.

The area between the Oubangui River in the south and the Chari River in the north was named Oubangui-Chari in 1903. Landlocked in the center of Africa, it is today surrounded by Congo, Cameroun, Tchad, Sudan and is called the Central African Republic, an independent state since 1960. The approximately 400,000 people in the colony in 1909, previously decimated by Arab slave raids and sleeping sickness, were the Banda, Baya, Mandjia, Zandé, and Sara speakers living in the savanna which dominates the country, and small groups like the Mbaka, Yakoma, and Banziri in the forest and along the rivers of the south.

Most of these people had little hierarchical authority, and the French eventually created chiefs who would supposedly act as aids to colonial officials. Shortage and rapid turnover of European personnel meant constant change and variation in the relationship between administration and chiefs. Many times administrators lost control of areas which revolted under local leaders, most of whom disliked the French-named chiefs. Graduates of "Colo" shunned Oubangui-Chari. An unstable, weak administration in a hostile, thinly populated area was surely unattractive. Few administrators had ever wanted to work in the country where Félix Eboué was to spend twenty years of his life.

ÉBOUÉ IN OUBANGUI-CHARI

Eboué arrived in Brazzaville 21 January 1909, four weeks after leaving Bordeaux. People said the town, situated along the Congo River, might become an important center as the headquarters for four colonies, but that year it was unimpressive. The small administrative capital, full of pretty bureaucratic intrigue and rough adventurers, businessmen, and officials who left most of their scruples back in France, had little attraction. Aperitif conversation consisted of boasting about cheating Africans out of ivory or rubber or recounting how an administrator had tortured an African to collect taxes. Having come to Africa without wives or families, most had set up house with one or several concubines. A

traveling white hunter whom Eboué met boasted he had nine
wives placed at strategic places along his usual itinerary.[4]

The capital also had a reputation among Antilleans and Creoles as racist. It would never be so bad as Leopoldville (formerly
called Kinshasa and now called Kinshasa once again), the Belgian
capital across the river, but Africans were rigidly segregated as the
city grew, and black Creoles might not be sure of a meal in a
restaurant or a room in a hotel because of strong racist sentiments
on the part of whites. This was definitely not the place Eboué
cared to stay; he had already made up his mind to go to the hinterland anyway, and he was assigned to Oubangui-Chari. He left
for Bangui less than twenty-four hours after his arrival.

The trip up the Congo and Oubangui Rivers took over two
weeks on small wood-burning steamboats run by the *Messageries
Fluviales du Congo*. The banks were lined with dense equatorial
forest that reminded Eboué of Inini region in Guyane. From the
narrow deck he watched the branches and vegetation typical of
the area float downstream, and he read—one of his favorite hobbies—the novels, philosophy books, and colonial publications he
had purchased in Paris and Bordeaux.

Eboué also talked with other passengers returning to Oubangui or going on to Tchad. Some had spent years in Africa and
told stories about the customs of the people as they claimed to
have observed them; they assured Eboué that the Oubanguians
were unredeemable "savages" without the least trace of civilization: "They are all cannibals, you know." and "You should see
how Oubangui women mutilate themselves!"[5]

Bangui was considerably smaller than Brazzaville, of course; it
had been established in 1889 as a post along the Oubangui River,
and by the time Eboué arrived twenty years later it still had only
a few scattered buildings with fewer conveniences than Brazzaville. The weather tended to be slightly cooler, in the low eighties,
and dryer which Eboué, who perspired profusely, appreciated. The

4 Interview with René Sadier, elephant hunter, Bangui, 12 July 1968.

5 One writer has suggested that such talk and the books written about Oubangui served a purpose. By removing the Oubanguians from the human community Europeans could do anything to them. See Pierre Kalck, *Histoire
centrafricaine des origines à nos jours* (Paris: University of Paris, Thèse pour
Doctorat ès Lettres, unpublished version, June 1970), Volume II, pp. 299-300.

atmosphere was more congenial because Emile Merwart, former Governor of Guyane, then headed the territory, and René Maran's father, Herménégilde, was still there as an official of such rank that he had recently acted as temporary governor of the colony.

Eboué, no doubt, told the senior Maran that he wanted an assignment in the hinterland far from the growing administrative centers, and elicited his help in getting the kind of post he desired. As for Merwart, he remembered having signed, eight years before, a decree granting Eboué a half-scholarship to study in France. They talked briefly, and Merwart named him to Bouca, the administrative center for Ouham *circonscription.*

In 1909 Ouham, located in the western part of Oubangui-Chari, was one of seven large administrative districts or *circonscriptions* into which the colony had most recently been divided, administrative reorganization being frequent. Four—Bangui, Kémo, Gribingui, and Ouham—were under civilian authority because they were not then in open revolt; three—Dar Kouti, Haut Oubangui, and Mbomou in the north and east—were under military rule because of war between colonial authorities and Mohammed es Senoussi, a Muslim leader, and others. In no area of the country could the French say they had complete control, however.

Ouham, like the other *circonscriptions,* was divided into two or three subdivisions, and the subdivisions were later divided into cantons. Administrators with the rank of administrator third class and above generally headed the large districts; deputy administrators third class and above headed the subdivisions, and French officials appointed African chiefs to the cantons. Cadet administrators like Eboué, expected to work as assistants to the head of a subdivision.

Although it was the dry season and the terrain to be crossed was savanna with high grasses and a few trees, it took Eboué one month to travel from Bangui to Bouca. He walked part of the way with the porters carrying his baggage and supplies but rode most of the distance in a *tipoye,* a hammock-like chair suspended between two poles carried by four Africans, which on a good day could cover thirty kilometers. He arrived on 20 March and, much to his surprise, had the responsibilities of a full-fledged administrator for two months in the absence of his superior.

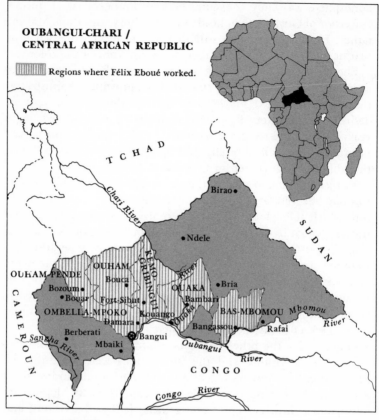

OUBANGUI-CHARI /
CENTRAL AFRICAN REPUBLIC

Regions where Félix Eboué worked.

Henri Vendôme, a Guadeloupan, arrived in May to take charge of the subdivision; he assigned his assistant to the post of treasurer or special agent to receive monies collected and make disbursements. Eboué and Vendôme may have been put together for reasons of origin; in fact, at least three Antilleans worked in the Ouham region, and the whites referred to the areas as "Creole Road." In any case, Eboué and Vendôme became good friends and, after they parted, corresponded until Vendôme's death.

Living conditions at Bouca were very simple. Eboué and Vendôme each had a thatched-roof mud house like those of the local Baya and Mandjia population. They had their own gardens but could purchase some canned foods from the Dutch-owned Ouhamé-Nana Company, then buying rubber and selling cloth and goods in the district. Hausa people coming in from Nigeria began to establish a trade network and sold cattle. Eboué did his own cooking but took a Mandjia-speaking woman into his house, an arrangement that went on for at least two years. Photographs taken around this time show that Eboué had kept his "Kruger" beard, was still quite thin, and dressed in the usual pith helmet and colonial attire. He must have become, by this time, a chain-smoker, for most photos show him holding a cigarette.

At the end of a year, in 1910, Vendôme recommended that his treasurer be accepted as deputy administrator third class, the proper first rung on the administrative ladder for a graduate of the Colonial School and approximately equivalent to lieutenant in the navy. The lieutenant governor then put him in charge of the subdivision at nearby Bozoum for two years.

The year that Eboué took over Bozoum, Martial Merlin, governor general of a renamed French Equatorial Africa, set out to organize the four territories under his authority. He ordered the complete conquest of the country by force where necessary and its organization under the direction of more qualified administrators than in the past.[6] In pursuit of Merlin's orders, Eboué was to obtain the cooperation of the people of the Karé mountain area, getting them to pay taxes and to abstain from attacks on

6 Kalck, *Histoire Centrafricaine* pp. 201, 206. After reorganization the governor general's immediate subordinates were the lieutenant governors who headed the non-autonomous colonies of French Equatorial Africa. They all had the rank of governor and belonged to the "corps des gouverneurs et gouverneurs généraux des Colonies," whose members could occupy—or not—various posts (*emplois*): first, gouverneur-général or résident général (French West Africa, French Equatorial Africa, Madagascar, Indochina); second, gouverneur (Guadeloupe, Martinique, Réunion, Guyane); third, résident (individual colonies of Indochina); fourth, lieutenant-gouverneur (individual colonies of French West and French Equatorial Africa like Oubangui-Chari); fifth, commissaire de la République (Cameroun and Togoland); sixth, secrétaire général de la fédération ou du gouvernment général (AOF, AEF, Madagascar, Indochina); and seventh, later on, inspecteur général des affaires administratives. "Thus, lieutenant-gouverneur was not a rank; it was the name given to the governorship of a non-autonomous colony whose chief was subordinate to a gouverneur général. . . ." Letter, Pierre Alexandre to Brian Weinstein, 11 January 1971.

French people and property. An example of the latter was an attack on a Frenchman traveling with cattle through the Karé area. Eboué went out with a detachment of seventy African guards, under orders from Lucien Fourneau, the new acting governor, to seize and imprison the leader of the Karé people. Eboué, however, disregarded the order, preferring to negotiate over a meal with the chief in his redoubt.[7] He justified his refusal to seize the man by writing that it would be better to have local authorities as allies rather than as prisoners and adopted this rule for the rest of his administrative career.

The best remembered local leader was the Baya-speaking Nakouen or Nakouéné. According to one account,[8] "he knew everything that was going on at Bozoum. The administrator called Nakouen to tell him what had to be done, and Nakouen called all the chiefs and did what was necessary." The Baya leader apparently decided he would work with the French:

> When Mr. Eboué arrived, there were two office buildings only. One had a roof, and one had no roof. Mr. Eboué wanted to live in the building without a roof. The building needed a roof, and Mr. Eboué asked for workers. . . . It was Nakouen and his men who came to Eboué to fix the roof. Eboué said: "Merci, you are going to work with me. . . ."

In answer to the question whether there were ever any local wars between Nakouen and others, the informant said: "The Karé people hid in holes in the mountain when they were asked to work. Nakouen received the order from Mr. Eboué to go to find them and make them work. Nakouen then organized his men and went to fight and find the Karé to make them work."[9]

To obtain the cooperation of the neighboring Baya and Mandjia peoples and specifically to get the Africans to collect rubber,

[7] He told the story to his friend, Jean Cazenave de la Roche, who wrote about it in *Le Gouverneur General Félix Eboué,* manuscript p. 57.

[8] That of Mallam Boka, a former Hausa trader at Bozoum, approximately eighty-five years old, who may actually have arrived a couple of years after Eboué's departure, although he claimed to have known Eboué (Interview in Hausa language with help of interpreters, Bozoum, 10 June 1968).

[9] According to the "Calendrier historique de Bozoum," Nakouen fought the Karé people in 1916, well after Eboué's departure, but the oral account is nonetheless interesting to show French dependence on chiefs.

Eboué traveled about much of the time for Merlin had ordered that this was the only way to organize an administration. Tours lasted up to a month, and often involved fighting Africans determined to resist demands that they collect rubber.

In one month Eboué, a West African corporal assigned to Bozoum, and a clerk, Narcisse Simonin, who worked with him could collect at most a ton of rubber for the Ouhamé-Nana Company. Even such a small amount was collected with the greatest difficulty, for in those early days the colony had no trees to be tapped, only vines growing wild very far from the villages. Africans had to find the vines, drain them and treat the sap, then return to their villages where the rubber was collected or walk to the administrative center to sell it for the money or tokens given to the administrator for taxes. The merchants who dealt in rubber —often British, Belgians, or Portuguese—constantly complained about the supposed lack of cooperation from the Africans and colonial officials.

They really had little to complain about because in Ouham region free competition among businessmen did not exist. The Ouhamé-Nana Company had the right, as the former concessionary, to purchase an established minimum quantity of rubber. Any rubber beyond that could be sold to the highest bidder. The lieutenant governor set a base price, and administrators supposedly supervised transactions between sellers and buyers, but local merchants agreed among themselves to keep the price as low as possible. European businessmen and some of their African agents also tried to cheat the Africans, using light scales to undervalue the rubber or avoiding payment. Africans countered by mixing stones with the rubber to increase its weight. In the event of conflict the Europeans called on the administrator to punish the Africans, no matter who was at fault.

Around Bozoum Eboué had other tasks too, like building his headquarters, making maps, and organizing his administration according to the instructions from Governor General Merlin. He planned a new route to Bangui in order to reduce the travel time from one month to seventeen days. He organized a small school where fifteen African children studied French, although classes were very irregular, depending on how much free time Eboué or

some other Frenchman had.[10] Eboué learned, from his pupils
and their families, as much as he taught; he was full of questions
about their customs and languages.

The young administrator wrote his first impressions of this
work to his uncle, Maximilien Liontel, who had retired to Paris
after serving as a President of the Court of Appeals. These letters
do not survive, but Liontel's responses indicate that his nephew
wrote him something about the customs he observed.[11] The earliest of Eboué's extant monthly reports also show his interest in
language, population movements, and histories of different ethnic
groups; he included detailed observations even when there was
little space given for such information in the official forms used.

Although René Maran shared Eboué's interest in African culture and had arrived in Oubangui-Chari in 1909, the two friends
were at first posted too far apart for their old and easy communication. Eboué shared his ideas and observations, therefore, with
Narcisse Simonin, his assistant at Bozoum; together they made
notes on the customs of the Baya people and prepared a short
article on them, "Les Bayas de l'Ouham Pendé," published several years later.[12] Neither man had any training in anthropology,
and the work seems quite elementary now, but it was, at the time,
a modest pioneering effort, more than ten years ahead of official
recognition that such studies were important; indeed, at the time
many administrators derided colleagues who studied African cultures. Merlin himself had said in a speech that the peoples of
equatorial Africa had no social organization at all and were, in a
sense, "new peoples" without culture.[13] Frenchmen interested in
such research communicated quietly among themselves and with
Maurice Delafosse who was writing on African civilizations and
teaching at the Colonial School. After a career in West Africa,
Delafosse had changed "Colo's" curriculum by emphasizing the

[10] Archives Nationales de France, Annexe des Archives d'Outre-Mer, Aix-en-
Provence (Infra, Arch. Nat. Aix), Afrique Equatoriale Française, Oubangui-
Chari, "Résumé des Rapports Mensuels arrivés à Bangui en December 1910."
[11] Archives Eboué, Letters of Maximilien Liontel.
[12] In Bulletin de la Société des Recherches Congolaises, No. 9, 1928, pp.
32-38.
[13] "Les Problèmes de l'Afrique Equatoriale Française," reprinted in La
Quinzaine Coloniale, Vol. XIV, 25 March 1910, p. 225.

study of African cultures. Eboué knew about Delafosse, having read his books and even class notes taken by younger colleagues who came to Africa.

Eboué hoped to meet Delafosse during his home leave, which began early in January 1912. Eboué left Bozoum and his pregnant housekeeper to take his expected leave in France and in Guyane. (Administrators had the right to six months' leave for every two years in Africa.) He had not seen his mother in ten years, and after a visit to Paris he sailed for Cayenne.

At home Eboué celebrated his return with his mother and sister who had married. He walked about his hometown, which had grown to 15,000. The center of Cayenne had not changed very much, however, and the concerns of its residents for development and assimilation had not changed either. One journalist wrote that France seemed to care for Eboué's French Equatorial Africa more than for Guyane:

Can we hope that France, which is interested so much in French Equatorial Africa (no one here is reproaching her for this), will agree to become interested even a little bit in French Guyane? Guyane, an old colony inhabited by Frenchmen, has furnished men who have served France, and she aspires to have relations with the metropole other than . . . those of a prison dumping ground.[14]

Eboué visited old friends and relatives. Camille Lhuerre had returned to Guyane to enter the prison administration, and Eboué attended his June wedding. Asked when he would marry, Eboué responded that he expected to do so during his next leave. He also visited the Collège de Cayenne to give the boys a short speech about Africa and the colonial service, encouraging them to think about it as a career.[15]

Eboué quickly spent the money he had put aside for leave and traveled back to France. On board ship he met Gratien Candace, just elected deputy from Guadeloupe and a friend of Max Liontel. They talked about blacks in the colonial service, and Candace promised to help Eboué. They parted cordially in France; neither could, of course, predict what odd turns their relation-

---

14 *L'Oeil* (Cayenne), 8 September 1910.
15 Interview with President Gaston Monnerville, Senate, Paris, 30 July 1967.

ship would take in the next twenty-five years. In September or
October Eboué requested the Ministry to send him back to Africa
before the end of his leave, but he had to wait in Paris until December for an authorization.

The delay gave him the time to meet some old friends or get
news of their activities. Yvon Delbos was rapidly becoming involved in the Radical Party and journalism; Hellier and Spas,
former classmates, had posts in the colonial administration, and
Méneau was holding a rather modest position in a bank. Eboué
spent considerable time with the Sporting Club, but he also had
more serious projects.

Waiting in Paris for his authorization to go back to Africa and
to Oubangui-Chari in particular, he considered his unsystematic
studies of African languages and tried to teach himself research
methodology by reading every study he could find about linguistics, for he hoped to prepare a guide to Oubangui's languages. He
made an appointment with Maurice Delafosse at the Colonial
School and presented very modestly his findings. Delafosse, obviously impressed with Eboué and the seriousness of his work,
promised to do some bibliographic work and write to him.

At the end of November Delafosse wrote a four-page list of articles and books he thought Eboué should read: "You will find
above, my dear colleague, the information I promised you. I may
have left out some items but not very many. With regard to the
proposed classification of idioms, what I am giving you is only
provisional and sometimes hypothetical."[16] Eboué kept this letter
carefully, and six years later he added to Delafosse's impressive
list his own little book prepared during his second very long assignment in Oubangui-Chari. On 9 December Eboué left for
Africa and arrived four days after his twenty-eighth birthday to
work in Ombella-Mondjo division.

OMBELLO-MONDJO: 1913-1914

At the end of 1911 France agreed to cede part of its colony in
Equatorial Africa to the Germans in return for the Kaiser's rec-

[16] Archives Eboué, Letter from Maurice Delafosse to Félix Eboué, Paris, 23
November 1912.

ognition of French pre-eminence in Morocco. Ouham area of Oubangui-Chari with Bozoum was included in the deal, and German troops entered Eboué's former post in April 1913.

The loss of part of A.E.F. forced the fifth reorganization of Oubangui-Chari since 1907, and by the time Eboué reached Bangui on 20 January 1913, the colony had been divided into twelve divisions, five under civilian administrators and seven under the military because of continuing revolts or the fear of them. Eboué, recently promoted to deputy administrator second class, was one of two hundred and seven French civilian and military functionaries of the colony.[17]

Before he proceeded to his new post at Diouma in Ombella-Mondjo division, he probably went back to Bouca, where his Mandjia housekeeper moved when Eboué went on leave; she had given birth to a son 14 July 1912. Eboué recognized him as his own, thus giving him French citizenship, and decided to educate him, an unusual decision at the time for few administrators did the same. He named the baby Henri Yves Félix Eboué, after himself, his own father, and probably after his friend Henri Vendôme. The mother must have cared for the baby for two years, but by 1915 she disappeared. The child stayed with René Maran for a while.

Maran and Eboué had seen more of each other as communications in Oubangui-Chari improved. Fort-Sibut, Maran's post for almost three years, was not far from Diouma, or from Damara to which Lieutenant Governor Estèbe reassigned Eboué in March 1913 after closing the post at Diouma.

Damara, a three-day walk from Bangui, was on the main inland route going east to Sibut; it was an easier assignment than Bozoum because French authority seemed more firmly established and because people seemed to pay their taxes and at first provided porters without resistance. In most divisions Africans fled to the Belgian Congo or revolted because of the five-franc annual head tax and because of the program in 1914 to recruit 5000 porters. Prices for rubber and ivory were down as a result of a depressed European economy, and it was therefore more difficult

17 Arch. Nat. Aix., A.E.F., Oubangui-Chari, "Rapport d'Ensemble sur la situation générale de l'Oubangui-Chari en 1913," p. 46.

for the Africans to collect enough rubber to pay their taxes. By the middle of 1914 Eboué complained that large numbers of the estimated 21,000 residents in his subdivision were also crossing the river into the neighboring colony. He put many in prison— so many in fact that Ombello-Mondjo was the second highest *circonscription* in the number of prison sentences given to Africans.[18]

To recruit porters and collect taxes Eboué toured a great deal, with little notebooks to record his compass readings, distances covered, and landmarks in order to complete maps started by predecessors. He put down the times and distances in such a way —"arrived at 12:03, left 12:17"—that he appears obsessively precise, even more than is necessary in surveying and map work. Small affairs also made up his daily existence. One village preferred to move into another subdivision when Eboué drew maps establishing administrative boundaries. One of the increasing number of Portuguese merchants moving north from Angola and Congo requested land for coffee cultivation which Eboué had to delimit. He regrouped villages along the route to Bangui and named canton chiefs.

Eboué's best Africans friends were at first the chiefs. The word "friend" is not an exaggeration, for Eboué genuinely liked and respected many of them. His scrupulous and courteous dealings with chiefs distinguished him from many other administrators who considered them petty clerks and petty tyrants which they sometimes were. Eboué took them quite seriously as leaders or potential leaders, and he occasionally supported unpopular chiefs for the sake of order. He regretted and feared the decline in local customs and authority with the advent of the colonial administration, and he recommended that local authorities, even those without a traditional basis, be strengthened, although French colonial policy generally advocated the suppression of local authorities. Chiefs with some traditional legitimacy provided Eboué with information about the customs of their people and kept a level of order within the society that Eboué regarded as crucial; chiefs without a traditional basis of authority were often useful aids and

[18] *Ibid.*, p. 48, and "Rapport d'Ensemble pour l'année 1914."

even confidants who gained power from their association with the colonial administration.

A typical relationship between Eboué and a chief was with Soumoussi, a chief living about eleven kilometers from Damara, a three-hour trip by *tipoye*.[19] The chief came once a month to the post to talk to Eboué, to remit tax money or porters. Eboué went to the chief to visit and asked Soumoussi questions about himself, just as he had done with others in Bozoum. The two men spoke in Sango, rapidly becoming the common language in the colony, and Eboué wrote down vocabulary and useful phrases for his projected book. At the end of their sessions they drank and ate food that one of the chief's wives had prepared, and Eboué offered the African a gift purchased in nearby Bangui.

Being close to Bangui meant that Eboué could get news faster from Europe than he had been able to in Bozoum. The news in 1913 indicated an increase in tension at home. Anti-German feeling grew, and a bill extending military service to three years passed the Chamber of Deputies. The socialists' leader, Jean Jaurès, called for general disarmament to prevent war, but many Europeans were eager for conflict and were not disappointed when it came in 1914.

World War I brought confusion to the colony. Some administrative posts had to be closed because French civilians went into the army, and the military left for the fronts. Eboué, like many of his colleagues, wanted to leave for Europe to fight for France, particularly after news came that the government had fled Paris for Bordeaux. Governor General Merlin protested that the empire would collapse if any more administrators left, and Eboué had to remain to contribute to the war in Africa.

Europeans in Oubangui during the war years recruited thousands of Africans as porters and soldiers to join French military forces moving west to reconquer the ceded territory of French Equatorial Africa and German Kamerun. These years were a time of great hardship for the Africans who produced food for the military, fought as soldiers, or traveled great distances on short rations, carrying weapons and equipment for a war they cared

19 Archives Eboué, Notebooks from 1913 and 1914.

nothing about. Many fled the colony, hid, or revolted against the French; the revolts were so serious that troops had to be called back from the front to put them down.[20]

In December 1914 Lieutenant Governor Estèbe feared that revolts in the area of Kouango, a key post for communication between Bangui and the hinterland, would seriously jeopardize the war effort. Under ordinary circumstances he would have sent in some troops, but he had no more to spare. In considering alternatives he noted in his personal files that Eboué's superiors from 1909 to 1914 had praised him for his ability to bring order to difficult situations; he also knew Eboué personally because he had been governor of the colony for three years. Estèbe therefore decided to name Eboué to Kouango.

KOUANGO: 1914-1917

To get to inland towns like Bambari in the center of the colony, administrators, soldiers, and merchants traveled up the Oubangui River to the post of Kouango, a subdivision of Kotto-Kouango division, and then north along the Kouango River (now called the Ouaka). All during 1914 most of the Langbassi, a Banda-speaking group who made up about two-thirds of the subdivision's 20,000 population, revolted against French authority, refusing to pay taxes and blocking the river routes. The Yakpa also resisted, but the Banziri people who lived along the Oubangui cooperated with the French, Estèbe told Eboué.

Eboué's mission was to suppress the revolts all over the area, collect taxes, and organize the first civilian administration. Estèbe warned him he could expect little help from Bangui; because of the war European personnel had been greatly reduced in the whole colony to less than a hundred. In all of French Equatorial Africa there were only 413 French administrators and clerks; two years later the number had dropped to 320 with only 48 for all of Oubangui.[21] Eboué was to have one European assistant and about thirty African guards whereas before 1914 Kouango had been occupied by half a dozen French soldiers and no less than

[20] Kalck, *Histoire Centrafricaine*, p. 290.
[21] Archives Nationales, Section d'Outre-Mer, A.E.F., VII, 6, "Personnel 1916."

two hundred African troops. Henri Vendôme, his old friend from Ouham, and now head of Kotto-Kouango *circonscription* in which Kouango was located, and Narcisse Simonin, who had his own post at Alindao, promised to help, but they were far from Kouango and had problems of their own. Eboué realized he needed the support of some key local leaders more than ever before.

At Kouango, Raymond Sokambi, a Banziri leader, and Singuéré and Pierlat, two Langbassi leaders, had been named chiefs by the French military in 1912. None had any particular claim to leadership in local tradition but had cooperated with the French by providing canoers when needed and by collecting and selling rubber and ivory to the Compagnie du Kouango Français (CKF) which monopolized commerce in the subdivision. Sokambi, who lived closest to Kouango, was the most important of the three.

According to family tradition, Sokambi was born in what was the Belgian Congo: ". . . having lost his father, [he] had come to Kouango, his mother's country. Because he was a courageous man, the first Portuguese merchants noticed him and hired him as an assistant. There Sokambi sold cloth and beads which his boss entrusted to him in exchange for rubber. After the departure of these Portuguese, who went from place to place to buy rubber, Sokambi remained and went to build his village not far from that of his uncles on the Gbabiti near the Ouaka River."[22] The Banziri chief and Eboué became inseparable friends and allies.

The two men looked like brothers, people said: "tall, deep black, strong, with similar features." Eboué visited Sokambi's household frequently for conversations with his friend's aged mother, who apparently told him a good deal about Banziri history and customs. Not being at all fluent in the language, he used an interpreter with her. Occasionally, Eboué went with Sokambi on canoe rides, and the chief organized canoe races

22 Told by Madame Clémentine Sokambi in the language of the Banziri to a Banziri schoolteacher in Kouango, who translated it into French and wrote it down, 3 June 1968, Kouango. Brian Weinstein, "Félix Eboué and the Chiefs: Perceptions of Power in Early Oubangui-Chari," *Journal of African History*, Vol. XI, No. 1, 1970, pp. 114-15.

along the Oubangui River, which was quite secure from attack, and put on dances for Eboué.

Administrators took advantage of the Banziri canoe-making skills and let Sokambi organize races for their amusement. The Africans' canoes were so large they could take as many as a hundred men each. Once Sokambi and Eboué challenged Vendôme and Juste Poujade, a Guyanese in charge of the river post of Possel, to a race from Kouango to Possel, a distance of about ninety kilometers. The Sokambi-Eboué canoe, *Aha-Gba* (which in Banziri means "You can do anything you like, but you won't be successful")[23] carried forty-two men, according to Eboué. Vendôme's took sixty men; Poujade's canoe was the smallest, with thirty canoers. The race downriver to Possel took six and a half hours. Vendôme won by a length. The three friends then spent the evening with their whiskey, which had been recently imported, and a large meal. A fourth administrator joined them for a few hands of bridge, one of Eboué's favorite games.[24]

In Kouango, Eboué met also Bada Marcelline of the Sokambi household. She was a beautiful petite woman whose color was a brown that people in the area call red. He gave the dowry to her brother, correct procedure among the matrilineal Banziri, and the Banziri considered them married. Everyone then considered Eboué a member of the Sokambi family, and it is clear that Eboué had a great deal of affection for his African relatives with whom he maintained ties until his death. He seems to have sincerely loved Bada Marcelline; he built one of the rare cement houses in the area for her, and he cared for her for the rest of her life. With all these links with Sokambi, Eboué could always count on the chief's help against the Langbassi and Yakpa.

One of the most important leaders of the fighting Langbassi was Amba, a young bearded chief. Even today he is remembered by the Langbassi as a hero, just as the Banziri think of Sokambi as a hero. According to local tradition, he was a simple peasant cultivator in the village of Mono before deciding to lead the

---

23 Interview with Jean-Marie Sokambi, Bangui, 19 August 1967.
24 Eboué wrote about the race in "Le Sport en Afrique Equatoriale," *Le Monde Colonial Illustré*, No. 103, March 1932.

Langbassi. (According to one account, a French administrator named him chief shortly before his revolt, but I have found no record of it.)[25] Amba and his followers refused to collect rubber and ivory to pay their taxes. They attacked convoys going from Kouango to Bambari, and they raided Langbassi villages that cooperated with the French.

To suppress this resistance and revolt Eboué had to depend on Sokambi and whatever men Sokambi could recruit. With a guard of only thirty men, the administrator could not adhere to any French policy of downgrading chiefs and hope to survive at Kouango. Sokambi helped him, and Eboué repaid his alliance and friendship with responsibilities, support, and gifts. With the men Sokambi recruited, Eboué traveled on many missions in attempts to catch Amba.

Amba evaded his enemy successfully for most of 1915. On one tour from 7 September to 21 November 1915, traveling over 1000 kilometers on foot, *tipoye*, and canoe, Eboué tracked the "rebels" to villages where informants, probably provided by the cooperative Langbassi chiefs, told him they were installed.[26] The enemy laid ambushes in the high grasses to catch Eboué. At night small units harassed his camp.

One night while Eboué slept in his tent Sokambi, who must have gotten up to take a walk, noticed something in the dark move near Eboué. He quietly approached and saw a man crawling under the tent. The chief, a powerful man, seized him and shouted for help. Some of his men rushed to the place and captured the intruder, an armed Langbassi whose mission was to kill the black whiteman, or "tobacco" as the Langbassi called Eboué. With the commotion Eboué awoke, and Sokambi told him the story. Afterward Eboué grasped the chief's hand and

25 Account of a Langbassi, about sixty-five years old, who had fled from Kouango as a youth and who did not know Amba personally. Cited in Brian Weinstein, "Félix Eboué and the Chiefs," p. 113.

26 Archives Nationales, République Centrafricaine (*Infra,* Arch. Nat. RCA) Kouango, "Rapports Mensuels." All information concerning Kouango comes from Eboué's own (handwritten) monthly reports from 1915 to 1917, interviews with members of the Sokambi family, and interviews with one elderly Langbassi man.

said, "You are truly my brother." Sokambi replied, "Vive la France."[27]

In the next weeks Eboué moved rapidly about the area. In small battles with the Langbassi hiding in the grasses or forest, Eboué's men shot many and took prisoners turned over to Sokambi. The Langbassi appeared to have gotten two or three old muskets, but they depended mainly on the iron knives and arrows they had been making for centuries. Eboué captured so many men that finally, according to local tradition (mainly Banziri local tradition and Eboué's accounts), the Langbassi leader found himself alone. He continued to travel about in the protection of the high grasses of the savanna trying to organize villages to fight. He succeeded for a time. Eboué returned to Kouango where, he wrote, Amba finally came by himself to surrender after losing his most important allies and relatives. (That Amba came by himself to Kouango seems uncharacteristic. It may be that Sokambi captured him and brought him to Kouango.) The lieutenant governor sentenced him to prison in Brazzaville, where he died, though still a young man.

The influence of Eboué's enemy must have been great because Eboué noted in a report that "with the submission of Amba's group, all the people of the region presented themselves to the head of the subdivision and declared their willingness to satisfy our requests [for rubber and peace]." Once word of Amba's arrest and imprisonment spread, "chiefs whose villages had not been visited came spontaneously to Kouango to see that [Amba] could no longer harm anyone."[28]

From then on Eboué and Sokambi worked to collect taxes from the Yakpa who had also resisted French demands and authority. Tax collection in Kouango increased to 77,609 francs in 1916 from 47,100 in 1915 and 34,933 in 1914.[29] To reward Sokambi for his cooperation Eboué made him chief of a total of three cantons out of the six in the subdivision. He therefore had authority over the

[27] Eboué told the story to Madame E. Barat who mentioned it in her unpublished manuscript, "Musique indigène." It is also important in the memories of the Sokambi family who have many versions of it. The Langbassi called Eboué "tobacco" because he smoked so much.

[28] Both citations from "Rapport Mensuel," November 1915.

[29] "Rapport Mensuel," December 1916.

Langbassi and Yakpa as well as over his own people, the Banziri. The governor also approved Eboué's idea to give him permission to purchase a rapid-fire modern rifle, to exempt him from taxation for a year, and helped him obtain materials for the construction of a cement house which still stands at Kouango. Eboué gave him cotton plants for experimentation as well as school materials for the little school the chief had opened and paid for. The success of pacification, as it was called, also brought Eboué an increase in rank to deputy administrator first class and then to full administrator third class at the beginning of 1917, equivalent to commander in the navy.

Similar operations had gone on elsewhere in the colony, and the efforts brought some success in terms of tax collection. In 1917 the colony collected 2,215,963 francs in taxes of which Africans paid about 2,000,000 or 100,000 more than originally expected.[30] One of the results of the campaign, however, was suffering and disease, to the apparent surprise of the administrators.

At Alindao, Eboué's friend Simonin wrote that "The region is in part subdued, but the population is plunged into an indescribable misery."[31] At Kouango a terrible epidemic struck the subdued Langbassi. The people called it *grou*. At first Eboué thought it was bronchial pneumonia. A military physician from Mobaye up the river said it might be beri-beri. He wrote that one cause of the disease (also called "rubber sickness" by the Africans because they got it after spending much time collecting rubber) may have been lack of protein. Looking for rubber took so much time and effort that the diet of the Africans suffered. Therefore, the disease may have been kwashiokor. In any case, the physician advised stopping the vigorous collection of rubber for the time being and urged an effort to enrich the diet of Africans.[32]

The disease spread at Kouango, and Eboué calculated that in the eleven months from June 1916 to April 1917 about 2500 people died from it. He got some medicine and attempted to treat people

---

30 Arch. Nat. Aix, A.E.F., Oubangui-Chari, "Rapport Annuel 1917."

31 Arch. Nat., RCA, Mobaye, "Rapport Politique 1918," cited by Kalck, *Histoire Centrafricaine*, p. 307.

32 Arch. Nat. Aix, A.E.F., Oubangui-Chari, 1917, "Rapport du Medécin Major Bablet sur l'état sanitaire de la Région Langbassi (19-21 March 1917)."

without much effect. "The health situation continues to be un-satisfactory. Beri-beri is working a terrible havoc among the Langbassi. This situation is agonizing."[33]

The governor worried about this situation and stopped rubber collection for some months; he also began to worry that Sokambi, like other chiefs, had gotten too much power for himself. One administrator suggested to him that the Banziri chief and others who had cheerfully helped the administration, shouting "Vive la France" all the while, had actually used the power gained from such collaboration for their own benefit and to settle old feuds. Once the Langbassi came under Sokambi's authority, he may have been selling them as slaves according to one administrator: ". . . Sokambi, Alindao, Otto, under color of helping the administration collect taxes, are killing, pillaging, and carrying off slaves. The abundance of human game is such that a slave is ex-changed often for a basket of manioc or two baskets of corn."[34]

But the administration could not afford to alienate its sup-porters, and Sokambi had a secure position for the rest of his life. From 1912, the year the French appointed him chief, to his death in 1957 Sokambi clearly manipulated the administration and perhaps the church for his own benefit as much as they manipulated him. His descendants, who occupy important posts in an independent Central African Republic, have fond mem-ories of Félix Eboué and others. The Langbassi clearly do not.

All during this period at Kouango, from the end of 1914 to the middle of 1917, Eboué heard little from his family because of the war. Cut off from the metropole and Guyane, he knew nothing of the German siege of Verdun and its heroic defense by French troops in 1916, until it was over. His closest relations were with René Maran who returned to Oubangui-Chari in 1916 after re-cuperative leave. Maran was less than eighty kilometers from Possel where Eboué sent his son Henri to Catholic School, and he and Eboué visited there or at Kouango.

Maran and Eboué discussed their own writing and colonialism in Africa, sharing their thoughts with Vendôme, Poujade, Si-

[33] "Rapport Mensuel," February 1917.
[34] "Confidentiel Mobaye," cited by Kalck, *Histoire Centrafricaine*, p. 309.

monin, and Robert Hermine, another Guyanese whom Eboué
had known in Paris. Maran still had time for his poetry, but like
Eboué had become fascinated with African civilization. Although
always an outsider, Maran tried to understand and communicate
to the world through the novel some things he saw, while Eboué
did the same through anthropological research and linguistics.
Maran was, in fact, preparing a novel around the story of an
African chief, and Eboué had nearly finished his manuscript on
the languages of the colony. He sent his own document through
administrative channels from Kouango to Bangui to Brazzaville
to Paris, and the government sponsored its publication as *Langues Sango, Banda, Baya, Mandjia* in 1918.

A COLONIAL PHILOSOPHY

Part of what emerged from conversations with Maran and a
few other friends was Eboué's developing colonial philosophy.
Most of his colleaugues, like other bureaucrats the world over,
seldom considered the broader implications of what they did, day
in and day out, or the historical significance of the system to
which they contributed. A few men, however, debated ideas
among themselves, wrote, and tried to influence policy choices,
some out of personal intellectual interest, and some from a desire to mobilize public opinion to force the government to spend
more money in Africa. Their discussions and articles revolved
around the ideas of assimilation and association.

The assimilationists believed that it was possible and desirable
for Africans to become black Frenchmen in culture and citizenship, and for the African colonies in the new empire to become
at least as closely integrated with France as the four old colonies.
The associationists, on the other hand, said that Africans would
never become Frenchmen because they had civilizations of their
own within which they could evolve, under the control of France,
to enter the modern industrializing world. (Although both groups
held genuine concern for African development, it is safe to say
that they had French interests uppermost in their minds.)

The white, Paul Dislère, a teacher at the Colonial School during Eboue's student days, propounded assimilationist doctrine; so
the black, Blaise Diagne, the Senegalese deputy to the French

parliament, who said he was a living example of the success of assimilation. Henri Labouret, an associationist who also taught at "Colo," made fun of schools which taught African children about "our ancestors the Gauls." Robert Louis Delavignette, an administrator in West Africa, argued that in a colonial situation there was always some assimilation and some association no matter what official policy might be. Delavignette insisted that France should think about its relationship with African societies and develop a coherent "native policy" or *politique indigène* which would be "based on men as they are, in the countries where they live. It should constantly adapt itself to them and not attempt to reduce them to some major category—economic, religious or racial."[35]

Eboué kept up on the running debate on these questions and read the books of Frobenius, one of the first Europeans to write about African civilizations; he and his friends, Antillean and white, discussed the issues in person and in letters. In correspondence with blacks from the old colonies Eboué envisaged assimilation of these four areas, on the grounds that black Creoles had been cut off from Africa and were searching for new values. In Africa, he believed, the only people in a similar situation were a small elite with some schooling, which might be assimilated and might serve as a link between France and the African masses; for their own good, Eboué believed, the masses should remain loyal to their basic tradition.

In his discussions with whites Eboué felt more relaxed talking about Africa than about Guyane. In Oubangui-Chari he shared his thoughts with René Isambert whom he first met in 1914 and who served under his orders later. He corresponded with Yvon Delbos and Roger Dévigne in France; Dévigne was a journalist friend of Delbos who had studied Frobenius' writings on Atlantis and introduced Eboué to their study. He himself had written books on the subject, and thought that this land mass had once been the center of a unified world civilization. The idea appealed to Eboué, who already had the stoic belief in human unity.

---

[35] Robert Delavignette, *Freedom and Authority in French West Africa* (London: Cass, 1968), pp. 49, 54.

This belief was, indeed, an important pillar of Eboué's approach to colonialism, and the idea of Atlantis supported it. If a great civilization shared by all men could have existed on Atlantis, a now-sunken land mass that had once linked Europe, Africa, and America, it would mean that mankind had fled in different directions from a single place, and developed differently from a single base. Those who believed in Atlantis believed that a few symbols, like the pyramids in Egypt and in Mexico, a few similarities in religious beliefs, and a few words in different languages remained as testimony of mankind's lost unity. Eboué was so taken with the idea that he made lists of words from African languages of Oubangui that resembled the ancient Greek he had studied in school.

If one believed that with separation each continent developed civilizations, one could not consider Africa blank slate, waiting for the so-called civilizing mission of France or any other country. *La Mission Civilisatrice* was nonsense, Eboué believed. The African peoples had their values, their social structure, and their leaders—all of which served to maintain order and give meaning to life. Colonialism could disrupt these systems and cause disorder: "Because of this latin mania to disorganize everything in order to facilitate assimilation, the natives are caught between their traditions . . . and our civilization which is poured into them with an eye dropper. . . ."[36]

Instead of trying to make Frenchmen out of Africans, Eboué thought, France should take the industrial age and modern organization to an Africa associated with it. For this goal government funds and private investments were needed. He believed further that Africans must be shown what he considered rational ways to work to make money and thus transform the material conditions of their lives while becoming linked with other countries in such a way that the resources of all continents could be used for the benefit of mankind: "The obligation to enrich the native masses will continue . . . to be my credo. I believe I am following the right path and consider all the rest to be useless and sterile. . . ."[37]

[36] Archives Maran, Letter from Félix Eboué, 24 July 1928.
[37] Archives Maran, Letter from Félix Eboué, 10 November 1927.

That the African might suffer in the course of enriching himself was probably unavoidable, Eboué thought. He once wrote in the little notebooks he carried:

> Love, love in itself, leave it to Tolstoy. Man must live and life means blows. But, if we have the iodine to dress the wounds, we agree with our existence which is to live and to fight—all the rest is nonsense. That is all Colonization is—more Nietsche than Tolstoy. It is necessary to know how to suffer. Only suffering permits organization.[38]

Material development would result from the introduction of cash crops so that Africans could cultivate instead of being forced to collect rubber; second, it would come from the extension of communication facilities and the insistence on regular working hours. The requirement to work certain hours meant, of course, forced labor, one of the most hated aspects of the colonial system. Eboué, who clearly believed, along with his white colleagues, that an outsider could know what was best for a people did not oppose forced labor, as long as the African was protected from abuse:

> I don't know any man, any people who has been able to lift itself in dignity and decency without the application of the law of effort, the obligation to work. . . . [O]ne loves or one does not love the native; those who love him truly and sincerely favor the obligation to work. Others will adopt another view because of their disdain for the black man or by false humanitarianism.[39]

Many years later Barthélemy Boganda, an African nationalist leader in Oubangui-Chari, pointed out that abuse is difficult to avoid in a colony:

> Colonization is a need for economic, intellectual and moral expansion. In this sense it is humane work, praiseworthy in itself and necessary. . . . It is not against this colonialism that we protest but against the humiliating subordination and the discrimination which is the immediate consequence of it.[40]

[38] Archives Eboué, Notebook, entry, December 1927, my translation.

[39] *La Conférence Africaine Française* (Brazzaville, 30 January 1944), February 1944, transcript.

[40] Barthélemy Boganda, "Discours prononcé par Monsieur Boganda, Président du Grand Conseil à la séance inaugurale de la première session ordinaire du Grand Conseil de l'A.E.F.," Brazzaville, 21 October 1957.

Eboué was aware of humiliation and discrimination but believed the colonial system could be reformed. In his view, abuses could be corrected by enlightened and educated administrators and by the provision of adequate funds for development. With material change Africa could advance peacefully in association with France without the destruction of its own civilization, he believed. These thoughts of the future evolved with time, and the idea that Africa might be independent occurred to him, but he was so preoccupied with the material condition of man that it was difficult for him to believe that an undeveloped area could be politically independent. Developed countries had an obligation toward the others to ensure their development, an obligation that could not be met without control.

The belief that one knows best for the African contains the elements of tyranny even when it is benevolent, although Eboué would not have liked such a judgment. Bolstered by a stoic philosophy, admitting the need for others to suffer for a high goal, the tyranny could be worse than if one professed no love at all for the people concerned. Rarely, however, are men completely governed by a single philosophical system, and Eboué's stoicism was tempered by other aspects of his character.

LEAVE: 1917-1918

By mid-1917 Eboué had been in Oubangui-Chari for four and a half years without leave because of the war. The only way he could get back to France was for the physician at Mobaye or Bangui to request sick leave for him because of the malaria attacks that all administrators suffered from after a sojourn in equatorial Africa. With the use of quinine the characteristic attacks of nausea and chills and fever were fewer, but it was something they had to get used to. Eboué was not particularly ill that year, but the doctor requested the leave that he wanted.

Eboué left Kouango in August 1917 and picked up Henri at Possel, for he had decided to take him home. The two left Bangui at the end of the month for Brazzaville where they spent ten days, staying with friends or in administrative lodgings; they then took the Belgian train from Kinshasa to Matadi, where they had a brief, unpleasant stay, being refused hotel lodgings because of

color. Their ship soon called, however, and they arrived in
Bordeaux in early October.

World War I was still in progress, its outcome still in doubt;
one reason that Eboué wanted to go on leave was to try to join
the army. Although the United States entered the war on the
side of France in April of that year, the new Bolshevik government in Russia sued for peace. In France debate about the conflict divided the country, and in November the strong-willed
Georges Clemenceau became Prime Minister, mandated to end
the war. The new leader inspired his compatriots with denuncia-
tions of pacifism in France and told them that all efforts must be
concentrated on winning the war: "A single and simple duty:
abdicate everything not concerning the homeland . . . the war,
nothing but the war. . . ."

Colonial governors, shorthanded as they were, tried to prevent
their administrators from joining the army. The only way open
to them was to get to Paris on sick leave and to try there for
intercession by influential acquaintances. Governor General Merlin wrote in vigorous protest to the "rue Oudinot" after one such
incident:

> It is necessary not to lose sight of the fact that after 30 months of war,
> I have arrived at the limit of personnel reduction. I am administering
> a territory of 2,000,000 square kilometers, a population of 6,000,000
> inhabitants with 128 administrators and 87 clerks of the civil services
> only. The result is that many posts have had to be closed since the
> declaration of war.[41]

However, Eboué asked Senator Lucien Hubert, closely associated with colonial circles, to intervene for him. The senator
wrote to the Minister of Colonies, but the Ministry, at the governor general's objection, refused Eboué permission. He then
turned to Herménégilde Tell, a high-ranking official in the penal
administration of Guyane and soon its first Guyanese director;
Tell's approach was also ineffective. Eboué gave up, and sailed
with Henri for Cayenne.

Back home after a five-year absence, Eboué entrusted Henri to
Man-Lie, who soon introduced her grandson to church attend-

41 Arch. Nat. SOM, A.E.F., XVIII, 6, Letter, Brazzaville, 7 December 1915.

ance. He then made the rounds of visits, quaffing Guyanese rum punch and catching up on happenings during his long absence.

Man-Lie, sister Cornélie, and Cornélie's husband, Félix Gratien, thought that Eboué should marry, particularly since he had a son to take care of. He had turned thirty-three in December and was considered a rather old bachelor already, but he broke his previous engagement because he had heard his fiancée had not been faithful to him. He then decided he would never marry and left Cayenne by himself for the metropole at the beginning of 1918.

On board ship news came that the war was coming to an end. French troops were moving north into Flanders and reconstruction was beginning in northern France. Eboué talked about the war with other Antilleans he met; with the exception of Eboué in first class, all were traveling in third. One evening there was to be a reception open to all passengers regardless of class. Eboué had planned to attend in a white suit, but the Antilleans begged him to appear in his full-dress uniform as none of them had his rank. One of them told Eboué that "we want to show the metropolitans that we Creoles have as high-ranking officials as they." Eboué refused initially but gave in when several people asked him again. The reception was well underway when he strode into the ballroom in his uniform, and was ostentatiously welcomed by the Antilleans and Creoles.[42]

After a couple of months in Paris Eboué left again for Oubangui. He arrived in July 1918, his twenty-four pieces of luggage carefully listed in his notebook. A new period in colonial history was beginning under Lieutenant Governor Lamblin.

THIRD ASSIGNMENT

Auguste Henri Lamblin had worked his way up the ranks of the colonial bureaucracy from the lowest-ranking clerk to acting governor in 1917 and then lieutenant governor of Oubangui-Chari in 1919. Known as a hardworking and efficient administrator, he began an ambitious ten-year roadbuilding program in the colony and encouraged the introduction of commercial crops to

---

[42] Interview with Jules Agénor, Paris, 31 July 1970.

change the economy of the country. Even André Gide, the famous French writer traveling in Africa to investigate complaints about colonial administration, had a kind word for Lamblin: "How pleasant, this modest man whose admirable work shows what an intelligent and continuous administration might accomplish."[43]

The governor believed that exactions and repression belonged to the past; a more numerous personnel and à decrease in patrols by uncontrolled troops were part of his policy. He realized this was true when the people of the Karé Mountain area—Eboué's first post and one supposedly subdued—revolted. After a bloody repression Lamblin correctly noted that the Oubanguians feared and disliked the French more than ever, and that something must be done about it. Lamblin may have done his best, but there is no proof that African attitudes changed.[44]

Lamblin tried to be careful in his assignments of administrators; in considering Eboué, who could now have a whole district under his authority as a full administrator third class, Lamblin apparently thought well of his record, for he named him head of Kouango *circonscription*, one of the largest of the thirteen in the colony. (Although the names are the same, this post was not the same as his previous assignment at Kouango subdivision.) Administrative headquarters were in Bambari, in the midst of Banda-speaking people, and the Ippy, Moroubas, and Grimari subdivisions were in the district. Shortly after Eboué's nomination the lieutenant governor changed the name of the district to Ouaka, a Banda name, and added Eboué's old post of Kouango to it.

By this time Eboué had been associated with Oubangui-Chari for ten years and had many friends there. Henri Vendôme remained at Mobaye struggling with another revolt; Narcisse Simonin had returned to Ouham where he and Eboué had first met; Robert Hermine worked at Ippy and then Bambari and was probably Eboué's closest friend; René Isambert, also under Eboué, commanded the Bambari subdivision and then Moroubas. Ajax Saint Clair, a Guyanese acquaintance, worked in the south,

43 André Gide, *Voyage au Congo* (Paris: Gallimard, 1927), p. 51.
44 Arch. Nat. Aix, A.E.F., Oubangui-Chari, "Rapport Annuel 1920," pp. 7-8.

and René Maran acted as administrative accountant at Fort Crampel in the north; Maran left the colony for Bordeaux at the end of the year, having been accused and fined for mistreating an African. Eboué made another friend, de Courseulles, head of Gribingui subdivision; the two shared an interest in the Banda-speaking people and had frequent conversations about their customs. Some of these friends gathered at Bambari in November to celebrate the end of World War I; they toasted the future at Bambari where economic innovation was beginning.

Economically and politically, the years at Bambari were good for Eboué. At the time it was becoming the second most popu-lous town in the colony and a pleasant place. It had administra-tive offices located on a hill overlooking the commercial quarter in the valley, along the Ouaka River. The Roman Catholic mis-sionaries chose another hill, and built their church there. Africans lived just across the Ouaka. Distances between these various quarters were considerable, and most Europeans traveled by *tipoye* or *pousse-pousse,* a wheeled chair similar to a rickshaw.

Eboué began work at a time of new conditions and new pol-icies. Although world rubber prices had dropped, the economy of the country had grown less dependent on it. In any case, re-ferring to Ouaka, the lieutenant governor wrote: ". . . in no way must the people . . . be forced to collect rubber, work which disgusts them, and wears them out for a derisory salary. In ad-dition, such work is in no way indispensable for the economy of the country."[45]

In Ouaka Eboué left rubber and introduced or expanded pro-duction of groundnuts, sesamy, rice, and ricin from which castor oil is made. He searched for minerals and when a subordinate discovered gold, he urged the government to develop it. He also promoted the production of cloth for sacks to transport other goods to market. He felt that he could take other initiatives be-cause Lamblin, like himself, believed that administrators working in the hinterland knew the problems of their regions better than officials in the capitals or the Ministry and should be able to make important decisions affecting these regions. The two of-

[45] Arch. Nat. Aix, A.E.F., Oubangui-Chari, "Rapport Annuel 1920," p. 25.

ficials shared a belief in the value of decentralized bureaucracy,
quite the opposite of French administrative tradition. Eboué, in
a happy mood, wrote his sister about the work with Hermine:
"Robert Hermine (did I tell you in my previous letters that he
has been with me for two years?) is still at Bambari. He is my
closest collaborator and helped me to realize here an economic
program the brilliant results of which brought bouquets from the
governor."[46]

Roadbuilding took some of Eboué's and Hermine's time, and
they celebrated the opening of a road between Bambari and
Bangui in 1920. It was three years before anyone saw the first
automobile on the road, but it gave hope of future development,
a hope also encouraged by the establishment of the Agence Economique de l'Afrique Equatoriale Française in 1919-1920 to promote investment and development. By 1926 there were 4200
kilometers of road in the colony of Oubangui-Chari.[47]

For economic and political tasks such as the introduction of
crops and the recruitment of road workers Eboué continued to
depend on African chiefs, partly because of his belief in their
value as leaders and as forces of cultural and social cohesion,
partly for the very simple reason that there were not enough administrators. In 1920, for example, only thirty out of the forty
subdivisions of the colony had European administrators; ten
were not occupied, and vast areas escaped administrative control.[48] Kouango had an administrator, but Sokambi, with whom
Eboué had re-established contact, actually ran Kouango subdivision at times, and the administration bolstered his authority
by giving him permission to purchase gunpowder. Eboué requested the lieutenant governor for the authority to permit all
chiefs to purchase gunpowder as a reward for their loyalism and
as a way to protect their plantations and to hunt.[49] Because very
few Africans had modern weapons, the possession of a gun with

[46] Archives Eboué, Letter, Félix Eboué to Cornélie Gratien, 27 December
1920.
[47] Kalck, *Histoire Centrafricaine*, pp. 322, 325.
[48] Arch. Nat. Aix, A.E.F., Oubangui-Chari, "Rapport Annuel 1920," p. 4.
[49] Arch. Nat. de France, Section d'Outre-Mer, Affaires Politiques 338, d. 3,
"Colonie de l'Oubangui-Chari, "Rapport du premier trimestre 1918."

a permit to purchase gunpowder gave Sokambi and other chiefs far greater power than the administration knew.

Sokambi's activities expanded toward Bambari; he opened a shop and hunted. This apparently brought him into competition with the Compagnie du Kouango Français trading company which objected to the administration. Eboué defended Sokambi and counterattacked by informing the governor and colleagues that CKF used paddlers from the Belgian Congo to transport rubber from Bambari to Kouango, thus depriving French subjects of money, and was refusing to accept certain varieties of rubber. He suggested the administration store unbought rubber for the Africans, or that it not force them to bring it to market, but that if they brought adulterated rubber to market, they must be fined or jailed immediately under the *indigénat*.[50] Sokambi also came to Bambari to see Eboué and greet his relative Bada Marcelline, who had moved to Bambari with Eboué. On 18 May 1919 she gave birth to Eboué's second son, named Robert Max, possibly after Robert Hermine and Maximilien Liontel. Following Banziri custom, Sokambi sent his eldest daughter, Clémentine, to help take care of the baby.

The child was born in the midst of the world-wide influenza epidemic which also struck French Equatorial Africa. In the area of Bambari people called it *dangola*; both Europeans and Africans were hard hit. The colony, already suffering from a shortage of European personnel, lost some of its men. Eboué worked under considerable handicap when de Courseulles died, and Isambert and others left for Bangui for medical treatment. Eboué kept in fairly good health these years except that he suffered from terrible earaches; once he requested permission by telegram (a telegraph system was built as far east as Sibut) to see a physician in Bangui. The pain had receded in his right ear but had left him a little deaf.[51]

In spite of his own discomfort, he cared for his European colleagues and distributed medicine among the Africans during the influenza epidemic. The Ministry of Colonies gave him a medal,

50 Arch. Nat. RCA, Bambari, "Correspondance Confidentielle," 12 September 1919.
51 Arch. Nat. RCA, Bambari, "Correspondance Confidentielle," Telegram No. 4C, Félix Eboué to Lt. Governor, 25 May 1920.

Médaille des Epidémies en Argent, and in 1919 raised him in rank to administrator second class.

In 1920 French Equatorial Africa got a new governor general in the person of Victor Augagneur, who, unlike his predecessors, was not a professional administrator. Trained as a physician specializing in veneral diseases, Augagneur had taught at the University of Lyon, been elected mayor of that city, and then represented the region in the French parliament. In 1905 he left France to become governor general of Madagascar where he was considered quite liberal. He returned to French politics after 1910, held important posts until an electoral defeat after World War I, and was appointed governor general of French Equatorial Africa as compensation for his defeat.

Augagneur had written several medical books and contributed to a growing body of colonial literature with articles and a rather well-known book, *Erreurs et brutalités coloniales.* He was dynamic as governor general, traveling often to Paris to encourage investments, to persuade the Ministry of Colonies to propose legislation that would allow his colonies to borrow money for the construction of a railroad from Brazzaville to the ocean, and to encourage the legislature to pass a proposal. He succeeded in getting the money, and work on the project officially began in February 1921, a tribute to Augagneur's effectiveness.

The governor general, a Freemason, was such an interesting person that one might have assumed that he and Eboué would have gotten along well. Augagneur, however, sensitive to any use of force against Africans, criticized Eboué for what he considered to be excessive use of the *indigénat,* which gave administrators the authority to imprison Africans for two weeks and to fine them without trial; Eboué had filled the prisons in Ombella Monjo in 1913. Augagneur also thought Eboué had worked the people too hard in Ouaka and stopped Eboué's expected advancement to administrator first class.

Lamblin continued to support Eboué, believing him to be one of the best administrators in equatorial Africa. Eboué himself, unaccustomed to being criticized in this way, defended himself to Lamblin by saying there had been no disturbances in his region since his arrival because of his policies and that if he had used the *indigénat* somewhat more than most colleagues, the reason was simply that the population of his area was greater than theirs. On the positive side Eboué had the largest school in the colony with three hundred students.

The accusations made against Eboué may actually have been based more on the actions of subordinates whom he trusted than on any actions he himself took. He believed that heads of sub-divisions knew the problems of their areas just as he had known the problems of his areas when acting in that capacity, and he also believed in the primacy of friendship. His friend Isambert, whom some others considered mediocre, was head of the Bambari subdivision and had gained a bad reputation among the Africans for putting people in prison. The latter nicknamed him "Tom-bou," a local snake which bites after little provocation.[52] Eboué protected Isambert as long as he was under his orders. Eboué was angry about Augagneur's accusations, and somewhat depressed, although only a few friends knew his feelings. He decided to go on leave and try to get back to Cayenne.

Cornélie wrote from home that Henri enjoyed Guyane but that he had trouble with other children who made fun of his African background; she also wrote he needed discipline. Eboué wrote her about Henri and Robert: "Tell Henri to continue to work hard. Little Robert is growing; he cries, has two teeth and is beginning to eat tapioca with milk."[53] After learning about Robert, "Cono" wrote encouraging her brother to think about a proper marriage to a Guyanese and took the liberty of putting forward the name of her good friend, Eugénie Tell.

At first, Eboué's responses were not enthusiastic and he said he would make no decisions until arriving home. He left the colony in July 1921 for what was unexpectedly the longest leave of his career. He did not see Bangui for two whole years, and when he returned he had a Guyanese wife and a baby daughter.

52 "Calendrier historique, Bambari," and informants at Bambari, 1967, 1968.
53 Archives Eboué, Letter, Félix Eboué to Cornélie Gratien, 4 February 1920.

III

RETURN TO CAYENNE, 1921-1923

ON HIS WAY to France Eboué spent three days in Brazzaville, a city much changed in twelve years: a few automobiles now, buildings of concrete, and a feeling in the air of economic change with Augagneur as governor general and the development-minded Albert Sarraut as Minister of Colonies. Even as prices for colonial products drifted down, more businessmen visited the capital, and a new group of men, the railroad construction engineers, particularly attracted Eboué's notice. Over their afternoon whiskeys they talked of bridges, tunnels, laying track, for in February the governor general had turned the first shovel of soil to begin work officially on the railroad from Brazzaville to the future seaport of Pointe Noire.

When Eboué arrived in Europe in August 1921, a different kind of change was beginning, but few people noticed it. A group of Africans and men of African descent met in London, in Brussels, and in Paris as the Second Pan-African Congress. Blaise Diagne, Senegal's deputy, presided, although the movement, like that of Marcus Garvey's Universal Negro Improvement Association, had few French-speaking members. Most delegates came from the English-speaking countries of Africa, the West Indies, and North America, but Antilleans and Creoles followed their deliberations.

Eboué was in Paris during the Pan-African meeting and had at least indirect contact with it. There is no proof he attended any sessions, but the black community was so small and close-knit that the Congress and its participants were a major topic of conversation. Some West Indians had known Diagne from the time he had worked in Guyane as a customs official before his election; Eboué had been introduced to him. Eboué knew Guadeloupe's deputy, Gratien Candace better, having kept up with him since they first met on ship in 1912. From Candace who attended and from others he heard about what went on at the meetings.

Resolutions drawn up that September in Paris put the accent on political change. They proclaimed the equality of races, admitted that one group might "lag a few hundred years behind another" with regard to "its industrial techniques or social organization," but essentially denied the right of one country to control another indefinitely. They demanded "Local self-government for backward groups, deliberately rising as experience and knowledge grow to complete self-government under the limitation of a self-governed world."[1]

With the possible exception of the African and Antillean members of the Ligue Universelle de la Défense de la Race Noire, founded in Paris after 1921, most French-speaking black leaders had a less radical view of the evolution of Africa and the West Indies.[2] Shortly after the Pan-African meetings, and possibly as a reaction to them, a French masonic federation to which Antilleans belonged "resolved that natives should be educated to be on a level with the Whites and that natives in the colonies should be represented in parliament."[3] Instead of political change toward self-government, Diagne, Candace, and others Eboué knew favored closer association of Africa and the old colonies with

1 Quoted in W. E. Burghardt Du Bois, *The World and Africa: An Inquiry into the Part Which Africa Has Played in World History* (New York: International Publishers, 1965, enlarged edition), pp. 238-39. See also Lamine Guèye, *Itinéraire Africain* (Paris: Présence Africaine, 1966), pp. 52-53.

2 For a discussion of the Ligue, see J. Ayo Langley, "Pan-Africanism in Paris, 1924-1936," *Journal of Modern African Studies*, Vol. VII, No. 1, 1969, pp. 69-94.

3 Mildred J. Headings, *French Freemasonry Under the Third Republic* (Baltimore: Johns Hopkins University Studies in Historical and Political Science, Series LXVI, No. 1, 1949, Vol. 66, Johns Hopkins University Press, 1948), p. 190, note 93.

France, extension of rights, and possible assimilation through education and economic progress. W. E. B. Du Bois, a leader of the Pan Africanists, considered these French-speaking blacks as lost to his cause. For him Diagne was "a Frenchman who is accidentally black"—a judgment that Diagne did not object to, and he wrote that Eboué's acquaintance, Gratien Candace, was "virulently French. He has no conception of Negro uplift, as apart from French development."[4] Candace would doubtless have considered that a compliment.

Eboué agreed more with Diagne, Candace, and the masons than with the political Pan-Africanists, at least concerning assimilation of Antilleans and Guyanese, but his ideas about Africans differed even from theirs. In the 1920's moreover, Eboué does not seem to have taken a strong political stand on any issue. He said that he sympathized more with the Socialist Party (SFIO) of the late Jean Jaurès than with the Radicals, but there is no extant evidence he was a dues-paying member.[5] The partisan spirit of French politics was not for Eboué. Because of his long absences and work in the colonies, elections came and went before he knew much about them. His own concern with colonial economic advance and administrative reform made him discount the primacy of politics and eschew dogmatism in political matters. He was thus able to keep on good terms with people of quite different political views.

These friends and relatives in France were getting older and in some cases more important. He celebrated with uncle Maximilien Liontel the latter's seventieth birthday and realized that the white-haired jurist whom he had first known as a dynamic attorney general was going downhill. He himself celebrated his thirty-seventh birthday at the end of the year with Liontel and friends.

Old teammate Yvon Delbos had been working in the Radical

---

[4] W. E. B. Du Bois, "The Negro Mind Reaches Out," *Foreign Affairs*, Vol. III, No. 3, reprinted in Alain Locke, editor, *The New Negro* (New York: Arno Press and The New York Times, reprint, 1968), p. 397.

[5] Maran says he "adhered to socialism according to Jaurès from the first years of the twentieth century," but there is no proof he belonged to the party. René Maran, *Félix Eboué: grand commis et loyal serviteur 1885-1944* (Paris: Les Editions Parisiennes, 1955), p. 18.

Party and writing in his newspaper, *L'Ere Nouvelle,* which he founded in 1919. He told Eboué that he might run for election as deputy. René Méneau, still in banking, gave Eboué some advice on his finances for he had some unpaid bills and wanted to help pay off the mortgage on his mother's house in Cayenne. Spas from his graduating class at "Colo" was in the colonies, but Roger Hellier had a job at the Ministry in Paris. Roger Dévigne invited Eboué to a drink at his little apartment on the Ile Saint Louis in Paris. He saw others, but he missed René Maran.

Maran had left Bordeaux in February after spending about eighteen months in France. The governor assigned him to the post of Archambault, alternately part of Oubangui-Chari and part of Tchad. Because he passed through Oubangui-Chari, the two might have met before Eboué's own departure for France; Maran would doubtless have given him a copy of his newly published novel, *Batouala,* his third book and first novel, the story of a Banda chief.

Maran was thirty-four in 1921, when *Batouala* appeared; its success made Maran famous. In the provocative preface, which appealed to the Pan-Africanists, he criticized the abuses of the colonial administration in Oubangui-Chari: "With regard to the natives, they have been weakened by incessant, excessive, and unpaid work which had prevented them from devoting the necessary time to their own planting. Disease has come; famine has invaded; their numbers are decreasing."[6]

Both Maran and Eboué had seen disease and famine and the forced labor which they themselves had unavoidably been involved in because of their positions; like others they had followed orders to recruit and to collect taxes. They saw and talked about the abuses but believed in the possibility of reform. Maran's critical preface made no call for revolution or Pan-African struggle and seems moderate by our standards, but some Frenchmen were shocked and regarded the author as a traitor to France. In the long run, though, the book's importance lies in its being an early sympathetic view of the African experience in the colonial situation.

6 René Maran, *Batouala* (Paris: Albin Michel, 1921), p. 17.

René Maran inscribed this photograph of himself in 1927 as a gift "To my old friend, Félix Eboué." Courtesy of Madame Eboué.

Eboué contributed information about Banda customs (which he knew better than Maran), translations of Banda words, and suggestions about a secret society called "Somali" which figures in the book. He was pleased with Maran and his own contribution. The book was selling, and was under consideration for the annual Prix Goncourt, awarded the best French novel of the year.

A committee of literary figures made the decision in December, and for Maran's friends, in 1921, the tension seemed unbearable. It was the first time in memory that a black's work was being seriously considered, and when Gratien Candace told friends that he wanted Maran to get this prize to show that a black Frenchman could do anything a white Frenchman could do, he spoke for many people.

On 14 December, the day of the expected announcement of the decision of the judges, Eboué felt ill—not the last time for him that sickness coincided with tension—and Paris was in its December gloom. He nonetheless got up to purchase a newspaper in the afternoon and was thrilled to catch sight of his friend's picture at the newsstand. He returned to his rented room, sat for a moment thinking about his friendship with Maran and the significance of the prize. He looked at his own copy of the book in which Maran had written: "To Félix Eboué, and old friend, who knows that I am not a bad or excited fellow, but simply a man endowed with character who does not want anyone to step on his toes." Then Eboué got up: "I finally had enough energy to read the newspapers, and dashed to the post office [to cable you], before returning to collapse in bed."[7] Eboué felt joy for his friend and the race, for the Prix Goncourt represented another step toward the assimilation that Antilleans and Creoles wanted to reach.

Shortly after this, Eboué made reservations on a ship to Guadeloupe and then on another to Guyane, for there was still no direct link between France and Cayenne. He could have spent his whole leave in France, indeed some of his colleagues never returned to Guyane once they left it, but he felt a need to touch Guyanese soil, to see his mother and sister, and to take Henri back to France. He hoped that somehow he might be returned to Guyane as an administrator or that he might run for deputy from Guyane; he wanted to be in a position to contribute to the economic development of his home colony, to do for Guyane what he was trying to do for Oubangui-Chari.

With all these thoughts in mind, he still made time before leaving for home to scour the bookshops of the Latin Quarter for copies of *Batouala*. Enough for friends and relatives in Cayenne, and for Yvon Delbos and Isambert.

7 Archives Maran, Letter, Félix Eboué to René Maran, 20 November 1922, reprinted in part in Albert Maurice, "René Maran et Félix Eboué, Une Amitié," *Hommage à René Maran* (Paris: Présence Africaine, 1965), p. 216.

Man-Lie's house on the rue Richelieu was crowded with children when Eboué arrived at the beginning of 1922. In addition
to the nine-year-old Henri, Cornélie's children lived with their
grandmother; Félix Gratien was not making enough to afford a
house. Eboué felt very close to all these children, and told Cornélie and Man-Lie about his second son, Robert, back in Oubangui-Chari. The child had had twelve teeth when Eboué left
Bambari, he said. Friends and relatives were urging him to marry,
and rumors persisted—rumors that were not discouraged by
Cornélie and her mother—that he might marry Eugénie Tell.

Miss Tell, born in Cayenne 13 November 1891, belonged to
the upper levels of Creole society. Her father, Herménégilde Tell,
born the son of a black prison official, taught himself law and
moved through the ranks of the penitentiary administration until,
in 1919, the Ministry named him director of the prison system,
the first Guyanese to attain such a rank. Monsieur Tell, a tall
handsome man, had a wide circle of friends in Guyane, the Antilles, and in the metropole because of his position and because of
his activities in French freemasonry. He was Venerable or head of
a lodge in Guyane and attained the rank of thirty-third degree,
the highest one can go.

Tell and his wife had three children, Guillaume, Eugénie, and
Charles, all sent to France in childhood. Eugénie went to a small
town in southern France to study music and become a pianist.
She and her younger brother Charles, whom she adored, practiced
their English by using it to write long letters to each other, and
Eugénie learned some German too. Charles died young in 1913;
Guillaume went into the army, and later became an official of the
Folies Bergères. Eugénie Tell returned to Saint Laurent, where
her father had his headquarters, to teach school. There she earned
herself a reputation as a very dynamic, independent young
woman interested in politics and women's rights.

Although the Tells had more money than the Eboués, such
differences were not so important in a very small community like
that of Guyane. Eboué and Miss Tell had first met ten years before at Camille Lhuerre's wedding but had seen each other rarely
since then. Cornélie first attempted to bring the two together

through letters; she wrote her brother before his return that people said they would be a good match, but Eboué, at first merely embarrassed by the gossip, objected that he had no money to match the promise of his career. And he had an important condition: "that the lady accept my children as well as the hazards of life in the colonies."[8] Cornélie and Man-Lie persisted, and Eboué said they could at least talk with Eugénie Tell to see how she felt about him.

In April Eugénie came to Cayenne; she and Eboué spent a week talking and getting to know each other. They decided to marry, and she returned to Saint Laurent. On 22 April Félix Gratien wrote a formal letter on behalf of his brother-in-law asking Herménégilde Tell for the hand of his daughter. A few days later Tell agreed to the proposal, and Eboué wrote his future wife in a tone which shows a complete change in his feelings.

> My pretty fiancée. I am bursting! My heart is swollen with a sublime joy and my soul breathes with the most intense emotion. . . . Did you feel it? At the precise moment when I got your father's answer—yesterday afternoon—I concentrated on you with all the force of my being, and the song of love . . . which went towards you from me must have been transmitted with all its force across space.[9]

They corresponded daily, sending their letters by the ship that went between Cayenne and Saint Laurent. Eugénie's first gift to her future husband was a cigarette holder, for he smoked constantly. They then exchanged rings; Eugénie gave Félix the ring that had belonged to her beloved brother Charles. They planned the wedding for June, and Eugénie traveled across the frontier into Suriname to purchase what she needed for it.

In May, Eboué visited Saint Laurent and brought his fiancée some silver thread, satin, and other articles she had asked him for. They began to know each other better. In her father's house Eugénie—or "Niette," his pet name for her—played the piano for her "Lix" and sang songs of Massenet: "I don't like Massenet, but

8 Archives Eboué, Letter, Félix Eboué to Cornélie Gratien, 4 February 1920.
9 Archives Eboué, Letter, Félix Eboué to Eugénie Tell, 27 April 1921.

I think you have reconciled me with your favorite musician. You sang with so much enthusiasm and sincerity . . . that sometimes I hum his songs when I think of you."[10]

After about ten days the future bridegroom returned to Cayenne to prepare himself and his family for the wedding. He had to arrange for best men and ushers and felt, in a moment of depression, that he had stayed away from Guyane so long that he had few friends there. This was odd for a man who always seemed to have many friends. But Eboué seems to have had such high ideals of friendship that perhaps many people who considered themselves his friends somehow failed to measure up. In any case, Eboué more than once said he had none when he needed them.

In Cayenne, he found enough to make up a complement of ushers. And he stayed busy enough to avoid wedding nerves. He gave a speech on *Batouala* at the local literary society, played bridge often, and went out with Henri and Cornélie's children. One day he walked by the sea with the children. Dropping his usual reserve, he began to run, running as he had when a schoolboy, but the years and the cigarettes had taken their toll, and he drew to a halt, feeling suddenly middle-aged: "Made young by a great love [I] believed [myself] young for good and gambolled with too much enthusism with the children on the beach—just like a young man. [I] was audacious enough to accept the challenge . . . a 100 meter race. But, just before the finish I felt pain and went back to the house."[11]

The second week in June the Eboué family traveled by boat to Saint Laurent (the colony still had no road connecting its two major towns), and the wedding took place in church on 14 June 1922. Eboué was splendid in full-dress uniform and had let his hair grow, parting it in the middle like a younger man. He had kept his mustache, but shaved it off shortly after the marriage.

The men and women in attendance dressed in the French fashions of the day, only Man-Lie, a traditionalist, kept her usual Creole head scarf and dress. After the ceremony the party was

---

[10] Archives Eboué, Letter, Félix Eboué to Eugénie Tell, 5 May 1921.
[11] *Ibid.*

At the marriage of Félix Eboué and Eugénie Tell in 1922, the bride and
groom are center front, with Madame Tell and Madame Eboué to the
right. Herménégilde Tell stands behind the mothers of the newlyweds,
with Eboué's sister, Cornélie Gratien, to the left in the dark hat. Her
husband, Félix, is the first man from the left in the back row. The only
other person identified is F. Halmus, the brother of Mrs. Tell, directly
behind Eugénie. Courtesy of Madame Eboué.

photographed, Eboué and his wife in the middle, the two mothers
on Eboué's left; an empty chair stood on Eboué's right to represent "Petit Camille" Lhuerre, a friend of twenty years, who could
not be present at the ceremony.

That the wedding had taken place in the Catholic Church was
a concession to the women, all practicing Catholics. The men
were indifferent or masons; Eboué himself had adopted stoicism
and abandoned organized religion, but decided to become a
Freemason during his leave in Cayenne in 1922.

Joining the Freemasons was a much more serious affair than
assuming a membership in one of the other clubs in which Eboué
delighted, and which provided him with the congenial com-

panions and intellectual stimulation he needed. In France he kept up his contacts with the sporting groups of his youth and discussion societies interested in the idea of Atlantis; in Cayenne he, with most Guyanese, belonged to Les Amis du Livre. But joining the Freemasons was, during the Third French Republic, a political as well as a social act.

During the Third Republic, from 1870 to 1940, opponents claimed that Freemasons had great power and accused them of plotting to accomplish everything from the destruction of French civilization and the Church to the provision of jobs for each other in the government and civil services. It is true that many politicians, educators, and civil servants belonged to lodges during this period, and indeed, that the Ministry of Colonies was known as the "masonic ministry" where supposedly one had to be a "brother" to move up to high rank. Although some important figures at the "rue Oudinot" were members, other were not; Yvon Delbos and Gratien Candace belonged while René Maran and Roger Hellier did not.

La France Equinoxiale lodge of Cayenne, founded in 1843, federated itself with the Grande Loge de France, an organization considered slightly less radical politically and theologically than the Grand Orient to which Eboué's father-in-law and Diagne belonged. Members of the Grande Loge, who often belonged to the Radical Party, believed that the universe had an order and a purpose determined by the "Grand Architect," meaning God, Science, or some other force beyond the control of man; the Grand Orient, many of whose members belonged to the Socialist-SFIO Party, rejected the idea of a "Grand Architect," and many considered themselves atheists. Although both federations or "obediences" were considered antipathetic to organized religion, membership did not prevent all members from being loyal churchgoers.

Tell and others probably encouraged Eboué to join, and 1922 gave him the first opportunity he had enjoyed to engage in the necessary study. After returning to Cayenne in July after his wedding, Eboué was initiated on the 13th and remained a member for the rest of his life. Although the organization in France was secret, Eboué never denied his membership and was not dogmatic about his beliefs, sometimes to the annoyance of more doctrinaire brothers. "Chacun à son goût," he said.

RETURN TO FRANCE

At the beginning of August, Eboué left Cayenne with his bride and son for France, with innumberable pieces of luggage, and more to come later, including the furniture that the Tells had promised to send them as a wedding gift. After stopping briefly in Suriname and Trinidad the Eboué's arrived in Fort-de-France, Martinique, to change ships. Before sending a cable to Eugénie's father to inform him of their safe arrival they found one from him with the news of the death of Bojotte, one of Eugénie's collection of dogs and cats.

The trip from Martinique to France was less pleasant than that from Cayenne to Fort-de-France; the family was a bit crowded on board the *Puerto Rico* because little Henri shared the cabin with his father and step-mother. He behaved well, but Eugénie Eboué was a little annoyed that the chief steward had forgotten his promise to find separate quarters for the energetic youngster.[12] They arrived in Paris near the end of August.

By October they put Henri in boarding school and moved into a spacious apartment at number 4, rue Chauveau Lagarde, just behind Madeleine Church and within walking distance of Saint Lazare railroad station. Because Eboué's own finances were quite limited, Mr. Tell appears to have paid the expenses of the apartment, which was to be their Paris address for fourteen years. They spent little time there, although Eboué overstayed his projected leave in 1922.

The Ministry gave Eboué an extended leave of absence. Eugénie was expecting a child and was understandably nervous about having it in Oubangui-Chari. Eboué inquired about the possibility of secondment to the Economic Agency for Equatorial Africa or to the central administration of the Ministry of Colonies to avoid the reduction in salary concomitant with extended leave. The Ministry refused the request, and he borrowed money from René Maran, still in Africa, to help meet added expenses.

12 Archives Eboué, Letters, Félix Eboué to Herménégilde Tell, 10 August 1922, Eugénie Eboué to Herménégilde Tell, 11 August 1922.

When he needed another extension of leave, he pleaded illness; the Ministry sent him to Val de Grâce hospital for a week of observation. He was in good health, but:

> The physician . . . realized what was going on but nonetheless declared me unable to return to my post. We thus got three more months to be renewed once again. That will take us up to 19 August when we must return to Congo where there is a need to make hay.[13]

While waiting for the birth of their child, both Eboué and Eugénie kept busy. She fixed up the apartment and had a bathroom installed. He decided to complete his law studies and attend courses that might help in the preparation of another book, even though at thirty-eight he was considerably older than other students. He attended lectures on "Experimental Phonetics," for example, by Abbé Rousselot at the Collège de France on Wednesdays and Fridays and courses at the Faculty of Law nearby, just up the rue Saint Jacques. On 19 July 1923 the Faculty of Law of the University of Paris granted him his law degree, the Licence.

The extended sojourn in Paris and his marriage to the daughter of Herménégilde Tell permitted Eboué much closer contact than ever before with people high in the administration, politics, and freemasonry. He got to know Blaise Diagne much better through his father-in-law; Diagne and Tell had become good friends when the Senegalese worked as a customs official at Saint Laurent before 1914, and they corresponded regularly. Diagne considered Eugénie almost like a daughter, and after her marriage wrote the following to Mr. Tell: "Please give a big kiss to my Nini and to her mother for me first and then for my family. Compliments to Eboué, the happy bridegroom, and tell him that I shall make sure he does not make his wife unhappy."[14]

Tell sent his son-in-law on various errands in Paris to see Diagne and others. He had discovered, for example, that people in the Ministry of Colonies were criticizing him because of an increase in the number of escapees from the penitentiary, and he

---

[13] Archives Eboué, Letter, Félix Eboué to Herménégilde Tell, 19 February 1923.

[14] Archives Eboué, Letter, Blaise Diagne to Herménégilde Tell, 28 June 1922.

thought they might send an inspection mission. Acting on his instruction, Eboué went to the Ministry and found out through Roger Hellier, his "Colo" classmate, that no inspection would take place. At the Ministry Eboué took the opportunity to help his own career along:

> I won't lose contact with the Ministry and shall watch over my nomination to first class. Last July . . . I was classed 18th whereas only 10 administrators were chosen. If I had been in Paris, I might have been able to make contact with the members of the Commission de Classement [which ranked the administrators] and get a better position.[15]

In January 1923 the Ministry promoted him to administrator first class as he wished.

Tell, not an old man at fifty-seven, was also thinking of going into politics in 1922, and Diagne, who had many ties with West Indian politicians, encouraged him. Jean Galmot, a white or metropolitan, represented Guyane in the French Chamber of Deputies, but new elections were to be held soon because Galmot had been censured for fraudulent business practices. Several men were under consideration as candidates, including Tell and Eugène Lautier.

Lautier, a well-known journalist in France and member of the Radical Party, edited *L'Homme Libre*, which had been former Prime Minister Georges Clemenceau's newspaper. Like some other whites, Lautier was considering a campaign for the position of deputy of Guyane, though he cared nothing about the colony and merely wanted a safe seat in the Chamber of Deputies. He suspected that Tell wanted the post too and asked Eboué to visit him for a talk in his sumptuous Paris apartment.

The journalist candidly admitted to Eboué he would rather not run for a seat to parliament from Paris because it would be less safe and voters would be so close that they could bombard him with requests. Guyane was far away. By making arrangements with governors and mayors one could always be elected without being bothered by local demands for personal favors and economic development projects. Eboué chain-smoked during the

15 Archives Eboué, Letter, Félix Eboué to Herménégilde Tell, Paris 27 October 1922.

interview, a sign of his nervousness, but he talked very little. He wrote to his father-in-law: "I was polite. . . . I listened for 20 minutes to his monologue. I was content to listen, practically without interrupting him. Gene, perhaps bothered . . . by my silence, felt the need to get up and continue his talk while walking around the room smoking."[16]

The effort to maintain his reserve and present a calm appearance was, of course, a way of drawing information out of others and characterized Eboué's administrative and personal style. Many years later inexperienced administrators mistook for ignorance or lack of initiative Eboué's way of listening quietly and carefully while others did most of the talking. This was the technique that allowed him, that day, to leave Lautier without having divulged any information about his father-in-law, much less with a commitment for support. He went home and immediately wrote a very long and very detailed letter to Tell about the interview and Lautier's plans and said in conclusion:

> He is one of three or four journalists of the Left whose articles permit us to forget those doctrines of radicalism which are hackneyed and out-of-date. . . . "Gene" is the third ace of the republican polemicists, one of the rare ones capable of answering with spirit the dangerous theories of those gentlemen of Action Française.[17]

Action Française was a royalist, racist, and outspokenly Catholic organization, the main organ of which was a newspaper of the same name; both had been founded in support of the military at the time of the Dreyfus affair, that is to say, both were opposed to a republican form of government. Most Antilleans, on the other hand, supported the so-called Radical Party, a left-of-center group devoted to sustaining a republican system. Many of Eboué's friends and the Grand Loge de France were identified with the radicals; Eboué himself stood somewhat farther left.

In 1924 Lautier won the election and remained deputy from Guyane until 1932. Eboué and others had occasion to regret his election, for he cared little about Guyane and his supporters did not hesitate to use fraud to elect him.

[16] Archives Eboué, Letter, Félix Eboué to Herménégilde Tell, 27 October 1922.
[17] *Ibid.*

While doing these errands for his father-in-law that autumn in 1922 Eboué received disturbing news from Africa. Because of *Batouala*, it appeared that threats had been made on René Maran's life, and in France a wave of criticism broke against his book and his career. Eboué wrote to Maran (via Robert Hermine because he feared letters might be opened) and encouraged him to leave Africa and the colonial service to defend himself, to dedicate his life to literature and to articles about the empire. In November 1922 Eboué went to see Candace for help: "I went to see Candace . . . and I wrote him the next day to ask him to insist that the Ministry permit you to return by English territory."[18]

The Ministry told Candace that nothing would happen to Maran, and Eboué wrote Maran to contact his friend, Henri Vendôme, as he went through Bangui. Vendôme presumably would provide Maran a safe place to stay if he had to return France via Bangui and Brazzaville. Eboué added that all leading black Frenchmen were concerned about his safety and his future career. In the Chamber of Deputies a white member attacked Maran, and Guadeloupe's representatives answered, Eboué wrote:

Did you receive the issue of the *Officiel* with the remarks of Barthel-emy against you and the energetic answers of Candace and Boisneuf. . . . I am currently in contact with Diagne, a friend of my father-in-law. A week ago he asked for news of you with a smile on his face. He seems to have an opinion about you similar to my own.[19]

Maran finally left Tchad and arrived in Bordeaux in August 1923, but he and Eboué may not have seen each other. Eugénie had, on 18 March, given birth to their first child, a beautiful baby daughter, Ginette, and Eboué could no longer prolong his leave. After settling Henri at the Lycée Michelet, Eboué, his wife, and daughter left France on 15 August for French Equatorial Africa.

TO AFRICA
In Africa, Governor General Augagneur, quite angry about Eboué's extended leave, had cabled the Ministry of Colonies early in the year asking for his subordinate's immediate return,

18 Archives Maran, Letter, Félix Eboué to René Maran, 20 November 1922.
19 Archives Maran, Letter, Félix Eboué to René Maran, 20 February 1923.

for by 1923 Eboué had a reputation as an excellent administrator. The head of French Equatorial Africa was desperately trying to fill vacant posts and solve the colonies' problems.

The economic situation in A.E.F. had deteriorated during 1922 and 1923 as prices for colonial products continued to decline. Collection of rubber completely ceased, for example, and the budgets of the colonies had a sizable deficit in 1923. Augagneur went to France to try to find money, hoping to complete the railroad thereby giving the colony a needed economic lift quickly. He also founded a research organization, the Société des Recherches Congolaises, to study the populations and local problems of this part of Africa—something Eboué and a few of his colleagues had long been doing.

In Oubangui-Chari Lamblin was still governor, actively pursuing ambitious roadbuilding programs and the introduction of industrial crops. The governor admired Eboué for his work in Ouaka region for the three years from 1918 to 1921. By 1923 it was one of the most prosperous and peaceful of the country, if not of all of French Equatorial Africa:

> Certain regions, like Ouaka, have begun a period of real economic prosperity based no longer on the problematical collection of products but rather on agricultural production. Vast plantations of food products, oil producing fruits (peanuts and sesame), rice, cereas constitute for the natives a source of profit.[20]

The situation in Gabon was much worse; the personnel office in Brazzaville apparently tried to assign Eboué there after his arrival on 8 September, but he did not want the assignment. He preferred a colony which, like Oubangui-Chari, had a completely civilian administration. Also, Gabon was in the grip of a famine, and the administration was under attack from *Jeune Gabonais* and the League for the Rights of Man and Citizen for abusive labor practices and the excessive power of some of the companies.[21] "What do these young Gabonese want? They demand representation, either a king, or elected officials dealing in their

---

[20] "Rapport Politique Annuel pour 1922," December 1923, p. 22.
[21] Brian Weinstein, *Gabon: Nation-Building on the Ogooué* (Cambridge: M.I.T. Press, 1967), p. 41.

name with the government, and this is what the government cannot allow," wrote the acting governor general.[22]

Oubangui-Chari had, in Eboué's view, not only a more enlightened administration under Lamblin, but also afforded the cooler and drier climate of the savanna by contrast to Gabon's heat and humidity. Lastly, and perhaps most important, most of Eboué's friends were in Oubangui-Chari, and he arranged to be reassigned there for the fourth time. After he, Eugénie, and the baby left Brazzaville, he wrote to René Maran: "I am, as you see, assigned to Oubangui, as I wished. It is true that I had to maneuver to return here."[23]

[22] "Rapport Politique 1922," p. 22.
[23] Archives Maran, Letter, Félix Eboué to René Maran, 5 January 1924.

IV

LATER DAYS IN
OUBANGUI-CHARI, 1923-1931

In Bangui, Eboué introduced his wife to Lieutenant Governor Lamblin and showed her something of the town. The September and October rains of Oubangui—often between 250 and 300 millimeters each month—were enough to discourage them from venturing every day into the capital with its unpaved streets, and Madame Eboué remained most of the time with her daughter in the quarters reserved for administrators. Eboué talked with Lamblin about the assignment to Bas Mbomou region that the government asked him to take and studied the monthly reports to brief himself on the region's problems and peoples.

Bas Mbomou, eastward up the Oubangui and Mbomou Rivers, then had about 90,000 adult inhabitants belonging to the Nzakara, Zandé, and Yakoma groups and spread out in four subdivisions: Bangassou, Bakouma, Rafai, and Ouango. Unlike the areas that Eboué had known in the western and central parts of the colony, local authority here before the advent of the French had been highly organized and hierarchized under Muslim kings or "sultans" who imposed themselves on local populations. By 1923 the French had abolished these sultanates with the exception of that of Rafai where Hetman, leader of the Zandé people, still possessed considerable authority, partly because the French trusted and respected him and partly because he was an extremely intelligent man who understood the politics of colonialism, using it to his advantage.[1] Most administrators found they needed his cooperation in carrying out their programs in Bas Mbomou in spite of a professed French desire to decrease the power of local leaders.

Lamblin told Eboué that the economic situation had been deteriorating in Bas Mbomou for several years because of the fluctuation in world prices for rubber and ivory. The previous administrator had failed to undertake the introduction of new crops, and had earned an infamous reputation among Africans for having molested small boys. Consequently, Eboué's job in this difficult area would be to develop a new industrial crop to provide the Africans with taxable income and to raise the morale—not to mention the morals—of the local administration. Cultivation was to replace an economy based on collection of wild crops.

Coffee, a cash crop, had been introduced into Oubangui-Chari, but Eboué and Lamblin thought about experimenting with something new in the comparatively rich soil of the region. They were aware of the fact that French political and economic analysts warned of the dangers of dependence on America for cotton products, and they knew that the Belgians nearby had begun to develop cotton cultivation quite successfully. So cotton seemed a good candidate.[2]

Africans had in fact produced a variety of cotton in Oubangui-Chari and Congo areas long before the arrival of the Belgians or the French, but the Europeans wanted large-scale cultivation of a strain acceptable to the European market. In the Congo, the Belgians had introduced an American variety and in 1922, the year before Eboué's return to Africa, they produced 1000 tons of ginned cotton.[3] Moreover, in 1922, Eboué's friend René Isambert, stationed at Ouango in Bas Mbomou, had experimented, though unsuccessfully, with some cotton seeds a Belgian had given him.

[1] Eric de Dampierre has written about this area in *Un Ancien Royaume Bandia du Haut Oubangui* (Paris: Plon, 1967).

[2] Much of my information on cotton comes from A. F. Eboué, "Le Coton en Oubangui-Chari: campagne du Bas Mbomou 1925-1926," *Le Monde Colonial Illustré*, October 1926, No. 3, pp. 224-26.

[3] Robert Mees, *Vade-Mecum du planteur de coton au Congo Belge* (Brussels: L'Afrique Belge, 1926), p. 109. The book was found in Eboué's library.

Accordingly, with the approval of Lamblin, Eboué agreed to seek
to introduce the cultivation of cotton to his region and, in effect,
to Oubangui-Chari. This decided, he left for Bangassou, administrative headquarters of Bas Mbomou, with his mind full of the
project.

Although the road east from Bangui to Bambari was open, travelers could not yet go all the way to Bangassou by car or truck
(not until later in the year would the road from Bambari to Bangassou be completed). The Eboué family—Félix, Eugénie, and the
baby—therefore took a *baleinière* or metal-covered canoe up the
Mbomou as far as Ouango, and because they had a great deal of
luggage as well as Madame Eboué's piano, they required at least
two large canoes. Sitting on deck chairs as the Africans paddled
up the river, Madame Eboué asked her husband many questions
about the new country during the eighteen-day trip. Though
the forest they traveled through was not so different from what
she had known along the Maroni River back home in Guyane,
the Yakoma villages on the banks of the Mbomou, with their
round thatched roof houses, were far different from anything
she had ever seen.

At Ouango, René Isambert was waiting for them, so when the
canoes slid into the landing, he took the Eboués by car and truck
to his own home beautifully situated on a hill overlooking the
river and the forest. Madame Eboué came to like Isambert during the comfortable visit, for she enjoyed his re-telling all the
local gossip; as a loyal Roman Catholic, she could not, however,
approve his increasing admiration for Protestantism. Soon the
talk had to end, and they were on their way by road to Bangassou, a distance of 78 kilometers, this time to settle down in the
very large thatched roof house reserved for the head of the district.

The house was situated in the administrative quarter of the
town, divided like Bambari into administrative, commercial, and
African sections. Previous administrators had built the house on a
high foundation necessitating a rather majestic stairway. Because the walls were thick stone, the rooms kept cool even during the hot dry season. Because the Bangassou area is a little
flatter than Ouango, the view was not so splendid as Isambert's

had been. The new head of the district soon invited his French and Belgian colleagues to the long verandah of the house for aperitifs and a celebration of the new year, 1924. He paid courtesy calls on Sultan Hetman at Rafai and on the Belgians across the river.

In 1924, a few months after his arrival, Eboué received from Belgian colleagues, with whom he established very good relations, four tons of seed for a Texas variety of cotton called "Triumph Big Boll." He proceeded cautiously with the June planting because the year seemed abnormally dry and cotton needed abundant rains to germinate and grow and because of the low quality of seeds. But with all his reading on cotton and his advice from the Belgians across the river, the attempt failed. Governor Lamblin was naturally not pleased and thought that if Eboué had traveled more that year to watch over the planting and weeding the result might have been different.

The governor's criticism was somewhat justified, for Eboué had not toured in 1924 as much as usual. Ordinarily, he would have toured the region for several weeks at a time, but he was no longer a bachelor, and his wife, quite worried and lonesome without him, asked him to stay close to Bangassou. Unaccustomed to the new country she was living in, she became nervous and sometimes frightened and was to write to him during one of his trips: ". . . my nerves are extremely strained for in addition . . . to your absence, Ginette has attacks of diarrhea several times a month, and she does not eat as she should. . . . I long to see you. . . ."[4]

In addition to Ginette, Madame Eboué had Eboué's five-year-old son Robert to take care of, for he arrived at Bangassou along with Chief Sokambi's eldest sons. (Eboué had written his old friend at Kouango to send him Louis, Paul Brazza, and Achille so that they might go to school under Eboué's direction.)[5] To make matters more difficult, his wife was also expecting her second child.

When Eboué did get out on tour, the two wrote each other

4 Archives Eboué, Letter, Eugénie Eboué to Félix Eboué, 18 April 1924.
5 Interview with Achille Sokambi, Bangui, 28 June 1968.

every day, and sometimes twice a day, sending the notes by relay runners: "I did not write you all day long," Madame Eboué once wrote when she missed a letter, "because I knew you were not far away. But tomorrow where will you be? Many kilometers . . . separate us; in spite of that you must feel my heart close to yours."[6]

During one short tour Eboué responded that she should try to understand the new country, but he nonetheless hurried home in April, leaving his work and complaining a little: "I don't see how I can administer my district without going on tour. . . . I shall be at Bangassou the 27th; to do that I shall be required to march night and day without stopping and at the same time do the great amount of work already undertaken. I shall drop the charting of the automobile road which will give me a little extra time."[7] In this case he arrived home in time for the birth of their son, born 14 May 1924, and named Charles after Madame Eboué's deceased younger brother.

Before their marriage Eboué had tried to explain what life in Africa would be like; now he once again had to tell Eugénie why he could not leave Africa. But he told her he could apply for a position in Bangui, although it might adversely affect his career: "there is only one solution . . . and this consists in asking for a change and an assignment in Bangui, for we cannot think, at my age, of abandoning my 16 years of service to look for something else. I have only my profession, and we must be satisfied with it."[8]

Trying to bolster his wife's courage, he hired servants to look after her and the house and asked Sokambi to send a trusted servant to act as "major domo." He also maintained good relations with local Frenchmen and with American missionaries, who tried to make sure his wife lacked for nothing. Robert Hermine, René Isambert, and his brother-in-law Félix Gratien, who had received his position through Eboué, also fortunately lived within visiting distance. They and others sent pieces of ivory which Madame Eboué had learned to make into hair brushes. Some

6 Archives Eboué, Letter, Eugénie Eboué to Félix Eboué, 17 November 1924.
7 Archives Eboué, Letter, Félix Eboué to Eugénie Eboué, 20 April 1924.
8 Archives Eboué, Letter, Félix Eboué to Eugénie Eboué, 23 April 1924.

brought fresh fruit and vegetables, abundant in this region, during their frequent, if brief, visits. And although Madame Eboué was a staunch Catholic, the American protestants, an independent group which had established headquarters on the edge of Bangassou, were very helpful. Although the distance between the mission and the Eboué house was considerable, a Negro missionary nurse, Mrs. Laura Bayne, came often to keep Madame Eboué company and help take care of the children. She served as midwife when Charles was born. Madame Eboué also went by *tipoye* to her new friend's house to listen to their radio.

To provide further diversion for himself and his wife, Eboué invited a traveling group of American missionaries sent by the Africa Inland Mission to his house. One of the Americans wrote: "Ralph [Davis] was able to accompany Madame Eboué on the grand piano while she sang. This pleased them [the Eboués] greatly. Most of the people who passed through could only play jazz, and they appreciated the fact that Ralph played classical music."[9] Other visitors came with the Citroën Mission crossing Africa.

It was lucky that Eboué could spend some time in Bangassou in 1924, because word came from Paris that Mrs. Eboué's mother, who had been staying in the apartment on rue Chauveau Lagarde, had died on Christmas Day, and his wife fell into deep depression. One last blow during the same year was the death of Eboué's uncle, Maximilien Liontel. However, with an enlarging circle of friends, the birth of her son, new hobbies, and encouragement from her husband, Eugénie Eboué began to feel, with the passage of time, she could get along better. With greater stability at home, Eboué could spend more of 1925 on his administrative activity and try once again to introduce cotton.

COTTON: 1925

The courses Eboué had taken at the Colonial School many years before had taught him nothing about tropical agriculture that he had not learned in Guyane. Before the cotton season be-

9 Cited by Kenneth Richardson, *Garden of Miracles: A History of the Africa Inland Mission* (London: Victory Press, 1968), p. 209.

gan again he zealously read everything he could find about it and consulted with the Belgians to avoid another failure. The latter were still cooperative and explained their problems: getting the Africans to work regularly at cultivation and protecting themselves as administrators from some powerful Dutch and Belgian businessmen, dependent on ivory, who objected if Africans spent their time cultivating instead of tracking elephants. Even worse, other merchants used numerous tricks to purchase cotton at the lowest possible price, thus defeating the administration's three goals: encouraging Africans to work on the new crop, stimulating local commercial activity, and increasing tax collections.

On the basis of his studies and interviews Eboué wrote several reports to Bangui, often working on them in the evening at home to be close to his wife who would play the piano or read to the children while he worked in the corner. Eboué apparently concentrated on his writing to the exclusion of everything, including the length of his cigarette ash, so that a number of his first-draft reports in the archives of the Central African Republic are distinctive for small cigarette burns. In the morning he gave the manuscripts to a secretary, accustomed to his unusual handwriting, to be typed. Eboué, increasingly known as an administrative perfectionist, was very particular that the reports follow correct form and made the secretary retype them for deviations from it. Many documents submitted to the governor show a comma added here and there by Eboué to improve the style or the clarity.

In his reports Eboué advised the governor to set minimum prices for cotton so that the highest prices might be paid to Africans. This suggestion was in line with Lamblin's plans for he had suggested in a circular to his subordinates that the officially designated market days which he had recently inaugurated for other products be carefully watched by administrators to make sure that the minimum prices established by them were respected. In principle no companies were allowed a monopoly of trade anymore, but they managed to invent clever tricks to keep prices low. Eboué also suggested export controls so that cotton would not be shipped to a foreign country. He suggested granting one company the exclusive right to purchase cotton, as in the Belgian Congo, in exchange for setting up cotton gins and baling machines; such an arrangement would mean, he thought, only a minimum investment of government funds.[10]

By June 1925 Eboué had plunged into cotton planting with all his energy. His reputation and career were at stake, he thought. During this period, one of worry, travel, and fatigue, another trait of Eboué's revealed itself: a tendency, justified or not, to believe that superiors and colleagues were waiting for him to make a mistake in order to remove him, damage his career, or refuse to give him credit for his accomplishments. During a long and difficult tour, Eboué wrote to his wife about his increasing disagreement with Lamblin:

> . . . this two-week period is so important for the success of cotton that I am forced to sacrifice my time. Don't forget that my position vis-à-vis L [Lamblin] does not allow for failure, for he would be only too happy—he and I, we don't view the cotton question in the same way. . . . Therefore, in order not to give him the chance to toast at my expense, I must do more than I thought to insure the success of the campaign.[11]

He wrote to René Maran in the same tone but, realizing he might be exaggerating, caught himself: "The truth is that my relations with Lamblin changed completely and to such an extent that we were at loggerheads. . . . I shall tell you in detail all my little troubles which are, to tell the truth, without importance."[12]

Eboué went on tour to supervise the preparation of the 1500 hectares designated for cotton. Touring, in 1925, was still strenuous, but much less so than it had been ten years before; the existence of some roads permitted the use of automobiles, mostly borrowed from local Portuguese merchants. Even so, tours to supervise cotton planting lasted two or three weeks, during which Eboué spent ten hours a day in the fields, accompanied by Mr. Pacilly, a government agronomist sent by Lamblin to help him.

Away from home, he wrote to his wife daily trying to cheer her up or explaining his work; he was going from place to place, showing Africans how to plant the seeds after the land had been

---

[10] Reports concerning cotton discussed in this chapter are in various archives of the Central African Republic.

[11] Archives Eboué, Letter, Félix Eboué to Eugénie Eboué, 26 July 1925.

[12] Archives Maran, Letter, Félix Eboué to René Maran, 9 November 1925.

cleared, then dividing the land into distinct family plots in an attempt to introduce cotton without disrupting local social structure or taking workers far from their homes. Each family was to be paid for its work as a family. "We shall have our 1500 hectares of plantations by sections of 1000 square meters, each one being separated by a ditch from that of the neighbor. It is a beautiful sight. . . ."[13]

In the midst of these tours Eboué often sat down to an impressive evening meal, the elements of which his wife sent him from Bangassou. He might first have a pâté de foie gras, then a main dish of chicken prepared by himself, a vegetable from his garden, and wine with a cake for dessert if some American missionary had prepared one for him. He once savored a bottle of champagne kept cold in a small stream.

Before retiring in the evening in one of the small buildings constructed for touring administrators, he read some of the dozen magazines and newspapers that René Maran regularly sent him. One of his favorites was the popular *Nouvelle Revue Française,* which he probably read more carefully than he did the political newspapers; he liked to be up on the French literary scene. He arranged the periodicals in chronological order before reading them and was very annoyed if one was missing. Once he thought the children misplaced a magazine, and Madame Eboué wrote to Félix Gratien of her surprise at his sudden anger: "Imagine. Lix accused the children of having lost some magazines he was looking for, and he was so silly when we sent them to him. He is still missing an issue. Do you have it?"[14]

He would also be put out if few letters arrived from France; he himself was a great letter writer, enjoyed hearing from friends, and expected faithful correspondence. In order to keep up his own end, he had his wife to take care of some correspondence while he toured.

In the evening by himself Eboué often expressed in letters an anger unrevealed in personal encounters. Reserved and always calm in appearance though he was, Eboué's letters show he tended

[13] Archives Eboué, Letter, Félix Eboué to Eugénie Eboué, 4 August 1925.
[14] Archives Eboué, Letter, Eugénie Eboué to Félix Gratien, 16 December 1925.

to brood and to imagine the worst would happen to him. His bitterness about not having received his promotion to administrator in chief, anger when instructions were not followed, annoyance at the loss of a magazine, frustration about not getting credit for something he had done are expressed only in letters, not openly. White colleagues, given double credit toward their seniority for the years spent in World War I, were being promoted faster than Eboué, for example: "My juniors from the Colonial School are now my seniors. . . . Can you imagine anything more disagreeable?"[15]

There were grounds for Eboué's concerns in 1925. Lamblin had turned critical of him, and Raphael Antonetti, named governor general of French Equatorial Africa in 1924, agreed; Antonetti criticized Eboué for letting subordinates, Isambert among them, run their own subdivisions with a minimum of direction from Bangassou. Eboué, however, believed a head of subdivision knew his area best, favored a decentralized administration contrary to French administrative tradition, and had thought that Lamblin was of like mind. His complete confidence in friends could also be abused.

On top of everything else, Madame Eboué had still not grown accustomed to Oubangui-Chari. Two days before his thirty-ninth birthday she wrote him that she could not bear this life: "I am profoundly sad and discouraged at times. At the time I insisted on going to Africa, I did not think I would shed so many tears. . . ."[16] Without noting that it was his birthday, Eboué responded 26 December. He begged her to be courageous during their separations and said he might be willing to give up his career if there was something else to do: "I see that it will be necessary to give up Colonial life, but where shall we go? Whether it is in Togo, Cameroun or in French West Africa it will always be the same thing. . . . But what to do in France? Do you see something? Tell me."[17] Saying that he would be willing to give

[15] Archives Maran, Letter, Félix Eboué to René Maran, 9 November 1925.
[16] Archives Eboué, Letter, Eugénie Eboué to Félix Eboué, 24 December 1925.
[17] Archives Eboué, Letter, Félix Eboué to Eugénie Eboué, 26 December 1925.

up his career as an administrator was really for the sake of temporary peace; he had no intention of leaving his profession
permanently, in spite of his complaining and jousts with pessimism.

Eboué cheered his wife by trying to keep her mind on Charles
and Ginette, who was beginning to learn local languages. He sent
ivory she could work with and encouraged her hobbies; he wrote
paragraphs about promotions, his own activities, and those of
Félix Gratien then purchasing rubber and ivory for the Compagnie des Sultanats. He wrote about Sultan Hetman, with whom
he had begun to work as closely as he had with Sokambi back in
Kouango.

Cooperating with local authorities and helping them to build
their own power was not only consistent with Eboué's beliefs but
also important for the success of the cotton program, Eboué
thought. He considered Hetman in particular to be a member of
the elite necessary to maintain order in any society, and he believed Hetman's sons could provide a new educated leadership
to meet the problems of a modernizing society without creating
chaos in the older society. To René Maran he wrote the following about Hetman: "A very good fellow, this Sultan Hetman—
intelligent, pure, savoir-faire, in brief, he has style. If he wants
. . . and if they don't send me back to Bangui . . . we shall
make something pretty out of his sultanate. . . ."[18]

Eboué got Hetman's cooperation in cotton cultivation. Indeed,
Hetman sent members of his personal guard, the *bazinguers,* to
work as "cotton boys" or teachers and surveyors of cotton cultivation. Hetman's son Binza worked as Eboué's assistant and
went on tour with him, and when there was no Frenchman to put
in charge of the Rafai administrative post, Binza took care of
the office and most duties like tax collection and census taking.
Hetman thereby gained power from an association with the
French and could always claim he was at least in part responsible
for the administration of Rafai in spite of French presence. Binza
and the *bazinguers* also assumed considerable power, and it is
said that they used it harshly. Hetman doubtless made money

[18] Archives Maran, Letter, Félix Eboué to René Maran, 5 January 1924.

Sultan Hetman of Rafai with his eldest son, Binza. Courtesy of Madame Eboué.

too, for lower-ranking chiefs received a bonus of two to four centimes for each kilogram of cotton produced in their chieftaincy and shared some money with the sultan.

After the planting season, Eboué hoped for the best. The rains were ample this year, and beginning in January 1926 the harvest looked good. By the time it was over, in May, the Africans had delivered more than 500 tons of raw cotton to the gins of the Ouhamé-Nana Company, and Eboué oversaw the sale of it. He suggested the company pay 1.50 francs per kilogram, but the governor and company settled for 1.25 francs. The cotton was

delivered in such quantities that Mr. Louckx, the company representative, once ran out of cash; Eboué knew that the Africans
would feel cheated if they were not paid, and that the result
could be refusal to work and the destruction of the program. He
sent a message to a group of chiefs to urge them to pay their
taxes, which they promptly did; Eboué lent the money to Louckx,
who then paid the Africans.

Louckx and an assistant trained Africans to work with the
American machines imported to gin and bale the cotton. Production increased from 40 kilograms per day in March 1926, when
ginning began, to 70 kilos a day in April. A hydraulic press produced about ten bales a day of cotton fiber. The bales were taken
by a little Ford truck from Bangassou to Ouango, where canoes
took them to Baugui. By the end of the cotton season they had
shipped more than 180 tons of cotton to Bangui, well over the
150 tons predicted. Naturally Eboué and his subordinates were
extremely pleased, celebrating with a party at which they were
photographed, talking about the next planting.

For the 1926-1927 season Eboué began to expand his program
by planting 5000 hectares of cotton at Bangassou plus 1500 at
Bakouma. He wrote the governor that the experience of the previous year proved the colony could become an important world
producer of cotton with private companies bearing most of the
expense. The Paris banker Marcel Bénard, interested in the development of French Equatorial Africa, formed the Société Coton-
nière Française (Cotonfran) which in a few years became a more
important purchaser of cotton than the Ouhamé-Nana.

The governor, on a trip to Paris, tried to interest other French
businessmen in cotton, saying that production might expand to
3000 tons per year and making promises about better quality.
Eboué's friends who knew about Lamblin's speeches reported to
him that the governor seemed to take credit for cotton himself
without mentioning the work done by administrators in Bas
Mbomou. This annoyed Eboué, and set him to worrying about
his position and promotion to administrator in chief:

> In spite of that, I continue to be interested in my métier. I say with-
> out false modesty . . . [that] I prepared and brought to a conclusion
> a cotton program which is the admiration of the Belgians, our teach-

ers in cotton matters. The young agronomist assisting me will collect the benefits for this cotton campaign which has launched him. . . . Antonetti and Lamblin will gain glory from it. I alone, the first worker, will gain nothing from it. That I knew before undertaking my campaign. I am above all else happy to have those I administer earn money. . . .[19]

Eboué's pessimism and annoyance were not unjustified for he was openly attacked, not praised, for the cotton, and some colonial publications many years later did not mention his role in its introduction even though the product became the country's most important export. In Lamblin's absence, for example, acting Governor Prouteaux wrote a report in 1926 criticizing Eboué's cotton program. Eboué himself wrote a short article on his program[20] and was attacked in another article by an agronomist, known for his interest in coffee production, for not paying the people enough for their work.[21] Another administrator, M. B. J. Montezer, made a damaging report in which he alleged that Eboué had neglected other tasks, including roadbuilding, and that his excessive stress on cotton had caused a famine.

Accounting for much of the difficulty was the Compagnie des Sultanats. Eboué had been on good terms with their Bangassou representative, Mr. Vialle, who had hired Félix Gratien, but official relations cooled after Eboué found out that company agents had been paying the Africans 1.50 francs per kilogram of ivory although the official price had been set at a minimum of 5 francs per kilogram. He warned them to pay more; and its executives undertook a campaign against him. The cotton campaign played a part in the conflicts; once it began, Sultanats feared, as the Belgians had predicted, a loss of ivory. The company went so far as to accuse Eboué of having a personal financial interest in cotton, and some colonial officials were prepared to believe it. The upshot was that Governor General Antonetti opposed Eboué's promotion to administrator in chief.

19 Archives Maran, Letter, Félix Eboué to René Maran, 9 November 1925.
20 "Le coton en Oubangui-Chari," *Le Monde Colonial Illustré*, October 1926, pp. 225-27.
21 Nême, "Situation actuelle de la Culture du Cotonnier et de Celle du Caféier dans l'Oubangui-Chari," *Revue de Botanique Appliquée et d'Agriculture Coloniale*, Vol. VII, 1927, pp. 585-86.

In a flurry of activity Eboué prepared reports for the governor
to counterattack, and requested a personal interview. With the
perspective that sixteen years in one colony gave him, Eboué
noted to the governor that private companies, thinking only of
their narrow immediate interests, had always objected to innovation in Oubangui-Chari on the grounds that new crops would
bring disaster. He had proof, in any case, that rubber production
had actually increased during his sojourn in the region. As for
Montezer's accusation, seconded by a physician, Eboué wrote a
report (a copy of which he sent to René Maran) in which he
stated that he was indeed very much concerned about food production: "The natives of Bas Mbomou have been driven to famine, Mr. Montezer pretends. . . . If Mr. Montezer had taken the
trouble to read . . . the cotton program prepared and approved
for Bas Mbomou, he would not have failed to be struck by the
fact that cotton was based solely on a large development of food
crops. Rice, peanuts, and corn are necessary for crop rotation;
cotton was possible only because of the cultivation of these food
crops."[22]

That food production had in Eboué's time been linked with
cotton instead of being diminished by it was confirmed twenty
years later by an administrator in Bas Mbomou after World War
II. He wrote that Eboué indeed set up a rotation scheme so that
fields not used for cotton would be used for food crops like
manioc, corn, and peanuts: "It is necessary not to abandon the
fields after the [cotton] harvest; it is necessary, as when the administrator Eboué resided at Bangassou, that young stalks of
manioc, corn, and peanuts take the place of cotton plants . . .
by the time the first rains come."[23]

Whether or not cotton cultivation can be blamed for famine,
there is no doubt that in the first place famine did accompany

[22] Archives Maran, Eboué report, 5 December 1927, p. 7. The fact that
Eboué sent a copy of an official report to Maran is a violation of administrative procedure, but was a practice nonetheless of administrators who thought
they might be calumnied by their successors. E. de Dampierre has an interesting account of the cotton dispute: "Coton noir, café blanc," *Cahiers d'E-
tudes Africaines*, 1960, No. 2, pp. 128-47.

[23] Jean Guibbert, "Le Coton en Oubangui-Chari," Mémoire 3283, Centre
des Hautes Etudes d'Administration Musulmane, 27 May 1949, p. 6.

most changes in the economy of Oubangui-Chari. Secondly, in spite of Eboué's efforts to make cotton cultivation a family affair, it is certain that the chiefs and sultan and *bazinguers* on whom he depended got more than their share of the profits, whether the administrator knew it or not. The African peasant, eventually forced to cultivate cotton, did not consider that he was working for his own benefit; he called the product "coton du comman-dant" and maybe "coton du chef."

The Africans had a keen sense of being exploited, but this did not prevent cotton from becoming the key to the economy of Oubangui-Chari and then for an independent Central African Republic. The Ministry of Colonies, happy to see the economic situation of a region improve, was less concerned about accusa-tions against Eboué than about reports from French and foreign writers concerning recruitment of labor.

In early October 1925 André Gide, on a tour of French Equa-torial Africa, included a stop at Bas Mbomou. No one knew why the writer was making the tour, but administrators were told to make sure everything was in order. Eboué, excited about Gide's visit, prepared a huge meal for him; Eboué, who had not forgot-ten the recipes for Creole dishes, prepared some of them for the honored guest. For one which called for a delicious blood sausage popular in Martinique, Eboué killed a pig himself and made the sausage. He also chose the wine, while his wife prepared other courses.

Both the Eboués wanted to talk to Gide; they had read his novels and had generally kept up with the French literary scene and placed their copies of the *Nouvelle Revue Française* in a prominent place so that he could see them. After aperitifs they sat down to eat, but Gide seemed to be a little ill; he later re-called the occasion thus: "Endless meal at the house of Mr. Eboué, head of the circumscription, originally from Guyane, (author of a little Sango grammar book that I have been studying for a week). A remarkable and friendly man. . . ."[24]

Gide did not reveal very much about the purpose of his trip, but Eboué, like most officials, thought he might be there to write

[24] André Gide, *Voyage au Congo: carnets de route* (Paris, Gallimard, 1927), p. 64.

some exposé of the situation. A colonial official accompanied him to, in his words, "try to put some blinders on his eyes because they don't know what he has come to do here. It would be a good idea to make sure everything is in order at the post and along the roads."[25]

As it happened, Gide did not see very much of what he was not supposed to see, but he did criticize recruitment of workers in the two impressionistic books written about this trip on his return to France. He could not have seen the worst aspects of treatment of African labor because of the "blinders." Moreover, the new abuses from recruitment for the railroad were just beginning.

Provision of workers for the Congo-Océan line began in February 1925, just eight months before Gide's arrival at Bangassou, and Eboué, like his colleagues, received his orders. That year, administrators in Oubangui-Chari recruited only 1000 men. Eboué supplied about one-quarter of them with the help of Sultan Hetman, who had the power to choose who would go. Hetman cooperated with Eboué and his successors in this task as well as in cotton until 1932 when recruitment ceased, being made a member of the Legion of Honor as a reward.

Between 1925 and 1932 about 42,000 men, or 9.2 per cent of all the men in Oubangui-Chari colony, had been recruited for the construction camps.[26] The suffering was just as bad as it had been during the earlier recruitments, if not worse. Many Oubanguians never returned home; some died along the way to the work camps, some at work because food was not adequate, more died because safety measures were minimal. Albert Londres, who specialized more than Gide in revealing scandals to the French-reading public, wrote about Sara workers from northern Oubangui that he saw:

> There was no name to give to the desolation of their condition. They dragged themselves along the road like sick ghosts. Shouts, blows could not revive them. I thought that, dreaming of their far away Oubangui, they were groping for the entrance to a cemetery.[27]

[25] Archives Isambert, Letter, Félix Eboué to René Isambert, 7 October 1925.
[26] Giles Sautter, "Notes sur la construction du chemin de fer Congo-Océan 1921-1934," *Cahiers d'Etudes Africaines*, Vol. VII, No. 26, 1967, pp. 258-69.
[27] Albert Londres, *Terre d'Ebène: la traite des noirs* (Paris: Albin Michel, 1929), p. 243.

René Isambert and Eboué in Oubangui-Chari after the successful cotton campaign.

Eboué complained to friends about the recruitment, but there is no record he objected to the administration. He complied with his orders.

In spite of this disagreeable task Eboué was generally happy in Bas Mbomou and proud of his work with cotton. With improved road communications he saw his friends more frequently. Isambert particularly interested him, for he had gone beyond the mere study of Protestant beliefs in 1923 to complete conversion in 1925. Under the direction of local American missionaries he studied the bible he always carried with him and talked with

Eboué, although the latter was a non-believer. He made his decision, and the Americans baptized him in the Mbomou River,
much to the amusement of local Europeans.[28]

Eboué found Isambert's sincerity moving. He wrote to Maran
with a significant reference to his own continuing stoic beliefs:

> . . . his conversion did not surprise me, for it is the logical conclusion
> of his Bible studies—either that or disbelief. Isambert likes me very
> much and would like to see me follow his footsteps, but he knows and
> is saddened by the fact that although I am an admirer of the Bible
> (and above all the Gospel of John whose esoteric form and initiatic
> scope please me) my mind has always refused to accept the Revelation.
> If I did not fear leading Isambert to doubt and perhaps even to dis-
> belief . . . I would encourage him to study closely the Mysteries of
> antiquity, Egypt and Eleusis. I am persuaded that then he could say,
> like the "Disabused Epicurean": Nothing new under the sun! But I
> am reluctant to do it; it is a bad thing to bring doubt to the mind of a
> believer.[29]

He believed that every person must discover his own religion and
thus refused to have Ginette or Charles baptized, saying they
would decide what to do about religion when they grew up. His
non-dogmatic approach to these matters set him apart from colleagues and even annoyed Freemason friends who during a discussion in Bangassou complained about Isambert's presence.
Eboué told him to stay: "He is my friend, and besides, he knows
more about these philosophical matters than we do!"[30] During
this period, Eboué also had cause to be pleased by the achieve-
ments of two other close friends Yvon Delbos and René Maran.
Delbos, elected deputy to the French parliament in 1924, entered
the government of Painlevé in 1925 as Minister of Public Education, from which position he promised to write to the Minister
of Colonies to urge Eboué's promotion. René Maran had published two books since *Batouala* and was working on others as
well as paying occasional visits to a now-attentive Ministry of
Colonies to get favors for Antilleans and Creoles. Eboué, proud
as ever of his friend, told him to concentrate on his literary activities instead of politics. His message to Maran was to devote

---

[28] Interview with Reverend Mr. Gust Pearson who baptized him. 29 June
1968, Bangui.

[29] Archives Maran, Letter, Félix Eboué to René Maran, 9 November 1925.

[30] Interview with René Isambert, Chartres, 5 July 1967.

his life to literature and show the white world what a black man could accomplish: "You will never succeed in rehabilitating the Negro by defending him. But, what a service you will render him if . . . you wanted to devote yourself only to literature."[31]

Maran responded that he was preparing a book to be called *Novel of a Negro* (which appeared later in fragments as *Journal sans date*). Eboué wrote: "I am waiting impatiently for *Roman d'un Nègre*. I don't like this title, which could (rather) be a sub-title. . . ."[32]

By 1926 Eboué felt he would like to see Maran and his own family. His wife longed for France and Guyane, and Eboué was becoming very concerned about his mother's health. Cornélie told him Man-Lie had been ill and that she was impatient to see her son. Eboué had been so involved in the cotton campaign and in other matters concerning his career that he had been careless about writing to his mother or to Henri in France. Feeling a little guilty, he began to find his thoughts turning homeward.

In March 1926 Eboué's mother became very ill. The diagnosis was pneumonia, fatal at her age and physical condition. Thinking of her religion, she called for a priest to administer communion, and thinking of her son she called, "Fé-fé, Fé-fé." The afternoon of 23 March the old lady died.[33]

Herménégilde Tell and Cornélie sent a cable to Oubangui-Chari and then wrote Eboué about the loss. "Cono" assured him that he had been a good son and that sacrifices made to send him to school in France had been rewarded:

. . . you must console yourself with the thought that you have always been for Her an affectionate and respectful son in the full meaning of the word. This model son that I shall always see in you in addition to the beloved brother I cherish.[34]

Too late to see his mother, Eboué, his wife, and three little children left the colony in June for France and a sad return to Guyane.

31 Archives Maran, Letter, Félix Eboué to René Maran, 9 November 1926.
32 *Ibid.*
33 Archives Eboué, Letter, Herménégilde Tell to Félix Eboué, 27 March 1926.
34 Archives Eboué, Letter, Cornélie Gratien to Félix Eboué, 31 July 1926.

FRANCE AND CAYENNE

With Man-Lie gone, Eboué had no reason to rush to Cayenne; he decided to spend the rest of the year in France at rue Chauveau Lagarde and at Vichy where he intended to go to the mineral waters considered a cure for the kidney trouble he had begun to suffer from. Family affairs there took up some of his time as well, and he met with his usual group of friends, enjoying to the full the excitement of Paris in the 1920's.

Henri was thrilled to see his father, for it had been three years since Eboué had left him in Paris. The boy was then fourteen, and although he had a good mind, was doing poorly in school, being a constant discipline problem. No wonder, for he had had very little parental authority since leaving his grandmother's house and yearned to be with a father who was absent most of the time.

Eboué had had little time for his children and gave them what could be called "bursts of attention." He might spend one day with them purchasing anything they wanted from expensive shops and being very affectionate, but then he would not have free time for weeks, leaving home early in the day and coming back from some dinner or meeting late in the evening. Madame Eboué took care of the children, looking after such things as the removal of their adenoids during the latter part of 1926.[35]

An unpleasant family matter then came up unexpectedly. Some years before Eboué had countersigned a loan given to a cousin on the Léveillé side of his own family. He had long since forgotten about it but, unfortunately, the cousin had not repaid the sum borrowed, and the creditor approached Eboué. Eboué, who refused to pay, sought the advice of René Méneau, his friend and financial advisor. The affair was settled somehow, but the question of the loan annoyed Madame Eboué, much more careful about money than her husband.

Cornélie also wrote about money matters from Cayenne, saying that Félix Gratien could not send enough money from Oubangui-Chari to support his family and asking her brother for help.

[35] Archives Eboué, Letter, Félix Eboué to Herménégilde Tell, 6 August 1926.

The Gratiens' eldest daughter was doing well in her studies, and Eboué promised assistance so she could come to France to study for a higher degree in science.

Eboué confided in Méneau and René Maran about his financial concerns, his anger over the attacks from cotton, and his discouragement about being passed over in promotions. He told them Governor General Raphael Antonetti did not appear to dislike him personally but that he did not push for promotions for his subordinates. As a result Eboué thought he and his colleagues in French Equatorial Africa were being discriminated against, not on account of color, but because A.E.F. was still the farthest backwater of the empire, and those who worked there were disdained by administrators elsewhere who discounted their abilities and their status: "Functionaries in A.E.F. are abused," Eboué wrote his father-in-law. "Mr. Antonetti thought it nice to say that we were the rejects of the corps [of administrators] the elite having been sent to A.O.F. or to Madagascar."[36]

Eboué went to Blaise Diagne for advice. The deputy had many contacts and talked to his young friend about a possible position with a business firm. Eboué investigated the possibilities but wanted something that would take him back to Oubangui-Chari; he thought a company planning to invest in cotton or coffee might want to use his knowledge. He did not, however, want to leave the administration without reaching the summit of his corps, administrator in chief. Promotion to this rank was always on his mind, and, in any case, 1926 was a bad year to think of a business career, for unemployment reached new high levels and capital flowed from France into neighboring countries. The government tried to introduce economy measures to save the franc, whose value steadily decreased, and private groups organized to contribute money to the government. Eboué still thought about a business career, but followed carefully the deliberations of the Commission de Classement meeting at the end of the year. He talked with friends about his dilemma.

In his favorite café, the Café de Versailles near the Ministry of Colonies, Eboué met with Roger Dévigne and Roger Hellier, who

---

[36] Archives Eboué, Letter, Félix Eboué to Herménégilde Tell, 6 August 1926.

told Eboué he would be appointed to a position in Guadeloupe, and others. Most of this time, however, he spent with René Maran.

Eboué told Maran about the possibility of going into business, but worried that at the age of forty-two and with business the way it was the decision might be the wrong one. Maran encouraged him to remain a colonial administrator and promised to do what he could in calls on the Ministry of Colonies about discrimination against Antilleans and Creoles and in articles in reform-minded Antillean publications.

Maran had gone much further in his political activities than Eboué wished him to, in fact. He joined the Ligue Universelle pour la Défense de la Race Nègre and then the Comité de Défense de la Race Noire of which he was the vice president. Some people considered these organizations to be radical and even communist affiliated, for in 1926 France was in the midst of a Red scare, the product of an economic and political crisis. That year governments changed with amazing rapidity; Aristide Briand, Raymond Poincaré, and Herriot tried their turn at forming a stable government.

From Indochina came new demands for locally elected assemblies, and in North Africa nationalist movements grew in importance. The following year the Freemasons called for reforms in the colonies and the "application to the colonies of French social laws."[37] The Grande Loge de France—Eboué's masonic affiliation —called for the nationalization of some domestic industry,[38] and two communist deputies were elected to the French parliament from Paris. For some conservatives all these demands and elections were a sign that the "Reds" were on the verge of taking over the motherland and its colonies.

The Ministry of Colonies warned the governors to watch movements in Africa which might be inspired by communists in France like the Amicale des Originaires de l'A.E.F., a Balali organization, or by Garveyism or Pan-Africanism from America. Eboué in their conversations warned Maran to be careful in his activities. He knew that the Ministry of Interior planted black spies in various

---

[37] Headings, *op. cit.*, p. 191.
[38] *Ibid.*, p. 192.

movements, and he knew that some people had considered Maran a communist ever since the publication of *Batouala*. Maran was, as ever, a reformer interested in abolishing those abuses of the colonial system which might push desperate Africans and Antilleans toward communism: "I must prevent certain groups of French Negroes from adhering to the demagogic utopias of communism," he wrote. "These Negroes from French colonies are very agitated now. Many, aggravated by the unintelligent methods of colonial policies are about to act rashly."[39]

Maran had, however, openly attacked Blaise Diagne as a traitor to the black race, and Diagne had sued Maran for libel for an article which appeared in *Les Continents,* a black publication he was associated with. The suit took place before 1926, in Eboué's absence; Eboué was usually on the fringes of such disputes anyway. He refused to take sides, remained friendly with both men, and generally adhered to his belief that friendship was more important than politics.

Eboué's association with Maran had brought him closer to some important movements like the Ligue and Comité, but he did not need Maran to be aware of the literary and artistic development that contrasted with the instability and fear in the Paris of 1926. There had been an influx of American writers and artists, many of them blacks, and black-consciousness was on the rise. Though America seemed, to the Eboués, a strange and distant place, they were delighted by the black American entertainers they encountered, and liked the few black Americans they met. They followed the career of Josephine Baker, who made her debut in the Revue Nègre at the Théâtre des Champs Elysées in 1925, and that of Paul Robeson. Through René Maran, Eboué met the Negro scholar Dr. Alain Leroy Locke, professor of philosophy at Howard University. Locke had praised French colonial policy in the early 1920's, and René Maran had criticized him for it; later the two men became acquainted during Locke's frequent trips to Paris and had grown to be friends.

Eboué was particularly pleased to meet Locke, for he owned his book, *The New Negro,* which had, in 1925, articulated the mean-

[39] Locke Archives, Howard University, Moorland Foundation, Letter, René Maran to A. L. Locke, 19 April 1927.

ing of the cultural renaissance then taking place among Negroes in the United States. Although Locke's spoken French was about as good as Eboué's English, they were able to have a conversation that both remembered many years later. Locke told Eboué how important a knowledge of African culture was for the Negro American, and explained how he was trying, through art, to destroy old myths about their ancestry.

Eboué promised to send Locke some art objects from Africa for a collection to be shown in Harlem; he kept his word later by shipping from Oubangui-Chari some iron knives. Locke wrote to Eboué to thank him for the knives, saying that they would help "show our people the ancient powers of our race. That is why I prefer old objects which don't show European influence." Locke signed his letter "Your friend and race brother."[40]

Locke also knew Eboué's colleague, Maurice Delafosse, who had just published his own *Civilisations Négro-Africaines*. Its publication and the establishment of the Institute of Ethnography at the Sorbonne marked the changes taking place in the study of Africa in France and drew African civilizations to the attention of French intellectuals.

At last, however, Eboué decided it was time to go to Cayenne. Seven-year-old Robert was put in boarding school with Henri in Paris, and René Méneau, who agreed to look after them, moved into the apartment at rue Chauveau Lagarde. Eboué, his wife, and the two younger children left at the very end of 1926 or the beginning of 1927.

In Cayenne Eboué first took care of the legal matters concerning his mother's death and decided to keep the house at the rue Richelieu. He had plenty of time to see old friends, like Lhuerre, and to take part in the many discussions about the forthcoming elections in 1928; many Guyanese hoped Jean Galmot would run against Eugène Lautier, who had ignored Guyane as he told Eboué he would during their conversation in 1922. He was doing nothing for the colony after having been elected by what most people considered fraudulent means.

Eboué re-established contact with his masonic lodge, La France

40 Locke Archives, Howard University, Moorland Foundation, Dossier African Art, copy of Letter, A. L. Locke to Félix Eboué, 30 July 1928.

Equinoxiale. After some study he thought he was ready to advance in grade, and on 14 February 1927 the lodge elevated him to eighteenth degree, the highest he ever attained, a respectable but not very high degree in Freemasonry. At about the same time he was named to the prestigious Legion of Honor which partly compensated for his failure to be named administrator in chief. Along with the good times, however, came new concerns.

Cornélie told her brother that the only hope for her and the children was to leave Cayenne for Paris, just as he had done a quarter century before. He agreed to help her, but Madame Eboué was opposed to spending so much money. She discussed the matter with her husband and then had what became a bitter argument with Cornélie, who had been her best friend. Eboué said little, but brooded over the dispute between his sister and his wife. The strain, however, began to affect his health.

Back in Paris before May, Eboué became ill. He had an attack of what he called *albumisme* or kidney trouble, which was to plague him for the rest of his life. He also occasionally heard a humming or buzzing sound and realized he was getting too tense.[41] Trying to relax and forget family troubles—Cornélie and her children traveled to France and relations with Madame Eboué were still not good—he visited with friends and absorbed himeslf in his career and current events.

The Paris of mid-1927 was as exciting as the year before. Lindberg's historic solo flight across the Atlantic in May was only one event which electrified the French. From across the sea came news of the condemnation and impending execution of the anarchists, Sacco and Vanzetti. Frenchmen marched through the streets of Paris protesting the punishment planned for these two men and condemned American justice. Lack of success in dealing with the war debts owed America also worsened relations between the two countries. Aristide Briand proposed a treaty along with the American Senator Kellogg to outlaw war; this project had a large place in the news along with the continuing "Red threat."

Eboué's notebooks testify to the fact that he saw a great many

41 Archives Maran, Letter, Félix Eboué to René Maran, 25 June 1929.

people and could not have spent very much time at home after returning to Paris. He saw old colleagues from Oubangui-Chari, talked with Gratien Candace, still deputy from Guadeloupe, and met Alcide Delmont, deputy from Martinique. He also saw Henri Vendôme, his first superior officer in Oubangui-Chari, and attended René Maran's wedding to a white lady, Camille, a match that Eboué approved of.

Both Governor Lamblin and Governor General Antonetti were in Paris at this time, and Eboué talked with them. They wanted him to return to Oubangui-Chari, and in order to get him there promised him a choice post at Fort Archambault in the northern part of the colony and their support for his promotion. They told him that Robert Hermine, one of his close friends, would probably be named to Fort Sibut, not far from Archambault; this news encouraged him to accept an unprecedented fifth tour of duty in the same colony. He gave up the idea of leaving the colonial service, and made plans for the forthcoming trip.

Arguments between Cornélie and Eugénie continued until the Eboués left for Africa with Eboué trying to keep on good terms with both. He gave Cornélie as much money as he could, but did not let his wife know about it; he asked his sister to watch over Henri and Robert who would be put in boarding school.

In October Eboué, his wife, and the two children, Ginette and Charles, waited in Bordeaux for a ship to Africa. A strike delayed their departure, but they finally set sail and arrived in French Equatorial Africa the first week in November 1927. After the usual short stay in Brazzaville they sailed to Bangui.

In the capital, Prouteaux, the acting governor of Oubangui-Chari, told Eboué he would not be assigned to Archambault as planned but that he would work in Fort Sibut, the headquarters for Kémo-Gribingui region, one of the most unpopular assignments in the colony. Eboué was furious but did not show his anger except in a letter to Boutin; in it he wrote: "The evil acting [governor] of Oubangui-Chari is a joker; in addition, he is a rotten jesuit plus a pervert. He heartily dislikes all those of us of color and on the Left."[42] He asked Boutin, a Freemason, to see if

[42] Archives Boutin, Letter, Félix Eboué to E. L. Boutin, 30 August 1928.

the lodges might be able to prevent Prouteaux's advancement to the rank of governor. He wanted someone to send a message to Léon Perrier, Minister of Colonies since 1925 and a mason; he wanted someone to see Gaston Joseph, another brother, in the key position of Director of Personnel in the ministry: "I am counting on you. Take care of it with Maran, and above all, bar the way energetically for Prouteaux, candidate for governor. He does not like us."[43] (Whether or not the Freemasons did act against Prouteaux is difficult to determine, but the acting governor, who then had the rank of administrator in chief only, was never raised to full governor.)

With all this worry and agitation Eboué suddenly became ill with what was diagnosed as pulmonary congestion—a rather vague term covering pneumonia, chronic tuberculosis, emphysema, in sum any disease which affects respiration. It is quite possible that there was a purely organic reason for the illness, but the disappointment over his assignment, the tension about his promotion, and the months of exhausting family disputes contributed to what he himself considered to be a psychosomatic disease. His stoic posture was catching up with him, and he knew it.

In a very moving and revealing letter to René Maran, Eboué analyzed the price he was paying for his struggle to keep his calm appearance:

> You remember the attack of albuminuria . . . and the pulmonary congestion which overwhelmed me. . . . People don't know me well. It was the worries from the dispute between my wife and my sister that were the only reason for my sickness. I react terribly to this kind of quarrel, and the fact that I found myself in the position of tightrope walker literally wore me out.

He said that the effort to keep his self-control was so great that he had two attacks of pulmonary congestion preceded by humming in his ears. In Bangui he tried to relax and to think about other matters without letting his family know how sick he felt: "The difficult thing for me was not to give rise to any worry among the family, and I succeeded."[44]

43 Archives Boutin, Letter, Félix Eboué to E. L. Boutin, 10 January 1928.
44 Archives Maran, Letter, Félix Eboué to René Maran, 25 June 1929.

Eboué was probably correct in his analysis for extreme tension can cause difficulty in breathing; breathing was a problem later in his life, particularly after personal conflict. Why he felt he could not let his immediate family know about his nervousness is a mystery. It appears the only people he really confided in were a very small group of friends, but only after brooding about what bothered him for a long time. For example, the attack in Bangui took place in November 1927, but he waited until June 1929 before writing to Maran, a full year and a half later. By the end of 1927 he felt better and left for his new post, arriving at Sibut on about 1 January 1928.

KÉMO-GRIBINGUI

For the first few months at Fort Sibut Eboué had mixed feelings about his assignment; he could not get used to the fact that acting Governor Prouteaux had named him to Sibut, and he suspected the official had sent in a secret report justifying what could be considered a humiliating demotion. Not knowing what people were saying or writing about him always worried Eboué.

In spite of everything Sibut was not so bad. It took only four hours from the centrally located post to get to Bangui by car, for example; the place had a telegraph station; and a physician had an office nearby, useful in case five-year-old Ginette or four-year-old Charles needed medical attention. The Mandjia and Banda population of the *circonscription* presented no problems, although Eboué lacked assistants. He took care of Fort Sibut, the administrative headquarters for the region, as well as the subdivision, and was obliged to watch over the affairs of Dekoa, 74 kilometers to the north. Europeans administered the two subdivisions of Fort Crampel and Possel, and seven African clerks and a hundred African guards stayed at Sibut. A single agronomist supervised agricultural programs, and Eboué absorbed himself in his work.

Eboué pretended to friends that he had lost his enthusiasm for his work because of the failure of the administration to reward him with a promotion or a better assignment. He saw the need to do something in Kémo-Gribingui, one of the poorest districts in the colony and one that had suffered because of recruitment:

"This poor Kémo-Gribingui. . . . I don't know yet if I shall not set about doing something for this unfortunate region in spite of the dirty tricks played on me. I must tell you that my zeal has chilled a little."[45] The letter continued with Eboué saying that if he innovated here as in Bas Mbomou, he might be courting attack. What was the use of making a big effort if one could never expect promotions, he asked. "I think I shall not bother about [the question of] promotions any more."[46] He wrote this, however, in a moment of depression and self-pity; he in fact worked hard in Kémo-Gribingui, proud of his tons of cotton and peanuts. And if preoccupations with promotion left his mind, it could only have been for a few minutes.

Later in the year Lamblin returned to Oubangui-Chari, after his leave in France, and sent his subordinates a circular in May 1928 telling them to emphasize family-based cultivation. Administrators should encourage the Africans to raise industrial crops and sell them for the most they could get. This had been Eboué's idea all along, and when he read the circular, he showed it to his wife, and underlined Lamblin's statement three times.[47]

The lieutenant governor was more friendly to Eboué now that cotton appeared a possible savior of the colony. Lamblin wanted to take much of the credit, it appeared. After asking Eboué to prepare another article for a colonial publication on cotton, Eboué heard, Lamblin did not seemingly object when the editors put his own name as author.[48]

In June Eboué planted cotton in Kémo-Gribingui with the help of Sultan Hetman's *bazinguers* that he had sent for. According to the account of Joseph Kabou, one of Hetman's men, the sultan sent Eboué twenty Nzakara "cotton boys." It took them one month to walk to Fort Sibut. "Mousseboy" (the name they called Eboué—from "Monsieur Eboué") chose land behind his house for the first cotton in Kémo-Gribingui, and the twenty men began to plant. Eboué assembled forty people from the area to

45 Archives Maran, Letter, Félix Eboué to René Maran, 10 January 1928.
46 *Ibid.*
47 Arch. Nat. RCA, Section Sibut, at Ecole Nationale d'Administration, Bangui, Circular, May 1928, Governor Lamblin to Chefs de Circonscription.
48 Archives Boutin, Letter, Félix Eboué to E. L. Boutin, 30 August 1928.

work with the cotton boys—two for each man: "Five seeds were put into each hole." Kabou then traveled about the region for five years teaching cotton cultivation. He received forty francs each month (at the time a shirt cost two to three francs).[49]

Eboué's success in Kémo-Gribingui also depended on the local alliances and friendships he established with chiefs. One was François Ngao, a Banda village chief named to his post in 1915. According to the Ngao family tradition, the chief originally came from the area of Damara. At Sibut he worked for European traders, first as a caretaker for animals, then as a dishwasher, and then as a cook. He tried being a tailor until he had enough money to request permission to purchase a rifle for hunting elephants.

Ngao came to the attention of the administration when the latter wanted a secret investigation of the activities of the Hausa traders in the region because the French suspected they were purchasing Mandjia slaves and selling them to traders from Anglo-Egyptian Sudan. Ngao made his investigation to the satisfaction of the French who made him a village chief. He continued to work with the French, and Eboué made him canton chief even though he was not originally from that canton.[50] Ngao worked closely with Eboué on the programs designed to improve the economy of the region.

Eboué tried to analyze the problems of Kémo-Gribingui in reports to the lieutenant governor for the production of rice, peanuts, and coffee decreased in 1927. He blamed the shortage of personnel, and, more important, pointed out that administrative and commercial practices demoralized the Africans: merchants paid them too little for the crops they raised; the administration distributed seeds of poor quality, meaning that only a small percentage germinated; and the collection of taxes from the money earned convinced the African he was working exclusively for the Europeans. "Everything that the native produced—or practically everything—served to satisfy his fiscal obligations."[51] Eboué feared

[49] Interview in French with Joseph Kabou, Fort Sibut, 20 June 1968.
[50] Interview in French with the chief's son and successor, Pierre Ngao, Fort Sibut, 20 June 1968.
[51] Arch. Nat. RCA, Section Sibut, Eboué Reports, 9 February 1928 and 6 June 1928.

Africans would never be motivated to cultivate industrial crops if companies were not forced to pay enough so that Africans had a surplus after paying their taxes to buy what they wanted. During the 1928 harvest at Kémo-Gribingui Eboué decided not to collect taxes immediately after the merchants paid the Africans for their products, the usual custom, in order to give them a chance to purchase things: ". . . it is important before all else to make the natives understand that they must produce . . . to increase their well being," Eboué wrote.[52] He thought that his agricultural program in Kémo-Gribingui would produce 150 tons of peanuts, 200 tons of sesame, 500 tons of rice, and 1000 tons of cotton, giving the Africans a total of two million francs; he was pardonably proud of the project.[53]

Although Eboué was often present when the Africans sold their peanuts, sesame, rice, and cotton to the merchants, his tours were not long, and good roads permitted him to return quickly to Sibut. Madame Eboué did not suffer as she had in Bas Mbomou, and as the children grew older she accompanied her husband when he traveled.

Because Sibut was only 200 kilometers from Bambari—all good road—Eboué traveled there to visit Sokambi, and it is certain he went there alone at least once to see Bada Marcelline, the mother of his son Robert. He had always taken care of her with money and clothing. By about 1928 she was dying from leprosy, people say, and Eboué went to say farewell. The Sokambi family knew Eboué had married someone from his own country; they considered it normal he should do so, but Bada Marcelline swore Eboué was the only man she ever knew and loved.[54]

If Madame Eboué had known about the money to Bada Marcelline, she would have been angry and justifiably so, for their financial position was not good. No one had subleased the apartment at rue Chauveau Lagarde, as they hoped, and Henri's and Robert's school fees had to be paid. They had traveled to Oubangui-Chari this time with so much excess baggage that the government which generally paid for all the personal effects of its administra-

52 Eboué Report, 6 June 1928.
53 Archives Boutin, Letter, Félix Eboué to E. L. Boutin, 30 August 1928.
54 Interview with Pierre Sondjio, brother of Bada Marcelline, 30 June 1968.

tors balked and required Eboué to pay some of the expenses. Eboué countered by requesting an adjustment in salary because he took care of Dekoa as well as Sibut, but the Ministry of Colonies or the lieutenant governor refused. Eboué must have been tempted to ask for a loan from René Maran, whose third novel, *Djouma, chien de la brousse,* had come out, or from René Isambert, who had transferred to Togo (which he did not like very much).

Financial problems having been settled for the time being by more careful budgeting, Eboué was finally glad he had not been named to Archambault because of its importance for the recruitment of workers for the Congo-Océan railway. The administrator there had to recruit many more men in one year than Eboué: "I shall furnish 520 workers," Eboué wrote. "I am sick of it, but I am better off here than at Archambault, directed by old man Joseph, who will have to furnish 2400 men!"[55] The colony furnished a total of 6075 workers that year.[56]

During the year 1928 Eboué joined the Ligue des Droits de l'Homme et du Citoyen which, among other things, had protested against abuses of the colonial administration. It is, therefore, surprising that Eboué wrote callously about recruitment: "It is necessary to recognize that an amelioration can be noted in the condition of the workers. As many people may die as before in the work camps, but the survivors who return . . . are in better condition."[57] The abuses were, in fact, reaching their apogee with Governor General Antonetti pressing relentlessly to finish the railroad; protests reached such a level that the Ministry of Colonies sent Georges Boussenot, a journalist, to investigate. Fortunately for Antonetti and everyone else except the Africans, Boussenot was a close friend and provided the Ministry with a convenient whitewash.[58]

In Kémo-Gribingui Africans fled recruitment, but Eboué went

---

[55] Archives Maran, Letter, Félix Eboué to René Maran, 21 March 1928.

[56] Giles Sautter, "Notes sur la construction du Chemin de fer Congo-Océan (1921-1934)," *Cahiers d'Etudes Africaines,* Vol. VII, No. 26, p. 259.

[57] Archives Maran, Letter, Félix Eboué to René Maran, 21 March 1928.

[58] My conclusion based on interview with Georges Boussenot, Nice, 14 April 1968.

on undaunted, evidently regarding the construction of the railroad as crucial to development and believing that suffering for the sake of the future was unavoidable. Elsewhere in Oubangui-Chari Africans made other administrators wonder if there was not a better way to develop the colonies.

Beginning in 1928 agitation against French rule grew, and administrators from widely separated posts reported so-called "fetishers" preaching against the whites. The Baya people in Haute Sangha, on the frontier with Cameroun, rose in revolt against recruitment and taxation. Bangui sent troops and put the area under military administration, but the revolt, called the *Guerre des Houes,* grew. Trading houses were pillaged, Europeans and their agents were attacked, and one administrator, surrounded in his office, "had to flee by placing himself in the middle of his guards who fired in all directions."[59] The French suppressed the uprising in 1929.

Governor Lamblin, surveying the situation in August, toured most regions of the colony. At Sibut he told Eboué he planned to send him back to Ouaka region and praised him for his work in Kémo-Gribingui. He also asked him to begin to prepare a study of the peoples of Oubangui-Chari. In September his replacement arrived, and the Eboués packed their trunks for the trip up the road to Bambari.

OUAKA

A return to Ouaka was homecoming for Eboué. This was the region he knew best, having served at a subdivision, Kouango, from 1914 to 1917 and then at Bambari as head of the whole district from 1918 to 1921. The region, one of thirteen in the colony, now had a population of about 74,500 adults, mostly Banda, whose language always interested Eboué.

Friends from the subdivisions of Kouango, Ippy, Moroubas, and Grimari greeted the Eboué family, and the four of them settled into the official residence on the hill overlooking Bambari town. Soon they invited the growing European community for aperitifs. French wine, brandy, and aperitifs, Scotch whisky, and

59 Archives Boutin, Letter, Félix Eboué to E. L. Boutin, 30 August 1928.

some canned goods were fairly easy to obtain, but like other administrators the Eboués had their own garden and animals.

The enlarged European community meant Eugénie would have more company, which pleased Eboué enormously. But the old problem of administrative personnel continued to plague him; at least one of Eboué's posts had to be officially closed at any given moment or run by African clerks.

Although the French were considerably behind the British in Africanizing the colonial bureaucracy, they had a growing corps of clerks (*écrivains*) and "interpreters" (*interprètes*). Africans from other colonies like Senegal, Dahomey, or Gabon had a higher level of French education than the Oubanguians generally and had the higher positions, but some local people also worked in the administration. They supposedly acted only on the orders of an administrator, but, like the chiefs and sultans, often had more freedom of action in fact than they did on paper.

In Ouaka two African men, Paul Domatchi and Michel Sodji, worked with Eboué. Sodji came from Dahomey and worked in Ouaka for many more years than any single Frenchman, black or white. He made frequent tours, doing census work and other tasks that the administrator himself had to do twenty years before. By 1928 most administrators traveled by automobile, thus avoiding some of the more distant villages, but the African clerks still traveled by *tipoye* or on foot to the most obscure corners of the area. In 1929 Sodji went on three long tours lasting up to a month each.

Domatchi, the son of a Banda-Linda chief, came from Ippy. Years before, Eboué, during his first tour of duty at Bambari, had asked Domatchi's father to send the boy to school at the administrative post. There he learned French and arithmetic, about the only subjects taught, and then traveled with administrators first as an interpreter and then as a clerk.[60] When Eboué returned to Bambari, he sent Domatchi to Kouango, without an administrator, to work with Chief Sokambi. At Kouango he became a kind of head of the subdivision.

Eboué and Domatchi corresponded almost daily. The head of

[60] Interview with Paul Domatchi, Ippy, 19 July 1968.

the district sent by runners little notes he wrote out in his inimitable and difficult handwriting; these are noteworthy in that Eboué used the respectful *vous* form when addressing his young African colleague, instead of the familiar *tu* form. Eboué also tried to move him up the hierarchy to better paying positions. Once he summoned Domatchi to Bambari to take an examination. Both Domatchi and Sodji assisted Eboué in his cotton program in Ouaka.

Eboué introduced cotton to Ippy and ordered the expansion of production to other subdivisions. Sensitive about possible criticism of cotton, he gave his subordinates in Ouaka very specific instructions: "You know already that cotton is the most controversial product that there is. We must not take sides in the debate but execute in good conscience and faith the program once it is decided." Eboué wrote that cotton would be the best way to provide the people of Ouaka with money "not only to permit the payment of taxes but to increase purchasing power, an essential factor of economic activity as well as social progress." He told them to observe the following principles: "1. We are not planting cotton for the sake of cotton. 2. Cotton must be part of an agricultural cycle known and already practiced. 3. Cotton must be considered a rotation crop with peanuts, rice, and corn. 4. In the preparation of cotton distinguish between savanna and forest which require different types of cotton plants."[61] During the month of June Eboué spent about three weeks overseeing the planting of 200 hectares of cotton at Ippy.[62] He suggested that cotton be tried at Grimari and Kouango the following year and then at Bambari and Moroubas the year after that.[63]

The success of cotton had been proved, and Eboué felt happy at Bambari. Changes over the past years ensured a better life for the administrator, too. A tennis court and a sporting club with Eboué as honorary president provided some relaxation at Bambari. A trip to Bangui by automobile took just a day, and a post

61 Arch. Nat. RCA, Section Ippy, Félix Eboué, message to heads of subdivisions, 27 October 1929.

62 Arch. Nat. RCA, Section Kouango, Letter, Félix Eboué to Lt. Governor, 18 October 1929.

63 *Ibid.*

office truck came regularly with letters, newspapers, and precious
magazines sent by René Maran.

Maran wrote Eboué about trouble in Cayenne after the elections. Jean Galmot had run against Eugène Lautier for his seat in
parliament. He lost by what his supporters considered to be fraud
and died several days afterward by what these same people believed was poison. There was a riot, the governor called in troops,
and several people were killed. Eboué was shocked and appalled.
He asked Maran for more information, and for some missing
numbers of *Nouvelle Revue Française* which he still read, and
Maran asked him to send information on the Banda to help him
in preparing another book, *Livre de la brousse*. He wanted Banda
stories, and Eboué replied that he would have to translate them
first, for Maran had doubtless forgotten whatever Banda he knew.
He added he planned a book himself but regretted that, in the
early days, no one had encouraged him: "Oh! If only the administration had encouraged us—you, Isambert, poor Michaud [a colleague in Bas Mbomou], de Courseulles and me—we would have
been able to determine and note everything. L [Lamblin] is thinking about ethnography a little late. And yet, how can they affect
him, these 'Negro' customs."[64]

Eboué delayed sending the material to Maran, perhaps because
he was getting a little deaf and could no longer hear the tonal
differences in Banda. In any case, Maran's book was overdue, and
the author complained about Eboué's slowness to friends:

> I am still waiting for news from Eboué. Each month I send him eight-
> een or twenty magazines or different newspapers. On the other hand,
> he is delaying a little too long in [sending] me the information I
> asked him for. . . .[65]

New arrivals in Bambari were also studying the Banda and
sharing their ideas with Eboué. Dr. and Mrs. Grall became interested in the tonal language, and Father Daigre, superior of the
Roman Catholic mission, did some studies too. Diagre visited
often with Eboué who had had a road built to the church to help

---

[64] Archives Maran, Letter, Félix Eboué to René Maran, 25 June 1929.
[65] Locke Archives, Howard University, Moorland Foundation, Letter, René
Maran to A. L. Locke, 8 April 1929.

the priest and who sent manioc to the school he ran, much to the annoyance of the Freemasons at Bambari.[66]

Visitors also made life busier. Lamblin, the most peripatetic governor in the history of the colony, often came through Bambari on his way to eastern Oubangui-Chari. The governor mentioned in passing that in the course of his tour several of the increasingly large group of literate Africans were presenting him with lists of complaints about the colonial administration. Eboué reminded his subordinates that they all lived in a glass house and must therefore be very careful in their application of sanctions and in watching that African soldiers not brutalize the population. If not, the situation might be exploited to their great disadvantage by the literate group or even by European businessmen always trying to find fault with the administration.[67]

Sokambi visited, the motion picture crew of Jean d'Esme came, Prouteaux, acting governor again, stayed in Bambari for a few days late in 1929, and Eboué rather took to him, in spite of his earlier feelings.

In January 1931 Antonetti visited Eboué during a grand tour of the colony, and Eboué gave a party and dance. Antonetti inspected the cotton harvest and the gins, and told Eboué how pleased he was with his work. The governor general also visited the gold mines recently opened by the Compagnie Equatoriale at nearby Roandji; Eboué's observations in 1919 had proved correct, and there was a significant quantity of the precious metal in the area of Bambari.

Eboué did not plan to remain in Ouaka much longer after Antonetti's visit for he wanted to go on leave. He was proud of his accomplishments with cotton, and his support of experimentation with coffee and with oil palm trees. In fact, he gave some tree cuttings brought or sent from the Antilles to Father Diagre for experimentation.[68]

The beginning world-wide depression had still not fully struck

66 Letter, R. P. Huck, missionary at Kouango, 1930, to Brian Weinstein, 9 April 1968.

67 Arch. Nat. RCA, Section Ippy, Letter, Félix Eboué to Chefs de Subdivision, 9 February 1930.

68 Interview with Father Ledriel, Bakala, 21 June 1968. Eboué wrote Daigre during World War II to find out what happened with the plants.

Oubangui-Chari, and production steadily increased from 1928 to
1931. Each African over thirteen paid a head tax of twenty francs
in Ouaka in 1931 and the colony's budget was 17,000,000 francs.[69]
Each European paid 120 francs. Eboué also increased food production, necessary to feed the workers; he instructed the canton
chiefs to recruit for the gold mine and for the railroad. (In 1929
his West African sergeant, Samba Sall, recruited 315 workers for
the railroad, and 372 in 1930.)[70]

Three years of Bambari's development was on Eboué's mind,
and the results could be seen; promotion was also on his mind,
and he finally was rewarded with it.

ADMINISTRATOR IN CHIEF

For several years Eboué had believed he deserved to attain the
rank administrator in chief. That he did not receive it profoundly
depressed him, especially as he saw younger men move ahead of
him. Louis Spas, a year younger than Eboué, had been the lowest
man in Eboué's class at "Colo" and had gone on to a respectable
but relatively undistinguished career; he was named administrator in chief early in 1930. Eboué felt he would never accede to
the rank without the help of highly placed friends.

Blaise Diagne and the West Indian politicians were all interested in seeing a black man reach the highest ranks. They
wrote letters to the Ministry of Colonies on Eboué's behalf, and
Gratien Candace even went so far as to inquire whether the
Ministry discriminated against Frenchmen of color. Yvon Debos
wrote, as did Marcel Bénard, the French developer of the gold
mines at Roandji and head of a cotton company.

Alcide Delmont, deputy from Martinique and a Freemason,
had been made Under Secretary of State in the Ministry of
Colonies under François Piétri, the minister. He did not know
Eboué well but was in a key position to help the nomination
along. Governor General Antonetti had come to change his mind
about Eboué over the past couple of years and now supported his

[69] *J.O.A.E.F.* 1930, pp. 1070-71, pp. 1040-41.
[70] Data on numbers of workers recruited for railroad from Letter, Professor
Gilles Sautter to Brian Weinstein, 2 December 1967.

promotion too. The last day of 1930 the Ministry of Colonies
therefore promoted Eboué to the rank of administrator in chief,
the highest rank in the corps, and equivalent to captain in the
navy.

Eboué and his wife celebrated the event with champagne and
wrote letters of thanks to various friends who had helped. They
then turned their thoughts to going home, to France and Cayenne. Two months after the announcement of his promotion he
turned the affairs of the district over to a successor, was honored
at the Sports Club of Bambari, and left with his family for the
port of Douala. It was March 1931.

A new road had been opened between Cameroun and Oubangui-Chari so that administrators could use the port of Douala
instead of going all the way to Brazzaville and then to the Belgian
port of Matadi. Eboué chose this route to see something of the
neighboring colony, and the family had a pleasant trip.

In Douala Madame Eboué received a cable informing her of
the sudden death of her father, Herménégilde Tell, at the age of
sixty-six. Tell, who had retired from the prison administration,
had been practicing law and had not been in particularly poor
health although he had fathered two more children.

The four Eboués then set sail on 23 March 1931 for their return to France; they looked forward to seeing friends but were
saddened at not having been there when their parents died.
Governor General Antonetti expected Eboué to return to French
Equatorial Africa at the end of the year, but he was fated not to
return to Oubangui-Chari for over nine years.

1909 TO 1931

The Oubangui-Chari Eboué left in 1931 was quite different
from the colony he had first seen in 1909. Roads instead of un-
charted paths; cultivation of industrial crops instead of collection
of wild rubber and ivory; administration instead of conquest; a
telegraph instead of runners; organization and planning—all this
an individual lived through and contributed to. For Eboué himself the years from age twenty-five to forty-seven meant success
in his chosen profession, from cadet administrator to administrator in chief; a family with four children; an apartment in Paris;

a large group of friends. But how completely can twenty-two years transform a country or a man?

French presence brought Oubangui-Chari into the current of the world economy, and an African elite—chiefs and clerks—saw benefits in an association of one form or another with France. But the masses continued to resist French authority, and could not see its advantages. Some revolted long after "pacification" had supposedly ended; some fled; the demoralized majority merely failed to do all the work demanded of them, although they did enough to produce impressive quantities of industrial crops.

Eboué had left one colony—his own—for another. He worked in east, center, and west Oubangui-Chari, from Bouca and Bozoum to Damara, Kouango, and Bambari, and then from Bangassou to Sibut and back to Bambari, an unequaled record. He had spent more time in Oubangui than at home, but everything he had done there he wanted for his own country. Africa, the land of his ancestors, showed signs of material development that were denied to Guyane.

V

MARTINIQUE: NEW HORIZONS
IN THE CARIBBEAN, 1932-1934

As soon as Eboué reached Paris in April 1931 he went to see Blaise Diagne, Under Secretary of State for Colonies since January, and now in a better position than ever before to help his protégé. Diagne's appointment and his own promotion to administrator in chief at the same time were a turning point in Eboué's career, for the way was now open out of the corps of administrators into a new profession or into a higher cadre in the administration.

Eboué told Diagne he wanted to be named to Guyane as a colonial official or to run for the post of deputy in the forthcoming elections. They talked about Guyane and the Caribbean in comparison with Africa. Eboué thought only about economic development in both places and repeated what he had written to a friend in Cayenne about what he would do if he had a position there: "You know my ideas—*forceful* economic action and calming the people to work better and realize something."[1]

Diagne urged Eboué to forget about a career at Cayenne. Eboué was no politician and with his father-in-law's death had lost an important source of support as far as an administrative

[1] Archives Eboué, copy of Letter, Félix Eboué to Albert Darnal, 10 April 1930.

appointment was concerned. Diagne warned him that he would be asking for trouble in Guyane, that friends would expect favors, and that he would become embroiled in petty local disputes. In any case, the Minister, then Paul Reynaud, opposed sending administrators back to their home colonies. Diagne told Eboué he would watch over his interests. For the time being, both men were busy with the International Colonial Exposition of 1931.[2]

PREOCCUPATIONS

The government was sponsoring the huge Exposition in Paris, and people came from many countries to participate in conferences, exhibits, and discussions about colonialism. A large building for the meetings had been constructed near the woods of Vincennes at the edge of Paris, and the colonies set up exhibits there.

In May the International Colonial Institute met in Paris, and in September the International Congress of Anthropology and Archeology. The following month the International and Intercolonial Congress of Native Society and then the International Institute of African Languages and Civilizations assembled. For a few months Paris became the capital of all colonial empires. Indeed the Italian Fascist leader Mussolini took the occasion to criticize French colonial practices and a new figure, Adolf Hitler, found a response when he claimed that the meetings proved the existence of a French plan to dominate the world.

Eboué went to as many meetings as possible, spending very little time at home. He reported to one congress by giving a paper, "Peoples of Oubangui-Chari," part of the book he had been working on since Governor Lamblin had asked him to do a study of the colony. Subsequently he talked with the editor of the colonialist publication *L'Afrique Française* and agreed to submit his manuscript for serialization in their monthly review.

Classmates and old colleagues from A.E.F. were in Paris for the Exposition, and when he was not in some meeting Eboué spent his time with René Maran, Roger Dévigne, Roger Hellier (back from Guadeloupe), Méneau, and Camille Lhuerre, on a visit to

[2] Interview with Camille Lhuerre, Cayenne, 23 December 1967.

France. In the meanwhile Madame Eboué enjoyed shopping for clothes she could wear at the receptions and dinners. In spite of the fact that the world economic depression had struck France, the designers still had enough spirit to argue about hemlines, skirt lengths, and hair styles. But Madame Eboué's taste in clothing was conservative and, in any case, she, like her husband, had become a little stout. She did not thus try the new dresses with the wasteline at the hip, a Patou innovation, or the Victorian bustle that one couturier tried to bring back, or even the "Eugénie" hat which, in spite of its name, had little appeal.

The hectic schedule of both the Eboués left little time for the children. Henry, who preferred to spell his name with a "y," and Robert were in boarding school. Henry, now nineteen, was still not doing very well, and Robert, twelve, seemed overly quiet. During most of Henry's adolescence the only contact he had with his father was through letters. In one he wrote of the troubling problem of identity: "There are 18 of us in the house, and among these 18 there is a diversity of races and countries: Bulgaria, Germans, a Russian, Persians, Austrians, Polish, Africans. Oh! One could say Africo-Americans, in speaking of my brother and me, on friendly terms with the French of France. . . ."[3] But letters were not enough. Henry needed his father. One day Eboué received a telegram from Henry asking him urgently to meet him after school: "Important." He rushed to the school and asked his oldest what was the matter. Sheepishly, Henry admitted that nothing was the matter: "I just wanted to see you."[4]

Eboué saw other members of his family from time to time. He watched over his nephews and nieces because of Félix Gratien's long absences and continuing inability to send adequate funds to Cornélie. Clérence Gratien, Eboué's eldest niece, became ill in 1931; and Eboué took her to the hospital himself, paid her bills, and later paid more expenses when Cornélie, who had taken a job, became too ill to work. He and his wife visited the Gratiens or the Diagnes on Sundays; Eugénie played the piano while Eboué and his sister sang.

3 Archives Eboué, Letter, Henry Eboué to Félix Eboué, 23 July 1931.
4 Interview with Henry Eboué, Paris, 25 May 1968.

Although most of the Eboué and Tell families were in France, Eboué and his wife traveled alone to Cayenne after the Colonial Exposition for a short visit to dispose of their property, leaving the four children in a boarding house in Paris. In Cayenne in September and October 1931 they lived in the house of the late Herménégilde Tell until they decided to sell it as well as the Eboué house in the rue Richelieu. A friend of the family, Philippe Saccharin, who had been particularly close to Tell, took care of the financial arrangements and sales.

Saccharin and Eboué talked about the situation in Guyane and the forthcoming elections. The Guyanese wanted to get rid of Lautier to replace him with a Creole. Saccharin planned to run for the seat in parliament, and so did Gaston Monnerville, a dynamic young lawyer. Eboué promised to support Saccharin because of old family ties and because Saccharin was from an old Guyanese family. Monnerville's family, in contrast, actually had come from Martinique, and many Guyanese resented a tendency to snobbishness among the Antillean community of Cayenne.

The prison still dominated Guyane, and Eboué thought that the colony had little prospect for development, unless a Creole became deputy. René Maran suggested a white person might have more influence in Paris than a black. In a letter, important because it shows Eboué's concerns for Guyane and expresses his feeling as a black man, Eboué wrote to a lawyer in Cayenne that both Diagne and Gratien Candace had done a good job representing their home colonies: "Why can't a Guyanese do as well? Unless you think they are innately incapable, it is impossible to agree with you [that a native-born Guyanese cannot adequately represent Guyane]." He accused some Guyanese of trying to stop others from running for the office out of jealousy and presented his own position: "As for me, I shall remain faithful to these two principles no matter what happens: (a) A Guyanese must represent Guyane. (b) Once a man has been chosen . . . everyone must support him."[5]

To ensure some measure of Creole unity Eboué met with E. L. Boutin, René Maran, Gaston Monnerville, and others a few

[5] Archives Eboué, copy of Letter, Félix Eboué to Albert Darnal, 18 April 1931.

months later in Paris, and issued a statement directed at Guyanese: For the sake of the "reputation and the future itself of the Colony, the Compatriots meeting this day" appealed to Guyanese to protest Lautier's candidacy to the Ministry of Colonies and asked their countrymen either to come together right away to support Saccharin or Monnerville or to get together for the run-off election.[6]

In Cayenne Eboué had time for things other than politics and family matters. He visited the masonic lodge where he had been initiated almost ten years ago and gave a talk about Africa: "Rites of Societies in Black Africa Compared with the Practices of Modern Free Masonry." He and his wife went to a meeting of Les Amis du Livre to hear a talk about music, and accepted several invitations. They left Cayenne at the end of the year with H. Tell's archives and library, and although Eboué planned to visit on a later leave, he never saw Cayenne again.

In Paris in December 1931 Eboué's career took a new turn. Blaise Diagne had been looking out for his friend's interests, and he knew he wanted to go to the Caribbean. An opening as secretary general of Martinique occurred, and Diagne supported Eboué for the post. Diagne had even greater ambition for Eboué because it appeared that the governor, Louis-Martial Gerbinis, already past sixty, the usual retirement age, would soon be recalled. The recall might permit the next secretary general the experience of being acting governor. And if Eboué were acting governor of Martinique at the time of Gerbinis' retirement, he might even be named governor if he had done a good job and if his friends like Diagne and Yvon Delbos supported him.

Gerbinis, governor of Martinique since 1928, was on leave in France, and Eboué went to see him in hopes he would not oppose his nomination. They talked about problems in Martinique, and then Eboué called on Senator Henry Lémery, the colony's representative in the upper house of the French parliament since 1920; Alcide Delmont, still one of Martinique's two deputies; and Victor Sévère, the mayor of Fort-de-France.

Diagne told Eboué that both Senator Lémery and Deputy Delmont supported Gerbinis and had exerted pressure to have him

6 Archives Boutin, Statement, Paris, 6 February 1932.

maintained in Martinique even though some people, like the socialists led by Joseph Lagrosillière, wanted him removed. Eboué had to avoid giving the impression that he was either particularly ambitious to succeed Gerbinis or linked with any opposition to incumbent Martiniquan politicians. None of them, it turned out, objected to Eboué's nomination, and all of them respected Diagne, so the Minister of Colonies, Reynaud, proposed Eboué's name, and a decree signed by President Paul Doumer, 28 January 1932, named him secretary general of Martinique.[7]

Between the nomination and his departure for the Caribbean Eboué had just two weeks. His schedule included luncheons, dinners, and têtes-à-têtes every day with Maran, Boutin, Roger Hellier, "Petit Camille" Lhuerre, and organizations like the Freemasons. He also found time to purchase books and to pick up extra copies of his own works.

Since the publication of his study of Oubangui-Chari he had been in touch with the Institut d'Ethnologie, presided over by the powerful deputy and sometime minister, Louis Marin. They met briefly and remained on friendly terms, though Marin was quite conservative politically. Marin encouraged Eboué to write to him and wished him success in Martinique, indicating he would help Eboué if he could.

Naturally the man Eboué spent the most time with before his departure was René Maran, who had many contacts in Martiniquan circles and introduced Eboué to one of the Nardal sisters. The Nardals were a distinguished Creole family; the father, an engineer, had sent his several daughters to France for their education, and they had all been quite successful. The daughters made contact with Antillean, metropolitan, African, and Afro-American intellectuals. With a Haitian physician, Dr. Sajous, they founded *La Revue du Monde Noir* as an organ of expression for Africans or persons of African descent.

Mademoiselle Nardal gave Eboué the names of some members of the lively literary community in Fort-de-France, and Eboué submitted an article on Oubangui-Chari to her *Revue*. Although

[7] According to administrative rules, the President of the Republic officially named secretaries general, governors, and governors general, after proposal by the Minister of Colonies.

Eboué already knew a great deal about Martinique, he asked Mademoiselle Nardal, Maran, and others about the problems and tensions there, both out of diplomacy and thoroughness.[8]

POWER IN MARTINIQUE

Martinique was the most important colony of the three French possessions in the Caribbean. Fort-de-France, the capital, had been founded as a naval base because of its fine natural harbor, and the French used the island as a center for their activities in the Antilles. It was a relatively small island with 1100 square kilometers and 230,000 inhabitants in 1932, compared with 300,000 people in Guadeloupe and the 25,000 to 30,000 of Guyane.

Governors in the old colonies had more power than their colleagues in Africa in some ways and less power in other ways. The head of Martinique colony was not a lieutenant governor reporting to a governor general; he could write directly to the Minister of Colonies. He also had more staff than most colleagues in the new colonies in Africa, for he had offices which paralleled those in the Ministry of Colonies—agriculture, labor, education, and so forth—and was assisted by a secretary general with the rank of administrator in chief.

The secretary general directed the administration, acted as an intermediary between the head of the colony and the various offices, prepared official correspondence and decrees, presented proposals to the governor, directed the preparation of the budget, and met regularly with the governor's Conseil Privé, or Privy Council. He represented the governor at meetings of the colony's elected assembly, the Conseil Général, and headed the Conseil du Contentieux, an administrative tribunal. He had to know the workings of the administration very well to be effective, and was extremely influential, even though only the governor could make policy decisions.

The Conseil Général tempered the power of the governor and his secretary general. These popularly elected legislative assemblies in the old colonies met in two sessions a year and had the power to vote the budget proposed by the governor. The Conseil

8 Interview, Paulette Nardal, Fort-de-France, 4 February 1968, and Archives Eboué, Eboué notebooks.

could affect the governor's programs, and other elected representatives could exert pressure on the Ministry of Colonies to affect the position of the governor.

The relations between elected representatives in a colony and the appointed governor were complex. The several cantons of Martinique elected the councilors. These men were often mayors of towns and controlled the quadrennial elections for deputy because they made up the lists of eligible voters; they had some control over the elections for senator, held every nine years, because senators were elected by town councilors and other notables instead of being elected directly by the people. Deputies and senators through party affiliation or friendship could then influence the Minister of Colonies to name or to remove a certain person as governor. One man might be a mayor, a member of the Conseil Général, and deputy all at the same time.

The governor had considerable power that he could use for or against an elected representative. As the official representative of the Republic—like the prefects in metropolitan France—he was the most visible source of benefits. For example, he had considerable patronage power and could put friends of friendly politicians in good jobs. He could influence elections by turning his back on ballot-box stuffing or, as the guarantor of public order, call out the gendarmes to watch elections or intimidate people. He also had the power to revoke mayors for wrongdoing, thus undermining the position of unfriendly politicians.

In the best of circumstances complicated mutual checks between elected legislators and appointed executives might ensure a just government, but in the worst of circumstances the various threats that different officials and politicians offered each other could create chaos and recrimination, preventing progress. A third force, and doubtless the most important, were the white-controlled sugar interests.

USINE AND RACE

The major source of income for most people on the two islands of Martinique and Guadeloupe was sugar cane. France purchased most of the semi-refined sugar, syrups, and rum made from the cane at prices above those of the world market in order to sustain the economies of her possessions. Martinique and Guadeloupe purchased most of their manufactured goods from the metropole at prices generally higher than similar products from nearby countries, too.

Each year the economic affairs section of the Ministry of Colonies fixed prices to be paid for sugar-cane products and set the quota for each colony. This meant some insecurity, for representatives from Martinique had to lobby in Paris for an increase in the quota for their colony which could only be done at the expense of Guadeloupe. Within each colony governors established a quota for each mill and by the 1930's began to intervene to set the wages paid cane cutters and the price for raw cane when sold by small independent planters to the *usine*.

The word *usine* in French simply means "factory," but in the Antilles it has always meant much more. In the old colonies *usine* symbolized all the economic, political, and social power of the privately owned sugar enterprise, the only industry in the islands. Owners were traditionally white and absentee in the case of Guadeloupe; they were white and often residents of a segregated suburb of Fort-de-France in Martinique. In Martinique the largest sugar enterprise belonged to the Aubéry family, and in Guadeloupe to the Darboussiers.

The mills owned large tracts of tax-free land on which they grew their own cane and hired men and women to plant and cut it; they also hired men to work in the mills. Small farmers who produced their own cane and cut it themselves or with the help of a few workers sold the product to the mills. All of these people depended on the sugar interests for their incomes from which, of course, they paid their taxes. The government depended on these taxes to pay administrators' salaries and keep the bureaucracy functioning. The *usine* thus had considerable economic and political power, to which governors and politicians had to pay attention.

The mill-owners might, they knew, encourage workers to vote for one candidate over another; they might furnish the funds a politician needed to support his partisan newspaper as an election approached. Corruption of local politicians by the mills was such that the man-in-the-street believed himself powerless. In the

words of the great Martiniquan poet, Aimé Césaire, they felt
themselves the mere plaything of others:

> mon peuple
>   *   *   *
> quand
> quand donc cessera-tu d'être le jouet sombre
> au carnaval des autres
> ou dans les champs d'autrui
> l'épouvantail désuet.[9]

Having powerful friends who could talk to the whites was the
only way to survive, many thought.

White owners and white officials in the administration formed
a separate caste in the Antilles. Middle-class Creoles might be
invited to Vieux Moulin, the governor's mansion in Martinique,
but they would find no whites there. Another reception on
another day might find white guests, but no Creoles. The governor tried to maintain good relations with Creole politicians, but
throughout most of Antillean history Creoles, no matter what
their status, never felt very welcome at Vieux Moulin.

Occasionally a white official's or white businessman's open
racism, particularly in Martinique, enraged the population. Early
in 1932, before Eboué's arrival, a European teacher in the Lycée
Schoelcher of Fort-de-France touched off a protest by giving to
her students the essay topic, "Why does the Negro make Whites
laugh when he dresses like a European?"[10]

Divisions in the population went further than Caucasian-
Creole for the Creole population itself had been plagued with a
great sensitivity to shades of brown and black. The fairer mu-

[9] Lilyan Kestleloot, editor, *Aimé Césaire, Poètes d'Aujourdh'ui*, No. 85
(Paris: Seghers, 1962), p. 184, "Hors des jours étrangers."

> my people
>   *   *   *
> when, oh when will you
> cease being the somber
> plaything
> at the carnival of others,
> or in another's fields
> the obsolete scarecrow?

[10] Reported in *L'Action Nouvelle*, newspaper published in Fort-de-France,
22 January 1932.

lattoes, who had family connections with whites and were sometimes received by them socially, often adopted the prejudices of
whites and openly disdained people darker in color than themselves. The three leading politicians—Lémery, Lagrosillière, and
Alcide Delmont—looked much more European than African but
attacked each other over the issue. Socialists wrote in their newspaper, *La Résistance,* that their very light opponent, Senator
Lémery, denied he had African ancestry; they referred to him in
print as a "renegade and mean Mulatto."[11]

The anomalous status of the old colonies, the sense of power-
lessness in the face of electoral fraud, the *usine* and a capricious
world market, and the prejudices brought by whites created most
divisions. Into this tense situation stepped Félix Eboué, a man
the deep color of ebony wood, who joked with friends that he was
"A Pure Black from Bordeaux."

SECRETARY GENERAL

On 11 February 1932 the whole Eboué family, including Henry
and Robert, sailed for Martinique. Charles was almost eight and
playing with model airplanes already, and his sister almost nine;
Robert was fourteen, and the eldest would celebrate his twentieth
birthday in July. They all could go to school in Martinique, an
arrangement that would take some of the strain off the family's
finances and reunite it for the first time except for leaves, in many
years. The six of them arrived 23 February and were cordially
but quietly greeted by subordinates and the governor while the
local press barely made mention of the event. They moved into
the secretary general's official residence, Les Tourelles. Eboué
quietly began his work as the governor's assistant.

During 1932 Eboué attended all forty-four meetings of the
Conseil Privé, during which he presented projects that the governor asked him to prepare. He also had daily meetings with
Gerbinis to discuss problems facing the colony. These problems
had put Gerbinis into conflict with the Conseil Général, composed of a majority of socialists like Lagrosillière who considered
the governor linked with their enemies, Delmont and Lémery.

11 *La Résistance,* 13 September 1934.

One afternoon a couple of days after Eboué's arrival, Gerbinis called Eboué into his office to talk to him about the sugar-cane harvest which, having begun as usual the previous month, would last until June. The governor gave his secretary general a letter from small planters who protested that, contrary to custom, the mills refused to furnish the usual number of trucks to haul the cane. The planters requested the governor to call into session the Commission Consultative du Travail, or Labor Advisory Commission, which had been created in 1927 to help resolve disputes between labor, small planters, and the *usine*. Such disputes had in the past led to disorders. The governor decided the administration must take action, but he decided not to call the commission. Instead, he asked Eboué to conciliate the two parties with the help of the labor inspector. An agreement was quietly reached, thus avoiding conflict.

A more important issue worrying the governor was that of the Grands Travaux, or special public works projects. Gerbinis had signed, on behalf of the colony, an agreement with a private company to extend electricity service, even though the Conseil Général had earlier "repudiated" the governor's project for the long-term electrification of all towns of Martinique. The Conseil was not in session, and the governor hoped the Commission Coloniale, or executive committee, would agree to fulfill the short-term obligations to the company. The governor told Eboué to explain the need for their accord. Two hours before the meeting Gerbinis instructed Eboué to emphasize the administration's desire to collaborate with the Commission and the Conseil. Gerbinis needed an agreement and sent Eboué to get one.

The meeting lasted from about two in the afternoon to seven in the evening. Eboué, realizing the complicated nature of the relations between the legislators and the governor, moved delicately. He insisted the governor wanted to cooperate on all matters with the legislators, and the chairman explained the point of view of the councilors. They spent most of the five hours discussing the problems of the electric company which, in the view of some representatives, was charging too much money. They raised other problems and Eboué, protecting Gerbinis, explained how the governor was trying to resolve them. Although the question of electrification was not completely resolved and plagued Martinique for a long time, the meeting closed on a note of cordiality; the chairman noted the secretary general's cooperative spirit. Later, one of Eboué's colleagues told him that it was the first time in memory that the legislators had been so conciliatory. Gerbinis waited in his office to learn the outcome, and Eboué told him the Commission seemed friendly and cooperative.[12]

Both major newspapers of the island approved Eboué's actions. The socialist publication said: ". . . he has shown much tact, propriety, and good will, thus contributing to the lowering of the implacable barrier between the executive and our assembly."[13] The radical newspaper of Alcide Delmont, sworn enemy of the socialists, also praised Eboué: "Mr. Eboué was preceded into the colony by a reputation that his presence has confirmed. We know he has the talent, the experience and the tact necessary to govern a colony like ours. It is also a pleasure to note that his colonial origins make him more apt than another to understand certain nuances and certain peculiarities of Creole character."[14] Eboué's practiced calmness brought good results in the tense atmosphere of Martinique, but elections put Eboué under great stress.

Elections for the Chamber of Deputies were scheduled for 1 May and 8 May 1932, followed by the Senate elections on 16 October. The socialists (SFIO) of Joseph Lagrosillière were pitted against the radicals of Alcide Delmont and against Henry Lémery. "Lagros," as almost everyone called Lagrosillière, was as eloquent as he was flamboyant. He had been a socialist deputy from Martinique and a member of the Conseil Général, but had lost his position because of accusations of fraudulent activities. At the end of 1931 parliament had voted a law of amnesty, including Lagrosillière. Therefore, he felt free to stand for re-election in May 1932 and won. Then, in October of the same year, he decided to stand for the Senate against his enemy Lémery, whom he accused of being a Fascist. Lémery, a very conservative man with a reputation for arrogance, had nonetheless the respect of many Antil-

---

12 Archives Eboué, Information from Eboué's notebook.
13 *La Résistance,* 26 July 1932.
14 *L'Action Nouvelle,* 30 July 1932.

leans and of Blaise Diagne for he was a brilliant man, the first Antillean to become a cabinet member, during the government of Georges Clemenceau. Lémery disliked Lagros and the socialists as much as they did him. The campaign was bitter.[15]

The two men traded accusations and may even have traded blows. Largo said Lémery was the puppet of the Aubéry sugar interests; Lémery countered, calling Largo the puppet of the Raimbaud-Hayot *usine*. There seems to have been some truth to both accusations.

Eboué's duty was to watch over the elections to ensure a fair vote. He told his subordinates to observe the balloting and write reports for him. He asked them to discuss their impressions of the atmosphere in the colony and the attitudes of the highly politicized newspapers. Were there any incidents of violence? Under what circumstances did the candidates arrive in a place? How did they conduct their campaign? The administration would prepare all necessary documents and arrange for voting places. The governor himself would oversee the actual election. The result of the elections was the confirmation of Lémery in his seat, and he remained senator until World War II.

For a number of reasons Eboué got to know and to like Lagrosillière better than the other two politicians. Roger Hellier may have introduced them to each other, for he knew all the Antillean politicians; Eboué felt closer to Lagro's political party, SFIO, than to the Radicals. He also liked Lagro's intense commitment and eloquence, and he never made a secret of their friendship, a troublesome mistake in the charged atmosphere of Martinique.

Eboué's relations with Lémery and Delmont were correct but cool. Lémery had been the least enthusiastic of the three Martiniquan legislators about Eboué's nomination to the colony because of his color. Once the senator requested Eboué's recall to France after he heard that dark-complected Martiniquans reportedly considered Eboué the champion of the darker peoples against the fairer ones and whites. He warned the Minister of Colonies that the situation in Martinique could degenerate into racial conflict if Eboué were not recalled and replaced by a white

[15] Interview with Henry Lémery, former senator and former minister, Paris, 8 July 1969.

metropolitan who would, in his view, be neutral between the mulattoes and the blacks.[16]

Alcide Delmont, never overly friendly but originally helpful to Eboué, began to be wary of him, for he believed that the friendship between Eboué and Lagrosillière threatened damage to his interests if Eboué were named acting governor. Continuing attacks by the socialists on Governor Gerbinis did not help matters, because Delmont began to suspect the socialists wanted to replace Gerbinis with Eboué.

ACTING GOVERNOR

In July 1932 the Ministry of Colonies instructed Governor Gerbinis to proceed to France. Gratien Candace, who had in June become Under Secretary of State for Colonies after one of the many government and cabinet changes that year, made sure no attempt was made to bring in someone from outside as acting governor. Diagne and Lagrosillière wrote to the Minister of Colonies, in support of Eboué, who became acting governor of Martinique on 15 July.

Eboué took care not to give Governor Gerbinis the impression he was anxiously waiting to take charge of the colony. He refused, for example, to move into Vieux Moulin, his right as acting governor, to use the governor's automobile, or to alter any of the secretarial staff, saying that, after all, the governor would return soon. Eboué wrote Diagne that the governor seemed suspicious of him.

Diagne warned Eboué about the governor and Delmont's suspicions: "Delmont, a strange one, is complaining you have not knelt down before him. Don't worry. Do your duty with grace for all, and forget the rest." Even if the governor is cold, Diagne wrote, don't worry about it. "Tell Eugénie not to hierarchize herself and be friendly and indulgent toward everyone. In this deuce of a country where the ridiculous arrogance of the Mulattoes has replaced, with the same stupid lack of intelligence, the out-of-date insolence of the white Creole, the most dignified attitude is to be sympathetic to everyone, above all to the humble people.[17] The advice certainly was not easy to follow.

16 Interview with Henry Lémery, Paris, 8 July 1969.
17 Archives Eboué, Letter, Blaise Diagne to Félix Eboué, 18 July 1932.

During the five weeks of his interim Eboué made some nominations that apparently convinced Delmont and Lémery that Lagro's friends could get jobs more easily than theirs. Secondly, students on vacation from schools in France brought back copies of a new radical publication, *Légitime Défense*, whose articles, written by young Martiniquan intellectuals, bitterly criticized French colonialism. Eboué considered the articles "abominable" but took no action against the writers, some of whom had scholarships from the colony.

This publication, only one issue of which ever appeared, apparently frightened some whites and conservative Creoles into believing revolution was close at hand. The Red scare had not abated in France, and when a Russian assassinated President Doumer early the previous May, it revived the specter of a communist plot. The continuing deterioration in the economic situation caused the government to increase use of the quota system to limit imports, and antagonisms between France and other countries arose; all these developments contributed their share to tension in France and its colonies.

Governor Gerbinis returned 23 August, and Eboué stepped down to the secretary generalship once again. Reflecting on his five weeks at the head of a colony for the first time, Eboué wrote to Maran: ". . . my first interim lasted exactly five weeks. I was really happy . . . I only ask to begin again. . . ."[18] It appeared, however, that he might not have another opportunity to have such a position in Martinique because his relations with Gerbinis deteriorated at the end of August, although Eboué did not understand why.

Gerbinis accused Eboué of not taking *Légitime Défense* seriously enough and said: "I have been obliged to write to the Minister about this. I don't know what he will do but you were wrong not to consider this matter serious." Eboué answered that he never underestimated the affair but "I did not panic."[19] Gerbinis' threats worried Eboué because he thought the governor may have requested his recall, and he cabled Blaise Diagne to

[18] Archives Maran, Félix Eboué to René Maran, 25 August 1932.
[19] Eboué reported his conversation to Blaise Diagne, Letter, 7 October 1932.

watch the situation. The Senegalese deputy told Eboué to keep calm, not to offend anyone, and "you will have nothing to fear from Gerbinis or anyone else. Act objectively and impartially. . . . I am watching over matters." As a postscript to his letter Diagne added one last warning: "Be careful. Confide in no one."[20]

For the next few months Eboué quietly did his work as secretary general following Diagne's advice. In a moment of optimism Eboué wrote Maran that rumors of his recall were false: "Here, everything is fine even if people say the opposite . . . consider that I 'am in control' of the situation and that I am experiencing no difficulty. I tell you this because people told my sister that I had troubles, etc., etc. Even if I had them, you know that I am resourceful enough to do like Horace: Flee in order to fight better."[21]

By the end of May or beginning of June in 1933 Gerbinis knew he would soon go on a much longer leave than before, but it appears he recommended that Eboué not be named to replace him. Delmont and perhaps Lémery, fearing Gerbinis might be forced to retire, agreed, but friends at the Ministry informed Diagne, Candace, and Lagrosillière of the plan. The three men began to act together to save Eboué, Diagne and Lagrosillière papering over their differences temporarily.

Albert Sarraut, Minister of Colonies, received a barrage of communications supporting Eboué. Gratien Candace claimed that Gerbinis' dislike of Eboué was really racial, white versus black. In addition to this, there was also a *sub rosa* conflict between blacks and mulattoes. The fair-colored Delmont accused the darker Diagne and Candace of mixing in the affairs of Martinique, and Candace angrily replied that Gerbinis and his friends (Delmont and Lémery) were against Eboué because "he had made the error—in their opinion—of being indisputably Negro. . . ."[22]

Diagne and Lagros wrote Eboué promising their support. Yvon

20 Archives Eboué, Letter, Blaise Diagne to Félix Eboué, 29 November 1932.
21 Archives Maran, Letter, Félix Eboué to René Maran, 15 December 1932.
22 Archives Eboué, Letter, René Maran, 30 July 1933. Maran here cites an article he wrote.

Delbos and Roger Dévigne, both of whom had worked with
Maurice Sarraut at the newspaper *La Dépêche de Toulouse,*
asked him to influence his brother Albert to name their friend.
René Maran, now writing in several newspapers, published
articles hinting at plots against Eboué.

On 4 June 1933 a decree made Eboué interim governor of
Martinique. "There you are! Governor p.i. of Martinique. My
warmest, my most fraternal congratulations" wrote René Maran,
thrilled to see a black man and a friend in such a high position.[23]
"This success constitutes, in my opinion, a new victory for our
race. . . ."[24] Eboué was happy: "I ardently wanted to be where
I am today, and [this is] where I want to be kept."[25]

This time it seemed Gerbinis would not return to the colony
so Eboué moved into Vieux Moulin, enjoyed the governor's official automobile, and organized his own cabinet. He asked René
Isambert to come to Martinique to be his secretary general, but
Isambert, on leave from a new post in Tchad, refused because he
said he was too tired. In the absence of old friends he was fortunate to have found new ones whom he could confide in.

Two companions in Martinique soon became Jean Cazenave de
la Roche, a white devout Roman Catholic who had been Gerbinis' private secretary, and the elderly Abel Sainte-Luce-Banche-
lin, a white Creole and Freemason who had taught for many
years in Antillean lycées. Others were the Wiltords.

Eboué and his wife often visited the Wiltords, Antoine and his
wife "Baby," who had become their most intimate friends in
Fort-de-France, Antoine Wiltord, a young black administrator,
had a household in which Eboué could feel completely at ease.
An evening might begin with four of them standing and singing
around the piano in the Wiltord's modest sitting room, proceed
to a rum punch and a West Indian meal with highly spiced rice,
and end with a hand of bridge.

Like his predecessors Eboué went to the usual official receptions, but he moved around a great deal more than they, and his
wife was finally much happier than she had been those early
years in Bangassou, although she still needed hobbies to fill up

[23] Archives Eboué, Letter, René Maran to Félix Eboué, 1 July 1933.
[24] Archives Eboué, Letter, René Maran to Félix Eboué, 14 August 1933.
[25] Archives Maran, Letter, Félix Eboué to René Maran, 21 November 1933.

the day. They entertained a great deal and made a special effort to attend marriages, burials, baptisms, and so forth, visiting the homes of Martiniquans proud to see a man of his color at the head of the colony, even though he still did not have the rank of governor.

On 11 November 1933 to celebrate Armistice Day, and perhaps to celebrate the publication of his book *Les Peuples de l'Oubangui-Chari*, Eboué decided to have a rather special dance. He loved to dance, and he tried something which had happened only once before in the memory of most Martiniquans—an inter-racial party. For the fête Eboué invited colleagues in the administration and leading members of local society, both white and black Creoles. He enjoyed planning for the event and showed his subordinates where he wanted the decorations put and what kind of refreshments to prepare. Many people declined to come, and in one case a white planter or businessman practically insulted Eboué, but the dance was held with well over a hundred people in attendance. Whites and Creoles came, and the ball was a great success; those who attended still remember it vividly.[26]

The four children, enrolled in school, saw more of their father but not much because of his occupation, his social activities, and because, for the first time, he was working in a colony with a large and active masonic community with whom he spent time in the evenings.

His home lodge, La France Equinoxiale of Guyane, made Eboué a kind of goodwill ambassador to Les Disciples de Pythagore Lodge in Fort-de-France, affiliated with the Grande Loge de France. He joined Les Disciples, which was also Lagrosillière's lodge, and he paid his dues for many years. He also visited other lodges, affiliated with the Grand Orient, Alcide Delmont's federation. This was friendly "socializing" but it also served to keep him on good terms with different political factions.

Eboué considered, however, that politics had no place in freemasonry and refused to attend lodge meetings for some months because members began to discuss political matters concerning his administration. In a speech to the masons he told them they

---

26 Eboué saved all the invitations and responses he got. The one rather insulting reply he tore up, but either he or his wife saved the pieces. Archives Eboué.

should not interfere in political questions and that they must not let themselves be divided by politics. Madame Eboué, after long discussions with her husband about religion and philosophy, had given up her Catholicism to join Le Droit Humain, a masonic order which admits both men and women. Although Madame Eboué influenced her husband in matters of musical taste and perhaps in personal appearance, he must have had great influence over her in this decision.

Freemasonry also gave Madame Eboué something else to occupy her time, besides the children, the family's pets, and a few hobbies. She followed her husband's administrative activities closely and he talked a great deal with her about his problems in Martinique, some of which were very serious.

THE FOURÊT AFFAIR

Above all, an interim governor had to keep the peace while the governor was absent. In 1933 a dispute concerning Albert Fourêt, head of the school system, threatened the peace of the island. Fourêt, a French white, taught and lived for over forty years in Martinique with his fair-colored Martiniquan wife, and by 1932 was both the principal of the lycée and the superintendent of schools. Martiniquans linked him with the Radical Party of Delmont and accused him of bringing politics into the schools by persecuting teachers associated with Lagrosillière's socialist party, SFIO. In 1932, for example, he had accused a professor of writing, under a pseudonym, critical articles for the socialist newspaper and tried to dismiss him.

Rumor had it that Fourêt disliked Eboué because of his race or his reported friendly relations with Lagro and the socialists. He thought Eboué might try to appoint socialists to positions in the school system. A former teacher and member of the Radical Party claimed Eboué planned to name a socialist to head a school post he wanted; either he or Fourêt told Lémery about it, and the senator complained directly to Eboué: "My friends complain of being passed over for colleagues recommended by Mr. Lagrosillière."[27]

[27] Archives Eboué, Letter, Henry Lémery to Félix Eboué, Paris, 2 October 1933.

Eboué answered rather dryly that Lémery's friends had made an error concerning recent promotions "in spite of what certain impatient and disappointed persons may think, say, and write. . . ." The person who wanted to be head of a school was the youngest of three candidates, and the nominating committee had chosen another older man who had the respect of all, Eboué wrote. He concluded forcefully: "I don't want to tell you that everything is perfect in my administration, but I must remind you that I endeavor to be impartial and objective."[28]

Relations with Fourêt deteriorated further after the baccalaureate or high school diploma examinations of June 1933. Fourêt had insisted on correcting the philosophy questions instead of leaving the job to the teachers; he then flunked many students, particularly those of a Creole teacher he disliked. Students had demonstrated their displeasure in July and vandalized the superintendent's automobile while the socialist newspaper attacked him for passing children of friends and flunking children of enemies. Examinations would normally be given again in October.

At the end of September Eboué, who had by then been acting governor for about four months, called Fourêt into his office. He began the conversation by asking him questions about general problems in education, then delicately brought up the question of the baccalaureate examinations of the previous June and asked him if he planned once again to correct the philosophy test. Fourêt replied he had the right to do so and would indeed correct the October examinations. Eboué agreed he had the right to correct any examination if he really wanted to do so, but new disorders might result and he as acting governor had the responsibility to maintain public order. The elderly superintendent answered he was not a coward and that he felt an obligation to correct the examinations because the Creole philosophy teacher had been inadequate. He said he was sure, in advance, that many students would again fail. Eboué strongly advised him to leave the grading to others.

Fourêt responded that he would correct the examinations, in-

28 Archives Eboué, copy of Letter, Félix Eboué to Henry Lémery, 2 November 1933.

cluding that of Henry, Eboué's son. Eboué asked him to use self-restraint in a tense situation. The discussions became more heated, and Eboué accused Fourêt of promoting disorder. At the end of their meeting Eboué asked Fourêt to think about his decision for twenty-four hours. He agreed but returned the next day to tell Eboué he had not changed his mind. Eboué then said: "All right, but you do it at your own risk."

The examinations took place on a Monday, 2 October, and Fourêt failed thirty out of thirty-eight students in philosophy. He also wrote a rather sarcastic note to Eboué informing him that Henry was among the failures. Shocked parents complained that the principal had again been too severe and had shown favoritism. The tension grew. On 5 October, as Fourêt left his office, two students struck him, and he called the police.

The colony went into an uproar after the examinations and the attack. Eboué stayed up late writing long reports to the Minister and requested the recall of Fourêt to France, for he believed Fourêt was part of a plot to make the acting governor seem incompetent to maintain order; he also took the opportunity to complain that educational facilities in Martinque were overcrowded and with too few teachers. Fourêt, in the meanwhile, reportedly told his friends he thought Eboué had something to do with the attack because of Henry. Eboué, furious at the suggestion, demanded in a note to the principal that he prove what he had been saying; he also sent Henry back to France to enroll in a special course to prepare himself again for the examinations.

At the trial of the students, held in December 1933, the young men admitted having attacked the principal, and Fourêt dropped the charges against them, possibly because his position in the island would have become impossible had he not. He corrected no more examinations and retired a year later. The relations between Eboué and the radicals worsened.

THE RED FLAG AND ANDRÉ ALIKER

Delmont and his friends thought they saw in other actions Eboué's links with the socialists and even with the communists. In November 1933 Eboué went to the town of Sainte-Marie to attend the inauguration of a monument to Martiniquans who had died for France in the First World War. Someone at the ceremony raised the red flag of socialism with the letters SFIO on one side of it. The flag did not remain very long, but Alcide Delmont's newspaper, *L'Action Nouvelle*, accused Eboué of involving himself in politics; "In seeing the governor pass, the crowd acclaimed in him not only the personification of France but also and above all 'The governor that Lagro sent.' . . . To make of Mr. Eboué the governor of a party is to do him a wrong, and he must understand this himself. Mr. Eboué must be careful of his friends."[29]

Eboué watched the newspapers very carefully for any comment concerning his administration and was highly sensitive to what people said about him. He saved copies of Delmont's newspaper and sent one to the Minister of Colonies as well as a report from the commandant of the gendarmerie who wrote that the red flag was up only briefly and that the tricolor was most prominent. A photographer had caught a shot of Eboué standing by the red flag, however. Events such as this one made Eboué edgy and convinced him his career was in jeopardy. For most of the time, however, the colony was relatively quiet, its economic situation improving under Eboué, and the relations between the executive and the Conseil Général never better. Into the lull suddenly exploded a series of dramatic events which showed the full force of Martinique politics.

One of the most controversial men on the island was André Aliker, manager of the local communist newspaper, *La Justice*, and a revolutionary. He relentlessly attacked colonial policy, Alcide Delmont, and Senator Lémery whom he called "puppets of the capitalists." He denounced Antilleans who believed empire could be reformed, calling them fools. He denied their assimilationist goals and called for a struggle for independence. In November 1933 several unknown men attacked Aliker and nearly killed him. Even though he claimed his life continued to be endangered, no steps were taken to protect him. Other assassination attempts were made, and rumor attributed them to the Aubéry sugar interests. Early in January 1934 Aliker was found drowned, and his body bore marks of a severe beating. Some people said

29 *L'Action Nouvelle*, 2 December 1933.

Eboué should have given him protection after the first attack, but he was no longer governor in January; his role in this affair is, in fact, unclear.

The communists themselves implied that Eboué had not been properly informed about the possible danger to Aliker,[30] but they never attacked or particularly praised Eboué for anything; he never openly attacked them either and, in fact, once he asserted in public that a man had the right to belong to the communist party if he chose to do so just as he had the right to belong to any other legal party. In March 1934 the radicals put forward the strange accusation that Eboué had protected Aliker, contrasting Gerbinis' supposed hostility toward the communists: "Gerbinis according to the communists is only worth an insult. . . . Gerbinis' subordinate found favor with *La Justice* because the local apostle of communism . . . found protection and support from this person."[31]

Delmont's hints may have been an attempt by the radicals to attribute to Eboué the leftist beliefs of his eldest son Henry, for back in France after the Fourêt affair Henry had begun to associate with many Antillean and African intellectuals. They formed clubs and study groups and began to agitate for change in the empire. Some of these young men, Aimé Cesaire of Martinique, Léon Damas of Guyane, and Léopold Sedar Senghor of Senegal, would soon become important poets of negritude as well as political figures in their own right.

After Aliker's death Henry attended a protest meeting with his Antillean and African friends and signed a petition calling for justice: "It is our duty to stand up to affirm our will to organize the struggle for the maintenance of liberty and the revenge for the one who died for that liberty."[32] Eboué was angry when he read the petition; he had been seriously concerned for some time with his son who had also begun to associate with communists, friends reported. Fearful for his career in the colonial administration, which was increasingly sensitive to nationalist demands in North Africa, Eboué thought he might be compromised and

[30] *La Justice,* 17 May 1934.
[31] *L'Action Nouvelle,* 14 March 1934.
[32] Reprinted in *La Justice,* 27 March 1934.

wrote what must have been an extremely angry letter to Henry. He forbade him to associate with reported communists and warned him he would have nothing more to do with him if he dragged the family name into dishonest affairs or communist-linked activities.

Henry responded begging forgiveness and swearing on the name Eboué that he would have nothing more to do with politics. Eboué remained very angry with Henry, although he joked about "my leftwing son" in public. Soon he would leave Martinique, but the change probably had nothing to do with Henry's activities.

REASSIGNMENT

In December 1933 it was rumored that Gerbinis would return shortly, thanks to Delmont and Lémery. If a governor had been recalled to France for an extended period, it usually meant the Minister of Colonies was displeased with him. Even if he were to be retired, his friends worked to have him sent back to the colony for a month or so to prove to his and their opponents that the Minister had confidence in him. The gesture, a tradition, was an expensive one, but Gerbinis benefitted from it. Diagne was ill, and others who might normally have been expected to help Eboué did not act to prevent Gerbinis' return, and he arrived in Fort-de-France on 7 January 1934. Eboué's interim finished.

In February 1934 the French government changed. Gaston Doumergue became Prime Minister with Senator Lémery as Minister of Justice, Marshal Pétain as Minister of Defense, and Pierre Laval as Minister of Colonies. The world-wide depression convinced the Minister of Colonies of the need to economize, and he therefore removed and retired a total of ten colonial governors and ninety-three administrators. He included Gerbinis, then sixty-three years old.

Friends thought this was Eboué's chance to be raised to the rank of governor and maintained in Martinique. But Delmont's newspaper then began to criticize Eboué, hinting he had communist friends. Eboué's own supporters had no particular influence with Laval, particularly with Lémery in the same cabinet. On 19 April the Minister announced Eboué's reassignment to

Soudan in West Africa; it was bad news, but the worst was yet to come. In May news reached Martinique that Diagne was dead. When Eboué heard, he lost control of himself and wept openly: "My father is dead."[33]

In deciding to remove Eboué as well as Gerbinis the Minister bowed to political considerations, not the interests of the colony. Laval removed Eboué to satisfy Delmont and Lémery, who doubtless complained that the socialists would see in the recall of Gerbinis a victory unless Eboué were recalled at the same time. The decision was, however, inopportune for the colony because the Conseil Général was scheduled to meet; without a governor or a secretary general no one could officially open the meeting and present the policy speech. After some confusion another administrator arrived in the island to head it.

Eboué and his family sailed from Fort-de-France 23 May 1934. On board ship he tried to relax with René Maran's most recent book, *Livre de la brousse*. Eboué had helped him with it, and Maran had dedicated the book to him. Eboué also talked with his wife about the bittersweet experiences in Martinique. They liked the Caribbean but disliked the intrigues of local politics and conflict. Eboué felt he had accomplished something, if only proving that a black man as governor in the Antilles could be just as good as a white man, if not better. He had not had the time or the power to begin policies of his own but had known what it might be like to be governor. At times he dismissed the idea he would ever accede to the rank, but he continued to hope, and even inquired about it at the Ministry after his return. He wrote Maran: "You and I both know that I shall never be governor any more than we shall see a black have the same duties as I again in the Antilles . . . the death of Blaise Diagne is significant. I have no more illusions."[34]

[33] Interview, Madame Antoine Wiltord, Fort-de-France, 6 February 1968.
[34] Archives Maran, Letter, Félix Eboué to René Maran, 8 July 1934.

VI

SOUDAN: WEST AFRICAN
INTERLUDE, 1934-1936

THE CITY of Paris was installing air raid sirens when the Eboués arrived home the first week in June 1934. Hitler and his Nazis, in power across the Rhine, were rearming Germany. Some voices in France still talked of disarmament; amid growing tensions between Left and Right and a succession of governments weakened by scandal, Marshal Pétain, Minister of Defense, urged preparedness, and parliament voted increased military expenditures. In Germany there were demonstrations for the return of their former colonies, including Cameroun. Louis Marin, Minister of Health, told Eboué in a conversation shortly after his return that the time had come for France and her allies to intimidate the Germans, and that such a step might be the only way to avoid war.

Eboué went to see Laval and got two months leave so that he could rest at Vittel mineral springs. Perhaps because of the tensions and conflict in Martinique, Eboué felt ill; in addition, his hearing was deteriorating. Physicians had found enough uric acid in his blood to "build the foundation of a house" in his own words,[1] and they prescribed treatment at Vittel. The diet was boring—milk, lean meat, special mineral waters, cooked fruit, and

1 Archives Maran, Letter, Félix Eboué to René Maran, 2 July 1934.

no alcohol—a miserable program for a man who usually ate and drank heartily. The regime made him temporarily slimmer and rather well below the two hundred pounds which became his usual weight as he approached fifty. Five feet ten inches tall, he carried himself with the grace that one would expect of a former athlete. But he felt his years and grieved deeply when friends died. Henri Vendôme was gone after serving at his last post in India. Diagne was gone too, and so was Robert Hermine. Back in Paris in the middle of July Eboué visited with Isambert, Joseph Lagrosillière who regretted what had happened in Martinique and who swore revenge, René Méneau, and Roger Dévigne. Relations with René Maran were no longer on the old familiar footing however.

René Maran and Eboué had been devoted to one another for thirty years, but their wives did not get along very well. Money was another reason for the strain of relations. Eboué had always been very relaxed when it came to personal money matters and had not made the careful calculations and programs typical of his approach to his work as an administrator. In addition, Maran was a friend, and as schoolmates back in Bordeaux they did not keep track of who "owed" the other a drink or a sandwich. In 1922 Eboué had been forced to borrow from Maran and later repaid the debt. Either in 1931 or a couple of years later Maran's wife apparently had borrowed from Madame Eboué.

The details of what happened are not clear, but there seems to have been a disagreement concerning the repayment of the loan. The two ladies became angry at one another and strained the relations between their husbands. No formal break took place between Félix Eboué and René Maran but they saw less of each other and by the end of 1934 ceased corresponding regularly. Both Maran and Eboué hoped to re-establish their former intimacy in the course of time, but Eboué's 1934 leave was too short, and he was too busy trying to find a house to effect any improvement before sailing.

The apartment at rue Chaveau Lagarde was now too small, and Eboué's income justified the purchase of a house even though economic conditions in France did not encourage large investments. Looking for a house suitable for his family of six, Eboué and his wife found one in the suburb of Asnières, a few minutes by train from Paris. Asnières was not a fashionable suburb, but the house pleased Eugénie Eboué immensely, and she liked the name of the street, Michelet, the same as the name of a school she had attended as a young girl.[2]

The Victorian, stucco and stone, three-story house had a large sitting room and dining room, five bedrooms, and a study. A courtyard with circular driveway in front of the house and a yard behind it provided room for flower gardens and for their dogs and cats to play. They moved in, and Eboué began to arrange his study on the second floor. He purchased cabinets for his rather large collection of books. He and his wife also had the books which had belonged to her father, and the Tell family papers, as well as their own extensive correspondence which they kept meticulously. The need to pack and to deal with the Ministry of Colonies about his new assignment did not leave much time for settling into the house, and, in fact, Eboué never would have the time to arrange his affairs at Asnières the way he wanted to.

A delicate administrative matter took up some of Eboué's time. The Ministry's clumsiness with regard to Eboué had continued; Laval had removed Martinique's two highest officials at a bad moment and had failed to consult with Jules Brévié, governor general of French West Africa, about Eboué's assignment. Consultation with the governor general about such an appointment was a matter of courtesy, something Laval cared little for, and rumor had it that Brévié wanted a friend to be named to the post. Eboué, therefore, made an appointment to see Brévié, and after a talk about problems in West Africa, believed he could work in his new post without fear of antagonism from him.

Eboué looked forward to his new post although he was not sure where it would lead him, he had few friends in Soudan and had little of the kind of basic knowledge about it that one gets from working as a subdivision head. Soudan was, however, an attractive and interesting assignment for a man interested in African history and culture. Parts of the territory (present-day Mali) were included in the three great medieval empires—Ghana,

2 Interview, Eugénie Eboué, Asnières, 10 May 1968.

Mali, and Songhai. Here was the famous city of Tombouctou, known for its community of scholars during the height of these pre-colonial civilizations. The empires had declined by 1878 when the French moved northeast from Senegal to conquer the area, a task completed by the end of the century after energetic resistance from local leaders.[3]

At first the French integrated the area with other possessions as part of Afrique Occidentale Française (A.O.F.), or French West Africa, but by 1920 they had made it into a separate colony within the A.O.F.; and had a lieutenant governor dependent on the governor general of French West Africa whose offices were in Dakar, Senegal.

The economy of the country, two-thirds of which was the Sahara, depended on exports of peanuts, cotton, and cattle shipped via the Dakar-Niger railway, completed in 1924 between Dakar and Bamako, the colony's major city. With the depression, markets and demand for the products fell off to levels disastrous to the colony's economy. The budget, dependent of course on local taxes, was one of the smallest in West Africa although the colony had a comparatively large population.

In 1934 Soudan colony, divided into twenty-four *cercles* or districts, had a population greater than that of the four colonies of French Equatorial Africa combined. Its 3,500,000 people, nearly a third Muslim, were Maninka, Foulbe, Bambara, Soninka, and Touareg. It was a diversified population; rule-making was difficult because the centralized decision-making habits of the French administration were not always flexible enough to deal with the hierarchized authority of local populations. Eboué knew that he would head this administration for at least a few months because Lieutenant Governor Fousset planned to leave.

The Eboués left Paris for Bordeaux the last week in July. They had decided that Ginette, Robert, and Charles would accompany them. Ginette, then eleven years old, had completed her C.E.P. or primary school diploma and could continue studying in Soudan. Robert and Charles, then fifteen and ten, could continue

[3] Much of my information on the background of Soudan/Mali comes from William I. Jones, *Malian Economic Policy and Planning*, unpublished manuscript, Université de Genève, 1970.

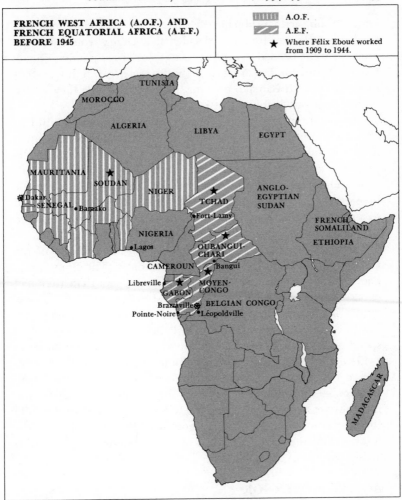

FRENCH WEST AFRICA (A.O.F.) AND
FRENCH EQUATORIAL AFRICA (A.E.F.)
BEFORE 1945

A.O.F.
A.E.F.
★ Where Félix Eboué worked
from 1909 to 1944.

their studies at the lycée in Dakar. Charles was already sure he
wanted to be an airplane pilot, and Robert told his father he
wanted a career in the diplomatic corps. Eboué bought Charles
model airplanes but told Robert that a black Frenchman would
never be able to make a successful career in the Ministry of
Foreign Affairs.[4] What to do with Henry, then twenty-two, pre-

4 Interview with Robert Eboué, 5 April 1968.

sented Eboué with problems; he talked with Cornélie, who had tried to watch over him, and decided that Henry would join the army for some needed discipline. On 31 July 1934 the five Eboués left Bordeaux for Dakar aboard the *SS America*; at Dakar they took the train to Bamako arriving 16 August. There they settled in their spacious cool house at Koulouba.

The usual tendency for the French administration to build its offices and administrative housing in a section of the city away from the business district and local population was especially pronounced in Soudan. The *quartier administratif* had been built at Koulouba, a few miles from Bamako, high on a hill where a breeze and a beautiful view of the Niger River valley contributed to a rather comfortable life by the 1930's. There was, in fact, even a swimming pool, reserved for Europeans.

Lieutenant Governor Jacques Fousset, a 1904 graduate of the Colonial School, greeted his comrade cordially. The Eboués also had the good fortune to find more acquaintances than they had expected, including also Captain and Mrs. Monlouis of Guyane. Frédériska Halmus Monlouis, vivacious and intelligent, was Eugénie's first cousin, and the two ladies could look forward to spending much time together in the absence of their husbands.

Eboué at first remained in Koulouba, however, while Fousset toured the colony in October and November. The secretary general immersed himself in political and economic reports from previous years and discussed them with other administrators. By the time Fousset left Soudan in December Eboué had familiarized himself with the colony and was ready to assume the position of acting governor.

ACTING GOVERNOR

Eboué went on tour immediately after taking over the administration on 12 December 1934. He wanted to see all the districts as soon as possible, and he wanted to know everyone working under his orders: "It has been necessary for me to find out rapidly what is going on in order not to run the risk of being accused of deficiency. To find out what is going on, as you know, there is nothing like going out to see people on the spot. Thus, I have been able to visit carefully all the *cercles* of Soudan, no mean feat

because there are 22 of them."[5] Formalistic as he was about administrative procedure, he believed in the efficacy of personal contacts and communication outside the bureaucratic channels. He
therefore encouraged his subordinates to write him personal un-
official letters to explain current problems in terms not possible
in the official reports. Because of his own experience, he was
convinced the heads of *cercles* knew the basic problems of the
country better than officials in Bamako. He was ready to listen
to them and to trust them.

For almost a year—from 12 December 1934 to 20 November
1935—Eboué acted as governor. His position was not very secure
because he did not have the rank of governor; Paris had also decreased salaries by 10 per cent for all colonial administrators because of the economic crisis and had retired as many administrators as possible. Nonetheless, promotion was on his mind.

Rumors abounded about the forthcoming retirement of five
men with the rank of governor, and friends in Paris wrote that
Governor Deitte, who had replaced Lamblin in Oubangui-Chari,
might be one of them. Thinking of the French Equatorial Africa
that he left four years ago, Eboué wrote E. L. Boutin, who had
replaced Maran as his epistolary confidant, that he would not
mind being governor at Bangui: "Don't you think that if the
facts are correct, I ought to try my chances?"[6] Candace, Lagrosillière, and Yvon Delbos, now vice-president of the Chamber of
Deputies, wrote the Minister of Colonies, but nothing was decided
about Eboué. He absorbed himself in work.

As an acting governor, lacking experience in Soudan and
knowing another man would replace him, Eboué was not in a
strong position to initiate programs, but economic development
and the role of African authority still concerned him. Governor
General Brévié had abolished the *indigénat* (which gave administrators arbitrary judicial power) for women, but maintained
forced labor throughout French West Africa. Eboué did not oppose it; on the contrary, when African men refused to work, he
used the *indigénat* to put them in prison for the need to work was

5 Archives Boutin, Letter, Félix Eboué to E. L. Boutin, 17 May 1935.
6 *Ibid.*

still part of his creed. In his view firmness was particularly necessary in dealing with the Touareg nomads, who had not accepted
French rule as late as 1934, and some Muslim sects which opposed it.

At the end of 1934 Soudan's economic situation looked slightly
better, and it improved further during 1935 as cotton production
increased and the demand for peanuts grew. The Compagnie du
Niger Français and the Société Commerciale de L'Ouest Africain
purchased the products, and during Eboué's administration sales
increased by over 14,000 tons. He encouraged the extension of
peanut cultivation.

In order to help local European businessmen during the depression an Agricultural Credit Fund lent to sisal planters almost
2,000,000 francs the year before Eboué came to the colony. The
Europeans could not pay back the loans, and the administration
decided to give them a moratorium and to lower the interest rate
from 6 per cent to 4 per cent. Eboué, who served as president of
the administrative council of the Fund, wrote to Brévié to defend
the change in the conditions of the loans. The governor general
in Dakar criticized the action as too lenient and thought the
Soudanese administration should be more conservative in money
matters.

Brévié then went on leave and left his secretary general, Pierre
Boisson, in charge. Eboué, thinking of the economic development of a region on the frontier with Mauritania, wanted some
salt deposits to be part of Soudan. Eboué contended that the
region of Tinioulig could be developed by the Sudanese and that
a former trading town, Oualata, would benefit. Chazelas, the
lieutenant governor of Mauritania, protested that the routes followed by nomads with whom the administrations in Soudan and
Mauritania were concerned demanded that the area be part of
his colony. Frontier questions with Mauritania were never satisfactorily settled, and there are occasional difficulties between the
two countries, now independent, even today.

Most hopes for development of Soudan came not from salt
deposits or sisal but from the huge irrigation project under the
Office du Niger, in which the French government had invested
heavily. The French hoped to create a large productive popula-

tion center in the Soudan, linked with Algiers by a trans-saharan route and a trans-saharan railway. By 1934 it was indeed possible to travel from Bamako to Algiers by automobile and airplane, but French hopes were far from being realized.

Emile Bélime, the dynamic general director of the Office du Niger, later said to be more enthusiastic than knowledgeable about water or agricultural engineering, got on poorly with the colonial administration which he considered hostile to his projects. He had a canal built just up the river from Bamako to irrigate the plains of Koba, Baguineda, and Tanima. By 1934 some 3800 African peasants had moved to the area to cultivate the land, and the Office hoped to augment the population by another 1200 on 3500 hectares of irrigated land.[7] An inspection mission sent by the Ministry of Colonies and headed by Robert Bargues (an acquaintance of Eboué's, later governor general of Madagascar) pointed out considerable problems concerning recruitment of Africans for the projects, distribution of land, payment by the Africans for the land, and suitable crops and marketing.[8]

Bélime disliked administrative interference. After the inspection he and Eboué got into an argument about colonization of the irrigated area by Africans, Bélime contending that the Office du Niger needed no intervention by the administration to ensure settlement, Eboué countering that the local administration wanted to cooperate with the Office du Niger and that persuasion on the part of the administrators encouraged settlement. Then Bélime complained that colonial officials had encouraged one village to move to the new land even though the people were not suitable for the type of agricultural work envisaged. Disagreements between the Office and the administration continued for years.[9]

Eboué's relations with Bélime were less delicate than relations with the Christian churches in this Muslim country. Although

[7] Sources: various unpublished reports and documents the copies of which are in the Archives Nationales, Republique du Mali, Bamako.

[8] Interview with Governor General Bargues, Paris, 26 March 1968.

[9] Some of my information also comes from Jones, *Malian Economic Policy and Planning*.

the Roman Catholics had helped the administration by implant-
ing the French language in the beginning of the colonial period,
they came into conflict with it later, when the colonial officials
realized that disorder could come from the social change promoted by the missionaries. They also feared that the Church
tried to undermine local authority.

During Eboué's interim, difficulties came up over the missionaries having instructed female converts and children that they
need no longer follow the family choice of a husband. The administration, concerned about African reactions to such preaching, warned the churchmen that they lacked sufficient knowledge
about African society and should not weaken it by such advice.

The head of the Soudanese Catholics was Monsignor Thé-
venoud, a man sure of his mission and apparently convinced that
any opposition to the Church's activities came not from an administrative desire to preserve order but came from a masonic
plot against the Church. Eboué, a Freemason, was not in a very
good position to approach the prelate, but in fact he had donated
money to the Church to soften relations. During a meeting with
Eboué the Monsignor insisted that girls should have the right
to choose their own husbands and were under the protection of
the Church once they converted or worked at mission stations.

Eboué defended the African tradition and explained he
thought there had been a misunderstanding between missionaries
and the many African fathers who brought their children to mission stations when they needed money to pay their taxes; they
thought they were temporarily hiring out the children to the
priests, who paid them. Church authorities then proceeded to
baptize the children and considered that their fathers had no
more authority over them. When their fathers asked for the children's return for marriage, the priests would refuse or stall; the
Africans became angry, and the administration often intervened
to prevent disorder. Eboué considered the problem impossible to
solve until new policies concerning African society were articulated; a new "native policy" or *politique indigène* was needed.
Some Africans were being caught between traditions represented
by chiefs and their own fathers on the one hand and education
and the Church on the other. Eboué thought a new status be-

tween citizen and subject was necessary and mentioned the term *notable evolué*, perhaps for Christians, in his reports.

French administrators, Freemason or Catholic, were not any more enthusiastic about the conversion of adults than they were about that of children. Because political authority and religion were extricably linked, conversion weakened loyalty to the village chiefs on whom the administration depended for the collection of taxes, recruitment of workers, and administrative tasks. In one case, a recent convert had refused to pay his taxes and found protection in a mission station.

Many canton chiefs, appointed solely on the basis of their loyalty to the French, had no more traditional basis for legitimacy than their colleagues in Oubangui-Chari, but a change in attitude began. In 1929, Maginot, the Minister of Colonies, had warned that without traditional authority African society would collapse, opening the way for communism. Partly as a consequence of this line of thinking the French created Conseils de Notables at the level of the *cercle,* and Robert Louis Delavignette, who became head of the Colonial School, wrote that these councils could take on more responsibility in the administration.[10]

In Soudan the ambiguity of French policy toward the councils was manifest. Conseils de Notables existed by the time Eboué arrived—one per *cercle*—but they had no significant powers. Chiefs were often chosen with sensitivity to tradition but administrators could still treat them like minor subordinates. Even Eboué, respectful of Sokambi and Hetman in Oubangui, could write: "We find no ill will on the part of the chiefs. For the most part they are collaborators who, in spite of their lack of education are obedient. . . ."[11] What the administration never resolved was the problem of how chiefs could be leaders and a cohesive force in their own societies while serving as "obedient" clerks to the French. Eboué named at least five canton chiefs during his governorship and requested increases in salary for them. He also directed subordinates to treat chiefs with respect and ordered that

[10] Robert Delavignette, "La Politique et l'administration indigène en A.O.F.," *L'Afrique Française,* Vol. 43, No. 1, pp. 7-11.

[11] Colonie du Soudan Français, "Rapport de présentation du project de budget de 1935," p. 6.

the tombs of the kings of pre-colonial empires be cleaned and maintained at the expense of the colonial administration, but these were rather minor actions.

In a more important decision the French grouped cantons together, beginning in 1933, to create provinces. Chiefs were to be chosen for these large entities on the basis of the will of the people, custom, and the capabilities of the person. Where people refused to obey these chiefs the French would move in to punish them; Governor Fousset, for example, sent forty Africans to prison for refusing to pay their taxes to their chief.[12] The idea of province chiefs was tried in other colonies too, but without much success.

The French set up a *médersa* or training school for sons of chiefs in Tombouctou and had 117 students in 1934. Another school had 61 students, most of whom were from nomadic tribes.[13] Eboué believed that the French must base their economic and social policies in the Soudan on this chiefly elite. The elite, once trained and convinced, would carry along the masses without social disorder. It was therefore important to Eboué that children of chiefs get the type of education that would help them rule in a changing world. In the schools run by missionaries and the colony there was a high percentage of children of chiefs during Eboué's administration: "In order to raise the intellectual level of chiefs, we undertook a judicious choice of children to admit in the schools so that those destined by their origins to become chiefs were among them." In 1933-1934 approximately 1500 students out of 12,000 were sons of chiefs.[14]

Governor General Brévié agreed with these programs but disapproved another and most interesting project to elect village chiefs. Fousset and Eboué had submitted in October 1934 a project providing for village commissions composed of all heads of families. By majority vote the commission would "designate" a chief. The governor general was startled by the word and changed

[12] Colonie du Soudan Français, "Rapport Politique annuel—année 1934," p. 112.

[13] Colonie du Soudan Français, "Rapport de présentation du project de budget de 1935," p. 11.

[14] Colonie du Soudan Français, "Rapport Politique 1934," p. 120.

it to "present" a chief, meaning suggest a chief to the administrator who might or might not then name him. In the towns, neighborhoods or *quartiers* would have chiefs designated by the commissions also. Brévié disliked this idea very much; in the urban areas trouble was feared from the educated and such elections might crystallize political movements: "It is more opportune not to put forward the principle of elections for the neighborhood chief. . . ." And he noted incredulously, "Well, elections?," thereby missing an opportunity to be ten years ahead of his time, for such elections came later.[15]

As in Oubangui-Chari Eboué talked seriously and courteously with African leaders about their role. Unlike Oubangui-Chari, however, Soudan had a relatively large group of educated men who worked as schoolteachers, military men, or chiefs. Some had gone to the William Ponty school in Senegal to prepare for teaching, the administration, or medicine. One man that Eboué knew was Fily Dabo Sissoko, a schoolteacher and then a canton chief, later an important politician. Sissoko was closer to Eboué in his intellectual interests than Sokambi had been, and the two men discussed the role of tradition in the country, and on Eboué's urging Sissoko wrote about the customs of the Soudanese.

Judging from the notes Sissoko sent Eboué, they considered each other linked by race. For Sissoko, Eboué was always a "race brother," a *frère de race*.[16] They talked about the black race, and Sissoko told Eboué of his pride in seeing a black man at the head of a colony.

It appears that in Soudan, however, some whites clearly disliked the idea of a black as acting governor. Some white administrators began saying that Muslims had no respect for a "descendant of slaves," and unhesitatingly explained to the Africans the slave ancestry of their Antillean and Creole colleagues. Some claimed that Eboué could not govern without white subordinates who had authority because of the color of their skin. One went so

15 Governor General, Afrique Occidentale Française, to Lt. Governor, Soudan Français, 9 March 1935.

16 Dedication written by Sissoko to Eboué in an article by Sissoko, "La Géomancie," in *Etudes Soudanaises*, 1937: "A M. F. Eboué, Très respectueux hommages et excellents souvenirs d'un frère de race." Signed 3 March 1937 and put into the Eboué library.

far as to claim that the Touareg could not bear the sight of Eboué and that he could reassure them only by lying that Eboué was not really the governor but that he merely advised the head of the colony in the way that low-caste ironmongers advised Touareg leaders.[17]

Eboué knew about these rumors and the antagonism of white administrators, but at the time did nothing about them. He apparently wrote to Philippe Saccharin, however, for Saccharin responded from Cayenne: "Certainly there is no lack of people unhappy to see you so highly placed. But, at least . . . you know your position; you know you are struggling against a century-old adversary who is pursuing one goal—namely not to find himself in a position inferior to that of a man of color."[18]

A visiting British official was pleased to meet Eboué and was not afraid to accept the hospitality of a man of color. Sir Arnold Hodson, governor of the Gold Coast, traveled through the Soudan in November 1935. Delighted to meet a British colonial official and talk with him about the British system of indirect rule, through chiefs and African kings, Eboué planned a meal that Hodson, like Gide, remembered as one of the significant events of his long trip from Dakar to Accra: "a long affair like all these French luncheons" with several different courses and wines, finishing with champagne. Photos show that Eboué had rapidly gained back whatever pounds he lost at Vittel.

After their discussions, with Madame Eboué helping translate, Eboué took Hodson on a tour of Bamako's schools and then to the sports club where Eboué often played cards. When he arrived in Accra, Hodson wrote an article about the trip for the London *Times* and *West Africa*. Eboué impressed him, and he noted that he was "a West Indian, and I believe the first colored man to act as governor. He and wife carried out their duties with dignity and tact."[19] Eboué got a copy of the article and underlined the words "with dignity and tact."

---

[17] Governor General R. Bargues heard this story during his tour of Soudan while Eboué was acting governor. Interview, Paris, 26 March 1968.

[18] Archives Eboué, Letter, Philippe Saccharin to Félix Eboué, 15 December 1934.

[19] *West Africa,* 20 June 1936, in Archives Eboué.

Other visitors and social events provided occasions for entertainment in the Eboué home. Governor General Brévié visited Soudan and inaugurated the Ecole Normale Rurale of Katibougou; the Eboués prepared receptions for their visitor, soon to be named governor general of Indochina. They also traveled to Conakry, Guinea, for the inauguration of a monument to a governor in May 1935.

Aside from trips Madame Eboué kept busy in Soudan. Ginette was growing up and well, except for a bout with pneumonia, and Charles and Robert took their studies at the Lycée Faidherbe in Senegal seriously, but Henry worried his father for he had not joined the army until about October 1935; Eboué sent him money but he apparently asked for a loan from his aunt Cornélie who did not have very much herself. Félix Gratien, then working for the Ouhamé-Nana Company, was more successful than he had been but Eboué still sent his sister money when he could. He also sent her copies of the occasional articles he was publishing on African civilization.

ANTHROPOLOGICAL STUDIES

Eboué never lost his early interest in African civilizations. Most of his earlier colleagues had cared little about these matters, but by 1934 more administrators were doing studies of the peoples among whom they worked. By then publication was a point toward promotion, for the Ministry of Colonies now realized the importance of the studies for effective governance and development.

The forms used by the administrators for their monthly reports in the early 1900's first provided little space for ethnographic information, but Eboué's writing in a section called "Population" filled the margins with copious remarks on what he saw and heard. In a typical report at Kouango in 1915 he wrote:

> The Langbassis have practically the same customs as the Banda. . . , but the dialect spoken by them differs from the other Banda dialects in its pronunciation, which is gutteral instead of palatized, in its vocabulary many words of which are unknown by the other Banda, and the roots of which are very difficult to find, and finally in its syntax which caries a little. In spite of these differences, we must class the Langbassis in the Banda group. The same is true for the Yakpas and

the Boubous. . . . As soon as the condition of the country permits,
the head of the subdivision will write down [more] linguistic and
ethnographic information about the Langbassis and compare it with
the work already done by him about the other Banda tribes.[20]

He had spent hours with Sokambi, Hetman, Soumoussi and
others to prepare his language manual and his little volume on
the whole country, *Les Peuples de l'Oubangui-Chari,* originally
titled *L'Evolution sociale, politique et economique des peuples de
l'Oubangui-Chari.*[21]

Les Peuples is a modest and rigorously honest publication.
Eboué said what he knew and admitted what he did not. Anthro-
pologists have had the benefit of more sophisticated techniques,
more money, and more time to collect data and are doing the
definitive studies of the peoples of Central Africa, but administrators like Eboué working without the benefit of official support
and in their spare time often did a respectable job.

In the first section of the book, Eboué sketched general charac-
teristics of the country and its history, as far as he knew it. Then
he dealt with the ethnic groups and the Banda in particular.
Lastly, he examined in summary fashion a few economic and political problems concerning the occupation of the country by the
French and the future, which he considered to be one of economic expansion and development. He said nothing about political change.

The book is very carefully footnoted, for Eboué gave credit
where it was due, mentioning the work of his friends Father
Daigre and Madame Grall who worked at Bambari. Even after
his departure, he carefully purchased articles and books about
Oubangui. Father Tisserant, another missionary, published a
book on the Banda without mentioning Eboué's prior work in the
bibliography. Eboué was so annoyed that he protested to the government of French Equatorial Africa, which had underwritten
the cost of publication.

Another writer, A. M. Vergiat, published a book called *Les
Rites secrets des primitifs de l'Oubangui* and Eboué read it carefully, noting in the margin many disagreements. He found sec-

[20] Arch. Nat. RCA, Section Kouango, "Rapport Mensuel," April 1915, Félix
Eboué.
[21] Archives Eboué, manuscript.

tions he thought were plagiarized from his own book, and his copy is amusing to examine because of his comments. In a section of mythology, for example, Eboué noted in the margin in several places: "See Eboué. Stop thief!" or "You joker! Come on. Look up the etymology of the word."[22] He did not object to Vergiat's interest, but he considered it dishonest work. He wanted others to do research in Oubangui and Soudan and encouraged them.[23]

Eboué's contribution to knowledge about African cultures was particularly important in the area of language and music. Since school days he had a penchant for these subjects, and in Oubangui discovered the connection between the two in tonal languages. Although he was not the first person to recognize that alterations in tone changed the meaning of words and phrases, he was the first to elucidate it in Central Africa.

Eboué claimed correctly that musical instruments like the linga or "talking drum" of the Banda could transmit any message that a human being might articulate: "In fact, every day they use their drummed language, the faithful reproduction of the [spoken] language with all its richness and all its nuances. . . ." With a linga, he wrote, "one can express absolutely all the ideas possible with spoken language."[24]

Eboué corresponded with several scholars about his ethnographic work. Louis Marin was particularly interested, and a German linguist, A. Klingenheben, wrote: ". . . what you have said about the languages . . . interested me very much . . . the musical tone and its representation by the 'linga.' . . . I am taking the liberty to send you some pages on the Vai."[25]

In West Africa Eboué and his wife made comparisons with what they previously discovered in Equatorial Africa. They traveled to the town of Koudougou, now in Upper Volta, to study the reported tonal languages in that district after Raphael Saller, a

22 Library Eboué, A. M. Vergiat, *Les Rites secrets des primitifs de l'Oubangui* (Paris: Payot, 1936).

23 An administrator in Soudan published his correspondence with Eboué: F. Lem, "Musique et art nègres, lettres addressées à M. Eboué," *Bulletin de Recherches Soudanaises*, No. 3, September 1936, pp. 73-83.

24 Eboué, *Peuples de l'Oubangui-Chari* (Paris: Comité de l'Afrique Française, 1933), p. 80.

25 Archives Eboué, Letter, A. Klingenheben to Félix Eboué, 7 December, 1933.

Martiniquan administrator, told them about his observations. They stayed in Saller's house, and he provided them with informants and an interpreter.[26]

Because of Eboué's ear trouble, he feared he might be making some mistakes in transcription, but fortunately Eugénie Eboué's musical training permitted greater accuracy, for she reproduced the tones on the violin she carried and then wrote them down. They then published an article, "La Clef Musicale des Langages Tambourinés et Sifflés: Essai de Linguistique Musicale." Eboué sent the manuscript to Louis Marin so that it might be read at a meeting of scholars in Belgium: "It is the fruit of some work done a little rapidly but which continues studies begun in Oubangui."[27]

Eboué had less time for African literature and poetry in Soudan. With the help of African teachers in Oubangui he had collected stories about Tere, the central figure in Banda oral literature. He planned to publish one day those that he did not send to Maran but never did, apparently not having had the leisure to get them in order. He made time, however, to help other scholars.

A Dahomean, Maximilien Quenum, prepared a study called "Au Pays des Fons," a study of an ethnic group in Dahomey which the Eboués looked over very carefully; they worked so closely on it that the criticisms are written one or two paragraphs in the hand of Eboué and then one or two paragraphs on the same page in the hand of Madam Eboué. Madame Eboué also prepared a study on African music which she presented to a meeting of the Freemasons, and Eboué corrected that and made a few additions.[28]

In Oubangui-Chari an ethnographic society had supported research, and Eboué thought it a good idea to set one up in Soudan. He proposed that other researchers do a general study of traditional methods of education, and had an assistant make up a questionnaire. He also told his subordinates that the study of African customs would convince them of the need to respect their continuing efficacy to maintain order.

[26] Archives Eboué, Letter, Raphael Saller to Félix Eboué, 6 September 1935, and interview with Governor Saller, Paris, 7 July 1969.

[27] Archives Eboué, copy of Letter, Félix Eboué to Louis Marin, August 1935.

[28] Archives Eboué manuscripts.

Eboué found that traditional law and order clashed with French ideas. In pre-colonial society secret organizations served an important order-maintaining function and upheld the values of the society. In Oubangui-Chari, Eboué had highly respected the Banda Somale. Once, after a member broke an important rule, the Somale called for his execution and designated an executioner who carried out his task. Eboué, refusing to ignore the African social-legal structure, merely gave the murderer a prison sentence, not the death penalty. Similarly, in Soudan, he faced the case of an administrator who desired to punish severely an African for having mutilated the hands of another who had stolen from him. Warning his junior colleague to be careful of the punishment meted out, he argued that such mutilations in Soudan were part of a larger system of beliefs and order-keeping mechanisms which held the local societies together. He had punished the murderer in Oubangui-Chari, but here in Soudan he strongly urged the government to undertake a study of Soudanese conceptions of thievery before punishing those who had applied traditional sanctions.

TO FRANCE, BRIEFLY

The Eboués had no complaints about this year in Soudan. He had gotten a sense of problems in another area of the empire and had done some thinking about policy toward the question of chiefs and the need to create a new status for educated people. In November 1935 Matteo Alfassa, who had perviously worked in Equatorial Africa and Martinique, arrived to take up his duties as lieutenant governor of French Soudan, meaning Eboué would not become governor there. Fousset went to Martinique for a brief period and then retired.

Alfassa and Eboué worked well together and became friends. Although Alfassa was close to retirement age, thus presumably giving Eboué a chance at the governorship, Eboué requested permission to go on leave. One reason may have been that he was again suffering from kidney trouble. The family assembled at Dakar to take a ship 2 September 1936 for France, looking forward to a long leave. They arrived in France one week later; much to everyone's surprise, leave would last only one month.

VII

GUADELOUPE: POPULAR
FRONT GOVERNOR, 1936-1938

REPORTS OF CONFLICT dominated French newspapers in September 1936. The Italians had defeated and annexed Ethiopia, and the Spanish civil war had erupted in July. Even more disturbing was German occupation of the Rhineland by an enlarged German army. This aggressive move called forth demands for a military build-up in France where, a government just three months old was trying to unite a deeply divided country with social reforms that Félix Eboué, for one, was enthusiastic about.

A period of great instability and polarization had begun during the winter of 1933-1934. The so-called Stavisky scandal, implying corruption in high places of the Republic, along with severe economic depression, encouraged right-wing, anti-democratic groups in France. Their activities culminated in Paris on 6 February 1934 with a massive demonstration which, some people believed, would finish with an attempt to overthrow the government and to change France back into a monarchy or a dictatorship.

Left-wing groups responded by organizing against what they considered to be a Fascist threat. The communists called for a coalition of democratic forces opposed to Fascism. On Bastille Day 1935 communist and non-communist participants in a huge demonstration pledged their unity in the defense of democracy and swore "to provide bread to the workers, jobs for youth, and for the world a humane peace."[1]

The socialists, whose programs Eboué increasingly agreed with, joined the radicals, the communists, the two largest trade unions, and four organizations, one of which was the League for the Rights of Man, to form what the members first called a Rassemblement Populaire, or Popular Rally. A representative committee then began planning a program published in January 1936, well in advance of the next legislative elections.

Political demands of the program included action against rightist organizations called the "Leagues," measures to protect the Republic, an end to corruption, greater freedom of the press, recognition of the freedom to join trade unions, more support for public schools, and extension to age fourteen of obligatory schooling, academic freedom, control and decrease in armaments, support for the League of Nations and collective security, and nationalization of war industries. Economic demands included a call for a fund to help the unemployed, a reduction in the work week, adequate retirement funds for the elderly, extension of public works projects, reduction in the cost of living, support for cooperatives, control of bankers, and prevention of secret agreements between civil servants and businesses.

The elections of 3 May 1936 gave a majority (376 seats out of 618) to this alliance of parties, trade unions, and organizations in the lower house of parliament, the Chamber of Deputies. Léon Blum, leader of the largest party, the socialist SFIO, formed a cabinet and named Yvon Delbos, Eboué's friend, Minister of Foreign Affairs; Marius Moutet, a socialist deputy long interested in colonial problems and critical of colonial abuses, became Minister of Colonies; and Maurice Viollette, a former governor of Algeria, Minister without Portfolio. There were no communists in the coalition cabinet.

The program of the new government emphasized economic and social change. A few days after Blum had officially organized his

---

[1] Georges Lefranc, *Histoire du Front Populaire* (Paris: Payot, 1965), p. 82. General information about the Front Populaire comes from this book as well as from Daniel Guérin, *Front Populaire: révolution manquée* (Paris: René Julliard, 1963).

cabinet he and his ministers met with representatives of labor and business to bring about reforms and to bring a halt to a wave of strikes which occurred all over France. Management agreed to the principle of collective bargaining, freedom for trade union organizing and activity, raises from 7 per cent to 15 per cent in salaries, elections of workers' delegates to represent worker interests, and no action against strikers. Workers agreed to respect the law. Shortly after this agreement the government promulgated a law instituting paid annual vacations for workers, and the legislature passed a law introducing the forty-hour work week and another law concerning collective bargaining. Workers and farmers thought a new day had come, although French morale was shaken by the devaluation of the franc, considered necessary by Blum because of the world-wide depression.

Although solutions to internal metropolitan problems clearly interested the government more than change in the colonies, Eboué and some of his colleagues who also believed colonialism meant economic development found encouragement in a speech by Marius Moutet:

> Colonization for us means the development of the colonial masses by the raising of their material, social, economic, intellectual and cultural level. That is the primary work of colonization. . . . [and] I say that the policies of the Front Populaire can be profoundly colonial.[2]

They were also pleased by Moutet's nomination of men known for their progressive views. Marcel de Coppet became governor general of French West Africa, and Moutet's cabinet included René Barthes, "considered a communist sympathizer" and negrophile by conservatives, and Robert Louis Delavignette.[3] Eboué wanted very much to participate in what promised to be a new orientation in France and the colonies. He heard that the post of governor of Niger was vacant and asked friends like Yvon Delbos and Gratien Candace to write to the Minister on his behalf. From Soudan Matteo Alfassa wrote a strong recommendation, and Gov-

[2] Journal Officiel, *Débats Parlementaires, Chambre des Députés,* No. 104, 16 December 1936, p. 3626.

[3] Charles-André Julien, "Léon Blum et les pays d'outre-mer," in *Léon Blum, Chef de Gouvernement 1936-1937,* Collogue, Cahiers de la Foundation Nationale des Sciences Politique, No. 155 (Paris: Armand Colin), p. 377.

ernor General Brévié commented very favorably on his interim. Suddenly a crisis gave Eboué his chance.

He had barely begun his leave when Maurice Viollette, acting as Minister of Colonies in the absence of Marius Moutet who had gone to Africa to investigate nationalist disturbances, asked him to become interim governor of Guadeloupe. A volatile situation, involving the then governor had developed in the islands, and Yvon Delbos, influential because of his cabinet position, and others like Barthes suggested Eboué might be able to bring back order. Barthes told Eboué that if he accepted this difficult assignment, he would certainly be raised to the rank of governor. He accepted.

Joseph-Louis Bouge, a white metropolitan and governor of Guadeloupe since 1933, faced economic and political problems he could not solve. By 1936 the economic situation in the colony had deteriorated sharply. Prices paid to Guadeloupans for sugar declined, but prices they paid for manufactured goods increased in the white-owned shops. Newspapers attacked the governor for not putting some controls on prices and for allowing a private company to take over the operation of electricity plants with rates higher than those in France. The newspaper *Nouvelliste,* edited by a supporter of the Popular Front and a friend of Guadeloupe's white Senator Henry Bérenger, attacked Bouge, while *La Démocratie Sociale,* Gratien Candace's publication, defended him. *La Voix du Peuple,* the newspaper of Maurice Satineau, recently elected deputy, supported Bouge too.

Even if the economic situation were excellent, the colony had difficult problems, possibly even more difficult than those of Martinique. Race tension, the power of the sugar mills, dependence on sugar and bananas, and an intensely personal politics were always problems. The fact that the colony consisted of several islands—two major islands, Grande-Terre and Basse-Terre, plus a half dozen small dependencies—instead of one made communication difficult and encouraged local politicians to establish fiefdoms whose tangled relations and feuds were almost impossible for an outsider to understand.

In September 1936, the month that Eboué went on leave, Governor Bouge had called for municipal elections in the town of

Saint-Louis on Marie-Galante island, a fiefdom of two enemies of Gratien Candace, Raphael Jerpan and Furcie Tirolien. Bouge had previously suspended Jerpan, the mayor, and the other members of the town council because of irregularities in elections the year before. At the end of September Bouge sent gendarmes to Saint-Louis to protect a commission he named to supervise the elections. Jerpan's friends, who were all black, attacked the gendarmes, who were all white. A gendarme fired into the crowd killing two and wounding several. Jerpan fled and went into hiding after the governor ordered his arrest. The Ministry of Colonies feared the situation might get worse with riots and general disorder and recalled Bouge to France for "consultations." A decree of 29 September named Eboué interim governor.

Before leaving for Guadeloupe Eboué had only eleven days. He spent a great deal of time with Cornélie, then quite ill, with no sign of Félix Gratien. He saw Lagrosillière, Gratien Candace, and old friends, including Roger Hellier, by then director of the Agence Centrale des Banques Coloniales, which represented the banks of the old colonies, since his return from the Antilles.[4] Eboué also saw René Maran once at lunch.

Eboué and his wife decided there was no point in the family accompanying him because it was not sure how long he would remain in Guadeloupe in spite of promises. Ginette enrolled at the girls school of the Legion of Honor. Charles had passed his last examinations, but Robert had failed; both could go to school in Paris, Eboué thought. Henry signed up for a second tour of duty, much to his father's relief. Madame Eboué decided she would have the heating system repaired at Asnières.

In Bordeaux awaiting his ship, Eboué talked with his friend René Isambert who, on leave from his post in Tchad, had the latest gossip about Equatorial Africa and the Ministry. Louis Courbain, a half-brother of Madame Eboué, had done brilliantly in his law studies and worked in Guadeloupe; he talked about the island. Eboué departed aboard the SS Cuba which left 10 October.

On board Eboué had a restful time. The crew was extremely courteous. He wrote letters to his wife and friends each morning and played bridge or talked with fellow passengers afternoons.

4 Interview with his son, Christian Hellier, Paris, 16 June 1969.

A gallery of French Caribbean politicians important to Eboué's service in Martinique and Guadeloupe. Top: L, Joseph Lagrosillière; R, Henry Bérenger. Bottom: L, Gratien Candace; R, Maurice Satineau. Photograph of Bérenger courtesy of the French Senate Archives. Others courtesy of the Archives of the French National Assembly. All photographs taken around 1937.

Jean-Baptiste Alberti, the Corsican governor of Martinique, was returning to his post and Eboué talked with him about promotions, honors, problems in the Antilles, and other matters of concern to administrators. He met Furcie Tirolien, the politician from Marie-Galante, and Eugene Graëve, the white businessman who had formerly represented Guadeloupe in the Chamber of Deputies. Graëve had run against Gratien Candace in the recent elections and was a good friend of Lagros.

As a matter of courtesy Eboué sent greetings by radiogram to Governor Bouge and to the three men who represented Guadeloupe in parliament—Candace, Satineau, and Bérenger. Only Bérenger responded. Before arriving in Pointe-à-Pitre he also sent a communication to Jean Cazenave de la Roche asking him to be in his cabinet in Guadeloupe.

No word came from Guyane during the trip. Eboué thought he might receive some congratulations on his nomination even though this would involve sending a radiogram to the ship. A Guyanese family told him, however, they were proud to see him treated so courteously on the ship and that his compatriots were happy to see him advance in his career: "I shall see in the tone of the letters I hope to receive from Guyane," he wrote his wife.[5]

The *SS Cuba* arrived at Pointe-à-Pitre, Guadeloupe's major port, the afternoon of 20 October, and the Guadeloupans greeted their new governor with enthusiasm. Demonstrations were frequent in the islands, but the fact that Eboué was black increased the interest and excitement of the people who turned out in great numbers to catch sight of him. What he appreciated most was a group of schoolgirls dressed in Guyanese fashion who presented him with flowers. Cazenave de la Roche had already arrived.

Before leaving the next day for Basse-Terre, his official point of disembarcation, Eboué made a quick trip to visit Rolland René-Boisneuf at nearby Gosier. Boisneuf, the local politician and mayor, was the son of a former deputy, Achille René-Boisneuf, and the godson of Lagrosillière, so the visit was an act of friendship. But since friendship and politics in the Antilles were inseparable, it was probably a mistake. Boisneuf had challenged

[5] Archives Eboué, Letter, Félix Eboué to Eugénie Eboué, 19 October 1936.

Jean Cazenave de la Roche, a photograph taken in Guadeloupe in 1937. Courtesy of Jean Cazenave de la Roche.

Satineau in the recent elections, and the two men were sworn enemies. Satineau's partisans doubtless noted Eboué's excursion.

Basse-Terre had no docking facilities in 1936, and a small boat took Eboué from the *Cuba* to shore, from which he was escorted to the official residence of the governor at Saint Claude, a white residential quarter along the slope of the dormant volcano La Soufrière. Bouge and Eboué chatted amiably about problems facing Guadeloupe and its 300,000 inhabitants, and Bouge invited Eboué, Cazenave de la Roche, and a few others to dinner.

Eboué stayed at a new government building with residential quarters as well as offices on the edge of Basse-Terre town. Cazenave de la Roche stayed there, too, for Eboué wanted someone trustworthy around all the time to talk to about his plans, his impressions, and, in a more official way, plan his speech to the forthcoming session of the Conseil Général:

> I have a great deal of work and, for the time being, only one man I can rely on. Therefore, I must work at double time so that as soon as I take over, the day after tomorrow, I shall truly be in charge. I have no intention of letting myself be manoeuvred around.[6]

Bouge left 24 October, and Eboué was in charge.

6 Archives Eboué, Letter, Félix Eboué to Eugénie Eboué, 22 October 1936.

PEACE AND THE "SOCIAL MINIMUM"

Eboué's first task was to restore confidence and order, do something about the economic situation, and explain the goals of the Popular Front government. He did not know how long he might be kept in Guadeloupe but presented the image of a man sure of himself and planning to remain.

On 29 October he had distributed throughout the country a poster-size "Message to the People." In the message he proclaimed his respect for the Guadeloupans, his intention to resolve in an orderly fashion problems facing the colony, and he called for unity to make everyone prosperous through honest work:

> Everyone will find in the Representative of a Republican France an impartial arbitrator, and the working people in particular can count on my solicitude for the amicable solution to questions of interest to them and of importance now.[7]

He then revoked the order to arrest Raphael Jerpan, and introduced the price controls that Bouge had refused; he also arranged the recall to France of the white commander of the gendarmes, a reputed racist and considered responsible for the shootings on Marie-Galante.

On 31 October members of the Conseil Général escorted the acting governor to the palace of the council to open its second annual meeting. Unlike some of his predecessors, he insisted on walking through the town of Basse-Terre to greet the onlookers. The town was and is one of the most beautiful in the French West Indies, built on a mountainside along the sea, with two-story wooden houses in the colonial style.

As was his custom, Eboué spoke to the councilors from a text that he and Cazenave de la Roche had prepared. Some legislators were surprised by his rather soft voice. Eboué was not the familiar Antillean orator who spoke with great ease and dynamism to large groups of people. He wrote all his speeches carefully, even those given on less formal occasions, and they reflected the painstaking work that went into them. His occasional smoker's cough,

---

[7] Reprinted in *Journal Officiel de la Guadeloupe* (Infra, *JOG*), No. 46, 29 October 1936, p. 859.

detracted from his speechmaking abilities, but that day in Basse-Terre people inside and outside the hall strained to hear him.

The new head of the colony opened the meeting by referring to "this beautiful land" and by expressing his pride to have been chosen "as provisional manager of Guadeloupan interests."[8] Supporting the application of Popular Front reforms of metropolitan France to Guadeloupe, he explained his idea of a "social minimum" program, which meant more than a material minimum. It meant intellectual and moral satisfaction which might come from increased technical education opportunities, worker housing, cooperatives, mutual aid societies, a minimum wage, and a sports program.

The forty-hour week, paid vacations, and collective bargaining would be applied to Guadeloupe, he said.[9] He proposed easy credit for small independent planters and the sale of land owned by government at prices the peasants could afford. After some praise for the French educational system he encouraged the council to vote funds for increased educational programs and for new primary schools so that all children could eventually be required to attend school until the age of fourteen.

The speech also revealed Eboué's view of the place of sports in the education of young people. He saw it as a key not only to physical development but also to the development of a spirit of cooperation, fair play, and teamwork among young Antilleans, who were as divided as their societies. He said, therefore, that he wanted obligatory exercises and gymnastics in all schools to begin immediately, and he promised the councilors that they would soon receive a report concerning the construction of physical education buildings and a stadium. Such a view was common in America or Britain, but it was unusual in France at the time. He admitted that some budget-cutting, necessary because the low price of sugar meant lower taxes, would affect this program but wanted to begin it as well as open a tourist office.

[8] Guadeloupe, *Conseil Général: Deuxième Session Ordinaire de 1936,* Basse-Terre, p. 5. All references below come from this source, pp. 4-24.

[9] Application of the forty-hour week meant little for the cane cutters who by necessity had to work more than forty hours during the harvest, but Eboué thought other industries might benefit, and eventually the sugar cane workers might find the law helped them too.

In concluding his speech Eboué said that the motto of his administration would be: Legality, Neutrality, Equity. He would be successful, he added, if the people united in peace: "in spite of all the factors of discord which appear as soon as men live side by side and which a wise man vainly advised to 'flee with horror'," he was convinced the people would act with "fraternal tolerance" toward one another.[10]

The Conseil Général showed its friendliness by frequent applause, and the crowd outside cheered the acting governor when he departed immediately after the speech. In the afternoon, M. Méloir, President of the Council, called on him to introduce the other councilors to him.

After the council meeting satisfaction of wage demands was Eboué's first Popular Front project. From 29 October to 9 November, dockers, banana harvesters, and building masons struck. Working with the divided leaders of the weak unions, Eboué decided to meet directly with strikers. As soon as he heard of a dispute or strike he went out for face-to-face contact with the participants; he wrote about one to his wife: "I had to interrupt the letter begun this morning at 7:30 AM, and I have been busy ever since—until this moment, 9:30 PM. What a rush! I am worn out. Imagine, building workers got it into their minds to strike, to induce those who wanted to work to strike, etc. I had to go to the work site that they seized in order to lecture them and tell them that although I am a friend who will support those demands which are just, I am in favor of order and cannot tolerate disorder in the streets."[11] Both workers and managers agreed that Eboué should arbitrate, which he did promptly by raising wages. He was proud that the strike had been resolved peacefully, a rare event in the island.

To get further information about strikes and the reasons for them Eboué depended on a number of sources, including André Haliar, Guadeloupan police commissioner at Pointe-à-Pitre, Marius Larcher, Martiniquan attorney general at Basse-Terre, Jean Cazenave de la Roche and M. Guillet, who had been with him in Soudan, from his cabinet, and his private secretary, Jean

[10] Eboué's reference was, of course, to the *Golden Verses* of Pythagoras.
[11] Archives Eboué, Letter, Félix Eboué to Eugénie Eboué, 7 November 1936.

Sainte-Luce Banchelin, the son of Eboué's white Creole friend from Martinique. That Eboué had three whites close to him annoyed some Guadeloupans, but Eboué, who was angered when he heard that, said the choice of his personal staff was his own business. Suspicious that he was being watched for mistakes and possibly remembering Blaise Diagne's advice about not trusting anyone in the local administration, Eboué confided in no one outside his small circle of friends and his wife to whom he wrote daily letters.

Various informants told Eboué that the strikes were not completely spontaneous, that gangs of partisans of Maurice Satineau and perhaps Candace were making the circuit of sugar mills, especially those of the large Darboussier *usine,* forcing workers to strike and generally causing disorder. On 20 November 1936 he was informed of trouble at Bonne-Mère sugar and rum distillery. He drove there immediately to speak to the workers and to arbitrate their differences with *usine* managers: "I told them to have confidence in me, but that I would not hesitate to call upon judicial authority in case of infractions of the law; I told them that obstacles to individual freedom and freedom to work would not be allowed and that property must be respected," he wrote to Marius Moutet. The workers agreed to wait for Eboué's talks with the factory-owners and seemed to be satisfied with the increase in wages they received. "I have succeeded once again in controlling the situation," he wrote.[12]

Eboué began to believe the strikes were encouraged by unnamed enemies who wanted to provoke him, a black governor, into using white gendarmes against black workers. The resulting bloodshed, with its racial overtones, would bring about his recall to France. His feelings had some basis in fact; conservative newspapers in France opposed the Front Populaire, complained about a supposed decrease in law and order in France and the colonies, and Gratien Candace showed some hostility to Popular Front programs:

In France the situation is becoming more complicated from day to day. Where are we going? No one knows. On the exterior the wind is

[12] Archives Eboué, Félix Eboué to Eugénie Eboué, 23 November 1936.

blowing a tempest; on the interior we have convulsive movements of
a social policy completely justified if we were in a period of calm. . . .[13]

Later, Candace wrote more openly: "With Léon Blum and ex-
tremist elements of CGT [trade union federation] which influence him, France might sink into anarchy."[14] Eboué feared he
might not be named governor, but he was wrong.

GOVERNOR

After Bouge left and order was restored, no word came from
Paris about a raise in rank to governor. Eboué, acting as governor,
still had the rank of administrator in chief; he grew depressed,
fearing that if the government of Léon Blum should fall, he
would never be named governor. He thought about going back to
Soudan as secretary general. In his moments of great depression,
which he was as always careful to conceal, he felt that his friends
had deserted him.

During this period Eugénie Eboué became more than wife and
mother; she became a collaborator in the full sense of the word.
She wrote him daily, long letters about luncheons and meetings
with various political figures and friends to find out why the titu-
larization was being held up. Everyone claimed to be working for
Eboué, she wrote.

Gratien Candace had told Madame Eboué in early October
that the Minister of Colonies had been planning to name another
person, but that he himself had insisted on Eboué. He also hinted
that Senator Bérenger opposed Eboué, while Bérenger's office
hinted that it was Candace. Another rumor attributed opposition
to Gaston Monnerville, Guyane's deputy, supposedly because he
feared that if Eboué were named governor, he might one day
challenge him for the seat of deputy. E. L. Boutin went to see
Monnerville, but the latter claimed to support Eboué. Another
rumor blamed Satineau, and yet another white business interests.

So absorbed were the two Eboués by Guadeloupe and the promotion that international politics was not even mentioned in
their correspondence. In October Paris had experimented with its

[13] Archives Eboué, Letter, Gratien Candace to Félix Eboué, 9 November
1936.
[14] Archives Eboué, Letter, Gratien Candace to Félix Eboué, 9 July 1937.

new air-raid sirens and blackout plans; the Nazis consolidated their power in Germany; the newspaper *Action Française* was accused of calling for the assassination of Léon Blum. In mid-November Roger Salengro, Blum's Minister of the Interior, attacked as a traitor by rightists, committed suicide. The only way in which the event entered into Eboué's available correspondence is that Lagrosillière reported to Madame Eboué that he spoke to Gratien Candace on Eboué's behalf during the funeral.

By mid-November the Ministry of Colonies had raised others to the rank of governor, but not Eboué. He wrote his wife that he had given up hope of ever becoming governor. Lagros, in reporting the bitter news that René Maran had apparently suggested to Marius Moutet that he name as governor a white administrator friend, offered to try and have Eboué transferred to Martinique.

The reasons for the delay may have been either simple bureaucratic inefficiency or opposition from someone, but the decision finally came. On 25 November Senator Bérenger's office telephoned Madame Eboué that Yvon Delbos, who was quite close to Bérenger, had just called to say that the Ministry of Colonies had just written a decree promoting Eboué to governor third class, the proper first rank and approximately equivalent to rear-admiral. A colonial official and Freemason in President Lebrun's cabinet could be expected to speed up signature. Moutet told colleagues he was pleased with the promotion because of Eboué's excellent record as an administrator who brought peace to Guadeloupe; in addition, he said it was "a manifestation of my feeling, my convictions that a man of color could fulfill such functions as well as a White. It was a political action too, as a challenge to Hitler, who had dared say that Blacks were 'half-apes.' And, I also knew—probably from Lagrosillière—that Eboué was a socialist."[15]

Madame Eboué immediately cabled her husband the good news, and on 4 December President Lebrun signed the decree officially promoting him. Once the news of his appointment came Eboué's mood changed, of course, and he wrote his wife instructions concerning the house, the children, some shopping, and other household matters. Eboué ordered foods from Martinique, engaged more servants, and planned some social events: "I am

15 Interview with Marius Moutet, Paris, 30 June 1967.

planning a luncheon and a bridge party. You will be invited. . . . I love you."[16]

The men Eboué and his wife considered responsible for his success were Yvon Delbos, Henry Bérenger, Lagros, Barthes, plus Roger Dévigne, and Victor Sévère, the mayor of Fort-de-France who replaced Alcide Delmont as deputy from Martinique. Eboué thanked them and Gratien Candace whose attitude toward him he was not sure about. To his old friend Delbos Eboué wrote: "I know about your numerous and insistant requests to Marius Moutet. . . . The Event came about by means of your friendship, as living and faithful as in the past." He then wrote that he saw the action of the Ministry as important in the assimilation of the Antilles: "Our people of the Antilles and Guyane has reacted with enthusiasm, and the feeling was put into words by a man in the street the other day at Basse-Terre who shouted [when he saw me]: 'Vive la France!' I found that beautiful and I was moved by it. This was my first recompense; I dedicate it to you. . . ."[17]

In a much more formal letter he thanked Bérenger and wrote a long letter to Candace expressing his feelings as a black man: "When I think of the brilliance of *Batouala* and of the distinction with which Diagne and you filled your roles as Minister, I am distressed at the idea of the heavy responsibility on my shoulders today. I am proud, full of joy, but a little frightened too. . . ."[18]

Candace responded that the event was an important symbol of assimilation and race harmony: "The important thing is that each Black who has a high post says to himself that he is an example for all. . . . True fraternity is being realized by work in equality and justice. We create, we work for tomorrow's generations. It is up to us to prove that our brain is not inferior to that of our white brothers. Let us thank France for permitting us to prove it."[19] Although René Maran apparently did not congratulate

---

[16] Archives Eboué, Letter, Félix Eboué to Eugénie Eboué, 10 December 1936.

[17] Archives Eboué, copy of Letter, Félix Eboué to Yvon Delbos, 9 December 1936.

[18] Archives Eboué, copy of Letter, Félix Eboué to Gratien Candace, 8 December 1936.

[19] Archives Eboué, Letter, Gratien Candace to Félix Eboué, 28 December 1936.

Eboué directly, he wrote an article about the appointment agreeing with Candace that it proved France made no distinction between black and white.[20]

And from "Cono," Eboué's sister: "You are the pride of our race and our family. Dear Man-Lie, what satisfaction this would have been for her who deserved it so much, and for Mr. and Mrs. Tell! . . . . Mr. Félix Eboué is Governor of Colonies!"[21] Finally, some reaction from Guyane. Friends sent copies of *L'Observateur*, a Cayenne newspaper which said that Eboué's new position showed that France wanted to show there are no inferior races. The paper deemed the appointment an honor for Guyane, for the Front Populaire, and for the black race. Men of color had held high posts in the colonial administration before, but this was the first time that a true black—a man dark black in color, "un véritable Noir"—had been named to such a position, the editors wrote.[22]

ELECTIONS AND SUGAR

Immediately after acceding to the rank of governor the Jerpan affair came back to haunt Eboué, and it affected his relations with Candace. He decreed that new elections would take place on 6 and 13 December 1936 for municipal councilors, mayor of Saint-Louis, and representatives to the Conseil Général from Saint Louis. Before the new elections Candace wrote to Eboué alleging that Jerpan and Tirolien would once again use fraud to ensure Jerpan's re-election. He warned Eboué not to favor them or to become friendly with his other enemy, Eugène Graëve.[23]

On 6 December voters chose between two lists of candidates, rather than between individuals, and Jerpan's list won easily. The new councilors then elected Jerpan mayor on 13 December, and the voters also re-elected him to the Conseil Général. The fact that only 507 out of 1584 registered voters actually cast their bal-

20 René Maran, "Autour d'une nomination de Gouverneur," in *Je suis partout,* 9 January 1937.

21 Archives Eboué, Letter, Cornélie Gratien to Félix Eboué, 8 December 1936.

22 *L'Observateur,* Cayenne, 2 December 1936.

23 Archives Eboué, Letter, Gratien Candace to Félix Eboué, 24 November 1936.

lots for municipal councilors is probably one indication that Candace was correct about fraud, and the elections were soon challenged.[24]

After the elections Candace began to criticize increasingly bitterly Eboué's handling of Marie-Galante. He thought that Eboué could have prevented Jerpan's election if he wanted to; he did not, he said, doubt Eboué's friendship but alleged that he was getting poor advice from his staff. Eboué responded that he could not prevent Jerpan from running, and that the law gave the governor no power to prevent the proclamation of the results. With regard to his staff, Eboué had wanted René Isambert as his secretary general; it would have been a significant promotion for his old friend, who had not yet reached the rank of administrator in chief. Candace said that he supported Isambert but that Marius Moutet wanted a better person; in the end, the Ministry chose Léopold Allys, who had already served in Guadeloupe.

In the course of 1937 some of Candace's friends in Guadeloupe were jailed for various offenses. This shocked the deputy who asked for and received Eboué's help. The election of Furcie Tirolien as president of the Conseil Général displeased Candace, who complained openly when Eboué nominated both Tirolien and Graëve to the Legion of Honor: "You have nominated Tirolien and many other slightly respectable people for the Legion of Honor. That will no doubt please the Senator [Bérenger]. Taking my turn, I ask you to nominate [the following]. . . ."[25]

Candace's relations with Senator Bérenger, his former friend, had begun to deteriorate as 1938 approached. Candace was insulted when Bérenger refused to attend a party in honor of Candace's twenty-fifth year in the Chamber of Deputies, but the basis of the growing antagonism between the two men and their allies was the forthcoming senatorial election. It was an open secret by 1937 that Candace, who had reached the posts of vice president of the Chamber and Under Secretary of State for Colonies, planned to finish his career in the Senate, as did many other politicians of the Third Republic. As in Martinique, senators were elected by the notables, including members of the Conseil Général. Jerpan

[24] *JOG,* No. 53, 17 December 1936, p. 1000.
[25] Archives Eboué, Letter, Gratien Candace to Félix Eboué, 9 March 1937.

and Tirolien, Candace's enemies, were two of the approximately three hundred electors, and Candace feared Bérenger might exploit Eboué's growing popularity to get more electors on his side.

It is true that Eboué's relations with Senator Bérenger were excellent, although the two men did not really know each other. They exchanged letters very frequently, Madame Eboué often writing for her husband after her arrival in Guadeloupe in early January 1937. Eboué was convinced that Bérenger had played a key role in his promotion to the governorship, and Bérenger continually warned Eboué of attempts by Candace and Satineau to undermine him, which was later true but may not have been in 1936. Eboué had complete confidence in Bérenger, probably because he considered him Yvon Delbos' friend. Bérenger was a powerful man, having been in the Senate for twenty-five years; he had been appointed ambassador to represent France during talks with the Americans about World War I debts, was part of the French delegation to the League of Nations, and served as president of the Foreign Relations Committee of the Senate. He was even mentioned as a possible candidate for the presidency of the Republic. He probably cared little about Guadeloupe except around election time, but he voted for the Popular Front reforms and supported the government more than Candace.

Eboué gave the senator as much information about his programs as he gave Candace, but his discussions with Bérenger and his assistant, Commandant Le Page, showed that Eboué wanted Bérenger to win the 1938 elections and that he was not neutral. Eboué thought the prospects for 1938 were so solid that no one would think of challenging Bérenger.[26]

As early as July 1937 Bérenger and his friend Tirolien calculated how many votes would go to the incumbent—201 out of 314: "The important thing is to maintain this majority and even to increase it," Bérenger wrote to Eboué. He added the list of his favored candidates in the next canton elections and asked Eboué his opinion, promising his own support for Eboué.[27] Eboué responded with gratitude, even obsequiousness, for the senator's support, and said with regard to the names suggested: "In prin-

26 Archives Eboué, copy of Letter, Félix Eboué to Le Page, 16 April 1937.
27 Archives Eboué, Letter, Henry Bérenger to Félix Eboué, 16 July 1937.

ciple I am absolutely in agreement with the names on the list. . . ." Eboué then warned Bérenger that the latter's position of appeasement toward the Italian invasion of Ethiopia in 1935-1936 at the League of Nations might be used against him in black Guadeloupe: "Because your position with regard to the Italo-Abyssinian war may be exploited here, I think it will be necessary to clip the wings of this canard, to prevent it from developing, with the aid of an article sent here and printed in the local press."[28] He also urged Bérenger, who had been excommunicated many years previously, to support his nomination of the head of the Catholic Church of Guadeloupe to the Legion of Honor.

Links with Bérenger angered Candace, and links with Boisneuf angered Maurice Satineau, whose position was much less secure than that of Candace. Satineau, who had edited the reformist colonial newspaper *La Dépêche Africaine* in the 1920's, had had a rather obscure career in France before returning to Guadeloupe in 1936 for the elections. He became mayor of Sainte-Anne, a town near Pointe-à-Pitre, and deputy. Two of his closest allies, Rajas Séjor of Saint Anne, and Dr. François-Julien, helped him and were his representatives in Guadeloupe. Satineau wrote the governor about Dr. François-Julien, director of the Pointe-à-Pitre hospital: "I confirm to you that he has my confidence, and I ask you to reserve a warm welcome to the steps he will take in the interest of my party and my friends. . . ."[29]

Eboué and his wife disliked Satineau, who had a bad reputation in France for dishonest business activities and quickly gave the impression of being interested only in helping his circle of friends. Their relations rapidly deteriorated because of an affair that had little to do with Eboué. Satineau and his friend Séjor had a falling out and became bitter enemies. Because Séjor was first assistant to the mayor, he took charge of affairs during Satineau's absence. When the two men became enemies, Satineau feared Séjor would undermine his interests at Sainte-Anne. Séjor on the one hand and Satineau and other friends on the other hand traded accusations. Satineau thought Eboué did not act to protect his interests, and after some of Satineau's friends were jailed for

---

[28] Archives Eboué, Letter, Félix Eboué to Henry Bérenger, 10 August 1937.
[29] Archives Eboué, Maurice Satineau to Félix Eboué, 9 October 1936.

common law violations, the deputy wrote Eboué bitterly: "I note with profound shock that your Administration is showing overt hostility toward my friends and me."[30] Eboué became convinced that Satineau wished to embarrass him during the sugar harvest beginning in January 1937.

After Satineau returned to the colony he went about speaking to sugar cane workers, boasting of his own importance as a deputy. It was he, the true friend of the worker, who would bring Popular Front reforms to Guadeloupe, he said. In February Satineau printed a tract complaining about the wages given workers: "I take the liberty of counting on the wisdom of the Head of the Colony and on the good will of *usine* owners so that they examine again, in the course of the sugar campaign, the possibility of ameliorating . . . the situation of the workers."[31]

The real meaning of Satineau's presence in Guadeloupe and interest in the workers was the forthcoming canton elections of some representatives to the Conseil Général. In April he printed another more open tract just before the election, scheduled for the 18th. Boisneuf, his old enemy, was, according to Satineau, the man of the *usine* and was supported by Eboué. Workers should demand higher wages and should vote against Boisneuf.[32]

In the elections both Boisneuf and Satineau lost to the socialists; Eboué did not interfere.

The demand for higher wages and general agitation supported by Satineau led to attacks by workers on company officials, and Eboué rushed about the islands trying to resolve each conflict. He was caught between the strikers and the *usine* which tried to undermine the governor's authority and break the strikes. Managers at the Darboussier mills brought in workers from Saint Martin island; although Eboué opposed the walk-out because he thought an agreement had been reached on wages, he ordered the workers sent back. Company officials paid no attention. Eboué then ordered the black police commissioner, André Haliar, to pro-

[30] Archives Eboué, Letter, Maurice Satineau to Félix Eboué, 19 February 1937.

[31] Tract, "Ouverture de la Campagne Sucrière," Maurice Satineau, 12 February 1937.

[32] Tract, "Rolland Boisneuf aux abois se cache derrière le Gouverneur Eboué," Maurice Satineau, 16 April 1937.

ceed to the mills with his men, round up the workers, and put them on a ship back to Saint Martin. This was done peacefully. Elsewhere Eboué found a factory manager cheating cane cutters with trick weighing devices and warned the manager to stop the practice immediately. The workers were convinced to resume cutting, and Eboué asked the Ministry of Colonies to send him a labor inspector to arbitrate in the future and to plan for the application of Popular Front labor reforms to Guadeloupe.

Pierre Pélisson, named labor inspector, arrived in May 1937. A metropolitan Frenchman, then only thirty years old, he had been working for the past few years at the central offices of the Ministry, rue Oudinot; he became interested, however, in the reforms of the Front Populaire and requested an overseas assignment. When he arrived, Eboué told him, as he told all subordinates, that he would be free to do his job without interference and that the governor would support him as long as he worked in the best interests of France and the colony.[33]

At the time of his arrival Pélisson had to deal with a dockers' strike that had gone on since April. The dockers had burned some houses in Pointe-à-Pitre, and they surrounded the company's offices to press a demand for higher wages. Inspector Pélisson, with Eboué's support, went quickly to see company representatives, and he advised them to agree to some worker demands; as the inspector and company representatives prepared to walk out of the offices, the white officials took up revolvers because they claimed to fear attack. Pélisson warned them against such provocation, which in the past often led to bloodshed, and they put their arms aside. The parties reached an agreement without further disturbances, and the peace which Eboué inaugurated in Guadeloupe continued,[34] although white business interests were always trying to maneuver Eboué into using force. Once, in an untypically frank letter, Eboué wrote to the Chamber of Commerce: "I burst into laughter in the face of the big industrialist who, in the course of a meeting at Pointe-à-Pitre, suggested that I requisition trucks, fill them with soldiers, machine guns, and in-

[33] Interview with Pierre Pélisson, Paris, 1 July 1969.
[34] *Ibid.*

struct them to cruise around . . . which would [supposedly] insure the reign of order in Guadeloupe."[35]

The maintenance of peace was helped by an improving economic situation in 1937. Exports of sugar, bananas, vanilla, and rum increased. In 1935 Guadeloupe had exported 38 million kilograms of sugar, but in 1937 the figure was 61 million. Similarly in 1935 the colony had exported 26 million kilos of bananas and 48 million in 1937. In light of such improvements Eboué thought he could begin some of his economic and social programs.[36]

REFORMS

On 29 May Eboué opened the first session of the Conseil Général for 1937. In his speech he called for unity within Guadeloupe and between Guadeloupe and Martinique for purposes of development. He criticized expatriation of profits by local businesses headquartered in metropolitan France or in Martinique. Unlike most of his predecessors he called for decentralization of the administration and more power for the locally elected municipal governments in the islands. He closed by saying that his new labor inspector was planning ways to introduce Popular Front legislation in Guadeloupe, as he had promised the previous session.

Pélisson was then asking different groups of businessmen, factory-owners, and labor organizations to submit any thought they had on the application of the forty-hour week, paid vacations, collective bargaining, public housing, and other proposed reforms. The Chambers of Commerce and Gratien Candace opposed the shorter work week and other changes, but in the next few months Eboué enacted the reforms, thus earning the enmity of conservative white businessmen, already annoyed by the price controls Eboué had instituted and the increase in wages paid their workers. In a sarcastic communication to the businessmen when they tried to raise prices in shops after the wage increases, Eboué said: "I will remember the brilliant and scientific report that you presented us: . . . that for each advantage received by . . . work-

35 Reprinted in Chamber of Commerce, "Interventions de la Chambre de Commerce," Pointe-à-Pitre, 2e et 3e Trimestre," 1937, p. 19.

36 Data from *Bulletin Mensuel d'Information*, Government of Guadeloupe, January 1938 .

ers . . . business is obliged to raise prices or lose its capital [you said]." Eboué told them he did not understand the reasoning behind such a judgment and that for peace in Guadeloupe they could not raise their prices. They answered that he did not understand economics, and Eboué said he found their opinion amusing. He insisted on price controls.[37]

Against the wishes of the Chambers of Commerce Eboué applied the forty-hour work week, by a series of decrees, to the building industry in November and the sugar refinery workers in December. He included shops in Pointe-à-Pitre and Basse-Terre a few months later. In July 1937 the governor created a Service du Travail et de la Prévoyance Sociale with three sections: one for the control and inspection of labor conditions, a second for dealing with cooperatives, mutual aid societies and labor unions, and a third for keeping labor statistics and archives. (He was one of the rare governors to instruct clerks to reorganize and keep in order the archives of the government.) Eboué created an inspection service to enforce safety standards for particularly dangerous or unhealthy work.

In September 1937 the governor prepared the decree about paid vacations:

> Article 1—The right to an annual minimum paid vacation either of two weeks including 12 working days or of one week including 6 working days is established for every employee, worker or apprentice who has worked continuously for a year or six months. . . .[38]

The labor inspector controlled the companies' calculation of vacations by a register of workers. In 1938 Eboué set up the rules for the payment of funds which would pay workers on vacation, the so-called Caisses de Compensation pour Congés Annuels Payés.

The explicit recognition of collective bargaining with the support of the government represented an important innovation. Although there were unions which bargained for their members with employers, they were weak and poorly equipped to deal with the well-organized businessmen and factory managers. Pélisson,

[37] Chamber of Commerce, "Interventions," pp. 19, 20, 51.
[38] *JOG*, No. 50, 14 October 1937, pp. 828-29, Arrêté of 22 September 1937.

with Guadeloupan unionists Mr. Edinval and Mr. Dessout, worked to strengthen union organization.

The decree concerning collective bargaining also provided for an important role for the governor. For example, when either a union or a business organization wished to write an agreement for a certain category of workers, they would, according to the decree, submit a draft to the governor, who would then inform the other prospective party to the proposal. Next, the labor inspector arranged a meeting between the two groups, but would not be present during the discussions. One of his subordinates could be there to prepare a transcript of the proceedings for the benefit of the two sides. If the two parties could not reach an agreement about the proposed labor contract, they would ask for the governor's assistance. The governor studied the matter and wrote a letter of advice to each party and suggested further discussion. If further discussion did not lead to agreement, the two parties went before a conciliation commission of high-ranking officials where an agreement had to be reached. A signed copy of the agreement would then be sent to the governor.[39] This intervention of the government could be of immense importance to unorganized weak workers' groups.

In his address opening the first session of the Conseil Général in 1937 Eboué proposed the colony construct low-cost rural housing for laborers to replace the flimsy structures typical of most areas in the islands. Peasants and agricultural workers need, he said, the special attention of government because they, "through stubborn work, and a faithful attachment to the soil, constitute the living force of Guadeloupan democracy."[40] He also proposed credit funds for fishermen and an expanded medical service. Concerned about water consumption at Pointe-à-Pitre, he suggested changing the method of payment to one based on quantity of water consumed rather than a flat fee. The governor reopened a school of agriculture to teach new methods of farming and to encourage young people to remain in agriculture instead of moving to the cities where few jobs were available. For young people he

39 *JOG*, No. 22, 21 April 1938, pp. 381-82, Arrêté of 31 March 1938.
40 Félix Eboué, Opening speech to Conseil Général, Guadeloupe, *Conseil Général: Première Session Ordinaire de 1937*, Basse-Terre, p. 19.

helped organize sporting clubs, and construction on two stadiums began. He asked a physical education specialist to come to the islands, and after this man prepared a program Eboué created a Physical Education Department in September 1937 to train physical education teachers.[41]

Although the economy of Guadeloupe was improving, funds for all these major projects were lacking, partly because of the Conseil Général's increasingly hostile attitudes. Even Eboué's plans to develop tourism went unaccomplished for the time being. He set up a tourism section in his cabinet and attempted to get the Conseil Général to vote funds for a full tourist office to attract foreign travelers. But the tourism industry was something new to Guadeloupan politicians, who did not fully understand how the colony would benefit, and some correctly feared the people could be transformed from cane cutters into bellhops and maids for plush white-owned hotels. Councilors from Grande-Terre also thought Basse-Terre would benefit most. A more positive achievement came when the governor succeeded in May 1936 in arranging for exchange visits between groups of Martiniquans and Guadeloupans to bring the neighboring colonies together and to encourage generally closer contact among Antilleans and Guyanese.

Eboué stirred controversy by urging changes in the tax structure of Guadeloupe to bring in more money to the treasury. In his speech to the councilors he asked: ". . . how is it that the different factors that contribute to our prosperity like sugar, rum, bananas and other agricultural products, whose prodigious export figures we are aware of, have such little effect on the receipts of our budget?"[42] But proposals to change the system of taxation met with strong resistance and confused discussions in the Conseil Général. Eboué's suggestion for a tax on luxury goods was rejected. In fact, the politicians knew very little about the finances of the colony and some were doubtless linked to the sugar interests which quietly opposed Eboué's suggestions; during 1937 they spent a great deal of time fighting among themselves. The newly

[41] "Eboué Le Grand Sportif," in *Le Dimanche Sportif de l'U.S.B.T.*, Basse-Terre, 26 May 1946, pp. 169-70.

[42] Conseil Général, *Première Session*, p. 3.

elected socialists, for example, accused Jerpan of not representing
the masses and tried to expel him; a leader of the socialists, Valentino, exchanged insults with Tirolien. During one session of the
Conseil the assembly nearly broke up:

> Mr. Valentino: "He has usurped a position that does not belong to
> him. Make him leave, gentlemen! Out, Jerpan!
> The socialists in chorus: Out, Jerpan! Out, Jerpan! Make him leave!
> President: Gentlemen, I beg you (he rings his bell for silence).
> Mr. Jerpan: And you, Valentino! Don't forget that you were the slave
> of the reactionaries. . . .
> Mr. Rinaldo: Who is the slave? It is you! . . . Out!
> The socialist group: Out! Out! The cheaters! Out, Jerpan!"[43]

Eboué was discouraged by the squabbling which only worsened
as time went on. In June during this session of the Conseil news
came that Léon Blum had resigned as Prime Minister and that
Camille Chautemps had replaced him 22 June. Blum remained in
the cabinet, however, which otherwise did not change signifi-
cantly. Yvon Delbos remained, and Marius Moutet was still Minister of Colonies. They named Gaston Monnerville Under Secretary of State for Colonies, the first Guyanese to hold such a
position, and in July Maurice Satineau appealed to him for
Eboué's removal.

Satineau now openly accused the governor of favoritism and
even corruption. He claimed he knew of links between the governor and the "reactionary forces" of big business, but once his attempts to get Eboué removed were known, everyone except white
business organizations appealed to the Ministry of Colonies to
keep Eboué in Guadeloupe. Labor organizations, parties like the
socialist SFIO, sports organizations, veterans, and the masonic
lodges wrote to Paris on his behalf.

Marius Moutet and Monnerville kept Eboué informed of the
attempts to remove him and asserted him of their support. They
also told him that Candace wanted him removed too, although he
was more subtle than Satineau, who wrote intemperately in his
newspaper *La Voix du Peuple*:

> Governor Eboué, in the service of Colonial Reactionaries, is keeping
> up . . . an extravagant and constant agitation around his name, an

43 *Ibid.,* pp. 337-38.

agitation directed openly against our two Representatives in the
Chamber. Out of jealousy he wants to lower their prestige. Thus, he
terrorizes the people, flouts universal suffrage . . . besmirches our republican and democratic institutions, and is leading the country
straight to anarchy.[44]

Candace kept up his surface cordiality but continued to warn
Eboué against Jerpan, Bérenger, and Boisneuf.[45] Eboué told Candace that he was not a man to turn the other cheek: "Satineau
has accentuated his break with me since publicly . . . he has denounced me as the man of the *usine* and the reactionaries. . . .
Can you believe it?" He added that if Satineau continued trying
to remove him from Guadeloupe, "I shall not fail to denounce
him to the people who know really that I am working for them
and that I ask nothing in return."

> I did not ask to come here. . . . My opinion about your colleague:
> he is a little man without education with base instincts. I shall not
> speak to you any more about it.[46]

In a later letter to Candace Eboué asked him what he had
against his friend Boisneuf. He warned Candace not to listen to
Satineau rail against Boisneuf and himself; he cited Boisneuf's
electoral loss as proof that he himself had not taken a partisan
role in the April 1937 elections. He reiterated his friendship for
Candace: "But sincere friendship is made of truth and confidence
. . . I *owe* you the truth . . . [it is] dangerous to continue to
support Satineau. . . ."[47]

FAMILY AND FRIENDS

During this difficult period Eboué depended on a small group
of friends for a respite. Evenings he might sit with Marius
Larcher, his attorney general, on the terrace of the Royal Hotel

[44] *La Voix du Peuple,* 20 November 1937.

[45] Archives Eboué, Letter, Gratien Candace to Félix Eboué, 8 April 1937.

[46] Archives Eboué, copy of Letter, Félix Eboué to Gratien Candace, 2 May
1937.

[47] Archives Eboué, copy of Letter, Félix Eboué to Gratien Candace, 25 May
1937.

Eboué playing cards with friends. Courtesy of Marius Larcher.

in Basse-Terre, drinking punch and watching the people go by. After dinner he might play cards or take an automobile ride with Cazenave de la Roche or Larcher. The driver would take them into the hills surrounding Basse-Terre, and they would discuss their work; the chauffeur would have to wake them when they reached their respective residences.[48]

The Eboués also entertained. They gave one of their famous dances to which both blacks and whites were invited, thereby causing a minor sensation as in Martinique. For dinners Eboué himself prepared the list of courses and chose all the wines; these extraordinary menus consisting of seven and eight courses were passed around after the meals and were the marvel of the colony; indeed some people considered Eboué too extravagant and were startled by his enthusiasm for good food. Near the end of a luncheon which had already lasted into the middle of the afternoon a man came with a pig which he offered the governor. Eboué insisted cooks prepare the pig immediately and proceeded to kill and dress it himself among much joking and laughter of all present. At another luncheon a man brought some rare and very delicious animal as a gift; this time Eboué had had enough to eat, but he said amid much laughter: "Don't touch it; let nobody touch it. I shall cook it myself."[49] In a more serious way Eboué entertained Englishmen from a neighboring island for political reasons to symbolize the increasingly close relations between France and Britain forming a common front against the Fascist powers. King George VI visited France after his coronation in 1937, and the French received him warmly.

The increasingly tense international situation was discussed everywhere, including the lodges Eboué regularly visited. He relaxed with Freemasons, and everyone knew about his membership. The two lodges in Guadeloupe were affiliated with the Grand Orient. Eboué continued to pay his dues to Les Disciples de Pythagore in Martinique, affiliated with the Grande Loge, Eboué's obedience; he liked the name, for Pythagoras was his favorite philosopher.

[48] Interview with Marius Larcher, Fort-de-France, 4 February 1968.
[49] Told by Alexandre Buffon, Director of Agricultural Services under Governor Eboué, Interview, Basse-Terre, 6 June 1969.

The news from sister Cornélie in Paris got worse. In spite of poor health, she continued to work; her daughter needed funds to complete her course in chemistry, and Eboué sent money, although this continuing generosity put a strain on his resources, and Madame Eboué objected. Henry got out of the army and into trouble over a tailor's bill, a bit of gossip seized on by the newspaper *Le Matin*. This deeply embarrassed Eboué who was sure the story—not a very important one—was planted by Candace, Satineau, or some businessman. Eboué wrote to Governor General de Coppet at Dakar to get Henry a job as a court clerk in West Africa. This was arranged, and Eboué's eldest son, now twenty-five, left for Senegal. Charles and Robert, forced to change schools in 1936 because of their father's assignment, attended the Lycée Gerville-Réache in Basse-Terre. Ginette still went to the excellent girls school of the Legion of Honor in which Eboué had been promoted to the rank of *Officer* on 11 June 1937. The governor now wore a little red rosette in the lapel of his favorite white suits.

Friends in France, Martinique, and Guyane sent him news of the political situation. Antoine and Baby Wiltord in Fort-de-France wrote that people missed him and hoped he might return one day as governor. Lagrosillière began to suggest that the two of them run together for deputy in 1940. News came of the death of his white masonic brother, Abel Sainte-Luce Banchelin, whose son worked as Eboué's private secretary. Banchelin had taught for twenty-five years in Guadeloupe before returning to Martinique. After his death Eboué made the rather unorthodox gesture of having his friend's obituary put on the first page of the official gazette of the colony. Roger Dévigne sent him some books and article references he wanted for speeches. Roger Hellier and E. L. Boutin kept him informed of gossip around the Ministry. With René Maran he exchanged rather formal and cold greetings for the New Year.

To all his friends Eboué sent copies of his numerous speeches in Guadeloupe, particularly his "Jouez le Jeu" address given to students at the Lycée Carnot of Pointe-à-Pitre, 1 July 1937. He probably gave more speeches than any other governor of the colony—and everywhere: at funerals, congresses, in towns celebrating their feast day or patron saint day, school graduations, marriages, funerals. He traveled everywhere, including the small islands like Désirade which had not been visited by a governor in almost twenty years.

These activities and the conflicts of 1936 and 1937 tired him. He was fifty-three years old and had not had a long vacation since 1932; he therefore planned to go on vacation at the beginning of 1938, but Lagrosillière told him to remain because someone might profit from his absence to name another governor in his place. Bérenger also wanted him to remain. He wrote: "Tirolien . . . [and] Boisneuf with whom I conferred yesterday evening don't think you should take a leave of absence in France next January. They believe the news would have a bad effect in Guadeloupe and even in Paris. Someone would exploit your departure and pretend it was a 'disguised recall'; they will try all kinds of manoeuvers for the nomination of an Interim, etc., etc. [Tirolien and Boineuf] asked me to speak to you about it immediately for they attach great importance to it and fear a discouragement of the Front Populaire [programs] in a year of the senatorial elections."[50]

Eboué responded that he hoped relations with Candace might improve and that the latter would decide not to run against Bérenger. He must have felt a little uneasy about his relations with Candace, who had been such a help to him ever since they had met in 1912 when Eboué's uncle, Maximilien Liontel, had asked Candace to help his nephew. Over all these years, however, Eboué and Candace never became very familiar and still used the formal *vous*. Eboué did not want to break relations with his former benefactor and kept up his correspondence with him until it became impossible. He agreed, in any case, to remain in Guadeloupe until October 1938, after the senatorial elections.[51]

That Eboué would remain in Guadeloupe even though he needed a vacation was much more convenient for Bérenger than for Eboué. The senator could be sure his friends would be well received; he also knew Eboué would never falsify election returns

[50] Archives Eboué, Letter, Henry Bérenger to Félix Eboué, 24 August 1937, attached to Letter dated 23 August 1937.
[51] Archives Eboué, Letter, Félix Eboué to Henry Bérenger, 8 September 1937.

in his favor or against him, whereas someone else might. Bérenger, after so many years in politics, had many highly placed enemies eager to remove him from the Foreign Affairs Committee.
Association with the black governor added to his own popularity,
and he would get support if people believed he kept Eboué in office. There was no doubt that by the end of 1937 Eboué was more
popular in Guadeloupe than any of the colony's three elected representatives, and Bérenger, Candace, and Satineau knew it.

CONFLICT

Conflict increased at the end of 1937. Sporadic strikes shook the
islands; the perennial feud between the socialists and Jerpan
came up; and the second annual session of the Conseil Général
was at times completely disrupted.

After the invalidation once again of elections at Saint-Louis,
Jerpan was re-elected in September 1937; he therefore attended
the Conseil Général, much to the anger of his opponents. Eboué
opened the session on 30 October 1937 with a speech urging tax
reform to get more revenue for the colony's budget, but the business of the councilors seemed to be more personal attacks and
conflict which immediately broke out after the governor left the
room.

The socialists tried to exclude Jerpan, and then they criticized
Tirolien's candidacy for the presidency of the assembly. Maurice
Satineau, a member of the Conseil, returned to Guadeloupe to attend this session and profited from the general confusion to attack Eboué as often as he was recognized. When the voting for president of the Conseil began, Valentino of the socialist group rushed
forward to stop it; Jerpan pushed him away from the ballot box,
but Valentino struck him in return and the ballot box crashed to
the floor, spreading the ballots about the room.

Gendarmes were called to protect the ballot box for the next
vote, and people crowded at the windows to watch the display,
the socialists shouting in unison: "Shame! Shame!"; the eldest
member who, by custom, presided until the election of a president,
ringing his bell for order; Tirolien and Satineau shouting at each
other in the general brouhaha. The gendarmes left because councilors said they would not deliberate in their presence. Most coun-

cilors applauded, and the socialists began to sing the Internationale.[52]

Jerpan and his friends tried to get Satineau's friend, Dr. François-Julien, removed from the Counseil, on grounds that his position as head of the hospital of Pointe-à-Pitre meant he would be voting on his own budget. Eboué consulted with the Ministry of Colonies, and a communication from Moutet confirmed the incompatibility of the two positions. Tirolien, who by then had been elected president, tried to remove François-Julien from the room; but he refused to leave. The decision about François-Julien left a bad impression for there were other members of the council with similar conflicts of interest; although Eboué said that something would have to be done about them too, the fact that the friend of Satineau had been singled out first implied that Tirolien and Eboué wanted revenge. The governor's relations with the legislature from this point on deteriorated sharply.

Eboué had asked the Counseil for its support in the use of land for a sports stadium. The socialists said that the governor was not acting in the interests of the workers because of his concern for sports, and Valentino openly threatened him with trouble during the forthcoming sugar harvest. He shouted: "I am breaking with the Administration and I declare that in Grande-Terre we are going to enter into an extremely agitated period."[53]

The budget was passed but Eboué's suggested innovations were defeated. He wanted the establishment of a fund to help redistribute tax monies from the richer towns to the poorer towns. He also wanted more money for sports and recreation projects, a property tax, and a program of public works. After the session Eboué was angry and downcast. At a meeting of the Conseil Privé, 15 December 1937, he gave a long rambling discourse on his problems; the other members sat and listened in amazement as he unburdened himself in uncharacteristic fashion. He complained about conflict in the assembly which even had made his secretary general, Allys, ill; that the removal of François-Julien

[52] Guadeloupe, Conseil Général, Deuxième Session Ordinaire de 1937, Basse-Terre, pp. 50-57.
[53] Ibid., p. 736.

was correct; that he had the right to choose his own cabinet officials; that some politicians wanted to place spies among his servants. In a moment of great depression he added he regretted having left Africa, but on the other hand, trying to find something positive, he decided there were some good points about the disturbances in Guadeloupe: "This boiling and this impatience, are they not a manifestation of a living and evolving organism?" he said.

At the beginning of 1938 a change of government took place in France putting Theodore Steeg at the Ministry of Colonies. But in March Léon Blum became Prime Minister once again with Moutet returning as Minister of Colonies, ensuring continued support for Eboué, who badly needed it. A difficult period had begun in February.

Two seats in the Conseil Général had to be filled by elections on 20 February because of the removal of Dr. François-Julien and the death of another member. Boisneuf ran against a socialist, and won. The socialists and friends of Satineau, fearful that now Boisneuf would be in a better position to challenge the deputy in 1940, accused Eboué of falsifying election returns to make sure his young friend won.

The evening of Sunday 20 February Eboué was in Pointe-à-Pitre at the office he maintained there, on the largest square in town, Place de la Victoire. When officials announced the results of the elections and the victory of Boisneuf, the socialist leader, Henri Rinaldo and a group of his men began a noisy demonstration, marching through the streets. As they approached the square, Eboué, Larcher, and a couple of others stepped out on the balcony to see what all the noise was about.

Rinaldo reviled Eboué, calling him the equivalent of "dirty nigger." The epithets had little to do with race; although Rinaldo was himself quite fair, Satineau was as dark as Eboué. They did not hesitate to use derogatory terms employed by white racists as well as the rough expressions of the Antilles. Larcher, the attorney general, charged Rinaldo with having insulted the Representative of the Republic, and the lawyer was suspended from the bar, creating a small uproar in the colony.

In April Blum's government resigned; Edouard Daladier, the

old radical socialist, replaced him and named Georges Mandel, the World War I collaborator of Clemenceau, Minister of Colonies. A new timid Government of National Defense, composed of radical socialists, took over the direction of French affairs one month after Hitler's annexation of Austria. The Front Populaire was no more.

Guadeloupe's Conseil Général met for its first session of 1938, and Eboué opened the meeting on 28 May with a very short speech indicating some insecurity on his part because of the change of government in France. He said defensively that he still had the support of the government and that he had always desired the unity of all. He said he was proud of his administration and noted that the economic position of Guadeloupe had vastly improved since his arrival. He told the councilors he would present a program of tax reform once again, a tourism project, and the Fonds Commun, all matters on which the assembly had failed to act during the previous sessions.

Instead of facing the colony's genuine problems, the legislature continued the electoral battles of the previous February. The socialists accused Boisneuf of fraud, and so much time was spent on mutual attack, criticism of the governor, defense of the governor, that Eboué's projects were not voted upon. The session ended in near failure 11 June 1938.

After the close of the Conseil session Eboué decided to visit Saint Martin island, a part of Guadeloupe colony in spite of its distance from Basse-Terre. Traveling with Tirolien, Larcher, and others, he was absent from 5 to 9 July, his last excursion before the new Minister of Colonies suddenly recalled him to France.

RECALL

Gratien Candace visited Guadeloupe in November 1937, supposedly on a mission, but everyone knew he had come to talk to some senatorial electors. Eboué invited him to the official residence for lunch and was courteous; they saw each other briefly after that.

The letters between Eboué and Candace—ambiguous in tone—continued into 1938 after Candace's departure. Candace swore he was not asking for Eboué's recall, although he admitted Satineau had. The governor repeated to Candace that he worked along the lines he thought they both believed in all their lives: "We all have a duty to work for the future of the race and of Guadeloupe. That is to say in the French context."[54] Eboué had information from Moutet that Candace and certain business interests wanted his removal.[55]

With Moutet no longer at the rue Oudinot, relations with the Ministry cooled. Georges Mandel, who was not at all happy about being named to the Ministry of Colonies, disdained the colonial governors as "potentates who needed to be taught a lesson once in awhile."[56] As proof of his feeling Mandel did not send the usual friendly greetings to governors—at least not to Eboué—and by June 1938 Eboué was discouraged and exhausted; he wrote at the end of the month to Bérenger: "A cable of encouragement from Mr. Mandel to the governor would be welcome. I accepted important responsibilities in Martinique, Soudan, as well as Guadeloupe. I have been working in these conditions since February 1932 and I am still waiting for the time to rest. I am at my 8th year of labor."[57]

In July the Minister of Colonies reportedly sent Eboué a secret telegram in which he asked him to estimate who would win the elections if Candace, still not declared, ran against Bérenger. Cazenave de la Roche discreetly made inquiries and estimated Bérenger would win by a large majority. Eboué forwarded the information to Paris, not knowing that Mandel, who had known both men since World War I, disliked Bérenger as much as he liked Candace.[58]

54 Archives Eboué, copy of Letter, Félix Eboué to Gratien Candace, 27 March 1938.

55 Interview with Marius Moutet, Paris, 30 June 1967.

56 Georges Wormser, *Georges Mandel: Homme Politique* (Paris: Plon, 1967), p. 210, and Interviews, Paris, Georges Wormser, Mandel's friend, 15 May 1968, and Max Brusset, Mandel's *chef de cabinet,* 18 June 1969.

57 Archives Eboué, copy of Letter, Félix Eboué to Henry Bérenger, 28 June 1938.

58 Interview, Jean Cazenave de la Roche, Juan-les-Pins, 13 April 1938. Mandel's feelings about Bérenger and Candace are confirmed by Mandel's friends Georges Wormser and Max Brusset, Interviews, Paris, 15 May 1968 and 18 June 1969.

On Bastille Day a telegram from Satineau in Paris arrived at the home of one of his partisans in Pointe-à-Pitre.

HAVE OBTAINED RECALL GOVERNOR EBOUÉ
BEST TO ALL—SATINEAU

The word spread quickly; and friends of Satineau began to shout their victory in the streets.

A friend of Eboué's, hearing the news, drove at top speed to the governor's residence at Saint Claude where Eboué was relaxing with his wife, Charles, Robert, and Ginette who had just arrived for her vacation. The friend told Eboué the news. The governor looked shocked but said nothing; he thought it a trick.[59]

The next morning Eboué heard that other telegrams had arrived and sent the following cable to the rue Oudinot:

YESTERDAY EVENING ALBRAND RECEIVED TELEGRAM SATINEAU QUOTE HAVE OBTAINED RECALL GOVERNOR STOP SAME TELEGRAM SIGNED CANDACE SATINEAU REPORTEDLY RECEIVED BY DEMOCRATIE SOCIALE STOP SEND INFORMATION URGENTLY AND EVENTUALLY TRY TO OBTAIN FROM MINISTER TELEGRAM OF CONFIDENCE TO REENFORCE AUTHORITY GOVERNOR.

Later that same day the Ministry sent Eboué the following coded telegram:

15 JULY
PLEASE TAKE NEXT SHIP AND CONFIDE INTERIM SECRETARY GENERAL GIVING HIM PRECISE INSTRUCTIONS TO KEEP THE STRICTEST NEUTRALITY DURING NEXT SENATORIAL CAMPAIGN.

It was followed by another recalling Marius Larcher, warning his substitute to be neutral in the elections too.

Eboué was shocked and humiliated at the treatment meted out to him, and he felt even worse the next day when his secretary general told him that Dr. François-Julien had written him a letter of congratulation on being named governor of Guadeloupe. Satineau's *La Voix de Peuple* crowed victory, and Eboué prepared to leave as instructed.

In the ten days they had, the Eboué's packed all their belong-

[59] Interview with André Gotte, 29 January 1968, Pointe-à-Pitre.

ings, and friends came to visit to console them with the conviction that after the election Eboué would certainly return. The masons sent telegrams of support for him to the Minister, as did other organizations, such as the Federation of Civil Servants: FEDERATION FUNCTIONARIES PROTEST AGAINST BRUSQUE RECALL GOVERNOR ÉBOUÉ. Sporting clubs honored Eboué with a ceremony at which they named their new stadium in his honor. The president of Basse-Terre Sporting Club said in a speech that all sportsmen of Guadeloupe were grateful for his interest in sports, were worried by his recall, and supported him: "[the Club] wanted to assure you that the young athletes of Guadeloupe who owe you everything and to whom you have given so much . . . are with you with all their strength and soul."[60]

On 26 July the governor and his family, accompanied by a great crowd of well-wishers, drove to the wharfs at Pointe-à-Pitre to board the *SS Cuba*. Eboué walked with Tirolien, Allys, and others to the ship in his full-dress uniform. The crowds shouted "Vive Papa Eboué! Vive Papa Eboué!" as the ship sailed.

The *Cuba* arrived at Le Havre on 5 August, and Eboué proceeded immediately to Asnières and wrote to Mandel requesting an interview. The Minister saw Eboué on 12 August and implied there had been criticisms of his administration, that his return was not yet decided, and that he ought to take a vacation. Marius Larcher also went to the Ministry where he was very coldly received and put on indefinite leave. Shortly afterward, André Haliar, Police Commissioner at Pointe-à-Pitre and the object of frequent attacks by Satineau and Candace because of his friendship with Eboué, was called to France, although he was not answerable to the Ministry of Colonies.[61]

Eboué felt ill and thought he would go to the mineral springs at Vichy. He first saw Senator Bérenger, who seemed cordial but a little cold, although he promised to do all he could to keep Eboué in Guadeloupe.[62] Eboué then had a dispute with the financial services of the Ministry, which did not want to give him the

60 "Eboué Le Grand Sportif," p. 171.

61 Interviews, Marius Larcher, Fort-de-France, 4 February 1968, and André Haliar, Paris, 1 May 1968.

62 Interview, Jean Cazenave de la Roche, Juan-les-Pins, 13 April 1968.

salary to which he was entitled. He had to borrow some money before leaving for Vichy.

It is difficult to believe that Eboué got much rest at Vichy. He was edgy and irritable, and was not out of range of letters about the maneuvering in Guadeloupe and the rumors abounding. And the European situation was unsettling and only somewhat less so after Daladier and Neville Chamberlain met Hitler at Munich at the end of August to appease the German dictator with Czechoslovakia for the sake of a few more months of peace.

Friends were sure Eboué had been recalled because of Candace, not Satineau. Candace had power but Satineau was generally considered his hanger on. One story circulating was that during the trip to Saint Martin at the beginning of July Tirolien had sent a telegram to Bérenger indicating that all was arranged on Saint Martin, thus implying that Eboué did the arranging for the elections. A friend of Satineau intercepted the telegram and sent it to Satineau who showed it to Candace. Candace then took it to Mandel as proof Eboué would make sure Bérenger won.

Candace arrived in Guadeloupe 4 September amidst cries of "Vive Eboué" and "Vive Bérenger." He later declared what had been common knowledge for two years, that he was running for senator. The campaign that he began was not against Bérenger, not even present, but against Eboué. In his newspaper Candace wrote of his long friendship with Eboué and his family: "Herménégilde Tell was my friend," he wrote; "I was Eboué's protector; he would not have been promoted to administrator in chief without me. I helped him get his interim in Soudan. I helped him get his appointment here, but Eboué took sides. He opposed Satineau and became friendly with Boisneuf. Eboué is a demagogue who spent money madly and engaged in electoral fraud under the banner of the corrupt Front Populaire."[63] From Vichy Eboué wrote to friends: "When the Guadeloupans understand their interests and the necessity to unite by forgetting everything that divides them only to retain the idea of the general interest, then work will be easy and fecund. . . . I am and I remain Governor of Guadeloupe, and those who thought they obtained my removal

63 *La Démocratie Populaire,* 24 September 1938.

and who even prided themselves about it have taken the trouble for nothing."[64]

The Ministry of Colonies sent an inspection mission to Guadeloupe to investigate charges Candace and Satineau made against Eboué and to watch over the elections, for Candace began to accuse acting Governor Allys of not being neutral either.

In October Eboué returned to Paris. He had lunches with René Isambert at the fashionable La Coupole on the boulevard Montparnasse, and saw Yvon Delbos, who promised to write some letters on his behalf, and Gaston Monnerville, no longer Under Secretary. Marius Moutet, Roger Hellier, and others gave him their impressions of Mandel. All indications were that Bérenger would win 23 October in spite of the opposition of Candace and Mandel.

At Asnières the day of the election Eboué played bridge. He decided to go to the Ministry of Colonies to find out if returns had come in from Guadeloupe. When the telegrams came, they showed that Bérenger, who arrived in the colony just before the election, had overwhelmingly won, 216 votes to 99.[65] Elated, Eboué went to his favorite café, the Café de Versailles, and bought champagne for his friends who toasted his return to the Caribbean in triumph. In Pointe-à-Pitre and Basse-Terre someone composed a song calling for Eboué's return:

Glory and Honor to Bérenger and Eboué
After this striking victory
You are stronger than ever.
Candace is no more than a ghost
For the Guadeloupans.
So that our joy may be complete
We ask our senator
The return of our beloved one:
Governor Eboué.[66]

Oddly, the ministry was silent. The difficulties with Mandel were not over, it seemed. The mission of inspection examined a long list of complaints of Satineau and Candace, and while ad-

[64] Letter, Félix Eboué to Alexandre Macal, 8 September 1938.
[65] *JOG*, No. 54, 27 October 1938, p. 987.
[66] "Gloire et Honneur à Bérenger et à Eboué," poster printed in 1938 at Pointe-à-Pitre.

mitting some indiscretions on the part of the Eboué administration on small matters, categorically denied political partisanship,
but the report brought no response from the Ministry. Satineau
claimed to friends that he had assurances from Mandel that no
matter what the outcome of the elections, Eboué would never return to Guadeloupe. Both Candace and Satineau, gloating in
spite of Bérenger's victory, claimed to know their enemy would
be sent to "some obscure corner" of Africa. Bérenger, safely re-
elected, seemed almost indifferent. He sent mimeographed letters
to constituents in October and November assuring them that he
had seen the Minister "in the best interest" of Guadeloupe.

Eboué's friends tried to comfort him. René Maran and he were
still not on very good terms, but Maran sent a note to his old
friend regretting the unpleasantness in Guadeloupe for he, perhaps better than anyone else, knew how it upset Eboué.

In early November Bérenger and Lagrosillière told Eboué they
were working to have him sent to Martinique if Mandel would
not send him back to Guadeloupe. Later, Eboué found out that
Candace's influence with the Minister was such that he seemed
able to prevent even his nomination to Martinique. On 16 November he wrote to Bérenger asking him to intervene in some
way.

On 17 or 18 November Eboué was called to Mandel's office,
where he found out that Candace and Satineau had indeed known
more about his future than he had. Mandel said: "I am naming
you Lieutenant Governor of Tchad in French Equatorial Africa,
and I am raising you to the rank of governor second class." Eboué
was shocked. Tchad? An inland colony, one of the poorest in the
empire, its governor would have a small staff and be subservient
to the governor general in Brazzaville. Mandel continued that
Tchad was an important colony because of its proximity to Italian forces in Libya and Ethiopia. Eboué did not express his dis-
may openly but suggested that he had not put in the required
number of months yet to be raised to governor second class. Mandel replied: "No one will know the difference when you and I
are dead."[67]

Eboué calmly agreed to go to Tchad and said that he would do

67 Interview, Eugénie Eboué, Asnières, 25 March 1968.

his best. He returned to Asnières in a fury, however, and, his hand shaking, scribbled a note to Bérenger: *"It is done.* I was received this morning by the Minister, and I was obliged to accept *my downfall* and to go to Tchad. People will no doubt realize the importance of the sacrifice that I have agreed to and the cruelty of it—you more than anyone else. I shall continue to play the game and be part of the team."[68]

Bérenger responded weakly that he had done his best and that he was pleased to hear of Eboué's promotion in rank. When Lagrosillière and others found out about it, they told Eboué that Bérenger had betrayed him. Lagrosillière tried other means to get Eboué transferred to Martinique. Others urged Eboué to resign from the administration to run against Satineau in 1940, but financial obligations—his children and keeping up the house in Asnières—made Eboué hesitate to retire. He also thought he should fulfill his assignment. On 19 November a decree officially named him head of the territory of Tchad.

The evening of the announcement Eboué, depressed and angry, went to the Café de Versailles in the company of a young Guadeloupan lawyer, Georges Céleste. He was looking forward to some comfort from friends who usually gathered there. No one was there. Eboué looked around and asked: "Where are my friends when I need them? Is this the meaning of friendship?"[69]

68 Archives Eboué, handwritten note to Senator Bérenger, n.d.
69 Interview, Georges Céleste, Paris, 28 August 1968.

VIII

RETURN TO AFRICA: TRIUMPH
AFTER HUMILIATION, 1939-1940

THE NEWS at the end of November that Eboué would not return to Guadeloupe shocked his friends there. By not sending him back to the Antilles, even for a few months, the Minister of Colonies disgraced him; the nomination to Tchad was considered demotion and punishment.

Eboué thought about his twenty-two months in Guadeloupe and tried to comfort himself with the idea that he accomplished something in the economic domain for the common man. When Léon Damas, Guyanese poet and journalist, came to see him for an interview, Eboué expressed pride with the application of Popular Front reforms to the Antilles and pleasure in the extension of sports facilities.[1]

What was done was done, and Eboué made plans to leave for Africa. He went to the socialist SFIO branch in the fifteenth arrondissement southwest of Paris to pay his dues and pick up his membership card and visited Lafayette lodge of the Freemasons

---

[1] Léon Damas, "La Flèche Outre-Mer, Guadeloupe 38, un entretien avec M. Félix Eboué, Gouverneur des Colonies," in *La Flèche*, 29 January 1939, p. 5.

to which he affiliated himself.[2] He and Eugénie finished their mortgage payments on the house, and he tried to arrange his books and papers in the upstairs study before his flight, scheduled for 22 January.

In a last conversation at the Ministry Eboué heard Mandel insist on the importance of Tchad if war came and, somewhat paradoxically, promise to give him another assignment after a few months.[3] Lagros and others still hoped to get him back to the Antilles in one capacity or another, and Eboué thought that because he had not taken a long leave in years, he would be entitled to ten or twelve months by about July 1939, thus permitting him to go home. He told "Petit Camille," visiting in Paris from Guyane, that they could go to Vichy or Vittel together and then return to Cayenne; it had been eight years.[4]

Joseph Lagrosillière and André Haliar arranged a farewell party for the evening before Eboué's departure. Over sixty colleagues and friends gathered at the Café de Versailles to express their affection for him. Roger Hellier, his classmate at "Colo," Marius Moutet, Governor Matteo Alfassa, who had given him such a good recommendation from Soudan, E. L. Boutin, Lhuerre, Blaise Diagne's widow, Madame Eboué, Ginette, Cornélie Gratien with her daughter and her son Elie who looked more and more like his uncle, and many others from Guadeloupe. Maran was not present, and Lagros refused to send Senator Bérenger an invitation.

In his booming voice Lagros proposed a toast, and Marius Moutet spoke briefly, praising Eboué as a Popular Front governor. Everyone then assembled behind Eboué for a picture. He seemed affable and cheerful, but the picture showed how he had aged since he had first left for Guadeloupe barely two years earlier. Amidst all the pleasantness he turned to Georges Céleste, who

---

[2] His card for 1939 is the first documentary evidence of his membership in the SFIO, although he reportedly joined earlier. The opposition of Guadeloupe's socialists to him had nothing to do with his feelings about the SFIO, because politics in Guadeloupe was so personalized that parties and party ideologies were not really part of the conflict. The fifteenth arrondissement branch attracted many intellectuals.

[3] Archives Lhuerre, Letter, Félix Eboué to Camille Lhuerre, 8 March 1939.

[4] *Ibid.*

had been with him the evening of the announcement that he would go to Tchad; Céleste remembers that Eboué gravely said: "I shall expect to see you tomorrow morning at the airport," as if he expected no one else outside his family to be present.[5]

At seven the next day a small group saw Eboué off at Le Bourget. He was traveling alone, for Madame Eboué was to join him in a few weeks, giving him time to prepare adequate quarters. It was a cold January morning, and a photo taken at the time shows Eboué bundled up against the weather, drawn and downcast.

This was his first plane ride and the speed amazed him. From Paris he flew to Marseille where a seaplane took him to Algiers. The next day he flew on to Soudan, his old colony. On 24 January he arrived in Niger colony for lunch and refueling, and the plane landed in Fort Lamy, capital of Tchad, in late afternoon.

Military and civilian administrators in Fort Lamy greeted him and drove him through the town. A cousin, Léon Léveillé, working as a communications clerk, his old friend René Isambert, recently widowed, and others had warned Eboué what to expect, but he was nonetheless taken aback by the town and his house. Lamy, built on a flat area overlooking the Chari River had about 14,000 inhabitants in 1939. Small government buildings spread out far apart at the end of a road, dusty or muddy, depending on the season. The route linked the African quarter with the administrative quarter, and the few businessmen—an assorted group of Greeks, Portuguese and Frenchmen—opened their dreary shops along that road. The larger companies which purchased the cotton or hides had their more imposing office buildings and warehouses nearer the administrative headquarters. The African market at the other end of the road reminded Eboué of Bamako's

---

At the farewell party for the Eboués, given 21 January 1939, at the Café de Versailles in Paris. Circled from the left are: 1. Rémonde Gratien; 2. Madame Cornélie Gratien; 3. Clérence Gratien; 4. Ginette Eboué; 5. Elie Gratien; 6. Madame Eboué; 7. Marius Moutet; 8. Eboué; 9. Dr. L. Lheurre; 10. Camille Lheurre; 11. Commissioner André Haliar; 12. E. L. Boutin; 13. Madame Blaise Diagne; 14. Georges Céleste; 15. J. Lagrosillière; 16. R. Hellier.

5 Interview, Georges Céleste, Paris, 28 August 1968.

market because of the cattle waiting for the long walk south and
the camels brought in by the nomads.

The governor's house was worse than anything Eboué had
lived in since his very earliest days in Oubangui-Chari. The large
cement building, its walls cracked, had two large rooms on the
first floor and two bedrooms and one bath on the second. What
furniture Eboué found was locally made, and although the administration purchased a generator for administrative headquarters, it had not allocated the money to set it up, so the house
lacked electricity. Servants pumped water each day up to the
bathroom. There was an oil refrigerator still functioning at an
advanced age, a homemade radio in poor repair, and there was
no piano for Madame Eboué; the only music would come from
an antique record player. The house was not bad for a young
bachelor beginning his career, but Eboué knew Niette would be
unhappy in it, and he was ashamed.[6]

After visiting the "Cercle" where administrators gathered for
drinks and bridge in the evening Eboué wrote some letters, one
asking the governor general, Joseph Reste de Roca, for money to
improve the house. Considering his present situation, he concluded that in spite of the humiliation, he would learn about
Tchad, contribute to its economic development, work for its defense. For these projects he needed reliable helpers and made
plans to bring Guillet, Cazenave de la Roche, Sainte-Luce Banchelin, Georges Céleste, and Allys to be with him.

The next morning the governor met with some of his subordinates. (There were 42 civil servants and 277 military men in the
Fort Lamy area.) He studied reports and in less than a week left
on the first of a series of tours. It took seventeen days to travel the
1000 kilometers from Fort Lamy to the post of Faya, north
through the desert toward Libya, because of the deplorable
condition of the vehicles used. Eboué began the trip in a ten-
year-old Citroen, the only automobile belonging to the administration, and two Chevrolet trucks rented from local merchants.
First the Citroen broke down in the sand dunes of the Sahara,
and everyone, including Eboué, pushed it out. It finally broke

<hr>

[6] Archives Eboué, Letter, Emile Buhot-Launay to Félix Eboué, 18 December 1938.

down completely, and they left it to the desert. Then one truck's pistons burned out, and everyone crammed into the one remaining truck which arrived safely in Faya. Eboué had fortunately taken the precaution of putting a wireless receiver and transmitter in the truck and was able to keep in contact with Fort Lamy.[7] "The trip was more of an athletic event than an administrative tour," Eboué wrote his daughter Ginette.[8] A consolation was finding fresh dates at the oasis of Faya, a fine gift for his wife, who was expected in his absence. Of course, he got his first close look at the colony.

TCHAD

Tchad, the largest of the four colonies of French Equatorial Africa, was divided into eleven departments in 1939, the most important of which in terms of population were those in the southern savanna. Like French Soudan, which Tchad ressembled in many ways, the savanna of the south faded into desert north of Fort Lamy, and the huge northern departments, Borkou-Ennedi-Tibesti, called B.E.T., were inhabited by about 32,000 nomads out of a total population for the colony of about 2,000,000. The peoples of the south, along the border with Oubangui-Chari, belonged to the Sara group; in the northwest, along the Camerounese-French Niger frontier lived innumerable Islamized peoples; in the east lived tribes related to others across the frontier in Anglo-Egyptian Sudan; the nomads of B.E.T. moved to and fro near Libya. The Muslims in particular had hierarchized political systems similar to those Eboué had known at Rafai and in Soudan; in 1939 there were four sultans whose power and prestige varied according to their own perspicacity about how to manipulate the French as well as the varying attitudes of French administrators.

The conquest of this country, barely finished by World War I, had given France an area two and a half times the size of the metropole with few resources and far from the sea. Cotton, pea-

7 Afrique Equatoriale Française, Territoire du Tchad, "Rapport," 28 February 1939.

8 Archives Eboué, Letter, Félix Eboué to Ginette Eboué, 25 February 1939.

nuts, cattle, cattle hides, and butter were the major exports going out through Brazzaville by the newly completed Congo-Océan Railway that Eboué had years earlier drafted workers to build or by rough roads and waterways through Sudan and Nigeria.

Because of the Africans' strong resistance to the French, the vastness of the territory, and the lack of resources, the country had undergone a longer period of military administration and was more neglected than Oubangui-Chari with regard to development. In 1938 the French government had put northwestern Tchad and northeastern Niger, both on the frontier with Libya, under military administration called the border areas or Confins Nigero-Tchadiens, and military officers administered its four departments. Defense plans also necessitated a large military contingent. Eboué on general principles wanted to have as many departments as possible under the control of professional civilian administrators; he believed that the military would not make good administrators, for they tended to form a separate caste and to disdain constituted authority.

He no doubt also feared a division of command between himself and the military leader, Colonel Grañier. In principle, the civilian governor was the highest ranking person in any colony with power to command the military as well as the civilians. In fact, here, as elsewhere, the military often resented civilian commanders in chief and sometimes refused to cooperate with them. Eboué's color was said to rankle the military more than it did the civilians.

At the end of 1938, before the arrival of Eboué, the civilian administration with many of these same considerations in mind took over Kanem department. From then on relations between civilian and militiary authority deteriorated and Eboué had to smooth them over when he arrived. In Ouaddai in eastern Tchad relations were strained between the military and the civilians over local African authority, and Eboué had to deal with that conflict too.

From his February tour Eboué got a better idea of Tchad's importance due its proximity to the Italian colony of Libya, its central location in Africa, and the increasingly tense international situation: "Basically Tchad could be interesting, but it has not been."[9] Things soon became more "interesting" in France and in Tchad.

In France agents from Italy and Germany, both encouraged by the victory of pro-Fascist General Franco in the Spanish civil war, were making trouble, agitating for the autonomy of Alsace and Lorraine. The government reacted vigorously, abolishing fascist organizations and purchasing American planes. In Africa the Italians, whom the French had originally hoped to appease by acceding to their occupation of Ethiopia, criticized French colonial policy and supported revived German claims on Cameroun. The French knew by the end of February that the Italian garrisons had been reinforced with fresh troops near the Tchad-Libyan frontier; Eboué received a secret report that a detachment of Italians had crossed into B.E.T. department on a reconnaissance mission and that they were building roads toward his colony.

During his sojourn at Faya, Eboué inquired about the feelings of the Africans toward the Italians, and took pains to see that refugees from Libya were comfortably settled. He followed the advice of Colonna d'Ornano, military head of B.E.T., keeping taxes down, enlarging the share granted chiefs, and asking for a special grant of 100,000 francs from the governor general to use in encouraging more Africans to leave Libya.[10]

He examined road work—or, rather, the tracks through the sand—and undertook a program to improve communications. Later, a civilian public works engineer, Mr. Ruais, took charge of road construction in the southern part of the colony and the military planned roads in the north. The government wanted a good communication network between Bangui and Fort Lamy so that three-ton trucks carrying supplies, troops, and arms could pass north in all seasons. By 1940 Ruais had under his command 8800 African men. They worked with little equipment but smoothed rough spots and cleared away underbrush; they also worked on the airstrip at Fort Lamy, destined to become extremely important later.

Eboué's program included filling in marshy areas near rivers in the capital, fixing buildings before the rainy season, construction

9 Archives Lhuerre, Letter, Félix Eboué to Camille Lhuerre, 8 March 1939.
10 Secret Letter, Félix Eboué to Governor General, 22 April 1939.

of a new hospital for Africans, a new market, new housing in
Fort Lamy. He also planned a ferry across the Chari River and
airstrips elsewhere. Funds were short and decisions were delayed
because he needed authorization from the offices of the governor
general for every step taken. To Isambert at Massenya he wrote:

> I have shouted so much about our criminal lack of preparation . . .
> that they are deciding to do something. . . . Oh, these offices! Mandel
> had to give specific orders to satisfy me so that the offices in Brazza-
> ville wake up. . . . If we don't have permanent roads, our brave men
> will be massacred. . . .[11]

In spite of all the talk of war preparation, other colonial officials
also believed they had little support. The discouraged governor of
Oubangui-Chari wrote Eboué: "It won't take you long to perceive
that no where else are Governors, deprived of means and initiative,
treated with such lack of respect [by the higher administration and
Ministry]."[12]

By the time Eboué returned from the tour Mr. Guillet, his *chef
de cabinet* who had worked with him in Soudan and in Guadeloupe, had arrived and so did Madame Eboué. Cazenave de la
Roche came from Martinique later, and Eboué wrote to the Ministry again to request a secretary general and the elevation of
Tchad's status to that of an autonomous colony, but the requests
became snarled in red tape.

Tchad interested Eboué more and more "because of the exterior situation." He changed his mind about departing, although he hated Fort Lamy because of the miserable living conditions: "I am not talking of leaving—I cannot even talk about it
because of the tense international situation. If worse comes to
worse, you know that Tchad will have a great role to play. I don't
want to seem to flee from my duties."[13]

Concerned about German claims on Cameroun, a parliamen-
tary mission arrived in Fort Lamy at the end of March 1939 after

[11] Letter, Félix Eboué to René Isambert, Fort Lamy, 24 March 1939, cited
by Albert Maurice, *Félix Eboué: sa vie et son oeuvre* (Brussels: Institut Royal
Colonial Belge, 1954), pp. 28-29.
[12] Archives Eboué, Letter, Lt. Gov. of Oubangui-Chari to Félix Eboué, 15
February 1939.
[13] Archives Boutin, Félix Eboué to E. L. Boutin, 16 March 1939.

visiting Douala and Yaoundé. Eboué's old acquaintance, Gaston Monnerville, headed the five-man mission;[14] Eboué invited the European population and African functionaries to greet the delegation the evening of their arrival, and took the occasion to introduce them with a highly patriotic and witty speech, asking the deputies to tell France that Tchad was "resolutely French." Adding a personal note, he said: "A symbol . . . of French dynamism is here in this assemblage . . . three sons of the oldest overseas province. Three Guyanese are here: . . . Gaston Monnerville who represents our little country in Parliament, . . . Paul Bernetel and . . . the only one of the three who came out badly since he became a colonial governor. . . ."

Eboué asked the visitors to tell Paris he needed money for the development and defense of Tchad. He wanted francs "in order to build roads . . . decent housing for our functionaries. . . , so that Fort Lamy, capital of the North, might have water and light and a sewage system, so that the medical program . . . can continue to develop." Making oblique reference to the defense of Equatorial Africa, the governor concluded: "It has been said that Fort-Lamy occupies a 'key position' in the defense of our African Empire. We only ask that this key be of gold; we are only asking for a little money. . . ."[15]

Monnerville looked at the roads, such as they were, and projects to extend air facilities. The mission then left for Paris, and Eboué, accompanied by his wife, went on more tours to see every department. In the south they visited with René Isambert, their cousin Léon Léveillé, and Dr. Adolphe Diagne, son of their dear friend Blaise.

Although Eboué originally thought he might be reassigned by June, no change in his status was made. Madame Eboué flew alone to Paris to be there during school vacation. Lagrosillière, always planning one project or another, told Eboué to remain in Tchad for the time being; the Martiniquan wanted him more than ever to run with him for the two seats of deputy. Friends in Guadeloupe begged him to resign from the colonial service to run against Satineau. He responded to all that although he had

14 Interview, Jules Ninine, Paris, 1 March 1968, and Letter, 31 March 1968.
15 Archives Eboué, copy of speech.

originally felt "deep sadness mixed with shame" because of the
assignment to Tchad, although his lodgings were terrible, although his powers as lieutenant governor were less than in
Guadeloupe, still he felt he had an important position "splen-
didly stuffed with responsibilities . . . and I shall remain here
as long as the international situation is not cleared up." In spite
of the fact he said he would have liked to see Satineau ("this
super dishonest man") beaten, he also felt financial obligations
toward his family for his salary as a deputy would be less than as
governor. He, therefore, suggested that his young friend Rolland
René-Boisneuf or some others could run, and he authorized the
use of his name to support Satineau's opponent, more proof, of
course, that Eboué was not neutral in Guadeloupe politics.[16]

Other news from Guadeloupe was that the new governor,
Pierre Alype, was in trouble. Strikes began again with the start of
the sugar cane harvest, and Marius Moutet wrote Eboué to ask
him what position the socialist SFIO should take with regard to
the resulting disturbances. Both Candace and Satineau supported
Pierre Alype, but this time Bérenger asked for the governor's removal, and the Ministry recalled the governors of both Guadeloupe and Martinique. Eboué could not suppress his satisfaction.
He wrote to his wife, "I have heard that my two comrades in the
Antilles wore themselves out in five or six months. We lasted 22
months in Guadeloupe and 27 in Martinique, and we would still
be there if they hadn't made us walk the plank . . . these are
delicate posts, and they cannot put just anyone there. You and I,
we are not just anyone."[17]

Madame Eboué sent news of the children and expressed her
worry as war tensions increased in Europe. Ginette would remain
in school, but Charles would go to the Lycée of Algiers. Robert,
who thrilled his father by winning a race in a track meet, had
almost finished his baccalaureate, but there was no news of
Henry in Senegal. Cornélie's health fluctuated, and she needed
money, as always.

Although René Maran and Eboué exchanged New Year's
greetings, they still had not re-established their old friendship.

[16] Archives Eboué, copy of Letter, Félix Eboué to L. Méloir, 3 June 1939.
[17] Archives Eboué, Letter, Félix Eboué to Eugénie Eboué, 25 June 1939.

During his wife's stay in Paris she did call on the Marans one afternoon, and Eboué was pleased: "You did well by going to see the Marans. At our age . . . we have no time to make new friends."[18] Eboué, like Maran, wanted to resume a relationship which looked back thirty-five years. Maran had decided that he would take the first step the next time Eboué returned from Africa,[19] but events unfortunately prevented the two from ever seeing each other again and resolving their differences and misunderstandings.

The situation in Europe in June and July 1939 deteriorated, and the French accustomed themselves to air raid drills and trying on gas masks. The economic situation in France had improved, but partisan squabbling continued. The communists, for example, following orders from Moscow after the signing of the Nazi-Soviet non-aggression pact, opposed war. Old friends fell out about questions of loyalty and patriotism—who was a "true" Frenchman. And for the first time questions of color were discussed; some right-wing newspapers attacked Eboué openly.

RACISM

By the end of 1938 questions of race were more prominent than they had been since the Dreyfus affair. French newspapers opposed to the Popular Front used Eboué as a target for their attacks on the socialist-radical government. In September 1938, for example, an Alsatian newspaper suddenly decided it had been an extraordinary thing for the Popular Front government to name a black man governor of Guadeloupe: this "Negro Citizen" ("citoyen nègre," a derogatory expression at the time) who "belonged to the cult of Blum and Stalin" was alleged to have created a terrible situation in the Antilles.[20]

With the increased tension between France and the Axis powers, German and Italian journalists, looking for an excuse to attack French colonial policy, also chose Eboué as a target. The Italian publication *L'Azione Coloniale* on 26 January 1939 published a disgusting open letter to Eboué: ". . . the cannibalistic de-

18 Archives Eboué, Letter, Félix Eboué to Eugénie Eboué, 23 July 1939.
19 Interview, Madame Camille René-Maran, Paris, 27 July 1970.
20 *Nouvelliste d'Alsace*, 3 September 1938.

sires of your illustratious ancestors might be reborn in you. . . ."[21]
A German journalist, writing about Eboué's nomination to
Tchad in the *Berliner Tageblatt,* said: "The Jew Minister, Mandel, named a Negro governor of the colonies for the first time in
the history of the European peoples."[22] Eboué had been governor
for two years when the article was written, and Louis-Placide
Blacher, a brown Martiniquan, had been named governor of Niger
in 1930, although Eboué was the first governor to be notably black.
But to the Axis journalists, truth placed a distant second behind
a malevolent, sneering tone.

In French newspapers with Fascist leanings like *L'Action Française* there reappeared the old canard that the Muslims of Tchad,
like the Muslims of Soudan, were black but considered themselves Arabs not Negroes, and disapproved of a dark black governor, seen as the descendant of slaves: "Our colonial administration has some mixed blood administrators. But, their intellectual, social, even physical francisation is sufficient."[23] Eboué read
such articles carefully, for they were sent to him by his wife and
by friends; he knew that the military personnel particularly said
that the sultans and Muslims would respect only a white administrator. Young African Muslim clerks told Eboué about these comments, but he told them he did not care. He knew that even if
there had been any antagonism toward him among the Muslims,
the whites were using it to serve their own ends because they
could not bear serving under a black.[24]

The French colonialist publication *L'Afrique Française,* in
which Eboué had published his articles on Oubangui-Chari almost ten years before, denounced the racists,[25] and high-ranking
white officials like Robert Delavignette, then director of the Colonial School, wrote him letters of encouragement and support.
But the attacks angered Eboué so much that he prepared a re-

21 Cited by René Maran, *Félix Eboué: grand commis et loyal serviteur*
(Paris: Les Editions Parisiennes, 1957) p. 93.
22 24 January 1939, cited by *L'Europe Nouvelle,* 18 March 1939, pp. 292-93.
23 *L'Action Française,* 6 March 1939.
24 His Excellency Mohammad Bechir Sow worked as a clerk in those days
and recalls Eboué's attitudes, Interview, Fort Lamy, 29 May 1968.
25 *Bulletin du Comité de l'Afrique Française,* February 1939, Vol. XLIX,
pp. 35-36.

sponse that may not have been published. In it he said that any-one from the old colonies was "as authentically French as the Presidents of the Chamber of Notary Publics and as the Angevin and Beauce region peasants."[26] But, by September 1939, Eboué had no further time to spend defending himself. World War II had begun in earnest.

WAR

On 1 September 1939 the Germans attacked Poland, and Brit-ain and France declared war on the Third Reich. A general mo-bilization for the armed forces took Henry, then twenty-seven, and he was sent to the European front. Robert, twenty years old, joined the army in October after having taken his examination for the secondary school diploma. "You have to do your duty," Eboué wrote.[27] Charles, at fifteen, wanted to join the air force but his age, of course, prevented him from doing so. Ginette, sixteen, and considered quite an adult by her parents, remained in France at the Legion of Honor school for there seemed no danger of invasion. In October, therefore, Madame Eboué flew from Paris for Algiers after closing the house; she left Charles at the lycée of Algiers, his entrance having been arranged by a friend in Yvon Delbos' office. (Delbos was then Minister of Education.) She pro-ceeded overland to Fort Lamy where she found her husband work-ing on an increased war program under the direction of Pierre Boisson, the new governor general, whom Eboué had known in French West Africa.

Eboué saw Boisson very briefly on 2 September 1939 when the newly appointed governor general's flight stopped over in Fort Lamy on its way to Brazzaville. Boisson returned at the end of the month to spend a day in Fort Lamy with Eboué, and then did some touring. He seemed cordial and promised increased funds to purchase needed vehicles for the heads of departments and to support Eboué's programs.[28] In the following months Boisson did not cooperate as Eboué hoped, however, and even criticized him

[26] Archives Eboué, copy of unpublished (?) article, "Racistes Stupides."

[27] Archives Eboué, Letter, Félix Eboué to Eugénie Eboué, 4 September 1939.

[28] Archives Eboué, Letter, Félix Eboué to Eugénie Eboué, 28 September 1939.

for some expenditures. Despite these difficulties, Tchad continued roadbuilding, and American observers reported that of all
French projects to prepare for possible war in Africa "The greatest activity at the present time . . . seems to be on the construction of a military road between Bangui and Lake Chad in French
Equatorial Africa."[29] Troop recruitment and training continued
so that there were over 2000 trained African troops in the colony.
Eboué's proposal to upgrade the colony so that he could communicate directly with Paris languished. His hoped-for secretary general, Allys, was named instead to Soudan, Banchelin could not
come to Fort Lamy, and Georges Céleste, on his way to join
Eboué, was drafted into the army. Mr. Guillet resigned. In December Léon Léveillé died. Cazenave de la Roche in Fort Lamy
and René Isambert, stationed to the south in Massenya, and
Maurice Adam, who worked as a type of secretary general even
though he received no compensation for the job, were of great
assistance, but Eboué soon chose Henri Laurentie, then thirty-
eight, to be his closest collaborator.

A Roman Catholic descendant of royalist philosopher Royer-
Collard, Henri Laurentie was different from Eboué, except for
the fact that he smoked heavily. A sharp featured man with a
shock of hair over the right forehead, his religion, cutting wit,
and a disarming modesty were as well known as his emotional
patriotism. Mr. and Mrs. Laurentie's house had the largest library in Tchad, and many said the young administrator wrote
poetry. He was certainly the most interesting and best read subordinate Eboué ever had had.

At Kanem Department north of Lake Tchad Laurentie's relations with the French military, whom he replaced in 1938, were
poor, but he got along extremely well with local African authority
and the growing cadre of African civil servants who remember to
this day that Eboué and he were practically the only Frenchmen
to address them with the respecful *vous* form in French.

Upon such merits Eboué, who met him during his first tour to
the north, based his decision to give Laurentie increasing respon-

[29] National Archives, United States of America, State Department (*Infra,*
U.S. State), Report on Defense Preparations in West Africa, American Consulate, Lagos, 8 June 1940, 848 L. 20/12.

Henri Laurentie, relaxing for a moment in wartime Brazzaville. Courtesy of the French Documentation Center.

sibilities. He had also discovered a man who shared his views on the role of traditional African leadership.

The governor thought that African authority had special importance in wartime. The chiefs recruited soldiers, collected taxes, and, most important, embodied order and discipline in their respective societies, particularly necessary during the crisis. When Eboué found that the French military in Ouaddai department had not followed the "policy of consideration," Marshal Lyautey's expression to describe his dealings with Moroccan authority, he asked Laurentie to take charge on this important area in the east along the frontier with Anglo-Egyptian Sudan.

Ouaddai's population in 1939 numbered almost 250,000, making it the second largest department in the colony; its land area equalled the size of Greece. The people of the area had strongly resisted the imposition of French authority in the late nineteenth and early twentieth centuries, but the French army finally captured their capital, Abéché, in 1909, and the sultan fled; military authorities then abolished the sultanate. In 1935 civilian authorities had enthroned Mohammad Ourada, a member of the original ruling family.

Ourada had studied in Algiers and Senegal, and seemed an ideal link between the traditional past and the exigencies of the present, which demanded, Eboué believed, loyalty to France. Rumor was that the Ouaddaians might attempt to declare their independence and raise an army against the French, certain disaster for the defense of the colony.[30] In order to build up the sultan's standing and loyalty the governor arranged for an invitation to Ourada to visit France during the celebration of the 150th anniversary of the French Revolution. The sultan, who traveled with Eboué's old friend Hetman of Rafai, met Georges Mandel and the Sultan of Morocco and wrote the governor several times during his trip: "Truly your protection has brought me all possible and imaginable honors."[31] After his return, Ourada told the Ouaddaians about the impressive sights of Paris and urged them to support France in the conflict.

Eboué also made it a matter of policy to support and to praise publicly leaders with a traditional basis of authority. "It is above all else necessary not to damage the prestige attached to his title by harassing or mocking him; on the contrary, consider him as a great chief. . . ."[32] Such a policy meant, of course, that if there were any conflict between the sultan and the people the administrator should ordinarily support the sultan.

Attempts to build up Ourada were successful in so far as Ouaddai's attachment to Tchad was concerned, and the region contributed heavily in men to the war effort, but Ourada himself, torn by conflicting demands and already an alcoholic by

[30] Archives of Tchad, file on Sultanate Ouaddai, and "Rapports Politiques 1936-37."
[31] Archives Eboué, Letter, Sultan Ourada to Félix Eboué, 13 August 1939.
[32] Ibid.

1939, could not function as an effective leader. One of Laurentie's successors, unaware of the impossible position in which the French put most traditional authorities, wrote a letter to Ourada revealing starkly the ambiguity of French policy:

> I fear you are somewhat confused. It appears you believe there is a Ouaddai Territory of which you are the hereditary possessor. This is an error because you know that . . . there is not any such Territory any more, but rather an administrative district called Ouaddai.
>
> Here, you are our direct collaborator for the administration of the subdivision, but the man who has responsibility before the Head of the Colony is me, and I am responsible for you. This gives me the right to give you orders, and this gives you the duty to follow them.[33]

Ourada died in 1945, still a relatively young man.

Laurentie's relations with the military in Ouaddai were no better than at Kanem in spite of the war. The antagonism extended to the relations between the African *tirailleurs* working with the French officers and the African guards working with civilian authority. At the beginning of 1940 the *tirailleurs* attacked the guards and some men were killed. Civilians and military blamed each other, and the incident necessitated a report by Eboué to the governor general in which he explained the difficult relations between the two authorities. He defended Laurentie as a brilliant administrator.[34] Eboué then asked Laurentie to come to Fort Lamy in February 1940 and replaced him with Maurice Adam, an administrator who, having gone to Saint Cyr military academy, served as a link between the two camps. In Fort Lamy Eboué gave Laurentie the title head of the office of political affairs, thus making him a type of secretary general even though he did not have the official position or the salary. Eboué's trust in his assistant grew and from February 1940 to July 1943 the two worked together on every major project affecting the colonies.

The first important task in 1940 was the order to recruit an additional quota of 3000 Africans to the army. This imposition by Brazzaville seemed to have been the last straw; the refusal to raise the status of Tchad, the absence of adequate funds, limits

---

33 Archives of Tchad, Sultanate Ouaddai, Dossier Sultan M. Ourada, Letter, Chef de Bataillon Montchamp to Sultan Ourada, 25 December 1940.

34 Letter, Félix Eboué to Governor General Boisson, 20 April 1940.

on his decision-making powers, worry about the war in Europe and the safety of his daughter, overwhelmed Eboué. His kidney trouble flared up and, when Lagros's new attempt to get him transferred to Martinique or Cameroun failed, Eboué decided he and his wife would leave Tchad.

At the end of March 1940 Governor General Boisson visited Fort Lamy, and Eboué requested permission to go to Europe. Boisson refused, telling him that Mandel had ordered all administrators to remain where they were until France's position in the war improved. Other administrators also wanted to leave. Eboué remained, although he had already shipped some of his belongings. At a meeting to commemorate the French victory over Sultan Rabah's resistance to the implantation of French authority in Tchad forty years before, Eboué spoke about the Frenchman, Commandant Lamy, killed in the last battle: "The memory of Lamy recalls here our present duty. Like him we accept the combat; like him we know that we can count more on death than on rest. Let us then fight by our will, our love and our blood for a great and proud France."[35]

By May 1940 the eight-month-old war in Europe was going badly for France and its allies. The Germans pushed into France, after crushing Holland and crossing Belgium, across the relatively unprotected northern frontier. At the end of the month the King of the Belgians negotiated an armistice with the Germans while his government fled into exile to continue the struggle, denouncing the monarch. On 3 June the British completed the evacuation from Dunkerque of their troops fighting on the continent, leaving the French to face the enemy alone.

The Germans advanced toward Paris. On the 10th the French government fled from the capital to Bordeaux, and the Italians, sure of gaining some French territory without making much of an effort, attacked along the Riviera. The situation seemed hopeless. In Bordeaux Prime Minister Reynaud submitted his resignation to President Lebrun, and Marshal Henri Pétain, World War I hero, replaced him.

[35] Speech, 22 April 1940, reprinted in *L'Afrique Equatoriale* (Brazzaville), 8 May 1940.

The colonies, cut off from regular communication with France, depended on shortwave radio broadcasts, particularly those of the BBC for information. They looked to the governor general for guidance. Boisson sounded courageous; he had lost a leg fighting the Germans in the previous war, and no one doubted his patriotism. On 15 June, after the French government moved to Bordeaux, Boisson spoke over the radio: Times are difficult but "We shall fight everywhere necessary until victory."[36]

Eboué in Tchad also urged his colleagues to be brave. The same day as Boisson's message Eboué and Laurentie prepared a circular to all European colonial officials in the capital warning them not to be pessimistic, at least in public. Defeatism would decrease the already lowered opinion the African functionaries and leaders had of France's power, he wrote. Those who said France was already defeated would be punished: "I don't want to finish on this note of menace. Here, we are more impatient, more sensitive than those in full action. Also, the war has arrived at a point of extreme tension and may confuse us. . . . Let us control ourselves; let us not forget ourselves and the natives who are watching us; let our firmness of soul and our hope be manifest. This is our duty as officials and as colonial Frenchmen."[37] Eboué and Laurentie followed the news together; they were both worried about their families. Laurentie's wife had returned to France a few months before to be with their four children, and there was no news of them. Ginette had planned to fly to Tchad but had found out too late that the dependents of colonial administrators were no longer permitted to join them. As for the older boys, Robert and Henry had already seen action in Europe. Only Charles managed to get to Fort Lamy before the end of the month.

On 17 June the French were shocked by a speech from Bordeaux. Prime Minister Pétain said he had requested an agreement with the Germans to end the combat; he asked the French to lay down their arms: "It is with deep sadness that I tell you today that it is necessary to cease combat." On 18 June French-

36 Printed in *Courrier d'Afrique* (Leopoldville), 16/17 June 1940.
37 Note-circulaire à tous les functionnaires européens de Fort-Lamy," 15 June 1940.

men in the colonies learned that their country had laid down her arms, and although leaders like Mandel and some senators thought of setting up a government in exile like the Belgians, Pétain refused.

On 22 June the French government signed an armistice with the Germans and two days later another with the Italians. The agreement with Hitler divided the country into a northern German-occupied zone and a southern non-occupied zone with an autonomous French government. The victors promised not to seize French ships and even said the French could continue to use them to protect the empire, but the British, fearing the Germans might use French ships against them, sunk on 3 July a large section of the fleet stationed at the naval base of Mers-el-Kébir in Algeria. Some 1300 Frenchmen were killed, a fact used by Pierre Laval (Pétain's vice premier) who, supporting the armistice, wished to prove that Britain was France's enemy.[38]

The armistice with Italy concerning Africa provided for the demilitarization and evacuation of zones along the frontier with Libya, including one extending 200 kilometers inside Tchad, Algeria, and Niger; it also gave Italy the right to collect French weapons that might be used against her and to send armistice commissions into French territory.

In the southern zone of France the French parliament and government installed themselves at Vichy. On 10 July, led by Pierre Laval, the parliament gave all power to Marshal Pétain and voted the end of the Third Republic. Only eighty men voted against this new dictatorship, including Léon Blum and Marius Moutet. No representatives from Martinique or Guadeloupe opposed the end of republican government in France. Bérenger, who feared for his life because he had helped Jewish refugees, hid at Bordeaux, while Yvon Delbos and Mandel went by ship to North Africa. Gratien Candace participated in deliberations and became a member of a consultative council of the new French State. Satineau voted for Pétain.

With the creation of *L'État Français* Marshal Pétain became Head of State and Pierre Laval became Prime Minister. They

---

[38] Robert Aron, *Histoire de Vichy, 1940-1944* (Paris: Arthème Fayard, 1954), pp. 109-11.

claimed they had followed the best path for France and the French people, who had been misled and deceived by governments of the Third Republic, particularly that of the Popular Front. They thought Germany had won the war and that it was only a matter of time before Britain too would surrender. In London and in Africa, for a time, optimism and the will to continue the war were stronger.

THE *BLOC AFRICAIN* FAILS

The day French soldiers were asked to lay down their arms by Marshal Pétain, Charles de Gaulle, recently promoted Brigadier General, spoke over the BBC from London to the French. Fight on, he said: "Nothing is lost for France. Struck down today by mechanized force, we shall win in the future by a superior mechanized force." He requested military men to join him in London and asked for the cooperation of Frenchmen who desired to continue the battle. France can continue the war, he said: "Because France is not alone. She is not alone. She has a vast Empire behind her. She can, united with the British Empire which controls the sea, continue the struggle. She can, like England, use without limit the immense industrial might of the United States."[39]

Most colonial officials in Africa had not heard the appeal of de Gaulle, and they did not know who he was anyway. The best-known soldiers of the day—Pétain, Gamelin, Georges, Weygand, and Juin—all supported the armistice. But immediately after 18 June most governors and military men in Africa expressed a determination to continue the war, for they knew about the substantial French forces in the Middle East and North Africa and could not believe France would surrender completely without calling upon these forces and the empire.

From Upper Volta a number of French troops and businessmen had left to join British forces in Gold Coast, and an administrator declared the colony would continue the war. The commander of troops in Djibouti, French Somaliland, said the British would give him help to continue the battle on the allied side; he

---

[39] Charles de Gaulle, *Mémoires de guerre: l'appel 1940-1942*, Vol. I (Paris: Plon, 1954), pp. 267-68.

swore he would not give up Djibouti to the Germans, or the Italians occupying Ethiopia. On 18 June Governor General Marcel de Coppet, who had been transferred from Dakar to Madagascar in 1939, telegraphed his colleagues throughout the colonies that Europeans and Madagascans favored continuing the war. Enthusiastic messages flowed from one colony to another for a week.

In French Equatorial Africa Boisson's enthusiasm manifested itself on 18 June. He sent telegrams to Governor Masson in Gabon, de Saint-Mart in Oubangui-Chari, and Eboué in Fort Lamy that "A.E.F. is remaining in the war." The next day Eboué sent Boisson a petition from members of the Fort Lamy Chamber of Commerce for the creation of an African Bloc, a grouping of French colonies which could ally with the Belgian Congo and the English.[40] And in a coded telegram Eboué asked Boisson for immediate instructions concerning liaisons with British colonies and French West Africa.

Boisson made contact with Brunot, high commissioner (governor general) of Cameroun, Cayla, governor general of French West Africa, and the French governors and residents general in North Africa asking them to inform him of the decisions they were taking. On 24 and 25 June Boisson cabled Morocco, Tunisia, and Algeria: "Are ready to unite with North Africa."

Governor General Boisson's resolve to continue was then shaken by the failure of the North African possessions to respond to his telegrams, for he regarded Tunisia, Algeria, and Morocco as the key. He hesitated while his subordinates pressed him to move; to the lieutenant governor of Gabon he wrote: "You must understand that we cannot throw A.E.F. by itself into some adventure." On the 27th Boisson changed his mind. To Cayla in Dakar and de Coppet in Tananarive the governor general first wrote that he and they might continue the war without North Africa and asked them what they thought. But a little later the same day he sent another telegram to Dakar and marked it "personal" for Cayla only. He said he had heard over BBC shortwave that changes in administrative positions had been decided and offered to meet the governor general of French West Africa to talk about them.

[40] Printed in *Courrier d'Afrique,* 25 June 1940.

In effect, what the BBC had been broadcasting was the news that the French government, still at Bordeaux, decided to name Boisson high commissioner (a newly created post) for all of Tropical Africa and to name Cayla governor general of Madagascar. Although Boisson received no telegram from Bordeaux because of poor communications, the news was indeed true, and he must have known it. Tezenas du Montcel, an inspector of colonies, arrived by air from France the same day and certainly must have told him about the nomination or brought him the message.[41] General de Gaulle, who clearly knew about the nomination of Boisson, tried to offset the government's initiative by asking him to be a member of his newly created Council for the Defense of the Empire and to organize the colony for a continuation of the war. De Gaulle also tried to hearten him by claiming American war matériel was already on its way to French Equatorial Africa and that Boisson could have anything he wanted in the way of weapons to continue the war.

The next day, 28 June, Boisson telegraphed his subordinates denying the news of the previous day: "Have received no communication relative to this nomination." But on 29 June Governor Cayla reportedly informed Boisson he would leave soon for Madagascar and that the governor general of French Equatorial Africa should proceed as soon as possible to Dakar which would be his headquarters as high commissioner. The Ministry of Colonies also transmitted the texts of the armistice with Italy, but Boisson does not seem to have transmitted them to Eboué, perhaps because he feared stirring up anger in Tchad.

The Ministry of Colonies installed at Vichy with Henry Lémery, Eboué's acquaintance from his days in Martinique, as Minister. Lémery forbade any contact with British agents then circulating through the empire with messages from General de Gaulle.

---

41 Médecin-Général A. Sicé, *L'A.E.F. et le Cameroun au service de la France* (Paris: Presses Universitaires de France, 1946), p. 89. It should be noted that Sicé and the other sources used disliked Boisson and opposed him in the next couple of years, but it still seems he must have known about the nomination before he admitted it. The point is important because he claimed that it was the inability of North Africa to lead the colonies into war and not personal ambition that made him go along with the nomination and give up the idea of continuing the war.

The British were, of course, worried that their former allies would become enemies, thus threatening the security of their colonies of Nigeria, and Anglo-Egyptian Sudan, and separating British West Africa from its most direct air route to the Middle East and Suez. They decided to blockade French colonies until they found out if they would work with Vichy or with General de Gaulle; they sent missions to Cameroun, Brazzaville, and Niger to talk to the French. In Gabon the British consul also attempted to make contact with people favorable to a continuation of the war under de Gaulle.

Boisson ordered a halt to British activities and Vichy sent Admiral Platon to offset British efforts. Platon warned officials to follow orders from Vichy and maintain their discipline. On 6 July Boisson refused to continue the war, using as an excuse the fact that North Africa, Morocco, Algeria, and Tunisia had not taken the lead, for reasons he admitted he did not know.[42] The May and June spirit to resist and to continue the war collapsed, and Boisson, admitting he was accepting a new post, left Brazzaville for Dakar 20 July. He passed through Fort Lamy where Tchad's leaders secretly made plans to act alone.

TCHAD'S INITIATIVE

Messages from the British and from General de Gaulle had begun to arrive in Fort Lamy shortly after the fall of France, but Eboué only informed Europeans, at that time, of the encouraging and rousing telegrams from Boisson which he read in public. Eboué's first reactions to the communications from London, transmitted via Northern Nigerian telegraph stations, were to answer respectfully and defer to his superior in Brazzaville. As a career administrator he could imagine no other procedure, particularly when he had no doubt that Boisson would provide the leadership necessary to continue the war. On 23 June Eboué telegraphed his response to one British message:

> Very happy to receive your message. I want you to know that resolution to continue the war on the side of Great Britain is certain but before taking action I must wait for directives from Governor General

[42] Speech, 6 July 1940, printed in *Courrier d'Afrique,* 9 July 1940.

of A.E.F. to whom I am transmitting your message. Be assured that
the feeling of the governor general will be at the same level as those
of the British Empire. I appreciate very much the nobility of your
message, and I think that soon we shall be able to begin joint action
on the basis of a common accord between competent authorities of
the Anglo-French bloc. My very best regards. Eboué.

That they should continue the war seemed natural to most
Frenchmen in Tchad. For at least a year and a half they had been
building strategic roads, recruiting troops whom they had
trained, listening to patriotic speeches, and given the chance, they
believed they could win handily against any Italian incursion
into Tchad. After 24 June, however, they wondered if an Italian
armistice commission might be allowed to enter their colony
without a fight.

On 26 June Eboué sent a forceful letter to Boisson to encourage the governor general who was still hesitating to act. He suggested the immediate organization of an African Bloc headed by
one person and assisted by a council composed of representatives
from the member colonies and subordinate to General de Gaulle
in London. He further suggested as much financial autonomy as
possible. Although England promised aid, the French should
raise taxes and find other sources of income to maintain financial
independence. On 29 June Eboué sent a message through Nigeria
to General de Gaulle that Tchad appreciated his stand, and
de Gaulle responded by saying that all colonies should name a
representative to serve as a liaison between himself and the colonial officials. Boisson remained inactive.

At the beginning of July Eboué and Laurentie talked about
what to do. Eboué had not communicated with the British about
possible cooperation since 23 June. They decided to take the initiative by making contact directly with the British to find out
how Tchad might remain in the war. Economic problems also
concerned Eboué, for trade with France due to the war and due
to a British blockade necessitated a rationing system in Tchad.
On 4 July Eboué sent a telegram to Kaduna, the capital of the
Northern territories of Nigeria: "Have asked Governor General
for instructions for liaison with neighboring colonies stop I have
received nothing stop Because of need to examine urgently ques-

tions affecting our colonies have honor to ask you to send as soon
as possible your representatives to Fort Lamy."

The Kano airport telegraph station received the message but
replied that they would send it to Lagos for de-coding in spite of
the fact that others report the message was not coded. On 5 June
Bernard Bourdillon, governor of Nigeria, sent Eboué a message:
"I received with great pleasure the invitation of Your Excellency
stop The governor [sic] of the Northern Provinces of Nigeria is
preparing to visit you immediately as my envoy."

T. S. Adams, Chief Commissioner of the Northern Provinces,
and his interpreter, the administrator L. C. Giles, had previously
gone on a mission to Niger to try to convince the French stationed
at a military base at Zinder to work with them, but having had no
success were unsure what they would find in Tchad. The two Englishmen arrived late on 5 July. The 5th and 6th were charged
with tension for Eboué.

The morning of the 5th a military representative of the commander of French troops in French West Africa had arrived from
Zinder to explain the Italian armistice. He visited Eboué's office
in the afternoon with Colonel Marchand who had taken command of French troops in Tchad just before the June defeat.
The representative explained that French troops would have to
be withdrawn from posts along the Libyan frontier and that Italians might enter Tchad to survey these posts. He said the Italians
would not come with soldiers and that Tchad would, in any case,
remain French.

Eboué responded dryly that although he appreciated the information, he could not consider the report as official for he did not
take orders from Dakar or Zinder. He also objected to the closing
of any posts and the removal of any soldiers, claiming that the
presence of soldiers was necessary to watch over the nomads. The
representative, who knew about the planned arrival of Adams
and Giles from Marchand, forbade any military man to go to the
airport to greet them. He then told Eboué the English had already
visited Zinder in an attempt to form an African Bloc and that most
recently the British had blockaded French Niger—a landlocked
colony like Tchad—by forbidding any commerce between it and
Nigeria.

Eboué and Laurentie then left for the airport to meet Adams and Giles whom they took immediately to the governor's residence.[43] Many Frenchmen had come to greet the visitors, despite the British attack on the French fleet just a few days before; that set a cordial note for the beginning of discussions, which started with Eboué's direct question: "If Tchad declares openly that she rejects the armistice and remains in the war, what can you give her for her defense? We consider that we need arms and above all a few 'planes and A.A. guns at once."

The British at this juncture stood alone to face the Germans in Europe, and as yet Nigeria was under-equipped militarily. They could not provide arms, but they could purchase Tchad's cotton and hides, thus giving the French colony needed currency to replace the unstable French franc.

In another house in Fort Lamy, that of Colonel Marchand, the representative from Dakar continued to speak to French officers.[44] He said that France, deceived once by British promises of help before June 1940, now had to submit to the armistice without counting on the British. By quietly building its forces the French in Africa might one day commence the war again. Several of the officers objected that it would be impossible to build up French forces under the eyes of the Germans and Italians.

A military delegation then went from Marchand's house to Eboué's house and asked Adams for his suggestion. Adams explained the British would like to see Tchad with General de Gaulle, that they would support the colony economically, and that they would even accept French refugees if worse came to worse. The delegation then returned to Colonel Marchand who after first refusing to meet Adams, agreed, finally, to speak with him.

In the course of the conversation between the British and the

---

[43] L. C. Giles very kindly wrote on 30 October 1967 an account of his relations with the French. I am relying on parts of it here. The whole document, called "First British Contacts with Eboué (1940)," is on file with the Oxford University Colonial Records Project. I am also relying on interviews with Governor General H. Laurentie Néron, 1968, 1969.

[44] This account comes from an unpublished manuscript, "Le Ralliement du Tchad" by Ronan, dated 1 March 1948, and has some unconfirmed information.

French a message arrived from Maurice Adam, head of Ouaddai department, that he had received a secret message from his British counterpart across the frontier in Anglo-Egyptian Sudan. The message, expressing concern about Italian troops reportedly massing along the Sudanese-Ethiopian frontier, asked what the French reaction would be if the British "should find themselves obliged to withdraw into Tchad."[45] The French and two Britishers were disturbed by the message, but decided to wait for a clarification from Nigeria. Marchand, who returned to his house, apparently told the military about the message, implying the British were far weaker than had been thought.[46]

Adams left 8 July, carrying with him Eboué's belief that Boisson might decide to continue the fight. Giles stayed on to work out economic agreements between Tchad and Nigeria, while Laurentie went with Adams in order to speak directly with Governor Bourdillon in Lagos.

For the time being Bourdillon wanted—or so Laurentie interpreted his thought—Tchad to serve as a quiet nucleus for an African Bloc wihch, once it was formed, could begin the battle against Germany openly. It still seemed, for example, that Brunot might lead Cameroun to the British side. He confirmed Adams' statements that the British would take responsibility for the economy of Tchad but wanted data on the colony's stocks and rate of production. He denied there was any possibility British troops might have to leave Sudan. After leaving Bourdillon Laurentie went to see the American consul, Percy Just, who reported to Washington that the governor of Tchad clearly planned to remain in the war on the side of the British.[47] Laurentie left Lagos thinking that for the time being Tchad's position should be one of friendly neutrality while establishing economic relations with Nigeria and waiting for coordinated efforts with other French colonies. He returned to Fort Lamy 10 July with an English officer whom Colonel Marchand refused to see. The latter had received objections from Niger to conversations with the British.

[45] Giles, "First British Contacts," p. 2.
[46] Ronan, "Le Ralliement du Tchad," p. 20.
[47] U.S. State, 740.0011, European War, 1939/4569, Telegram, Consul, Lagos, 10 July 1940.

The day of Laurentie's return Eboué wrote a report to Governor General Boisson, just after the head of French Equatorial Africa had said publicly that the group of colonies could not continue the war. His purpose was to offset Boisson's suspicions. Eboué wrote that many in Tchad wanted to continue the war alongside the British and that the visits of Adams had helped calm them, serving thus a useful purpose. Eboué added the idea that French forces in Ouaddai should be reinforced, for in spite of the armistice the Italians might cross Sudan into Tchad. Laurentie read the report and thought it would be a good idea to emphasize the economic aspect of relations with Nigeria in order further to obviate Boisson's suspicions and counteract any other reports he might have received from Marchand or anyone else not at that time in favor of collaboration with Britain. Laurentie added a few paragraphs to Eboué's report, writing that Nigeria had decided to purchase some cotton from Tchad; neither Adams nor Giles spoke about political or military matters, he claimed.[48] Boisson responded on 15 July that he saw nothing wrong with strictly commercial relations but that Eboué must avoid any political or military agreements with the British.

Giles began to work out the economic agreements with Louis Michel, an administrator of pro-Vichy persuasion. The two worked on "the import/export needs and possibilities of Tchad and the possibility of improving her meagre communications with Nigeria (a poor dry-season road to Maiduguri: dry-season roads to Garoua in French Cameroons and thence river-transport down the Benue)."[49] Giles, accompanied by Cazenave de la Roche and Laurentie also went to the Cercle for drinks and general discussion with the French who gathered there in the evening "without [his] being able to say too openly that Eboué would make a declaration at the right time. . . ."[50]

The next few weeks were difficult for Eboué and Laurentie. They had made no political or military commitments to the British who wanted "a guarantee of a completely friendly attitude to-

[48] "Note personnelle pour Monsieur le Gouverneur Général Boisson," Félix Eboué, 10 July 1940.
[49] Giles, "First British Contacts," p. 3.
[50] *Ibid.*

ward Great Britain" as Giles wrote Eboué on 19 July. But if they came out openly for Britain, they risked strong reprisals from Brazzaville or even an attack from Niger without being able to defend themselves; the British could not help militarily. But if they did not come out for Britain, the British might not help economically; and if they did not come out for Britain and de Gaulle quite soon, some of their own subordinates might take initiatives threatening the unity of action and command that Eboué wanted.

Some Frenchmen had left Tchad in order to join the British. Eboué had asked his subordinates to wait and have confidence in him, but their attitude toward him was similar to his attitude toward Boisson, and some acted on their own, just as he had done. At Abéché, for example, Maurice Adam sent a subordinate into Anglo-Egyptian Sudan to consult with British authorities about a possible union of their forces, and they continued consultations into July. Adam and his assistant "felt free to act to ally our department with Sudan because we believed the French government, humiliated and defeated, had no control over its own decision-making at Vichy."[51]

On 20 July Boisson arrived by plane in Fort Lamy. He told Eboué he had been appointed Vichy's high commissioner and was on his way to Dakar to take up his post. Eboué received him courteously and they talked about Eboué's children in France; Boisson advised him to ask the Minister of Colonies, Henry Lémery, for information about Ginette, Henry and Robert. He also told Eboué that Giles, the English representative, must leave,[52] and Eboué agreed to follow orders.

Eboué drove Boisson to the small city hall where a group of French officials and businessmen waited. Boisson told them there was no possibility of continuing the war and that colonies must have the discipline to follow government orders. His statements angered them. According to one account, at least one man wanted to shoot Boisson; according to another, someone urged Eboué

---

[51] Interview with Adam's assistant, Georges Tourot, Bangui, 31 July 1968.
[52] Governor General Henri Laurentie, "Le Refus du Tchad," in Edgard de Larminat, *Chroniques Irrévérencieuses* (Paris: Plon, 1962), Appendix III, p. 386.

to arrest him, but Eboué declined, saying that such an action might hurt Tchad more than help it.[53] As Eboué and Boisson walked out of the building, Eboué, lagging a bit behind, turned back to the crowd and signalled to them to be calm and patient. Boisson left.[54]

General Husson, military commander of French Equatorial Africa in 1940, had traveled as far as Fort Lamy with Boisson and became acting governor general the day Boisson left. On 21 July, the day Husson was to fly back to Brazzaville, he agreed to meet briefly with Giles, who had not yet departed for Nigeria: "Laurentie and de la Roche bundled me into my uniform and a car, and we drove to the airport. The engines of Husson's 'plane were already running. I stammered out my message with all the tactful eloquence I could, begging him in Great Britain's name to continue the fight against the common enemy." The sound of engines drowned out the conversation, and the plane was soon in the air. Giles left Tchad on 29 July with a letter of support from Eboué to General de Gaulle, and Giles and Eboué agreed that Tchad would rally to de Gaulle's movement when the general himself thought the time was right.[55]

Eboué signed no formal agreement with the British, for to do so would have been beyond his powers as lieutenant governor. He hoped that Cameroun's Brunot and acting Governor General Husson, who had the authority, would provide the leadership. At the beginning of August Eboué was expecting to receive British goods coming by boat along the Benué River through Cameroun. Adams telegraphed Eboué, however, that because Brunot forbade the visit of British ships and airplanes to Cameroun's port, Douala, the British had refused to allow boats to cross Cameroun via the Benué River to Tchad. Adams hinted Eboué should perhaps act toward Cameroun: "If you were in control of Garoua, the situation would not be the same. Please understand that the governor wants very much to help you. . . ."[56] Diplo-

53 Letter, A. C. Picut to Brian Weinstein, 23 July 1969.
54 Interview, His Excellency Mohammad Bechir Sow, Fort Lamy, 29 May 1968.
55 Giles, "First British Contacts," pp. 4-5.
56 Telegram, T. S. Adams to Félix Eboué, 11 August 1940.

matic relations between Britain and France had been broken, and Laval was by this time shouting that Britain, not Germany, was France's true enemy.

There was still no word from London about what coordinated action to take, and some of Eboué's subordinates, uneasy at the wait that they did not fully understand, began to doubt that Tchad would continue in the war. They argued early and late whether an administrator or a military man could disobey orders received from superior officers, for the Ministry of Colonies expressly forbade any relations between the French colonies and the British. Boisson, in a personal letter to Eboué on 10 August, seemed as ambiguous: ". . . to move towards the goal that we all desire, the more we are ourselves, the stronger we shall be, the more possibilities we shall have and the more they will be efficacious. . . . Keep the morale of everyone high without morbid excitement. Let everyone do his work . . . without intrigue. . . ."[57]

Husson, to whom Eboué wrote in August, repeated to him that he would do something about the economic situation and that any attempt to establish relations with the British would be severely punished. Husson did not specifically threaten Eboué, for it seemed that the Vichy government was worried much more by Brunot in Cameroun. A Vichy policy that affected Eboué more directly, however, was a request for a list of all Freemasons under his authority. The Nazis and some of the most important supporters of Vichy were violently anti-masonic, and the regime was preparing to abolish the Grand Orient and Grande Loge de France, which it did on 19 August 1940. Eboué ignored the request, and bided his time.[58]

THE "THREE GLORIOUS DAYS"

While he did so, General de Gaulle and the British in London formally agreed that the French leader would "proceed with the constitution of a French force consisting of volunteers [to be] utilized against common enemies." The British guaranteed to provide this force with the same equipment used by their own

[57] Archives Eboué, Letter, Pierre Boisson to Félix Eboué, 10 August 1940.
[58] Interview, Eugénie Eboué, 10 May 1968.

armies, and to pay French soldiers for the time being. The agreement implied that the French would repay such funds eventually.[59] What de Gaulle now needed of course was men, resources, and land he could use as a base. Carlton Gardens, where his offices were located, was really all that de Gaulle had at the beginning of August 1940. New Hebrides and New Caledonia in the Pacific, where a movement to rally to de Gaulle had begun, were minor outposts lacking the importance of Equatorial Africa.

To prepare the necessary group action in French Equatorial Africa and Cameroun—the only areas where a sizable number of Frenchmen had made their feelings known—de Gaulle sent three men on a mission to Africa on 5 August. They were Commandant Leclerc, a military man who had joined him in London and was to be headquartered in Accra as his representative to the British military; René Pleven, a businessman; and Captain Didier de Boislambert. They were to form a mobile team to act on their own.

In Lagos on 11 August they joined Colonel Edgard de Larminat, a career military man who had left his post with French forces in the Middle East to join de Gaulle;[60] the fifth member of the group was Colonna d'Ornano, Eboué's former subordinate who had left Brazzaville, where he had been reassigned, to find a way to continue the war. The five made their plans, buoyed by British offers of assistance.

They decided that de Larminat would go to Leopoldville to try to begin a movement in Brazzaville for de Gaulle; Leclerc and de Boislambert would go to Cameroun; and Pleven and d'Ornano would go to Fort Lamy. They further decided that because of Eboué, Tchad would be the starting point of the rally and that if Colonel Marchand offered resistance, d'Ornano, already known by the military of Tchad, would seize command.[61]

On 24 August Pleven and d'Ornano flew to Fort Lamy where Eboué, who had been informed of their arrival, assembled a large crowd to greet them. Although it was the rainy season, the day was clear and from the airplane Pleven saw the crowd, not sure if

59 Agreement signed 7 August, printed in De Gaulle, *Mémoires de guerre*, I, 279-82.
60 Edgard de Larminat, *Chroniques irrévérencieuses* (Paris: Plon, 1962).
61 Interview with President René Pleven, Paris, 20 June 1969.

they were there to greet them or arrest them. When they landed, Pleven and d'Ornano, somewhat apprehensive, stepped out, only to be rushed by a man who thrust into Pleven's hands a bouquet of flowers, blue, white, and red; the crowd erupted into cheers for de Gaulle's representatives.

Eboué escorted them to his residence, where he asked Pleven to speak to the Europeans about his trip and events in France as he and General de Gaulle saw them. In the next two days Pleven met with the European civilians; he explained that the catastrophe which struck France could be overcome with General de Gaulle's plan to keep France in the war, thus keeping France an active participant in any decision-making affecting the future of Europe. In the meanwhile d'Ornano explained de Gaulle's program to the military. Marchand was absent on tour before the mission's arrival but returned and was finally convinced to join with Eboué and most of the young military men whose enthusiasm for a continuation of the war had never waned.

On 26 August the European population was invited to the town hall of Fort Lamy. Pleven and d'Ornano stood at the rear of the room. At the front was Colonel Marchand with Eboué at his side; Marchand read a statement drafted by Pleven, Eboué, and Laurentie proclaiming the adherence of Tchad to General de Gaulle's developing movement and to an alliance with the British to win the war and save the colony from economic disaster: ". . . the restoration of French grandeur and independence require that Overseas France continue to fight alongside Great Britain [and we] proclaim the union of the territory and the troops that protect it with the Free French Forces of General de Gaulle. . . ."[62] Marchand, rather than Eboué, read the statement because his earlier opposition was common knowledge and de Gaulle's representatives wanted to give a military emphasis to the Gaullist movement.[63] Racism among the military men may also have had an influence on the choice of Marchand, who was white, over Eboué.

Eboué, apparently still hoping to change Boisson's and Hus-

[62] Reprinted in Jean Cazenave de la Roche, *Le Gouverneur General Félix Eboué, 1884-1944* (Paris: Hachette, 1957), p. 126.

[63] Interview with President René Pleven, Paris, 20 June 1969.

son's minds, telegraphed Dakar and Brazzaville about the action taken. He said that if they could not approve his action, he would administer Tchad as an autonomous French colony. Husson replied immediately that Eboué had taken a very dangerous step, and Lémery, the Minister of Colonies, stripped Eboué of his functions as governor of Tchad, naming M. Chazelas, who had been lieutenant governor of Mauritania while Eboué was in Soudan, to replace him. The decree had no effect because Eboué telegraphed Dakar that he would not permit Chazelas to land at Fort Lamy. Eboué telegraphed his subordinates on 26 August to explain his action:

> Have decided in agreement with Colonel, the Military Commander, to establish in Tchad a clearly French policy united with the Free French forces of General de Gaulle and in collaboration with our British allies. Economic agreements have been signed with Nigeria [and] similar agreements will be signed with Sudan. These actions will safeguard interests confided to us and will remove possibility of ruin which menaced us. It is necessary that all work at their posts in spirit perfect discipline knowing that our efforts henceforth only work to save France and to revive French spirit in Empire and conserve Tchad Territory for our country. Publish [this] and listen to French radio [from] London.
>
> Eboué.

The action in Tchad was quickly known elsewhere in Equatorial Africa, and that same night Leclerc and de Boislambert, with help from British secret agent, Major Allen, arrived in Douala, the Camerounese port, and seized the most important offices. The next day, 27 August, Leclerc declared Cameroun to be part of the Free French Movement: "I have taken, beginning today 27 August and in the name of the General the post of General Commissioner. Cameroun proclaims its political and economic independence. It is ready to take its place in the French Colonial Empire, free and decided, to continue the struggle at the side of the Allies, under the orders of General de Gaulle until complete victory."[64] When the news arrived in Fort Lamy about the Cameroun coup, necessary because of Brunot's hesitations, Eboué

64 Poster.

learned that his former Martiniquan colleague in West Africa, Raphael Saller, who had been interested in Eboué's studies in music was playing a key role with Leclerc.[65]

On 28 August young military men in Brazzaville—encouraged by events in Tchad, Cameroun, and by de Larminat across the river—and Médecin-Général Adolphe Sicé, recently appointed head of the health services of Equatorial Africa, seized power, captured Husson, and proclaimed their adherence to the Free French.[66] Oubangui-Chari followed a few days later, the delay due to resistance from the military commander. Gabon declared for General de Gaulle 29 August, but Lieutenant Governor Masson, under considerable pressure from the Catholic bishop and local businessmen dependent on German markets, changed his mind. Military operations from Cameroun, led by Leclerc, and one from Moyen-Congo, led by Commandant Parant, won the territory to the Gaullists during September and October. Masson then committed suicide.

In three days the movement of General de Gaulle became something more than a dispirited group of people gathered in London. With the adherence of French Equatorial Africa and Cameroun to his cause General de Gaulle had control of a vast, strategically located territory; over 7,000,000 people; and resources not as valuable as those in West Africa but valuable nonetheless. Most important de Gaulle could now more truthfully claim that France was still in the war.

The rally to Brazzaville and Cameroun depended on coups from outside; Oubangui-Chari depended on pressure from neighbors; and that of Gabon on military action. The adherence of Tchad depended on Eboué's decisive leadership.

This was, of course, also significant for his career and illustrative of his view of his purpose. He had believed that his role as an administrator was to bring about economic change and organization for modernization as the French defined it for their colonies. This view did not prevent him from thinking about some broad political questions, however; the contents of his li-

[65] For an account of Leclerc's actions see Henry Maule, *Out of the Sand* (London: Odhams Books, 1966), pp. 53-63.

[66] Sicé, *L'A.E.F. et le Cameroun au service de la France*, pp. 146-59.

brary were proof enough of that.[67] Although he believed political matters were secondary, he made a very important political decision affecting France and the war effort. Why he did when others did not is an interesting question that cannot be explained by a single factor. One writer says that he was a black man and could not see how he could continue his career under a regime linked with racist Nazi Germany; another that he was a Freemason and knew the Vichyists were taking action against the lodges; a third that he was a socialist and a Popular Front governor and knew of the hostility of those in power to the Popular Front; a fourth that he was compelled by the economic situation in Tchad to follow de Gaulle in order to open French trade with Britain. In any case, some still say, Eboué betrayed his role as an administrator because he refused to obey orders coming from Vichy and joined a "rebel" movement.[68]

But the question of disobedience was clearly irrelevant. Everyone had been ready to continue the war, and they did not because they felt themselves too weak to do so or saw personal advantage in adhering to Vichy. Ten years after the event, Marcel Peyrouton, resident of Tunisia, wrote simply that he did not rally because General Noguès, head of Morocco, did not. Noguès refused because he thought the navy would not follow him and that the weapons and men at his disposal in North Africa would be insufficient. The proximity of North Africa to Fascist-controlled western Europe ensured a German invasion of French territory if they tried to continue the war, he thought.[69] The question of being a "rebel" and disobeying came up later after each man, in that extremely difficult period, had chosen a path, then tried to justify the choice.

For each explanation of Eboué's action there were men similarly situated who chose to adhere to Vichy. Candace was also black; Marcel Peyrouton, later named minister and then ambassador of Vichy, was a Freemason. The Popular Front's Prime

67 Victor Cambon, *Notre Avenir* (Paris: Payot, 1919), p. 9.

68 Henry Lémery, *D'Une République à l'autre: souvenirs de la mêlée politique 1894-1944* (Paris: La Table Ronde, 1964), p. 260.

69 Marcel Peyrouton, *Du Service public à la prison commune; souvenirs* (Paris: Plon, 1950), p. 72.

Minister *chef de cabinet* Deschamps never denied his socialist
loyalties, but he followed orders from Vichy and was named governor of Ivory Coast. Niger was in as difficult an economic situation as Tchad.

If there were any factors about Eboué's personality or particular concerns which affected his decision they were his deeply felt
disappointment when the Ministry of Colonies prevented him
from joining the army to fight for France in World War I and
secondly his determination to follow through on policies which
he regarded as correct, like the introduction of cotton in Oubangui-Chari. Henri Laurentie, a firm, hardworking man provided
the support of a friend that Eboué always needed near him as
well as ideas that Eboué acknowledged in a tribute to him:
". . . my dear Laurentie who, you all know, was for me the best
of collaborators. His civic courage, his intellectual honesty, his
vast culture, his intransigence—all these qualities plus an extraordinary amount of work helped me greatly in the difficult tasks I
had to undertake." Laurentie played a key role, Eboué said, in
the adherence of Tchad. "It is with emotion and affection that I
say to him. Thank you."[70]

The heads of departments and other officials provided the
spirit to fight on in the African Bloc.[71] Eboué, very sensitive to his
proper role as a loyal Frenchman, which he always considered
himself to be, and believing the stoic phrase he often cited:
"There are some things that depend on us, and some that do
not," when it did depend on him acted to influence the course of
the war, despite the risk it posed to him and the possibility of
an attack on Tchad. "Jouez le jeu; take initiative," he said.

The men directly involved at the time saw the real and sym-
bolic importance of Eboué's role. General de Gaulle immediately declared that Tchad "has shown the path of duty and has
given the signal of recovery to the whole French Empire."[72] and
in February 1941 named Eboué to his newly created Order of
the Liberation with Leclerc and de Larminat. Leclerc signed a

[70] Félix Eboué, "Discours en Conseil d'Administration," Afrique Francaise
Libre, Brazzaville, 19 November 1942, pp. 7-8.
[71] Interviews with H. Laurentie, G. Torrot, and Médecin-Général A. Diagne.
[72] de Gaulle, *Mèmoires de guerre,* I, p. 289.

picture of himself "To Governor General Eboué whose position in 1940 will always be an historic example for all Frenchmen."[73] And, lastly, Richard Brunot, who faltered at the head of Cameroun but who joined the Free French after the "Three Glorious Days," wrote to Eboué: "I pay you the tribute . . . that is due to you, to you, my dear Eboué, more than to any other man."[74]

[73] Signed picture, 11 December 1942, Eboué library.

[74] Archives Eboué, Letter, Richard Brunot to Félix Eboué, 18 November 1941.

IX

GOVERNOR GENERAL, 1940-1944

IMMEDIATELY after the 26 August declaration Eboué told his assembled subordinates that if their loyalties lay with Vichy, they could sign a list and leave for Niger without fear of harm. One of the first men to step forward was Louis Michel, in charge of the colony's economic affairs; as he signed, another administrator, enraged, slapped him in the face. Eboué demanded calm, and others—some military men, administrators, and most physicians with the exception of Dr. Adolphe Diagne—signed.

In the next two days Eboué prepared to send to Dakar the personal files of the pro-Vichy administrators, thus permitting them to continue their careers in West Africa. In the case of Michel, the governor praised his administrative skills in spite of his political views and suggested his future superiors promote him.[1] Eboué's refusal to let political differences interfere with his opinion of an official or his relations with a friend had always been unusual, but in these circumstances it was surprising and annoying to his closest associates and his wife.

After the Vichyists left by truck for Niger radio broadcasts from France and West Africa unleashed a barrage of insults and threats to the families of those in Tchad who had rallied to General de Gaulle, for many wives and children remained in

[1] Interview, His Excellency Mohammad Bechir Sow, Fort Lamy, 30 May 1968. Sow was the clerk who typed Eboué's papers at this time.

France. Letters arrived advising administrators to change their position, seize the colony to follow Pétain, instead of following de Gaulle and "that Negro" or "that Mulatto" Eboué. The governor was at least as vulnerable to threats as others; his years as an administrator, a socialist, a mason, and a Popular Front governor had made enemies, any of whom could point out his highly visible family to the Vichy government in southern France or to the Germans occupying northern France. There was no news of the whereabouts of Henry and Robert and no response to the desperate letters Madame Eboué wrote to Ginette.

Instead of retreating, Eboué sent telegrams to the governor of Niger asking him to rally to General de Gaulle. He sent other communications to Léopold Allys, secretary general of Soudan and other friends; using Lagos as a communications center, Eboué asked the British to cable old friends whose names he provided in Guadeloupe, Martinique, and Guyane. To Philippe Saccharin he wrote: "Courage—Confiance—Vive la France Libre —Affections Eboué." Although Eboué, de Gaulle, and the others expected their action would begin a large movement in the other colonies, none adhered immediately to the Free French.

Laurentie and Eboué flew to Brazzaville to confer with de Larminat on 10 September. De Larminat explained his intended organization of the colonies, and Eboué asked him to send some physicians to Tchad and promised to keep up the propaganda toward Niger in the vain hope of a rally to General de Gaulle. Eboué, then recorded for later broadcasts an appeal to citizens and subjects in the colonies to follow the new leader. Referring to himself as a child of the empire he asked his Antillean and Guyanese compatriots and the inhabitants of all other colonies to think of themselves as Frenchmen and to reject the Vichy government: "France has drawn us closer and closer to her heart and her spirit. France has done more than adopt us; she has given herself to us. In return, we have entrusted ourselves, body and soul, to her genius; by feeling and by reasoning we are without reservations Frenchmen." He said that the Vichy government, prisoners of the Germans, was betraying the colonies and would lead them to economic ruin: "Enough of this treason. We shall remain French in spite of the illegitimate masters. Already

French Equatorial Africa has risen for national salvation. Everyone, follow its example. From the Caribbean to the Mediterranean, from the Gulf of Guinea to the Pacific. On your feet, Empire, that wants to remain French. On your feet, sons of the
Empire, for the salvation of the homeland. Stand up with all
your force and all your love for France."[2]

Eboué and Laurentie returned to Fort Lamy to await news
from General de Gaulle, then en route from Britain to Dakar by
warship in an attempt to seize or rally the capital of French West
Africa. The sad news arrived at the end of the month that the
French of Dakar, rather than rallying, had fired on the Free
French, killing some and preventing an effective landing. The
failure to win the administration and military in West Africa
threatened the safety of those who already joined de Gaulle; in
Tchad an invasion from Niger was feared and to block such a
move Marchand ordered troops to the frontier.

The apprehension had some basis in fact; during a meeting
between Hiter and Pétain in October, they discussed the possible
re-taking of Tchad and other Free French colonies.[3] Laval later
talked specifically about Tchad to his cabinet:

> One day, at the Council of Ministers, Mr. Laval took a small piece of
> paper out of his pocket. It was a tiny map of Africa. In an evasive
> way, he spoke about Tchad, occupied by the Gaullists, its strategic
> value, and the need to maintain the rights of the government over all
> the territory constituting our empire. Nothing more.
> Another day, he alluded to conversations with General Huntziger
> and General von Varlimont of the German General Staff. They con-
> cerned an action to re-take Tchad, a military operation. . . .[4]

There was, however, only one attack on Fort Lamy, on 22 January 1942 when an enemy airplane bombed the airport destroying gasoline supplies.

After the failure to take Dakar de Gaulle continued to Lagos.

[2] Archives Eboué, message from Brazzaville, 16 September 1940.

[3] Henry Lémery, *D'Une République à l'autre: souvenirs de la mêlée politique 1894-1944* (Paris: La Table Ronde, 1964), pp. 269-70.

[4] Marcel Peyrouton, *Du Service public à la prison commune; souvenirs*
(Paris: Plon, 1950), p. 176.

In his memoirs de Gaulle omits mention of his sojourn there; it was a disheartening one, for although he received encouraging news from de Larminat, the reaction of local Frenchmen was cold at best when he admitted his mistake in trying to rally Dakar and when he asked them for their support.[5] On 8 October he arrived in Douala, Cameroun, to a very warm welcome organized by Leclerc. The demonstration revived de Gaulle's spirits, convincing him of his mission.[6] He then flew to Tchad where Eboué called on the Europeans and Africans to greet him enthusiastically. In his speech of greeting, Eboué said that General de Gaulle alone denied France's defeat; de Gaulle alone proclaimed the need to continue the war, and Tchad would fight; "You have taken into your hands the salvation of France: Tchad is at your service for the war and for the victory."[7]

The supporters in Fort Lamy, like the enthusiasm at Douala, were important insofar as they buoyed de Gaulle's spirits: "I found in Tchad a vibrant atmosphere. Everyone had the feeling that the spotlight of History had just focussed on this land of merit and suffering."[8] The general sensed Eboué's loyalty immediately and realized he had a man willing and capable of undertaking more important responsibilities: "Eboué received me in Fort Lamy. I felt that he gave me, once and for all, his loyalty and his confidence. At the same time, I noted he was broadminded enough to understand the vast projects I wanted to involve him in."[9]

The general told Eboué of his plans to build more roads and air facilities for better communications between British West Africa and the Middle East and to open a new front against the Axis Powers: "My intention was to establish on the borders of Tchad and Libya a theatre of Saharan operations to wait for the day when events would permit a French column to seize the Fezzan [in southern Libya] and to move out from it toward the

5 United States National Archives, State Department files (*Infra*, U.S. State), 740.0011, European War, 1939/7218, Report, Consul, Lagos, 3 October 1940.
6 Charles de Gaulle, *Mémoires de guerre: l'appel 1940-1942*, Vol. I (Paris: Plon, 1954), p. 111.
7 Archives Eboué, copy of speech.
8 de Gaulle, *Mémoires de guerre*, I, p. 112.
9 *Ibid.*

Mediterranean."[10] The two discussed developments in France,
and de Gaulle promised to help find the Eboué children.

With Colonel Marchand, de Gaulle flew into northern Tchad
to visit French and African troops. When he returned to Fort
Lamy, General Catroux, former governor general of Indochina,
who outranked de Gaulle, had arrived. Eboué prepared one of
his dinners, during which de Gaulle toasted Catroux, who, rumor had it, might receive British backing to replace de Gaulle.
Catroux responded that he would follow orders from de Gaulle.[11]

On 24 October de Gaulle arrived in Brazzaville "very relaxed,
brightened up by the atmosphere of loyalty, confidence and reso-
lution. . . ."[12] He, de Larminat, and Pleven discussed the future
organization of the territory and the military operations then in
course in Gabon; de Larminat had been titled Head of the Free
French Africa, and Pleven, Secretary General of Equatorial
Africa.

FORT LAMY TO BRAZZAVILLE

But by the end of October Free French organization was still
practically non-existent. On 27 October de Gaulle issued a mani-
festo claiming legitimacy for his movement and began to organize a
type of government in exile. He accused the Vichy government
of not being independent; a "new power" was necessary to
"direct the French war effort"; "circumstances" chose de Gaulle,
he said, to lead. The general said he would act in the name of
France and created a Council for the Defense of the Empire
which would act as a type of government; he named Eboué, Leclerc, de Larminat, and six others to it. It was clear, however,
from the organization and powers of the Council that orders
would come from de Gaulle and that it would be purely advisory.

While his supporters were completing the conquest of Gabon,
the general decided to reorganize the colonies and to give Eboué
more responsibilities by naming him the head of French Equatorial Africa. Before making the formal appointment he told Gov-

---

[10] *Ibid.,* p. 111.

[11] *Ibid.,* pp. 113-14.

[12] Edgar de Larminat, *Chroniques irrévérencieuses* (Paris: Plon, 1962), p.
172.

ernor General Ryckmans of Congo of his intentions and told Lord
Hailey, a distinguished British official then visiting the French
and Belgian territories at the head of an economic mission. They
agreed with the nomination, and Lord Hailey, who told de
Gaulle that he knew and liked Eboué, was particularly enthusiastic.[13] The American consul in Leopoldville reported, however:
"While the appointment is looked upon with some misgivings
by the Belgians and the British, they all readily admit that Mr.
Eboué is a brilliant and cultivated man who has had years of
experience in African colonies and knows more about French
Equatorial Africa than anyone else on the scene."[14]

That de Gaulle might consult with the British and the Belgians before making such a nomination seems untypical of his
style and suggests some concern about the reaction to a black
governor general, for the Belgians, in particular, were known
as blatant racists. However, given the fact that any governor general of French Equatorial Africa would have to work very closely
with the British and Belgians, it seemed natural to let them
know in advance who the head of A.E.F. would be, and then to
reassure Eboué, which he did by letter.

On 9 November de Gaulle wrote a very long personal letter
to Eboué explaining first how he envisaged the future. There was,
he said, no chance the Vichy government or any of its supporters
would enter the war: "There is no more any doubt that Vichy
is definitely for 'collaboration' with Germany and Italy, a collaboration which will be complete slavery." With the usual
French sensitivity about Anglo-American intentions with regard
to French colonies de Gaulle asked Eboué's advice about "our
position in the Antilles vis-à-vis America," and told him that any
Englishmen in Tchad for a possible military operation against
Libya must understand "that they are on *our territory* and not
on theirs, and that they must go through you and through the
military commander for everything they do." He told Eboué he
planned to name Leclerc military commander of Tchad, replac-

13 Archives Eboué, Letter, Charles de Gaulle to Félix Eboué, 9 November
1940.
14 U.S. State, Letter from American Consulate, Leopoldville, 31 December
1940, 851U.001/7.

ing Marchand, who would work with de Larminat, named commander of Free French military forces in Equatorial Africa. As for Eboué de Gaulle said quite simply, "You yourself will come to Brazzaville as Governor General," adding that the British and the Belgians would accept him in this role.[15]

Eboué's personal ambitions had been satisfied by 1936; he had reached the summit of the administrative corps, administrator in chief in 1930 and succeeded in being named governor in 1936. He had thought that he would retire at the usual age of sixty in 1944, and possibly try his hand at politics in the Caribbean. The war, the Free French movement, and new nomination as governor general of the group of colonies where he had modestly begun his career were totally unexpected.

In Fort Lamy he and his wife read and re-read de Gaulle's letter, talking over the years gone by, the parents who had been ambitious for them, the friends whose help they had had. The conversation turned to their children: Ginette, Henry, Robert, and to Cornélie and her children. Where were they? Were they safe?

Late that night Eboué dictated to his wife his response to General de Gaulle. He wrote a report for de Gaulle on the Antilles and added "Guyane" separately even though de Gaulle, like most metropolitan Frenchmen, did not consider it separately. He accepted de Gaulle's nomination and swore his loyalty once and for all: "And now, general, in spite of my great desire to remain in Tchad, I am very grateful to you for having thought of me for the post of honor at Brazzaville. You know that you can count on my loyalty to you personally and on my devotion for the beautiful cause that we are all defending under your orders."[16] By the time Eboué's response reached Brazzaville, de Gaulle had already named him provisionally to the rank of governor general on 12 November and to the post of governor general of French Equatorial Africa (on 15 July 1941 Eboué became full or permanent governor general in rank, once equivalent to vice-admiral but in the circumstances much higher). The general named

[15] De Gaulle to Eboué, 9 November 1940.

[16] Archives Eboué, copy of Letter, Félix Eboué to Charles de Gaulle, 14 November 1940.

de Larminat high commissioner of Free French Africa, a newly created post, to coordinate activities of French Equatorial Africa and Cameroun.

During the rest of November Eboué and Laurentie blocked out the future organization of French Equatorial Africa. Although military matters would naturally be in the hands of soldiers like Leclerc, de Larminat, and Marchand, civilian authority would provide crucial support, and Eboué considered reform of the administrative structure crucial. He wondered if he would be able to do anything with a high commissioner over him, and he instructed Laurentie, whom he wanted to be close to him in Brazzaville, to fly to the capital to survey the most pressing problems and to begin reorganization if it could be done. Laurentie, named acting secretary general of French Equatorial Africa on Pleven's departure for London, became permanent secretary general; he wrote Eboué his impressions of the work and a series of witty character sketches of the men under Eboué's command. He was optimistic and reassuring: ". . . the ensemble of your projects: administrative simplification, decentralization, and the voluntary contribution—will not meet opposition. There are enough men of good will to succeed." Some re-education of administrators would be necessary, and there were other problems of organization which Eboué and he could undertake with hope of success.[17]

By 8 December the Eboués were ready to move south. Charles had already left for Cairo to enter a French Jesuit school, and the Red Cross was trying to locate the other three children. The evening of the 8th the administrators of Fort Lamy gave Eboué a farewell party and two days later Eboué, his wife, and Jean Cazenave de la Roche, whom he named to head his cabinet, left by automobile for Oubangui-Chari to visit those posts where Eboué had begun his career.

Eboué took his wife and Cazenave de la Roche to Bouca, his first post, and told them about Henri Vendôme, dead years before. At Bozoum he showed Cazenave de la Roche the Karé

17 Archives Eboué, Letter, Henri Laurentie to Félix Eboué, 18 December 1940.

Mountains, where he had fought Oubanguians refusing to cooperate with the administration, and at Damara he pointed out a
spring of fresh water that he had discovered in 1913.[18]

From Bangui they went by boat to Brazzaville, arriving 30
December, four days after Eboué's fifty-sixth birthday and thirty-
one years after the new governor general had first set foot in the
city.

REORGANIZATION AND REFORM

Brazzaville had changed greatly since 1909. It did not compare
with Leopoldville across the river but still had grown from a
mere village of a few hundred inhabitants to a town of over
25,000 in 1940, including about 1000 Europeans. As it grew, the
French divided it like their other colonial cities into commercial, administrative, religious, and African quarters: ". . . through
the trees the buildings of Brazzaville appear in scattered clusters,
for a space of 3 miles. The bank rises gradually to a distant
height of 150 feet, where the cathedral stands in a clearing."[19]
Paved streets, low permanent buildings in the commercial part
of town along the river, and the cement building used for
the administrative offices on "Le Plateau," the hill overlooking
the Congo River, left no doubt about material change. A new
railroad station in the business quarter testified to the completion
of the Congo-Océan Railway in 1934. Africans lived at each end
of the town in "Poto-Poto" and "Bacongo."

Eboué had changed even more, from the athletic young man
of 1909 to a man who looked older than his fifty-six years. He was
graying, stout, weary, and tense. He occasionally used a cane because of arthritic pain in his joints; and was soon to purchase a
hearing aid.

When Eboué's boat arrived in Brazzaville, the military and
civilian authorities greeted the governor general with full honors; he and his wife, accompanied by Laurentie, Cazenave de la

---

[18] Jean Cazenave de la Roche, *Le Gouverneur Général Félix Eboué, 1884-
1944* (Paris: Hachette, 1957), pp. 134-35.

[19] Naval Intelligence Division, *French Equatorial Africa and Cameroons*,
B.R. 515, Geographical Handbook Series (HMSO, Oxford University Press, no
date), p. 380.

Roche, and Georges Céleste, assigned to Brazzaville, quickly moved their belongings into the official residences in the administrative quarter and readied themselves for a series of receptions and conferences.

The day after his arrival in Brazzaville Eboué, his wife, and Laurentie went to lunch at de Larminat's residence. The high commissioner invited Lord Hailey, General Sicé, Hailey's assistant, F. J. Pedler, and a few others. The luncheon was extremely cordial, for British and Free French relations had been clarified for the time being by agreements between de Gaulle and Churchill in London and between Hailey and de Larminat in Brazzaville. In October, before Laurentie's and Eboué's arrival, the British and French signed an agreement providing for the purchase of all of Equatorial Africa's agricultural production then piling up in warehouses, and London agreed to give financial aid beginning at £200,000 per month. At first, of course, the British could not use all the cocoa, palm nuts, coffee, and bananas purchased and either dumped great quantities into the sea or burned them. Their purpose was "to keep things going in A.E.F."[20] Later, however, they and other allies depended on rubber, wood, cotton, and gold from the French territories.

Lord Hailey invited the governor general, his wife, and Laurentie the following week to Leopoldville along with some Frenchmen in the Congolese capital, and he told everyone that he and Eboué were good friends.[21]

Eboué and Hailey could have met sometime before for the Englishman, after a career in India, directed the African Research Survey and must have traveled to Soudan in about 1935, but they were hardly good friends. Hailey's statements, to the Belgians in particular, were designed to bolster Eboué's authority which, the British thought, might be weak on the Leopoldville side of the river.[22] The highest-ranking British officials, Lord Hailey, Sir Bernard Bourdillon, who visited Brazzaville in Feb-

20 Letter, F. J. Pedler to Brian Weinstein, 2 May 1968.
21 Letter, F. J. Pedler to Brian Weinstein, 13 May 1968.
22 Pedler Letters. In an interview with Belgian journalists just before he left Leopoldville, Hailey spoke about his "good friend" Eboué. *L'Avenir Colonial Belge,* 8 January 1941, p. 2.

ruary, Governor General Huddleston in Anglo-Egyptian Sudan, and the new consul in Brazzaville, Robert Parr, liked and trusted Eboué and Laurentie at a time when they still worried that Vichy pressures might have an effect on other Frenchmen. In those days of intense suspicion Eboué appealed to many Englishmen because of his lack of chauvinism. He told them about the French colonial system, and asked admiringly for explanations of the British system of indirect rule. He said that he hoped to visit Nigeria and Sudan. He became so friendly in fact that General de Gaulle later warned him to have less to do with the British.

If the British were concerned about Eboué's authority among the Belgians, they might have been concerned about his position in Brazzaville too, for the local white population of assorted merchants and low-ranking functionaries accepted a black governor general with difficulty. Accustomed to giving orders to blacks, they felt that their own rather insecure prestige as whites might be shaken in the eyes of Africans who saw them following orders from a black man. Some took out their feelings on African clerks or workers under them. A minor dispute between a white administrator and black clerks might end with the white saying, "If you don't like my decision, you can go see *your* governor general, le gros singe, to complain."

Like all small European communities in Africa, this one's members relaxed in the evening at cocktail parties and dinners that lasted too long; a favorite recreation at these was malicious speculation about Eboué, his wife, and the white people who visited them regularly. A number comforted themselves with the erroneous notion that Henri Laurentie, the closest white to Eboué, was really in charge. If the directives came from a white, they could follow them, they thought.

Eboué knew Brazzaville and its inhabitants, one reason he always preferred to work far away. In a town such as Bouca, Eboué had felt relaxed in his dealings with Africans and Europeans; there, he was the administrator making detailed decisions for the district, and the whites needed him just as much as he needed them for help and companionship. In the segregated capital of Brazzaville Eboué was not happy, but only once or twice lost his self-control and this concerned the British, not the French. On one occasion he heard a rumor that the British wanted Laurentie as governor general and were saying that Eboué's administration lacked energy. He wrote directly to General de Gaulle: ". . . the impatience to intervene is growing among them and is expressed a little too much. . . ."[23] Mostly, however, he kept his feelings to himself and worked on administrative problems—for the war and for his leader.

As governor general, Eboué represented General de Gaulle to the people and headed the administration providing support for the war effort the Free French engaged in. As the head of the group of four colonies, Tchad, Oubangui-Chari, Moyen-Congo, and Gabon, Eboué also defined the broad lines of policy on the basis of his profound knowledge of the area; he traveled about to keep morale high among Europeans and Africans and to urge them to give part of their salaries to a fund for the purchase of military equipment for de Gaulle. Henri Laurentie, like other secretaries general before him, transformed the broad statements into circulars and decrees, and he directed the day-to-day operations of the administration.

Very quickly after his arrival in Brazzaville Eboué instructed Laurentie to draw up three major circulars and supporting decrees: the reorganization of the administration, a new policy toward African society, and a request for a voluntary contribution of money for the war effort.

On 19 January 1941 Eboué made public his first circular.[24] He said that Africans and Europeans must work for victory under the leadership of General de Gaulle and that he would tolerate no lack of discipline; second, decentralization of administrative decision-making would take place to encourage local initiative for the solution of the different problems facing each colony; third, Europeans must not forget the Africans, who were neither irrelevant for the war effort nor irrelevant for their future development. The Africans have a civilization, he said, and they have leaders who must be supported.

23 Archives Nationales de France, Fonds de Gaulle (*Infra,* Arch. Nat. de Gaulle), Telegram, Arrival from Brazzaville, No. 239, 14 April 1943.

24 JO-AFL, 1 February 1941, pp. 86-90, and Cazenave de la Roche, *Le Gouverneur-Général,* pp. 137-39.

The next day, on 20 January, Eboué issued a decree clarifying the powers of the heads of the four territories. The governor general gave his subordinates considerable autonomy and delegated as much authority to them as he could, particularly over the control of order, matters of personnel, and African authority.[25] Individual governors probably had more authority to act on their own initiative under this decree than since the organization of French Equatorial Africa in 1910.[26]

A week later another decree re-established a Council of Administration for Equatorial Africa, composed of the governor general, the four governors, and other representatives, including four Africans to be elected, as they had been previously under Governor General Reste, by a limited African electoral college.[27]

At the beginning of March Eboué went on tour in Gabon, whose pockets of pro-Vichy elements needed watching, and whose new governor had been fatally injured in an airplane crash. Eboué traveled by road through the southern part of the colony, meeting with Dr. Schweitzer in Lambaréné, and in Libreville with Monsignor Tardy; although Tardy had supported Vichy and helped dissuade Governor Masson from rallying to de Gaulle in August 1940, Eboué refused to permit any action against him and tried to maintain cordiality toward him; he did not want to antagonize the Vatican or devout Roman Catholics and thereby to weaken the Free French movement. At a meeting of the four bishops of French Equatorial Africa at the end of the year, Eboué offered government help for Roman Catholic schools to help develop education. This shocked fellow masons but it was a clever step to neutralize Vichy propaganda that the Free French were a gang of Freemasons, Jews, and Communists. The Church accepted the aid and schools grew considerably in spite of the war.[28]

Eboué returned to Brazzaville in April in time for de Gaulle's

[25] JO-AFL, 1 February 1941, pp. 96-98.
[26] Interview, P. O. Lapie, former governor of Tchad, 1941-1942, Paris, 14 May 1968.
[27] JO-AFL, 15 March 1941, pp. 167-70.
[28] Interview, Henri Laurentie, Paris, 31 July 1967.

second visit and in time to hear the news of the fall of Yugoslavia to the Germans then moving into the eastern Mediterranean and threatening the Middle East. De Gaulle told Eboué of his concerns about possible British attempts to replace the French in Syria and Lebanon still under Vichy control. As de Gaulle returned again to Brazzaville in July, he and his colleagues learned of the Vichy French surrender to the British in the two Arab countries. De Gaulle was certain the British wished to replace French authority in this area as well as in Madagascar where they had landed, and their actions infuriated him. He also thought the Americans wanted French Caribbean possessions.

Although de Gaulle had the Middle East on his mind during his July visit, he was also obliged by circumstances to resolve a serious dispute concerning Eboué's attempts to decentralize the administration in accordance with the January circular and Eboué's conflicts with high commissioner de Larminat. It is likely the Free French decided to create the post of high commissioner because Vichy had done so, and it seemed a good idea to centralize in war; in the absence of very specific division of duties de Larminat's offices worked against Eboué's attempts to decentralize and duplicated some of the activities of the governor general's office. The resulting confusion lowered morale.

De Gaulle made appointments with Eboué and de Larminat the first week in July. He first met with de Larminat, who came with a large briefcase stuffed with papers concerning his program. After de Larminat left, Eboué walked in with a slim four-page report in his hand, winking at Céleste on guard at the entrance that day. Although Eboué had told him that he was preparing himself "to be angry" in discussions with de Gaulle, it is highly unlikely he let himself show much emotion with his leader. He complained, however, about the development of a complex bureaucracy in the high commissioner's office and the attempt to take power from the individual governors: "As far as the Governor General is concerned . . . centralization and control over details are outmoded methods which have killed all sense of responsibility and initiative. Let us continue our efforts towards decentralization. . . ." Eboué then said that if this situation con-

On 26 August 1941 at Brazzaville General de Gaulle pins the Croix de la Compagnon de la Libération to Governor General Eboué's chest. General de Larminat at left. Courtesy of René Isambert.

tinued, he would be willing to step down as governor general.[29]

A few days later de Larminat was raised in rank to general and left for the Middle East to head Free French military forces there. De Larminat and Eboué parted on fairly good terms; many years later the general wrote he liked Eboué and considered him a "more capable" administrator than himself.[30]

[29] "Note Confidentielle et Personnelle pour le Général de Gaulle," Félix Eboué, 4 July 1941. Interview, Céleste, Paris, 28 August 1968.
[30] de Larminat, *Chroniques irrévérencieuses*, p. 221.

General de Gaulle evidently thought changes in personnel resolved the problems, and he named Médecin-Général Sicé, the highest ranking military official in Brazzaville, to the post of high commissioner. He appointed General Legentilhomme commander of French military forces. The nomination of Sicé, a sincere patriot but without administrative experience, displeased Eboué, and in the next few months he became more tense. Relations with Sicé were worse than those with de Larminat, and Eboué quite explicitly threatened to resign in 1942. De Gaulle withdrew Sicé from his post and abolished the office of high commissioner in July 1942. But he named Leclerc his "personal representative" in Brazzaville, and Eboué inquired if this nomination meant another high commissioner under a different name. He made his feelings known to Leclerc who advised de Gaulle that he preferred to have nothing to do with administrative matters and would concern himself with military operations planned from Tchad into Libya.

Decentralization having been begun, Eboué turned to the issuance on 8 November 1941 of what became his best-known single measure, his circular on "Native Policy."

LA NOUVELLE POLITIQUE INDIGÈNE

It is clear from accounts of the war years, 1939 to 1945, that most Europeans considered Africans passive observers, and in many ways they were. The Africans of Cameroun and Equatorial Africa did not decide to join their lands to the Free French movement; the Europeans made the decisions and used their African subordinates to win cooperation of a group of educated Africans. Once the colonies entered the war again on the side of Britain, the African representatives to the Council of Equatorial Africa were passive onlookers. No African made policy, although the Free French would never have been able to participate in the war without African cooperation in the exploitation of mineral and agricultural resources, provision of workers, and recruitment of soldiers.

After early British financial assistance Equatorial Africa became self-sufficient and contributed in important ways to Free French finances. African gold and diamonds, sold to South Africa

or America, brought money to de Gaulle's treasury. After the
fall of Malaya to the Japanese, which cut off the British from
their primary source of rubber, and the entry of America into
the war in December 1941, the need for African rubber increased
greatly. In the four colonies of Equatorial Africa rubber production had decreased from 1750 tons in 1921 to 600 tons in
1941.[31] With the crisis old rubber trees were tapped and the
government forced Africans to search for rubber-bearing vines
and plants and extract the juice just as they had done thirty
years before. In the twelve months from 1 July 1942 to 30 June
1943 Africans produced 2500 tons of rubber, the largest quantity
produced in any twelve-month period in the history of the four
colonies,[32] and it increased the following year. The Rubber Control Board, set up to purchase the product, shipped it to Britain
for the manufacture of airplane tires.

Gabon produced wood for export for many years, particularly
the rare Okoumé, used to make high-quality plywood. During
the war a mill in Port-Gentil cut the logs into long wide sheets,
transformed in English factories to become parts of fuselages for
airplanes of the RAF which successfully defended Britain and
helped turn the tide of the war. Oubangui-Chari and Tchad increased their cotton production for the war effort, and the four
colonies contributed, according to some estimates, about 40,000
troops used in Africa and in Europe. The workers and troops
remember World War II with bitterness for they were obliged
to work and fight in a European war that seemed to bring them
little benefit, although many still receive pensions.

From the point of view of most Frenchmen all that was necessary was that the African do his work without complaint. Eboué
agreed with the need for peace and discipline, but he also wanted
to bring about reforms in policy toward African society during
the war.

The first problem concerning African society was that of the
Balali in the area of Brazzaville. For years they had rebelled
against payment of taxes, under the leadership of André Matswa,

[31] Report dated 7 September 1942.
[32] Arch. Nat. de Gaulle, Comité National Français, Telegram, Arrival from
Brazzaville, 8 July 1943, No. 361 AE.

founder of a mutual aid society, the Amicale, that Eboué had been warned about in the 1920's. For the Balali the beliefs of the movement were important in helping them come to terms with social changes.[33] By the 1930's the Amicale was demanding autonomy or even independence for their region. In 1938 Governor General Reste proposed the granting of autonomy to the region, but the Ministry of Colonies refused, and Boisson, his successor, prosecuted the leaders of the movement.[34] In December 1940 de Larminat had had some Balali leaders shot, and Laurentie reported to Eboué, still on his way to Brazzaville, "severity has given way to violence, which is, a priori, idiotic."[35]

After his arrival in Brazzaville Eboué said that he would consider Balali complaints but would demand "discipline" for the war effort. He then consulted with missionaries and the Belgians and held a series of meetings with the Africans, threatening them with loss of their schools if they did not cooperate with the administration and pay their taxes. The problems between the Balali and the French were not resolved, and Eboué kept Matswa in prison where he died in 1942. Some of the followers of Matswa blamed Eboué for their difficulties and suffering, "considering him a traitor to the black race."[36]

While Eboué ordered the use of police to exercise surveillance over the Balali, he asked Henri Laurentie to prepare a circular on general policy toward African society, a new "politique indigène."

As early as 1911 Messimy—during his three and a half months as Minister of Colonies—prepared a "native policy" which consisted in application of the idea of "creating new societies impregnated with our ideas."[37] The policy in North Africa would be one of

33 Georges Balandier, *Sociologie actuelle de l'Afrique noire: dynamique sociale en Afrique centrale* (Paris: Presses Universitaires de France, second edition, 1963), pp. 410-11.

34 Jean-Michel Wagret, *Histoire et sociologie politiques de la République du Congo (Brazzaville)* (Paris: Pichon et Durand-Auzias, 1963), pp. 42-53.

35 Archives Eboué, Letter, Henri Laurentie to Félix Eboué, 18 December 1940.

36 Placide N'Zala-Backa, *Le Tipoye doré* (Brazzaville: Imprimerie Nationale Congolaise, 1968). This is the story of a Matswanist. Cited by Claude Wauthier, Letter to Brian Weinstein, 23 November 1968.

37 P. Bourdarie, *La Revue Indigène*, 1911, Vol. VI, 30 March 1911, p. 131.

"fusion," in Asia "association," and in black Africa a policy of "education." These vague ideas were never worked out clearly.

One of the well-known proponents of a coherent "native policy" was Maurice Delafosse, the man who in 1912 had urged Eboué to study the languages of Oubangui-Chari. In 1921 he warned that the French should recognize the existence of African civilizations and help them evolve without destroying them. He advised administrators to study African society before making decisions and to avoid centralization.[38]

Eboué knew Delafosse's work and had discussed his feelings with Laurentie, who prepared a document reflecting the governor general's point of view. Eboué went over it carefully and presented it to a group of church and business representatives meeting in early November 1941. On 8 November 1941 he signed the document, a new circular, and sent it to the governors.

Like the 19 January document on decentralization, Eboué's November circular was written as an introduction to specific reforms he planned to propose. The fact that this message became better known than all his other circulars, speeches, or decrees would probably have annoyed Eboué; the importance of the document itself has been exaggerated because of the propaganda surrounding it.

The circular urged French administrators to plan for the future development of French Equatorial Africa, to make prosperity their goal. It said that to serve France the health, education, and general welfare of the African population had to be improved, new industries had to be introduced, a new dynamism had to transform the colonies for the benefit of all, Africans and Europeans.

Eboué said that a coherent policy must be shaped to raise the standard of living, but it must be shaped with the cooperation of local leadership rather than imposed by Frenchmen through French institutions. He cited Marchal Paul Lyautey, the first French resident general of Morocco: "There is in every society a ruling class, born to rule, without which one can do nothing."

[38] Maurice Delafosse, "Sur l'Orientation Nouvelle de la Politique Indigène dans l'Afrique Noire," *Renseignements Coloniaux, supplement to L'Afrique Française,* July 1921, pp. 145-52.

Eboué said that in Equatorial Africa, as elsewhere, the European administrator could not freely choose the ruling class or the leader and must not consider them as clerks: "There is a chief designated by custom; he must be recognized." Administrators must seek out the "legitimate chiefs" and restore them to their positions of dignity, he said.

These suggestions concerning chiefs are the most often cited part of Eboué's circular in spite of the fact that they were not original or feasible in 1940, and Eboué provided no specific decrees to implement them. Much of Equatorial Africa had no tradition of chieftaincy. The so-called "ruling class" was unknown among most peoples of Gabon and Moyen-Congo except for the Batéké whose king, the Makoko, had lost most of his importance before the coming of the French. In Oubangui-Chari Eboué himself did not appoint men who had traditional legitimacy as canton chiefs; he named Sokambi chief of ethnic groups different from his own, for example. Only at Rafai did a ruling family exist, and Hetman, the Sultan, died at the beginning of the war. Tchad was really the only one of the four colonies with hierarchized societies.

The importance of the document for 1940 lay first in the discussion of the *métis,* a person of mixed race, and next in the explanation of the need for a new status for a growing group of educated non-citizens, the call for the creation of urban communes to be run by the educated non-citizens, new customary courts under African judges, and a systemization of labor-recruiting practices.

The document dealt with the question of the position of the Eur-African *métis,* a matter of particular importance in Gabon where Europeans had been settled longer than most of the other colonies. French officials, feeling guilty about the growing numbers of children born of African mothers but abandoned by European fathers, tended to favor the Eur-Africans in schooling, accession to citizenship, and appointments to positions in the administration. This created antagonism in Gabon and the favoritism annoyed Eboué, possibly because he had always seen some favoritism shown the fairer colored in the Antilles and resented it. Eboué warned administrators not to favor the *métis,* although an effort should be made through team sports, for example, to help the fatherless children to find a sense of community.

In the weeks after the issuance of the circular Eboué directed the preparation of four projects to put into effect the other proposals, and he sent them to Pleven. Pleven had been named National Commissioner for the Economy, Financial Affairs and the Colonies in the newly formed Comité National Français created by General de Gaulle in September 1941 as a more formal government-in-exile than his previous organization.

The covering letter for the projects was more important than the November circular. It said that the British and Belgians were ahead of the French in colonial policy, incrusted as it was with old ideas. It went on to attack the idea of assimilation and citizenship as "sterile," creating only a separate petite bourgeoisie cut off from their own society and not part of European society; it proposed a new attitude toward French Equatorial Africa and new policies.

In the past, it said no administrator wanted to spend his career in this part of Africa, and the governors used appointments here as stepping stones to the more desirable posts in West Africa, Madagascar, or Indochina: "From now on the government must take measures so that this colony, the first that rallied . . . comes out from its obscurity," Eboué's letter said. The wealth could be developed, the population could grow, but a governor general willing to spend ten years of his life here must be named. Eboué said he would leave after the war to permit the nomination of a new man.

Continuing, he said, the future "success of native policy" would depend on administrators remaining a long time in one colony. Instead of a corps of administrators moving from colony to colony, they should work in one area all their lives, learning at least one major language spoken there. Apparently forgetting his own long leave of absence in 1922-1923, Eboué also suggested that the standard six-month leave for every two years of service be reduced.

He suggested that Africans be given increasing control over their own affairs: ". . . the future Minister of Colonies ought to

. . . orient himself towards the creation of native communities concentrating on their own affairs. . . ." Coming close to what, in the context of the time, was certainly a revolutionary position, the letter continued: "Colonial policy, being one of the things the French public is most indifferent about, it is possible that circumstances might be favorable enough to permit us to finish with all the ordonnances, all the Senatus-Consultes [used in the Antilles], all the laws and all the decrees which hinder the free rise of the colonies, and to have accepted a relative autonomy for our overseas possessions within which the natives will progress without leaving their natural setting."[39] Eboué, interested during the war years in shaking the government loose from old-fashioned colonial ideas, probably proposed such a radical idea of autonomy less in hope of having it adopted than to provoke discussion. There is no indication that René Pleven or General de Gaulle ever responded to the letter whose ideas were not made public.

The first decree created a labor office in such territory "to control the engagement and use of native labor." Eboué wanted government control of recruitment through an office in each capital and to force companies to take the families of workers when they recruited workers.[40] The second proposed the creation of the new status, *notable évolué,* to be granted some Africans by the governor general of A.E.F. or the governors. The *notables* would be exempted from the *indigénat,* or prison without trial, and they could be exempted from the forced labor such as road work; they would be members of the electoral corps which elected representatives to the advisory council of the colonies, and members of the governing body of the new "native communes." He apparently meant them to be an urban elite parallel to but not in competition with the traditional elite in the rural areas,[41] but it is difficult to see how both elites could exist side by side for very long. Third, the governor general would have the power to grant to urban areas a corporate status with an appointed council composed of *notables* and citizens. Such a council would

39 Letter dated 20 December 1941.
40 JO-AFL, 1 November 1942, pp. 372-573.
41 Félix Eboué, "Discours en Conseil d'Administration," *Afrique Française Libre, Afrique Equatoriale Française,* 19 November 1942, p. 10.

be consulted about the rate of taxation and it would execute orders of the administration and maintain order. If the governor
general gave his permission, it could have its own budget.[42]
Fourth, African courts would be composed of chiefs or other
local leaders chosen according to custom. They could travel outside administrative posts on their own and could inflict maximum penalties of five hundred francs or three months in prison.
Judges would be chosen by the governor from a list presented
by heads of subdivision.[43] The importance of this project was that
the courts would operate on their own, although the heads of
subdivision would watch their activities.

Pleven's offices were surprised by the projects. They liked the
November circular better than specific proposals because it could
be used safely to show that the French were thinking about reform, but did not rattle the status quo by doing anything definite
about it. They were particularly sensitive to the issue of leadership, for at the end of 1941 Churchill and Roosevelt signed the
Atlantic Charter recognizing the right of all people to choose
their own leaders, and the emphasis on traditional leadership
might show the French were in step with the Charter. The
French National Committee ordered copies of the circular to
which they gave a new name, *La Nouvelle Politique Indigène,*
and sent copies to America and Britain.

Pleven wrote High Commissioner Sicé for his opinion about
the projects. Unknown to Eboué, the high commissioner advised
against their application: "Certain changes envisaged by the
Governor General with regard to Native Society and our relations with it do not seem to have been sufficiently studied to be
applied."[44] No action was taken, and Eboué inquired about London's silence. In May the newly created Commission for Legislation examined the Eboué projects and objected that they did not
correspond to the November circular, that the labor-recruiting
project implied forced labor (forced labor existed already in fact),
that it would be dangerous to decentralize so much penal power
to Africans. The Commission first opposed the *notables evolués*

42 *Ibid.,* pp. 574-75.
43 JO-AEF, 1 August 1943, pp. 470-72.
44 Report dated 15 March 1942.

for fear of "creating a kind of native aristocracy" and equally disliked the idea of autonomous communes.[45]

Eboué's response was to threaten to fly to London to put his case to General de Gaulle after the exchange of a series of acrimonious communications. On 1 August 1942 General de Gaulle cabled Eboué that he was signing decrees about labor, *notables,* and the communes. A year later the decree concerning the African courts was also accepted, while Eboué prepared more changes affecting the status of African civil servants.

As a career administrator Eboué felt kinship with young administrators, European and African, just beginning their careers, although the relationship was more one of father to son than of brother to brother. Since the time he had helped Domatchi in Oubangui-Chari in 1929, he wanted to see African functionaries assume more responsibility and power. In West Africa he discovered better educated clerks and teachers, like Fily Dabo Sissoko, because of the superior school system. This experience apparently convinced him Africans could play a more important role in the administration.

By the time Eboué returned to Equatorial Africa in 1939 schools there had improved somewhat; he tripled the money spent for African educational institutions.[46] The Ecole Edouard Renard, organized by Governor General Reste in 1936 in Brazzaville, was beginning to produce teachers, civil servants, and medical personnel after the pattern of the Ponty School in West Africa.

In Tchad Eboué had known and encouraged a few African clerks who looked to him for guidance in their own careers. In Brazzaville he knew five African functionaries particularly well and worked to integrate them into positions previously held by Europeans. He was not the first to take such an interest, but in the past those favored had generally been the *métis.*

The three Gabonese, one Dahomean, and one Camerounese in whom he interested himself at Brazzaville he treated with re-

45 Report dated 16 June 1942.
46 Documents, Arch. Nat. de Gaulle. Also, Robert Pinhède, "Contribution à l'étude de la vie de Félix Eboué," Mémoire, unpublished, Ecole Nationale de la France d'Outre Mer, 1945-1946, p. 39.

Jean-Hilaire Aubame, far left, second row, and Jean-Rémy Ayouné, far right, first row, with other officers of the Union Educative et Mutuelle de la Jeunesse Africaine. Courtesy of Madame Eboué.

spect and helped. One wrote: "I discovered in him not one of those numerous Blacks who, once they succeed in life, forget their origins and the misery of their brothers, but rather a precursor, an older brother. . . ."[47] Eboué took a particular interest in Aubame, who had been of help to de Larminat during the August 1940 movement. The tall deep-voiced austere and devout Roman Catholic came from the northern Fang-speaking part of

[47] J.-R. Ayouné, "Pour la construction de l'Afrique nouvelle," in Henri Walker-Deemin, editor, *Ecrivains, Artistes et Artisans Gabonais* (Libreville: Institut Pédagogique National, 1966), p. 33.

Gabon; he joined the African corps of the customs services before the war and was transferred to Brazzaville in 1942. On Sundays he often visited the Eboué home.

Aubame and his colleagues became *notables évolués,* and Eboué encouraged them to form literary, discussion, and sporting societies. From the point of view of many French administrators such societies, like the Union Educative et Mutuelle de la Jeunesse Africaine, were "harmless" enough and kept potential leaders or "troublemakers" busy with their own mild "rhetoric." While Eboué had no revolutionary goals in mind for these societies, he envisioned them as mutual aid clubs for the African functionaries, and he asked his young subordinates their opinions of policies toward African society.[48] Out of such groups came the beginnings of some of the first political parties, all of this unforeseen by Eboué, however.

The governor general also tried to bring some coherence to the various decrees issued about African civil servants, and issued a series of decrees reorganizing the African cadres and creating Ecoles Supérieures des Territoires to train clerks and to prepare candidates for the Edouard Renard School. Eboué granted the status of *notable évolué* to over two hundred Africans, and at the beginning of 1944 created the commune of Poto-Poto, naming twelve African members of the Municipal Corps or Council with Aubame as president.[49] This seems like progress, but in spite of his status, Aubame, for one, still had difficulty getting admission to the local cinemas.

On 23 and 27 February 1943 Eboué integrated Aubame and three of his colleagues into the local cadre of Secrétariats Généraux, previously reserved for French citizens.[50] Two whites then challenged the legality of the decision, preventing the four from taking their positions. Eboué's successors abolished the cadre, effectively nullifying the integration, and some white administrators actively discouraged Africans from applying for the status

48 Interview with Jean-Rémy Ayouné, Minister of Foreign Affairs of Gabon, Libreville, 6 August 1968.
49 JO-AEF, 1 February 1944, p. 108, and 1 March 1944, p. 201.
50 JO-AEF, 15 March 1943, p. 183.

notable évolué. Considerable time was spent, however, in formulating requests, constituting dossiers, making decisions on accession to this "local citizenship," all of which were made obsolete by the post-war development of nationalism. Before they were obsolete they were contradictory.

The essential contradiction of Eboué's *politique indigène* and its related changes concerning *métis* and African civil servants becomes clear when comparing this panoply of circulars and decrees with the treatment of the Balali. Eboué called for decentralization, recognition of dynamism in African cultures, finding the "true chiefs" and so forth for the evolution of Africa. But he like other administrators was unable to recognize and accept a truly African movement like the Balali Amicale. He recognized African values but refused to allow them to be expressed in ways he did not determine. To allow their expression would, of course, have denied his own role as a foreign administrator and would have shown the paradoxes of colonialism itself.

WAR TENSIONS

Less ambiguous than a policy toward African society was Eboué's third circular asking for money. In a ringing call to patriotism on 9 December 1941 Eboué said that by contributing part of their salaries administrators could participate more actively in the war and help save France. Administrators and Africans, he wrote, had already contributed enough money to purchase four airplanes for Free France, and they should contribute almost double the amount already given. He praised Britain for having staved off the Germans in August and September 1940 and called on his compatriots to make sure that France would be with the victors at the end of the war: "France also will win the war. . . ."[51]

The colonies, and most particularly Tchad, had already made a contribution to the war. Without the cooperation of Tchad the British would have been obliged to fly a much longer route

---

[51] Afrique Equatoriale Française, Gouvernement Général, Circulaire, No. 143, 9 December 1941.

around Africa to get to Egypt which Rommel's Afrika Korps was trying to capture. According to a correspondent of the London *Times*: "It is not until one looks at the war map in a West African operations room that the importance of Fighting Free French Africa is seen in true perspective. With Brazzaville or Fort Lamy in enemy hands—or even in the suspect hands of Vichy—the whole structure based on Lagos, Takoradi, Freetown and Accra might be endangered."[52] The route through Fort Lamy was "the lifeline from Great Britain and the United States to the Middle East, to India and the Far East," according to another correspondent.[53] At times a hundred planes a day flew over Fort Lamy, and America, which did not recognize the Free French, although it recognized the importance of the colonies, sent a military mission to Equatorial Africa in October 1941 and began to supply steel and other materials via Britain under the Lend Lease program.

The preparation of the three circulars and the subsequent decrees, tours, and speeches had exhausted Eboué. He and his colleagues had worked under greater strain than ever before in their careers. Cazenave de la Roche fell ill at the end of 1941, and Eboué sent him on leave; after he left for South Africa, where white administrators went normally for sick leave during the war, Jean Poupel replaced him.

The tension Eboué felt was considerable. There was no telling what the Germans or the Vichy government would do to Ginette, Robert, and Henry if they knew who they were. Eboué fully expected some action against his children, not only because of his actions but also because racist legislation and the arrests of friends added daily to their fear for those they loved.

Indeed, the Pétain government had replaced the historic French motto of "Liberty, Equality, Fraternity" with "Work, Family, Country," reduced civil liberties sharply, and adopted racist regulations on the Nazi model.[54] The government put Yvon Delbos under house arrest and interned Léon Blum, Georges

52 *Times,* 21 July 1942.
53 *Times,* 22 January 1942.
54 Robert Aron, *Histoire de Vichy, 1940-1944* (Paris: Fayard, 1954), pp. 231-32.

Mandel, and the son of Marius Moutet, since they could not find Moutet himself.[55]

A special court condemned General de Gaulle to death, and at the beginning of June 1941 a military court condemned Eboué in absentia to death and ruled his property must be confiscated for "crimes against the homeland."[56] Free French offices in London sent Eboué a telegram of congratulations after the court ruling, and Eboué responded with thanks: "Distinction with which Vichy honored us only proves how efficacious our action is and commits us to pursue the struggle until the end."[57] Condemnation by Vichy honored Eboué in the eyes of the Free French, but it represented a threat to the welfare of his family and the house at Asnières.

It does not appear that the Eboués had any sure information about their children during 1941, but news came that Louis Courbain, Madame Eboué's half-brother, and several friends in Guyane and the Antilles had been interned by the Vichy government. At this time friends noticed that if the subject of his children came up in conversation, Eboué would nervously snap the nail of one finger against the nail of another, trying to seem very calm. He was smoking two packs of cigarettes a day, but these signs of tension were all there were; he did not slacken on his rounds of opening schools, attending receptions, giving speeches, and touring the four colonies.

Eboué tried to relax in small groups or with one or two friends. He reassigned René Isambert to Moyen-Congo from Tchad in August 1941 and invited him to dinner often. In spite of his long career, Isambert was still an administrator first class; with great effort Eboué got a promotion to administrator in chief for him. Antilleans like Georges Céleste visited, and Guyanese stationed in Brazzaville took their afternoon punches with the governor general and his wife. Much to Eboué's delight he found someone interested in music who could help him continue the

[55] *Ibid.*, pp. 233-34.

[56] *Etat Français,* Arrêt No. 8, "Arrêt rendu par contumace par la Cour Martiale séant à Gannat (Allier), 5 June 1941.

[57] Sent 31 June 1941.

studies he had begun many years previously. A young couple, Herbert and Eliane Pepper, had escaped occupied France to join the Free French movement. Graduates of the conservatory of music in Paris, they were sent in March 1941 to Brazzaville where they taught music courses and wrote a chorale sung in an African language. Eboué came to hear the performance and met the Peppers. He invited them to his house where he told them of his own work in the 1920's in Oubangui-Chari and later in Soudan on tonal languages. When Mrs. Pepper said she had no piano, Eboué found one and had it sent to her immediately.

As Eboué got to know the Peppers better, he relaxed with them and laughingly told them stories about himself and the reaction of local whites to his nomination. One of his favorite anecdotes concerned the arrival of a subordinate to the colony, probably Oubangui-Chari. Eboué, so the story goes, went to meet his official, and the white, mistaking Eboué, dressed informally, for an African, ordered the "boy" to take his valise. He obediently carried the valise to the man's quarters, and only later, when the administrator went to salute his superior officer, enjoyed the man's shock to discover that he was Eboué, the "boy." However much he may have told the story or similar stories, he told them so often that it is difficult to believe he did not think about the humiliation a great deal. Perhaps he was testing himself to see if the story still hurt.

Eboué decided to ask the Peppers to work for him: "Finally, I have some true musicians," he said. "I have research to be done." He decided they would continue the work he had begun and gave them lists of words he had worked with in Oubangui and the names of people with whom they should make contact. The list included Chief Sokambi at Kouango, Eboué's old friend, and a young French administrator in Tchad, Pierre Lami (later a governor of Tchad), who wrote Eboué about a whistled language he found while working among the Lélé people. The Peppers traveled, on Eboué's instructions, to Oubangui-Chari where they studied the linga, or talking drum, at Bambari to collect more evidence for Eboué's theory that among the Banda "speaking with the mouth and with the drum were the same thing." He also wanted them to examine his idea about the unity of music, lan-

guage, and dance as human communications.[58] In Oubangui-
Chari Eboué visited them and was thrilled to see them work with
the linga. The trip also was the occasion of a visit to Sokambi
whom he had not seen for ten years. In Bangui Eboué spoke to a
group of administrators and Africans about his memories of this
colony. He had thought about Oubangui-Chari, "the country to
which I dedicated my youth," and had even brooded about the
troubles that he had over cotton, now recognized as a success:
". . . work modestly begun has been magnificently continued
[and cotton] bitterly criticized and pursued at the expense of a
career against winds and tides . . . is now the number one
source of income in the colony. . . . To see all that after a long
absence following almost a quarter century of work in this country is for me a particular comfort and testimony to the certainty
of the destiny of my dear Oubangui."[59]

When the governor general returned to Brazzaville from his
tour, he found a letter from his daughter Ginette, safe and in
good health. In spite of the occupation of northern France, she
was continuing her studies for the baccalaureate. At the end of
1941 the Legion of Honor school had refused to let her continue
her studies, probably because the order had recently expelled
her father, but she matriculated at another school and passed
the first series of examinations.

With the help of some next-door neighbors at Asnières, Ginette hid the family valuables in the basement, under the coal,
and had successfully prevented the occupation of the house by
German soldiers. French authorities did not confiscate the house
as feared, although they were planning to put it up for public
sale. Some officials, charged with the task, were probably unsure
about the outcome of the war and feared making enemies; in
addition, Madame Eboué's brother, working for the Folies Bergères, got some scarce tickets for the official in charge of the
house. Whatever the reason—fear or the Can-Can—he did not sell
the house.

---

58 Interviews with Eliane Barat, Paris, 6 July 1967, and with Herbert Pepper,
Dakar, 9 September 1967. They wrote about their work in *Présence Africaine*,
Vol. I, No. 1, November-December 1947, pp. 149-157.
59 Handwritten speech in Archives Eboué.

Instead of living at Asnières, Ginette had stayed with her aunt Cornélie Gratien, Eboué's sister. In December 1941 Robert had escaped from the prisoner of war camp in which the Germans had kept him and Henry with other black soldiers and made his way to the Gratien apartment. Then he left for Lyon in Vichy-controlled southern France, where he enrolled in a lycée to complete his baccalaureate while working with the French underground. All this news from Ginette filled the governor general and his wife with joy, but she also had something very sad to tell her father: Cornélie—his "Cono"—and her eldest daughter, whose studies Eboué had paid for, had both died. Cornélie's health had been poor for years, and the food shortages and a severe winter were the final blow. Although her husband finally returned to France from his long sojourn in Oubangui-Chari, he came too late to see the wife he never adequately provided for.

In April 1942 German authorities released many French soldiers, including Henry, who claimed he was ill, but Vichy authorities still held Louis Courbain, Eboué's brother-in-law. By May the French National Committee established contact with Ginette and sent money to her through the Red Cross, which she shared with Henry. With the help of Portuguese friends, Gaston Monnerville, and the British Henry and Ginette crossed over the line dividing occupied and Vichy France. The three children made their way to Spain and then to Portugal. The British embassy gave them passports, claiming they were British subjects from one of their West Indian possessions, and the French National Committee arranged to send them by ship to join their father in Africa. Eboué, who paid all expenses, expected them at the end of 1942. In September Charles finished his diploma course, joined the air force, and traveled to Brazzaville to see his parents (and General de Gaulle, then visiting) before going to Britain and Canada for pilot training.

Just after allied forces landed in French North Africa in November Eboué called for a meeting of the Council of French Equatorial Africa. The governors of the four territories, representatives of business, and three African delegates (including Sultan Mohammad Ourada) met with him in Brazzaville. There was cause for optimism and self-confidence. Increasing the power of the radio transmitter at Brazzaville, renamed *Voix Libre,* released the French from their dependence on the BBC and permitted world-wide broadcasts. In these broadcasts the Free French could now boast of their new organization, for de Gaulle had made contact with underground forces, and they decided to combine in July into a new organization: "Free France and Captive France are from now on two constitutive elements of a single France which is Fighting France (France Combattante)." General de Gaulle named himself head of the new organization while maintaining his presidency of the National Committee in London.[60]

More important, the transmitter could boast to the homeland, completely occupied by the Germans since the American landings in North Africa, that at the end of the previous May Free French forces had held out against the vastly superior German forces of General Rommel at a place called Bir-Hakeim. The famous Afrika Korps, moving eastward through Libya toward Egypt, was stopped long enough by Free French forces to permit the retreating British forces to re-form in a good position to prevent the German invasion of Egypt.

Although the successful outcome of the war was in no way assured, Eboué spoke about non-military matters in his speech to the governors. He urged them to think about the long-term development of the colonies: "We have not failed to push this [war] effort to the maximum as much in personnel as in products necessary for the Allies. But the war is happily a transitory state, and we must think of the future and the complexity of problems. . . . I believe we ought not wait for Victory to set the general direction, philosophy, and action to take, as long as it does not adversely affect military needs."[61]

Following Eboué's instructions, Laurentie reported to René Pleven concerning economic development. He advised changes in the relationship between the government and private business, and assumed that government would take a more active role in

<hr />

[60] "Circulaire," 29 July 1942, in JO-AEF, 15 November 1942, p. 612.
[61] Afrique Française Libre, Afrique Equatoriale Française, "Discours en Conseil d'Administration prononcé par M. Félix Eboué," 19 November 1942, p. 12.

the economy than private investment. The biggest privately owned companies in Equatorial Africa were under British and Belgian control, and they never re-invested their profits in the colonies. The secretary general therefore suggested raising taxes to almost one-third of all profits above five million francs (about $110,000 then) and suggested that the French National Committee support the creation of a large government-backed French company for trading and investment.[62] Eboué read Laurentie's report after he returned from a tour, and wrote on the top of it, "Copy for the personal information of General de Gaulle," and sent it to him.

American authorities in Africa objected that Eboué had begun development projects with materials destined strictly for the war effort. One said in a report to the State Department that Lend Lease was "being stretched to cover belated improvements" in French Equatorial Africa. For example, an American tractor was being used to build a road without strategic value, he said.[63] As rubber became increasingly important to the Allies—rising to 4000 tons per year—the French hinted they should get something in return for the future of the colony and asked for a cement factory. The Americans thought this had nothing to do with the war effort and were annoyed.[64]

Family matters at this time preoccupied the Eboués, for the children were expected in December. Madame Eboué, overwhelmed at the prospect of seeing them, her daughter in particular, went to the port to wait for them. When they arrived, the children and Madame Eboué flew to Brazzaville for an emotional welcome by Eboué, on 20 December. Past differences between Henry and his father were forgotten as Henry, Robert, and Ginette told their father what they had lived through in prison camps and occupied Paris. Robert and Henry told their father they had been separated from the white prisoners, who did not protest this manifestation of racism. The three children

62 Arch. Nat. de Gaulle, Secrétariat Général, 253/CF, Brazzaville, 18 July 1942.
63 U.S. State, FW 851 U.24/48, 10 August 1943.
64 U.S. State, 851 U.24/97, Report, Consul, Brazzaville, 27 April 1944.

The four Eboué children and Madame Eboué. Courtesy of Madame
Eboué.

Robert   Henry

Madame Eugénie Eboué

Ginette   Charles

were also full of questions; they noticed that their father had aged a great deal and was unhealthily fat. He had begun monthly visits to the physician.

After three months Henry and Robert flew to join Free French forces in the Middle East. Ginette remained in Brazzaville, now far from war developments.

TURNING POINT

The American landing in North Africa in November 1942 precipitated a crisis in the Fighting French movement and sharpened the differences between Roosevelt and de Gaulle. American attitudes toward the Free French and its leader in particular had been ambiguous at best. In June and July 1940 American consuls in Lagos and Leopoldville had followed events in the French colonies closely and made contacts for the sake of information. After the "Three Glorious Days" of August the American consul in Leopoldville asked the State Department if he should make an official visit to de Larminat across the river. Washington responded that it wanted "to avoid as far as possible raising any question of principle in the matter of relations between this Government and the de Gaulle Committee" but advised the American representative to inquire about American nationals and property in French Equatorial Africa: "You will of course be careful in this connection to refrain from any action or statement which would commit this Government in any way."[65]

In 1941 the Americans were indirectly helping the Free French through Lend Lease but only because Churchill explained the importance of the colonies and because Washington could still pretend the Free French did not exist by shipping goods through the British. A supposedly private trading company in New York also purchased products from Equatorial Africa.[66] At the end of the year Eboué enthusiastically received an American military

65 U.S. State, Telegram from State to Consul, Leopoldville, 4 September 1940, 740.0011, European War, 1939/5334.

66 U.S. State, Division of European Affairs, Report, 16 July 1941, FW 740.0011, European War, 1939/11872.

mission in Africa to study military facilities and resources. The American government then tried to negotiate directly with Eboué without recognizing de Gaulle, but the governor general urged them to deal with his chief, and in all relations with the Americans Eboué followed instructions strictly.

Even after America came into the war in December 1941 Roosevelt acted as if de Gaulle did not exist. The French leader was offended when the same month the Americans signed the Pact of the United Nations creating an anti-Axis alliance without asking the French National Committee to join. Washington announced it considered France a neutral power,[67] and sent an emissary to speak to the Vichy high commissioner for the Antilles who agreed to the neutrality of Guadeloupe, Martinique, and Guyane. This action angered the Free French who seized French-owned Saint-Pierre and the Miquelon islands off the coast of Canada, thus angering the Americans.[68]

In July 1942 America officially opened a consulate in Brazzaville, even though it still did not recognize any government in exile. Eboué thought the occasion would be an important way to impress the Americans and get them to change their attitude toward de Gaulle. The governor general postponed an important tour he wanted to take in order to be present when the American consul, Laurence Taylor, arrived. Eboué greeted Roosevelt's representative with all possible honors. A police guard, lining the road from the boat landing to the city, played the American national anthem. The governor showed Taylor his furnished living quarters and an office equipped with everything down to pencils and paper, treatment that Taylor, a career Foreign Service officer, had never had in his life.[69] But Taylor's government, unimpressed, continued to look for someone other than de Gaulle to lead a French movement and thought they had found their man in General Henri Giraud.

Giraud, who outranked de Gaulle, had been commander of France's seventh army until his capture by the Germans in 1940. In a German prison from May of that year to April 1942, he

---

[67] de Gaulle, *Mémoires de guerre*, I, p. 184.
[68] *Ibid.*, pp. 185-86.
[69] Interview with M. L. Taylor, Santa Rosa, California, 20 October 1968.

made a heroic escape and returned to France before the allied invasion of North Africa. At Vichy, where he seemed safe from the Germans, Giraud talked with Marshal Pétain, whom he admired greatly and whose patriotism he did not doubt. Giraud told Pétain he believed America would win the war and that France would have to depend on America for help after the victory.[70] A small group of Frenchmen proposed that he attempt to bring the North African possessions of France—Morocco, Algeria, and Tunisia—back into the war, and Giraud left for North Africa.

After the allied landing in Morocco in November 1942 the American consul in Algeria persuaded the head of the French navy, Admiral Darlan, to sign an armistice with the Americans and to lead the colonies back into the war against the Germans. Darlan, caught between opposing forces, pleased no one and was assassinated. Giraud then became head of French forces in North Africa with the support of Washington.

Giraud never denounced Pétain and in fact had proclaimed his loyalty to him when he left France, thus managing to rally some Vichyists around himself. High Commissioner Pierre Boisson, Eboué's former superior, declared that French West Africa would join with North Africa, and he traveled to Algiers. On 26 December 1942 Boisson, General Noguès (whose hesitations in June 1940 had so undermined the Bloc Africain), and several others formally declared Henri Giraud to be high commissioner for all overseas France and their leader in the war. Giraud then considered himself the legitimate head of the French war effort. The declaration meant that there were three men claiming leadership—Pétain, de Gaulle, and Giraud. De Gaulle's partisans mobilized to support their leader. In a radio broadcast Eboué said that General de Gaulle was the only person capable of leading France, and he was the only man who had always fought the enemy.[71]

From London General de Gaulle offered to meet with Giraud,

70 Robert Aron, *Histoire de l'épuration,* Vol. I (Paris: Fayard, 1967) pp. 26-27.

71 National Archives, Transcriptions of Shortwave Broadcasts, Station: Brazzaville, Shinda, Record 05134, 30 October 1942.

but the latter at first refused. The two men met for the first time in Casablanca, Morocco, in January 1943, under the eyes of President Roosevelt, who backed Giraud, and Prime Minister Churchill, who backed de Gaulle. In spite of the coolness of their relations and the open antagonisms between their followers, Giraud and de Gaulle formed the French Committee of National Liberation and became joint presidents.

De Gaulle's supporters found the idea of working with Giraud and his associates extremely distasteful. They believed that they had risked their lives while Boisson and others accepted positions under Vichy, and they felt they had proved themselves at Bir-Hakeim and in Libya while others watched. In 1942 French and African troops under Leclerc had moved deep into Italian territory from Tchad. At the beginning of 1943 Leclerc moved his troops toward the Mediterranean coast and Tripoli while the British forces moved in from Egypt. As the Free French advanced north they met with other French troops stationed in North Africa but inactive until the armistice signed with the Americans. After battles with German forces the French arrived in Tripoli in January and in Tunis in May 1943. The 1600 mile march across the desert and the stand at Bir-Hakeim justifiably added to the pride and self-confidence of the Free French, deeply depressed by German victories of 1940 and the fall of France.

The Free French were in no mood after these battles to follow a man who still respected Pétain, and they feared the Americans might use their power to try to prevent de Gaulle from going to Algiers. A contest for supremacy began, and Eboué played a role in it.

In March 1943 Guyane finally rallied to the newly formed French Committee of National Liberation, and the Vichy governor left. Eboué's old friend, Philippe Saccharin, and the mayor of Cayenne, Ulrich Sophie, whom he had known as a schoolboy, cabled Eboué of their decision to join him. They took over the functions of governor until one could be sent and called Giraud and de Gaulle separately.

General de Gaulle kept Eboué informed, and Eboué sent telegrams to the Guyanese, trying to make them understand they must support de Gaulle, not Giraud. He spoke over the radio to

Guyane saying he was proud of his compatriots, that General de Gaulle was the single leader of the French, and that all must be united behind him. He spoke part of his message in Creole, the first time anyone could remember hearing him speak it.[72]

Unfortunately, Giraud and de Gaulle both named a governor of Eboué's home colony. Giraud chose Jean Rapenne who had supported Vichy as governor of Niger in 1940, and de Gaulle named Maurice Bertaut, then an administrator in chief in Cameroun. (Both men were members of the class of 1924 at the Colonial School.) A representative of Giraud arrived quickly from America, and Rapenne was thus able to become governor instead of Bertaut. This confusion infuriated Eboué.[73] The only immediately satisfactory thing about the adherence of Guyane, in Eboué's view, was the subsequent release of his brother-in-law, Louis Courbain, from Devil's Island.

On 30 May 1943 de Gaulle arrived in Algiers where he and Giraud served as co-presidents of the French Committee of National Liberation, each trying to outmaneuver the other. Eboué renewed his pledge of loyalty made in October 1940 in Tchad:

> For almost three years your heroic and unfailing will has been our guide. For almost three years, animated with an undying hope and always faithful, we have followed with you the difficult steps from a humiliated France which kept her pride. Today, the recompense arrives. The patriotism of General Giraud is a promise that there will henceforth only be a single direction for a unified Homeland. The day for punishment of traitors and victory over the enemy is approaching. Vive la France![74]

The African elite, represented by Aubame, who was probably advised by Eboué, expressed its support in a telegram to de Gaulle: "Black youth of French Equatorial Africa asks . . . National Committee to bring to attention of Allied government that French African Empire wants General de Gaulle, initiator

---

72 Arch. Nat. de Gaulle, Telegram, from Félix Eboué, 24 March 1943, 240/ INF.

73 For the point of view of the Guyanese, see Ulrich Sophie, *Le Ralliement de la Guyane à la France Libre* (Paris: Soulanges, 1964).

74 JO-AEF, 1 June 1943, p. 333.

of French resistance movement to be recognized by all Allies as Supreme Chief of Fighting France. . . ."[75]

In Brazzaville Eboué celebrated the arrival of de Gaulle in Algiers with festivities on 6 June;[76] but the tension between the supporters of Giraud and those of de Gaulle grew. On 18 July European residents of Brazzaville received an unsigned letter called "Letter from a group of French patriots in Brazzaville to General Giraud." The authors of the letter complained that many of de Gaulle's followers were extreme anti-American "leftists" like trade unionists, Freemasons, Jews, and Communists who would install an extreme leftist regime in France if de Gaulle took power. They concluded that only General Giraud could save France from such a group.

The tension grew that month because of the rallying in July of Martinique and Guadeloupe and the need to name a governor. De Gaulle told Eboué he wanted to name Bertaut to Guadeloupe because of the failure to install him in Cayenne. Giraud objected that it would not be a good idea to name someone who, according to rumor, was not "pure white" to a post so close to America. De Gaulle asked Eboué his opinion.[77] Eboué sent a long and extremely interesting reply in which he analyzed for de Gaulle some of the problems in Guadeloupe; for some reason he denied that the people thought very much about race. With regard to Bertaut, Eboué vigorously defended the appointment if de Gaulle thought him capable. Eboué said race should make no difference: "One must only consider his personal qualities and not the fact that he is or is not of the white race, which I don't know anyway. "Can he govern well one of the Antilles? This is the only question to ask."

Eboué gave no less than eight reasons why the French should not worry about American reactions to the appointment of Bertaut even if he had some African ancestry. First, America had changed some race attitudes. Second, Eboué said he was sure 15 million black Americans, who had already shown some in-

[75] JO-AEF, 1 January 1943, p. 2.

[76] U.S. State, Report, Consul, Brazzaville, 11 June 1943, 851.01/2321.

[77] Arch. Nat. de Gaulle, Secret Telegram, London, to Félix Eboué, 25 May 1943, COL 9272C.

terest in Africa through the NAACP, would protest any race-biased American action against Bertaut. Third, cordial relations existed between Haiti and America. Fourth, America, it was rumored, had a black consul general in Colombia. Fifth, America had cordial relations with Brazil, a mixed country. Sixth, Roosevelt recently invited the President of Liberia to visit Washington. Seventh, Eboué, as governor in the Antilles, never felt any American opposition. Eighth, a black journalist had recently visited him.[78] What the eighth reason had to do with American attitudes is not clear, but what is interesting is the vigor with which Eboué defended the possible nomination of a man with reported African ancestry to a high post. It was, of course, his assimilation ideal that any Frenchman could serve in any high post if he had the qualifications without regard to race. Bertaut was named governor of Guadeloupe.

In August 1943 America recognized the new French Committee, and soon de Gaulle outmaneuvered Giraud for the leadership position. In August General de Gaulle also planned to come to Brazzaville to celebrate the third anniversary of the adherence of the colonies as well as the progress made in the war. But he could not come. He had many plans to make in Algiers for the future organization of France and for the futures of his Vichy enemies. In September, for example, Boisson was relieved of his post in Dakar. A newly established Commission of Purification planned to see whether or not he should be tried, but his death precluded a decision.

At the beginning of November 1943 a Provisional Consultative Assembly met to discuss the future government of France. In spite of the role of the empire in the war, the French National Committee, prior to 1943, had thought very little about definite new directions, although Eboué was struggling to bring about changes. It was therefore decided to hold a conference in Brazzaville to formulate suggestions concerning the African empire and then to submit them to Algiers.

Pleven and de Gaulle scheduled the meeting for the end of

[78] Arch. Nat. de Gaulle, Telegram, from Félix Eboué, 30 May 1943 and 5 June 1943, No. 321.

January 1944, and Eboué would, of course, have to be there. Eboué felt tired and had a few bouts with minor illnesses. He also missed his two friends—Laurentie, who had left in July for Algiers to work with Pleven, and Isambert, who had gone to London. The governor general decided that he, his wife, and Ginette would take a vacation at the beginning of 1944, just after the Conférence Africaine Française.

X

TO CAIRO: A PREMATURE
ENDING, 1944

IN RESPONSE to Eboué's New Year's wishes for 1944 General de Gaulle cabled from Algiers:

Thank you, my dear friend, for your greetings and for sending me the feelings of confidence and fidelity of French Equatorial Africa united around you. The year 1944 will perhaps be the year of liberation but it will not be the end of the battle. I am happy to be able to count on the continuing effort of French Equatorial Africa and on you.[1]

Germany still dominated Europe and Japan the Pacific at the end of 1943, but North Africa had been liberated. In September the Italian government capitulated although Allied troops had still to fight the Germans in control of Rome and other major cities. Free French forces took Corsica. On the eastern front the Russians gradually pushed the enemy back toward the frontier. In the Orient the American forces were proceeding, island by island, to within striking distance of the Japanese mainland. Although Britain, America, and the Soviet Union did not include de Gaulle in their December 1943 meeting at Teheran, optimism prevailed in Brazzaville.

Eboué shared the optimism, but he had reason for concern about private family matters. All was well with Ginette, then

1 Telegram, 30 December 1943, Algiers, de Gaulle to Eboué.

twenty and finished with the baccalaureate; with Madame Eboué, occupied with a woman's auxiliary; and with Charles, happy with pilot training school in Britain and Canada. But Eboué was worried about Henry and Robert, both in the Middle East, serving with units previously inactive and loyal to Vichy; they suffered some racial discrimination and insults, and Robert, a quiet young man then twenty-four years old, was particularly affected. Eboué tried to have him transferred to Brazzaville, but he entered an officer training school instead; although he reportedly did well, he graduated at the rank of sergeant while his classmates moved higher. Eboué, angry, informed Laurentie, then in Algiers, and Laurentie promised to do what he could. He later requested Robert's transfer. Eboué had money taken out of his monthly salary (of about $1000) and sent to each of his three sons.

Because of these concerns and the fact he had not had a long vacation in years, Eboué felt and looked tired at the end of 1943. Each month the physicians in Brazzaville tested him and found a high level of uric acid; his joints were sore and stiff, and it seems that the problem was gout. His rich diet did nothing to help matters. In November he left the capital to rest in Pointe Noire, on the sea and therefore a little cooler than Brazzaville. André Bayardelle, who had replaced Laurentie, took over the affairs of the group of colonies. When Eboué returned, he prepared for the colonial conference scheduled to begin at the end of January.

BRAZZAVILLE CONFERENCE

In spite of the fact that the Free French movement could never have existed without the colonies, General de Gaulle and René

On the closing day of the Conseil d'Administration, in November 1943, Free French administrators and aides posed on a Brazzaville lawn. From the left in the front row are Governor Fortuné, Secretary General Bayardelle, Eboué, General Marchand, Governor Sautot. Behind Sautot is Governor Vuillaume, and between Marchand and Sautot stands Governor Rogué. Standing at the far left is Sultan Ourada. Courtesy of Madame Eboué.

Pleven do not appear to have given very much thought to specific change in the empire. It is true that de Gaulle says in his memoirs (written ten years after the events) that he knew change was necessary: "I intended that my government take the initiative without delay."[2] But no one in the French National Committee had first-hand colonial experience and most members concentrated mainly on the future of metropolitan France while assuming a return to the *status quo ante* in the colonies.[3] A decree of 2 December 1941 created commissions for the study of post-war problems, but none was designated to deal specifically with colonial issues. Eboué's circulars, the Atlantic Charter, the anti-colonial posture of America, and probably the independence of Lebanon in 1943 convinced the French leaders of the need to think about reforms. In July 1943 Pleven decided to call the governors together for a discussion of the future.

The National Committee could have chosen Algiers or even Dakar for the meeting, but to honor Eboué's role in the Gaullist movement they chose Brazzaville as the site. The conference date, January 1944, and the location were announced in October.

The idea of a convocation of governors in tropical Africa was not original; similar meetings had been held in 1934-1935 and in 1937. The war, however, encouraged some colonial governors to hope for significant change this time, even though they knew they would have only the power to recommend to the Consultative Assembly which had been meeting in Algiers since November 1943. Idealism and optimism prevailed among those planning for the conference when they received the preliminary program, which set forth the goal as "the definition of French colonial doctrine in Africa and the practical rules by which it will be applied."[4] Eboué's influence over the agenda was clear; four major subjects to be discussed—native policy, the *évolués*, eco-

[2] Charles de Gaulle, *Memoires de guerre: l'unité*, Vol. II (Paris: Plon, 1956), p. 182.

[3] See Roger V. Des Forges, *The Myths of Brazzaville: The War-Time Origins of the French Union 1939-1944*, unpublished senior thesis, Princeton University, 15 April 1964, pp. 162-64.

[4] Commissariat aux Colonies, "Programme général de la Conférence de Brazzaville, Janvier 1944," p. 2.

nomic development, and administrative reorganization—had been raised in his 1941 circulars. A fifth project, concerning political change, was new. The Commissioner of Colonies rejected self-government, at least in the foreseeable future: "If there is self-government, it will only perhaps be after long and strictly controlled evolution." But the fact that the empire must be included in the constitution of a new French Republic meant change—greater integration and assimilation than in the past.

Brazzaville prepared for the meeting and for de Gaulle's arrival on 28 January. The tricolor flew from every building in the central part of the town and on the administrative buildings overlooking the river. Nineteen governors and governors general arrived, as did Laurentie, now holding the rank governor; he would serve as secretary to the conference. On 28 January Eboué and these officials greeted de Gaulle at the airport where he reviewed the African and European troops. In the evening Eboué had de Gaulle, Pleven, Laurentie, and a few others to one of his overwhelming dinners. They discussed the world situation and the good news from France of increased activities of the underground.

The next day de Gaulle, accompanied by the various governors and Eboué, attended soccer games between African teams and between European teams at the new stadium; he spoke a brief tribute to Eboué, after whom the stadium had been named: "Nothing could be more appropriate than to give the stadium the name of your governor general, for reasons into which I will not go but which you know as well as I, and which I will summarize in declaring: He is a great Governor General; he is a great Frenchman!" When the cheers died down de Gaulle praised them for their war effort and led them in the signing of the Marseillaise.[5]

The 30th of January de Gaulle and Eboué took part in the unveiling of a monument to Pierre Savorgnan de Brazza, and then, in the first plenary session of the Conference Africaine Française, Pleven, the chairman, welcomed the governors and the guests and

5 National Archives, FSI Shortwave Broadcasts, Station Brazzaville, Shinda Monitoring Station, 29 January 1944, 61700F-12944.

re-emphasized that the conference would concern itself with the social aspects of colonization, not just the economic aspects. After another speech by Félix Gouin, President of the Consultative Assembly, General de Gaulle officially opened the deliberations.

He stated that France must "renew" herself, that her policies in Africa must associate the African with the progress that takes place: "You will study here for submission to the government what moral, social, political, economic and other conditions you think must be progressively applied in each of our territories in order that, through development and the progress of their population, they will be integrated into the French community with their personality, their interests, their aspirations, their future."[6] After his speech he departed for Bangui, Fort Lamy, and to Algiers.

From 31 January to 8 February the governors met in closed sessions, dividing themselves into seven commissions: 1. Social and family customs and labor. 2. Economic organization. 3. Administrative reform. 4. Education. 5. Hygiene and public health. 6. Personnel. 7. Custom reform.[7] Eboué interested himself particularly in the first commission and made a statement on African labor on 2 February. He summarized the history of development of French Equatorial Africa: the concessionary companies failed to bring about significant change, for, he said, they failed to get Africans to work regular hours, a necessity, Eboué felt, to foster the habits necessary to achieve development. Only high wages, he said, could help achieve what was necessary.

Since his earliest days in Oubangui Eboué had believed in some kind of forced labor; at Brazzaville he said that everyone should be honest enough to admit it existed and then to regulate it: "One reads in our rules and laws that work is free in French Equatorial Africa, but is it? We must have the courage to answer no! With the present system for recruitment of workers we have made veritable purveyors of labor out of our administrators." He proposed that administrators recruit labor for businesses working

---

[6] La Conférence Africaine Française, Brazzaville, 30 Janvier 1944-8 Février 1944 (Alger: Commissariat aux Colonies, 1944), p. 28.

[7] Mrs. Dorothy Shipley White is preparing a long study of the Brazzaville Conference.

in the interest of the colony, a rather vague statement, considering that all enterprises by employing African labor contributed to the collectivity by giving the African the wages from which he paid his taxes. He openly accepted forced labor: "I declare here that I am a partisan of the obligation to work which is the *right* to work. . . . I shall always remember the late Blaise Diagne, the Black Knight, discouraged and disappointed after his return from Geneva where before the Mandate Commission he pronounced the foul words, 'forced labor.' He was almost booed by the learned gentlemen who unfortunately knew nothing about the subject compared with Blaise Diagne."[8] Eboué believed that every adult male must work, but believed as well that the administration must protect him from abuse.

In a more interesting and important report André Latrille, Eboué's former subordinate in Tchad, by then governor of Ivory Coast, seemed to progress past Eboué, and to make Eboué's views seem dated. He said that there were many abuses in a forced labor situation in spite of attempts to control them, and that European employers disregarded minimum wage provisions. He proposed gradual abolition of forced labor.

In the same commission the next day the discussion turned to assimilation and association doctrines. Eboué defended the associationist position, i.e., that Africans had their own civilizations within which they could evolve; he argued against Martiniquan Raphael Saller's view that Africans could become Frenchmen and that colonial policy should encourage such a development. Eboué then introduced African opinion into the meeting. Fily Dabo Sissoko, the Muslim teacher and canton chief, had prepared a manuscript on African opinion and had sent it to Eboué.[9] In addition, Eboué had a statement from organizations of civil servants in Brazzaville, and a statement from Jean-Rémy Ayouné, a Gabonese working in his cabinet. Sissoko supported the idea of association and Ayouné the idea of assimilation.[10]

8 Transcript of meeting, 2 February 1944.

9 Archives Eboué, original manuscript. In his dedication he wrote: "To Mr. F. Eboué, Governor General of the Colonies, respectful wishes from a brother who has never lost hope in the Race. 25/12/1943.

10 *La Conférence Africaine*, pp. 100-101, 94.

No matter what the opinions of these Africans might be, the introduction of their views into the meeting was meaningful. Eboué served notice in his quiet way that French administrators should pay attention to the views of a growing African elite, that their views had relevance, and that the Africans should have a greater role in decision-making.

This commission and the other six met until 8 February when the Conference closed with a series of recommendations. Among them was the idea that the colonies be represented in a new colonial parliament or federal assembly and that decentralization of decision-making be undertaken. Decentralization meant more power to governors from central offices in the ministry and the creation of local assemblies which would deliberate on budgets for the colonies. More positions in the administration were to be open to Africans and the educational system was to be revised to train them for higher positions in the colonial administration. Inspired by Eboué's circular, the Conference suggested keeping African political institutions and encouraged West African colonies to adopt the statute concerning the *notables évolués*. A contradictory measure, that education should be exclusively in the French language, was also supported. The governors also recommended more control over labor and immigration of Europeans.

Some reforms were introduced in the months following the Brazzaville Conference: the *indigénat* disappeared, and Africans gained more freedom to organize. Two years later the new constitution of the Fourth Republic provided for the creation of local assemblies in Africa, an Assembly of the French Union, a very weak federal assembly with representatives from all African colonies and France, and the extension of citizenship. The reforms were small and outdated in the long run, and the French Union was merely an extension of the French empire under another name, but the Conference made an African elite of clerks, teachers, priests, doctors and others realize that change was possible. Jean-Hilaire Aubame wrote: "It was impossible to continue to think according to the old colonialist conceptions, and in this regard the Conference of Brazzaville can be considered a real declaration of the Rights of African Man. A

Declaration still perhaps timid, incomplete and sometimes ret-
icent, but rich in possibilities."[11] One then beginning nationalist
leader wrote years later: "[The] French Union . . . opened per-
spectives of equality in the relation between the colonized and
the colonizers." The decrees from 1944 to 1946 "permitted . . .
the promulgation of series of laws authorizing the constitution of
political parties and trade unions" in which future leaders gained
experience.[12]

Eboué, believing that the Brazzaville Conference recommendations vacillated between association and assimilation,[13] began to
set down his thoughts in an essay he called "The Future of
Africa." The "oldest continent" would, he said, see a renaissance
after the war. Such a change would depend on the farsightedness
of the Europeans, who should not draw back from comparing
their programs among themselves. The key of the future was
native policy and the development of a new bourgeoisie of
"African citizens" around his idea of *évolués*. Europeans and
Africans working together would "lead us in some time to an
Afro-European form of civilization." In a second essay called
"Economic Pan-Africanism" Eboué wrote that French territory
extended from Brazzaville to Dakar as much as from Marseille to
Paris and would continue to do so, but that after the war economic policy must change to permit more trade between Brazzaville and Dakar without passing through Paris or Marseille. "I
also think that these States, dominions, or federations ought to
be able to make agreements or develop exchanges of their products—without creating 'African Nationalism'—and that the form
of these agreements would not exclude or prevent economic relations with other continents." To coordinate such relations
among African countries and possibly with other continents, he
wrote, an organization was necessary: "It seems to me necessary
to create a permanent organism whose duty would be to co-

11 J. Aubame, "La Conférence de Brazzaville," in *Afrique Equatoriale Française*, Eugène Guernier, editor (Paris: Encyclopédie Coloniale et Maritime,
1950), p. 186.

12 Ahmed Sékou Touré, *L'Afrique et la révolution*, Vol. 13 (Conakry, 1967),
pp. 30-31.

13 Interview with Henri Laurentie, Néron, 7 May 1968.

ordinate and arbitrate the different interests concerned and
which would have its headquarters (a permanent secretariat) in
one place but whose members would meet periodically in the
different capitals of Africa."[14]

Eboué's statements had the elements of a profoundly anti-colonial revolution, whether he knew it or not. By not requiring
commerce to pass through the metropole there was a possibility
of breaking free from the so-called Colonial Pact in which
vertical trade strictly controlled by Europeans between the colony and the European power ensured that commerce would
always work to the advantage of Europe; this allowed the corol-
lary possibility of creating locally owned industry free of metropolitan interests. Eboué, not looking at the connection between
economics and politics, did not seemingly realize that if a country
became increasingly independent of France in the economic realm
—particularly if it were linked with other African countries—it
might be able to become politically independent.

TO EGYPT

At various times during the war Eboué planned trips either to
Nigeria or to Anglo-Egyptian Sudan, but he never left French
territory either because he had too much work or because the
vicissitudes in General de Gaulle's relations with the British
prevented courtesy visits. After the Brazzaville Conference, however, Eboué decided to go to Egypt, Palestine, Syria, and Lebanon, and Pleven agreed to a three-month leave. He particularly
looked forward to the pyramids of Egypt, for he was still interested in the idea of Atlantis, and one of the keys to believing
in it was the similarity of pyramids in Egypt to those in Mexico
and Peru.

Many of the Antilleans in Brazzaville, who considered Eboué
their protector, asked him not to leave for the Middle East, saying that they feared he would never return. There had been
rumors, spread by whites who still did not like him, that he

---

[14] Handwritten manuscript in Archives of Jean Poupel and Archives Eboué,
"L'Avenir de l'Afrique" and "Panafricanisme Economique." Also published
in part in Albert Maurice, *Félix Eboué: sa vie et son oeuvre* (Brussels: Institut
Royal Colonial Belge, 1954), pp. 47-48.

might be replaced by Laurentie or someone else, and other rumors that de Gaulle might make him governor general of French West Africa or send him to the Antilles. Eboué quietly responded he saw no reason for concern.[15] He had seen his physician who said he was in good enough health to travel, and after signing two decrees integrating two more African clerks into the European cadre of the civil service Eboué, his wife, Ginette, and an African driver left Brazzaville on 16 February in their Dodge motorcar for the Belgian Congo. André Bayardelle remained as acting governor general.

After numerous receptions and dinners in the Congo the family visited gold mines at Kilo-Moto and saw some industrial installations near Stanleyville where they remained for several days. There Eboué rested, read a few detective stories, and telegraphed the governor general of Madagascar to send a selection of seeds to Congo for purposes of experimentation.

Traveling by land gave Eboué the possibility to exchange views with these Belgian administrators. He also brought along writing paper and began to note more thoughts about colonialism in Africa; he had not done this systematically before; his previous studies had been about African music or general ethnography, but everything he wrote during this trip suggests that he sensed a great change coming even though he could not believe it would be political. He evidently believed that he would have an important role in the post-World War II era.

Still in the Congo he wrote, "It was therefore not a bad idea that I undertake this trip in order to judge the degree of evolution our friendly neighbors arrived at already. In addition, African matters are not so different from one country to another and at this great turning-point in colonial ideology—latent before the war but [overt now because] the war has shown the need for some revisions—it was good to compare methods and judge them. . . ."[16]

He continued his reflections after departing from the Congo. In mid-March the family drove into Anglo-Egyptian Sudan head-

[15] Interview, Georges Céleste, 28 August 1968, Paris.

[16] Archives Eboué, unpublished notes, "Impressions de voyage du Stanley Pool au Stanley Falls."

ing east on the White Nile and near the Sudan, Congo, and Uganda frontiers. They boarded a river boat at Juba on 18 March, Ginette's twenty-first birthday, and planned to go as far as Kosti where the train to Khartoum stopped.

The trip to Kosti was to last eight days, from 18 March to 26 March, but the second day out of Juba the boat became stuck on sand banks in the Nile. Eboué sat on the deck while the workers attempted to free the boat, and observed the life of the riverbank villages. In this area, subject to annual flooding and to centuries of slave raids by the Arabs to the north, Eboué judged that "The natives themselves are not happy; the villages are sad. One feels that millennia of horrible things which must have happened in these regions marked the country with sadness."[17] An Englishman confirmed that the people were the Dinka Eboué had read about.

Within two days, Eboué was bored; he noted in his diary: ". . . papyrus, hippos, crocodiles." From the ship someone fired a gun aimlessly. Eboué turned to a French translation of Wendell Willkie's recent and famous *One World*,[18] originally published in 1943. Willkie, the defeated Republican candidate for President of the United States in the 1940 elections, said that World War II was a revolution for world liberation "giving to *all* people freedom to govern themselves as soon as they are able, and the economic freedom on which all lasting self-government inevitably rests."[19]

One World stimulated Eboué to think about political topics. He thought it "very American" in outlook, but added "will look at it again." He thought about it in terms of the Dinka people whom he had been observing. They were simple cattle herdsmen who went naked, and Eboué asked himself about Willkie's ideas of independence for all in terms of these Dinka: "Really, Mr. Willkie, must the Atlantic Charter be applied in the Dinka, Shilluk, or X Republics? Have we the right to leave things in this state on the pretext of freedom? Or, on the contrary must we

[17] Archives Eboué, Diary, March 1944.
[18] Wendell L. Willkie, *One World* (New York: Simon and Schuster, 1943).
[19] *Ibid.*, p. 180.

intervene and help, out of love, these human beings to become men?"[20] He thus still believed in the primacy of economics and organization, to say nothing of stoic love.

On 27 March the boat arrived at Kosti. The Eboué family disembarked and boarded Governor General Huddleston's private railroad cars, which he had dispatched for Eboué. He was impressed with the great luxury afforded high British colonial officials.

Before the train left, however, Eboué had enough time to visit an African hospital. He was surprised to learn that there were African physicians, for in French Equatorial Africa there was not a single fully trained African physician: He was even more surprised to learn that native physicians operated—even on Europeans if necessary. He planned a visit, therefore, to the School of Medicine at Khartoum.[21]

They left for Khartoum, arriving early in the morning of 28 March. Governor General Huddleston met them with an honor guard, although Eboué was on a purely private visit. The family were Huddleston's guests at the governor's palace, and all the British received him with great courtesy and consideration. Eboué visited the medical school and toured the city of Khartoum, and the next day was interviewed by a reporter. Eboué praised the economic progress of French Equatorial Africa and said that France and the colonies were "indivisible."[22] The evening of 29 March the governor general of Sudan gave him an official dinner during which he presented Eboué with a specially bound English translation of the 8 November 1941 circular, *La Nouvelle Politique Indigène*. After more visits to schools the Eboués left Khartoum by train on 31 March for Cairo. Huddleston came to the station to see them off.

The family arrived in Cairo on 4 April where they were met by leaders of the Free French office, the Suez Canal Company, and several friends. The Eboués quickly moved into Shepheard's, the city's most luxurious hotel.

20 Archives Eboué, Diary, March 1944.
21 *Ibid.*
22 *Sudan Times*, 29 March 1944.

CAIRO TO 17 MAY 1944

The first evening in Egypt's capital Eboué wanted to visit the pyramids just outside the city. He, his wife, and Ginette drove to it although the hour was already late. The evening air was cool and clear; the moon illuminated the great stone structure. Eboué got out of the automobile, walked toward the pyramid and said nothing. The chill in the air bothered Madame Eboué, and she called to her husband. He remained almost transfixed before the pyramid, symbol of pharaonic history and, for Eboué, symbol of the unity of mankind: "This is true civilization, true civilization," he said quietly and returned.[23]

The following day Eboué visited the city and looked at his mail which had arrived from Brazzaville. One correspondent had depressing news: ". . . many too many things are done as if you were not supposed to return. Besides, there is a rumor to this effect that they let continue with satisfaction. The two decrees concerning the nomination of natives that you wanted to sign yourself before your departure have been stopped. . . ."[24]

Eboué also found a request to grant an interview to Walter White, the Secretary of the American National Association for the Advancement of Colored People (NAACP), in Cairo on a world tour. The intellectual leaders of the Negro community in the United States had been following Eboué's career ever since his governorship of Guadeloupe. Just after Mandel recalled him from the Antilles, for example, Dr. Mercer Cook, writer and university teacher, visited the islands and then wrote an article, "Guadeloupe Loses Its First Negro Governor," for *Opportunity* magazine, one of the leading Negro publications.[25] In the article Cook expressed his anger that black men, Candace and Eboué according to his interpretation, had divided themselves. Cook who regularly reported to the Negro American community on events in French-speaking countries continued to follow Eboué's

---

[23] Interview, Madame Ginette Fontaine-Eboué, Paris, 19 June 1967.

[24] Archives Eboué, Letter to Félix Eboué, 28 February 1944. I have no documents showing Eboué's response, and the person who wrote to him this letter refused further details.

[25] *Opportunity*, Vol. 17, No. 4, April 1939, pp. 112-13.

career and objected, in a 1943 article, that de Gaulle did not name Eboué to the Committee of National Liberation in Algiers. He wondered in print if de Gaulle had betrayed his loyal follower in spite of all he had done for France: "The war has made Governor General Félix Eboué the world's most prominent Negro. To us, as to the natives of his French Equatorial Africa, he stands as a symbol. What happens to him now is an indication of what may happen to us all later."[26]

Cook's colleague at Howard University, Alain Leroy Locke, whom Eboué had met in the 1920's, helped edit a special issue of the magazine *Survey Graphic* on color problems and included an article on the governor general. In slightly exaggerated prose the author, Egon Kaskeline, said that Eboué, "France's first Negro governor," served "the less fortunate members of his race" and desired the "liberation of the African Negro from oppression and exploitation."[27] Locke had sent Eboué a copy of the magazine.

The Negro *Pittsburg Courrier* had sent a journalist to interview Eboué before his departure for Egypt to get details on his early life and career. The American presented him with a very long list of questions, and Eboué spent a great deal of time writing out the answers. He also spent one whole day with the visitor, and members of his staff, who had no idea that the *Courrier* was a Negro newspaper, were surprised at Eboué's very friendly behavior toward the foreigner. Eboué also received White very cordially, giving him much of his time.

During two conversations Eboué and White managed in a mixture of French and English to discuss the adherence of Tchad to de Gaulle's movement in 1940, and then Eboué went back over his earlier career, telling about the introduction of industrial cotton to Oubangui-Chari about which he was very satisfied. White asked him about the future, and Eboué expressed a desire for a transformation of the colonies: "We must declare war on

---

[26] Mercer Cook, "Why Is World's Foremost Negro Snubbed by Allies?," *Chicago Defender*, Moorland Archives, newspaper collection, File "Félix Eboué," n.d.

[27] Egon Kaskeline, "Félix Eboué and the Fighting French," *Survey Graphic: Color—Unfinished Business of Democray*, special issue, Vol. XXXI, No. 11, November 1942, pp. 522-23, 548-50.

illness; we must abolish poverty and ignorance. . . . Africa needs
doctors, technicians, teachers, scientists to help develop its people
and its resources. And we are going to get them." White then
asked Eboué if he foresaw independence in Africa and noted his
own disappointment when Eboué quickly responded: "We are
Frenchmen, and we are loyal to France."[28] At the end of the interviews White asked Eboué to visit the United States for he said
it would be important to show black and white Americans a
black man who had reached such an important position in world
affairs. Eboué responded that he would like to visit America and
to know more about the NAACP.

Eboué would have liked to spend more time with White, but
he had to visit some Egyptian officials and make a few speeches.
On 11 April he went to see Prime Minister Nahas Pacha for a
courtesy visit,[29] and the evening of 15 April he gave a speech at
the French lycée on colonial history and French African policy,
"From de Brazza to General de Gaulle." Pleven had asked him
to give some publicity to France's efforts to reform the empire
and Eboué obliged. He was not feeling well but he finished his
speech. The next morning he felt feverish, and the family
thought it a good precaution to go to the hospital; on 16 April
Eboué entered the French hospital of Cairo for what everyone
thought would be a short stay.

The physicians gave Eboué an examination and discovered
what seemed to be "pulmonary congestion"—pneumonia—a re-
currence of what in the 1920's was a psychosomatic illness. It is
possible that the tension caused by the rally of Tchad, a year
without knowing the whereabouts of his children, the conflict
between himself and de Larminat and then between himself and
Sicé, the racism of Brazzaville, and worry about Robert and
Henry contributed to his illness.

Eboué, keeping very calm and quiet, did not seem very ill, but
he gravely requested the physician to order water from the Nile
brought to him, and he drank it without explanation. The Nile
had given life to Egypt, and he hoped it might help restore him.

---

[28] Walter White, *A Rising Wind* (New York: Doubleday, 1945), pp. 115-16,
121.
[29] *Le Progrès Egyptien,* 12 April 1944.

One of the last photos taken of Eboué. Courtesy of
Madame Ginette Fontaine-Eboué.

His condition improved, and sitting up in bed he began to write
again about tonal languages in Oubangui-Chari and succeeded
in preparing a short manuscript. The last thing he wrote was a

letter to General de Gaulle.[30] On 29 April he and his wife left
the hospital for lunch at his physician's residence. The next day
he went to lunch at another Frenchman's house, but he felt ill
and asked his host if he could lie down. That afternoon he went
back to the hospital. The doctor called a specialist who said
Eboué's heart was weak. The pneumonia continued. An English
physician administered the newly discovered penicillin.

The news of Eboué's illness traveled swiftly to Brazzaville and
to Algiers. From Brazzaville the bishop wrote: "Rumors are
circulating about the definitive departure of Mr. Eboué. We still
hope to see him again here. . . ."[31] Laurentie replied for Pleven:
"There is no basis to these rumors. . . ." But he admitted his
former superior officer was extremely ill. On 13 May Laurentie
became concerned about Eboué; he flew from Algiers to Cairo to
see him. This gesture from a friend and loyal colleague deeply
touched Eboué, and he succeeded in talking with him a little in
spite of his difficulty in speaking. Military authorities granted
Robert permission to visit his father, and with Madame Eboué and
Ginette he stayed by Eboué's bed reading to him from the daily
newspapers. Suddenly, Eboué developed uremia. He weakened
quickly. On 16 May Laurentie rushed to the hospital again. Eboué
knew he was dying and struggled to say something to Laurentie: "Henry, Robert, my children," he whispered, "Watch over
them. . . ."

On the 17th physicians installed an oxygen tent. Madame
Eboué, Ginette, Robert, Laurentie, and Philippe Pain, a distant
relative, stayed at his bedside. In the afternoon he began to
tremble and tried to say something, but no one understood. At
6:30, the evening of 17 May 1944, he quietly died.[32]

ÉBOUÉ THE SYMBOL

The day after Eboué's death René Pleven arrived in Cairo, and
Governor General Huddleston came quickly from Khartoum
with other high-ranking British officials. General de Gaulle could

---

[30] The letter is, as yet, unavailable.
[31] Letter, Bishop Bièchy to René Pleven, 30 April 1944.
[32] Archives Eboué, Letter, Eugénie Eboué to Charles Eboué, Letter, Ginette
Eboué to Charles Eboué, 19 May 1944, Interviews.

not travel, but he issued a statement: "The country, the nation, and the empire are in mourning for Governor General Félix Eboué of French Equatorial Africa, Companion of the Liberation. Every Frenchman remembers that by maintaining Tchad in the war at the worst period of our history, Félix Eboué put a stop to the spirit of capitulation in this land that borders the Sahara. Félix Eboué, a great Frenchman, died serving France." The commissioner for colonies promised Madame Eboué that after the liberation of French territory the nation would pay proper tribute to her husband, but he would have to be buried for the time being in Egypt. The funeral was held on 19 May, only two days after Eboué's death, in the church of Saint Marc de Choubrah, although Eboué was not a practicing Roman Catholic. Pleven and others said a Catholic mass would look better than the masonic ceremony, and Cairo cemeteries were arranged according to religion.

At the funeral Pleven gave the oration. He spoke about Eboué's career in Oubangui-Chari, in Tchad, and his work in Brazzaville; he did not mention the Antilles. He said Eboué made an important contribution to the empire and could have continued to influence colonial policy after the war: "I declare with sadness that the loss suffered today by France in his person weakens the homeland for the present and impoverishes it for the future." Eboué, the first man "of his race" to become a governor, he said, was a symbol of brotherhood for the French and proof that racism was not part of their culture. Addressing himself to the dead man Pleven said: "I promise you that the French and Christian ideal of human brotherhood . . . will continue to guide colonial policy that you helped us elaborate just a few weeks ago in Brazzaville. . . . You will remain for the whole Empire, where you were born, proof that France recognizes between its sons no distinctions other than merit."[33] The press and radio widely reported the death and funeral.

News reports of Eboué's premature disappearance distressed African civil servants and Antilleans for he had become a symbol for them too, and gave them hope for change after the war.

[33] Archives Eboué, Speech, René Pleven, 19 May 1944.

Many said he must have been poisoned for he seemed in good health and was only fifty-nine years old. In fact, of course, he had been ill, and there is no proof he died of anything other than a natural death, although some whites would have liked to see him replaced because of his attempts to integrate African subjects into higher positions in the colonial service, because of racist feeling, and because of the fear he might have an even more important position after the war.

Antilleans particularly thought Eboué might have been powerful after the war and would have helped direct development funds to the old colonies and grant them more rights as Frenchmen. In Guadeloupe, the same day as a ceremony honoring his memory, a newspaper lamented the loss: "The black race loses in Félix Eboué its star. For the black world his presence at the sides of those who are preparing the future of France and the authority that he had the right to have in the cabinet after the war were a guarantee. Fate has decided otherwise."[34]

The newspaper was incorrect, for in death as in life Eboué served the Antillean cause of assimilation. In July 1944, for example, a group of West Indians in Morocco formed a "Club Félix Eboué" to perpetuate the memory of a black man who devoted his life to France and through him "to make overseas French territories known and liked and to pursue their assimilation to departments of the Metropole."[35] For them Eboué was a link between the Metropole and the old colonies. His life, they said, proved that race did not count; his career proved Schoelcher, the liberator of the slaves, right, for as a free man Eboué worked sincerely for his country, helping to save it from Nazi domination: ". . . by his action [Eboué] made the men of his race and all Humanity understand there is nothing in the world superior to Liberty," a Guyanese wrote.[36] Antilleans then worked for the integration of Guadeloupe, Martinique, Guyane, and Réunion into France during the discussions concerning a new constitution after liberation in 1944.

The freeing of France from German control came quickly

---

[34] *Le Miroire de la Guadeloupe* (Pointe-à-Pitre), 25 May 1944, p. 1.
[35] Letter, Club Félix Eboué to René Pleven, 29 July 1944.
[36] *La Voix de la Guyane*, Vol. VIII, No. 17, July 1960.

after Eboué's death, permitting the organization of a provisional government on European soil in 1944. On the 6th of June allied forces landed on the Normandy coast, and in the next weeks moved east toward Paris, liberated by French forces and the city's residents who revolted against the Germans at the end of August. This permitted General de Gaulle to enter the capital triumphantly 26 August 1944 and, after "saluting the Regiment of Tchad," to walk down the Avenue des Champs Elysées in a sea of cheering Frenchmen, four years to the day after the adherence of Tchad to his movement.[37]

At the head of a provisional government General de Gaulle led discussions about a future constitution. Madame Eboué participated, because Guadeloupe, grateful to her husband for Popular Front reforms, elected her deputy to the French legislature; Ginette worked in the Ministry of Colonies; Charles continued in the French air force; Robert joined the colonial administration with the encouragement of Laurentie who became the highest official in the Ministry; and Henry involved himself in the theater and cinema. In 1946 the French adopted a new constitution creating the Fourth Republic and the French Union, as foreseen at the Brazzaville Conference. A law of 19 March 1946 made Martinique, Guadeloupe, Guyane, and Réunion departments of France. After Eboué's assimilation came the integration of his homeland. Citizenship was extended in Africa.

In the year after this change of status Antilleans and Guyanese asked the French government to redeem its pledge of proper tribute to Felix Eboué. They had already formed several organizations to prepare for the centenary in 1948 of the abolition of slavery, and one of their projects was the transfer of Schoelcher's remains to the Pantheon to rest among such French heroes and leaders as Victor Hugo, Emile Zola, Rousseau, and Jean Jaurès. Because nothing had been done about returning Eboué's remains to France from Egypt, they decided to call upon the French government to inhume him in the Pantheon at the same time as Schoelcher.[38]

---

37 de Gaulle, *Memoires de guerre,* II, pp. 310-12.
38 Interviews, A. Côme-Corneille, Paris, 25 June 1967, and President Gaston Monnerville, Paris, 30 July 1967.

Many of Eboué's old friends and associates worked for this project and others to honor his memory and, in some cases perhaps, serve their own interests. On 15 May 1947, three years after Eboué's death, supporters of General de Gaulle, then trying to organize a party after his resignation the previous year, arranged for him to place a plaque on the house where Eboué lived as a student in Bordeaux and to give a speech praising Eboué and calling for support for the French Union of which Eboué was, he said, "one of the best artisans."[39] Another plaque was put on the building at rue Chaveau Lagarde where the Eboués lived for years; streets were named in his honor; monuments were raised in Guadeloupe, Cayenne, Brazzaville, Fort Lamy, and Bamako, and books were written. Each occasion presented an opportunity to assure Africans the empire was progressing and working in their interests, and speeches made in the Assembly of the French Union invoked the name Eboué to justify new measures. Writers claimed a Eur-African federation was possible.

Among those working to perpetuate the memory of Eboué were his friends and associates: Yvon Delbos, who moved to the Senate and later ran for the Presidency of the Republic; Camille Lhuerre, who spent the rest of his life in Cayenne; Gaston Monnerville, President of the upper chamber of parliament; René Isambert, who retired after the war; Marius Moutet, Minister of Colonies once again; Louis Marin; Governor General Reste; René Pleven, who became Prime Minister; Emile Merwart, who as governor of Guyane in 1901 had signed the decree permitting Eboué to leave his homeland to begin his education in France; Roger Dévigne; E. L. Boutin; and René Maran, who prepared a book on the life of his friend.

A growing African elite of educated men and civil servants shared the views of these Antilleans and metropolitans for they saw in Eboué's career proof that a black man could succeed in the French system, and many hoped to do the same as he. They, too, could become governors or achieve other positions in equality with the whites of metropolitan France, they thought.

[39] Charles de Gaulle, "Pour sauver l'Union Française," 15 May 1947 (Paris: Société d'Edition et de Diffusion de Documentation, "Notes et documents," No. 2), p. 1.

Africans close to Eboué, like Jean-Hilaire Aubame and Fily Dabo Sissoko, became deputies to the French parliament, and others were admitted to the Colonial School. They supported all honors to Eboué's memory.

The point of view of the African masses of French Equatorial Africa was different. For most of his career Eboué was seen by them as another administrator who happened to be dark in color; "c'était un Martiniquais de France," they often said. Eboué had never called himself their brother or urged them to rise in revolt against European authority, for to do so would have been to encourage revolt against himself. The idea put forward in 1945 by the Nigerian Nwafor Orizu, that Eboué should have declared Tchad independent instead of following de Gaulle, was something that could never have occurred to him. He exercised authority as a French colonial administrator, his chosen career. His respect for African civilization, his support for African chiefs and civil servants, his efforts to bring Africa into the main current of the world's economy meant little to most of the Africans over whom he had authority. With the exception of Guadeloupe, where the masses benefitted from Popular Front reforms, only the elites associated themselves with Eboué, and they saw meaning in the decision to put him in the Pantheon.

By 1949 the various committees had succeeded in their project. A ship brought Eboué's coffin to France. After lying in state at the Colonial School he was carried up the rue Soufflot along with Victor Schoelcher. Parisians, Antilleans, Guyanese, and Africans lined the street. Gratien Candace caught the eye of Georges Céleste. President Auriol was there. The Minister of Colonies spoke. They buried Eboué alongside Schoelcher and Jean Jaurès. Félix Eboué, the only black man in French history to be officially recognized as a Hero of France by burial in the Pantheon, thus became a permanent symbol of assimilation.

Eboué was not the only black symbol of assimilation and a multiracial Eur-African community. Just before France's surrender in June 1940 German soldiers captured Captain Charles Ntchorere, a Gabonese French citizen, and ordered that he stand hands up with African troops instead of with the whites who were officers like himself. He demanded his rights as a French officer and refused German commands. One bullet through the skull killed him instantly.

African and some Antillean elites of later generations rejected the example of Ntchorere and Eboué. No longer interested in struggling for equality within the empire because they believed the goal impossible and undesirable, these men and women fought for separation from France and independence. No longer interested in leaving their homelands for careers in the so-called metropole, they began to build nations of their own, confident in the rightness of their purpose. Nonetheless, there is no doubt that Eboué's success contributed to their own sense of confidence even if they rejected him as a model. Eboué showed that blacks could have an impact on history, and he showed the meaning of participation.

Up to World War II the world considered Africans and those of African descent to be passive observers on whom history, directed by the whites, acted. Eboué was definitely not a passive observer; he acted and influenced history by introducing cotton in Oubangui-Chari; by fighting for reform in Guadeloupe where he is best remembered and loved; by rallying Tchad to General de Gaulle; and by pushing through reforms in French Equatorial Africa. At a time when no black man's picture or name appeared in a newspaper of Europe or America for having done anything —good or bad—there was Eboué with all the medals, earned in his chosen profession, pinned to his chest, and, "indisputably Negro," acting to influence the course of events. Even an anti-colonialist and pan-Africanist like George Padmore objected when anyone did not give credit to Eboué as a black man who influenced history, though he had once referred to him as a "lackey."[40]

No matter what names other blacks might have used to call him because he worked in Africa, the land of his ancestors, as a colonial official, Eboué never rejected blackness and never forgot Cayenne, his own colonial homeland. He had escaped the hope-

---

[40] Georges Padmore, "Way to Win Africans Against Nazism," *The New Leader* (London), 3 October 1940, p. 3; Letter to Daniel Guerin, cited by James R. Hooker, *Black Revolutionary: George Padmore's Path from Communism to Pan-Africanism* (New York: Praeger, 1967), p. 129.

lessness of Guyane to make something of himself, and he succeeded under very difficult conditions with his own intelligence,
a personal ideology, and a self-control which protected him from
some of the tensions of a man in his position living in his times.
Always thinking of himself as a black person within the French
nation, he would have liked to work for the development of
Guyane within the French nation. He had become assimilated
and wished to see his country fully developed and integrated;
but his premature death prevented him from exercising any direct
influence over the affairs of Guyane after the war.

The most important part of Eboué's view of his own role was
the belief in the need to participate fully in the affairs of the
French nation. Although he recognized the racism of many white
Frenchmen, the existence of discrimination, and he knew the
cutting pain of humiliation, he refused to withdraw from the
system like Jean Veneuse, the central character in René Maran's
Un Homme pareil aux autres, who says:

> I know now that neither education nor training can prevail against
> race prejudice. I know that most of my superiors never considered me
> more than a Negro, more than a "dirty nigger." . . . Well? . . .
> Well, what is there to do if not to isolate one's self from a world that
> rejects you, and to analyze it? Such has been my conduct to this day.
> And such no doubt will continue to be my conduct until death ar-
> rives to deliver me from the complex that is suffocating me.[41]

Eboué decided, rather, to participate in the game of life and
thought he could only realize his potential (helped by a few
friends) within the French nation.

It is, of course, true that France used Eboué for her own ends.
Every nation uses its participants, for it wants to survive as a
distinct actor in the world. To succeed it needs men and women
willing to act in such a way that it remains strong; to succeed it
needs men and women willing to give their lives so that the
nation—the "supreme loyalty group"—prevails. By refusing to
accept the participation of groups of people on the basis of race,
religion, or sex the nation stupidly weakens itself.

Participation also permits the individual to use the nation.

[41] René Maran, *Un Homme pareil aux autres* (Paris: Arc-en-ciel, 1947), p.
25.

This level of community is today the most effective order-maintaining organism known. In the absence of order the human being cannot survive to lead a productive life with an identity which gives him meaning for his existence. A weakening of the community thus threatens the individual. Eboué, like other superior individuals, made a more important contribution to the French nation than most of his contemporaries and he gained more than they from her, but the interaction between individual and community was the same. It continues to be the same for us all, trying as we are to realize our individual potential through the nations to which we perceive that we belong. As morally ambiguous as the participation might sometimes prove to be, individuals are allowed little choice in the matter.

This level of community is today the most effective order-maintaining organism known. In the absence of order the human being cannot survive to lead a productive life with an identity which gives him meaning for his existence. A weakening of the community thus threatens the individual. Eboué, like other superior individuals, made a more important contribution to the French nation than most of his contemporaries and he gained more than they from her, but the interaction between individual and community was the same. It continues to be the same for us all, trying as we are to realize our individual potential through the nations to which we perceive that we belong. As morally ambiguous as the participation might sometimes prove to be, individuals are allowed little choice in the matter.

Africans close to Eboué, like Jean-Hilaire Aubame and Fily Dabo Sissoko, became deputies to the French parliament, and others were admitted to the Colonial School. They supported all honors to Eboué's memory.

The point of view of the African masses of French Equatorial Africa was different. For most of his career Eboué was seen by them as another administrator who happened to be dark in color; "c'était un Martiniquais de France," they often said. Eboué had never called himself their brother or urged them to rise in revolt against European authority, for to do so would have been to encourage revolt against himself. The idea put forward in 1945 by the Nigerian Nwafor Orizu, that Eboué should have declared Tchad independent instead of following de Gaulle, was something that could never have occurred to him. He exercised authority as a French colonial administrator, his chosen career. His respect for African civilization, his support for African chiefs and civil servants, his efforts to bring Africa into the main current of the world's economy meant little to most of the Africans over whom he had authority. With the exception of Guadeloupe, where the masses benefitted from Popular Front reforms, only the elites associated themselves with Eboué, and they saw meaning in the decision to put him in the Pantheon.

By 1949 the various committees had succeeded in their project. A ship brought Eboué's coffin to France. After lying in state at the Colonial School he was carried up the rue Soufflot along with Victor Schoelcher. Parisians, Antilleans, Guyanese, and Africans lined the street. Gratien Candace caught the eye of Georges Céleste. President Auriol was there. The Minister of Colonies spoke. They buried Eboué alongside Schoelcher and Jean Jaurès. Félix Eboué, the only black man in French history to be officially recognized as a Hero of France by burial in the Pantheon, thus became a permanent symbol of assimilation.

Eboué was not the only black symbol of assimilation and a multiracial Eur-African community. Just before France's surrender in June 1940 German soldiers captured Captain Charles Ntchorere, a Gabonese French citizen, and ordered that he stand hands up with African troops instead of with the whites who were officers like himself. He demanded his rights as a French officer and refused German commands. One bullet through the skull killed him instantly.

African and some Antillean elites of later generations rejected the example of Ntchorere and Eboué. No longer interested in struggling for equality within the empire because they believed the goal impossible and undesirable, these men and women fought for separation from France and independence. No longer interested in leaving their homelands for careers in the so-called metropole, they began to build nations of their own, confident in the rightness of their purpose. Nonetheless, there is no doubt that Eboué's success contributed to their own sense of confidence even if they rejected him as a model. Eboué showed that blacks could have an impact on history, and he showed the meaning of participation.

Up to World War II the world considered Africans and those of African descent to be passive observers on whom history, directed by the whites, acted. Eboué was definitely not a passive observer; he acted and influenced history by introducing cotton in Oubangui-Chari; by fighting for reform in Guadeloupe where he is best remembered and loved; by rallying Tchad to General de Gaulle; and by pushing through reforms in French Equatorial Africa. At a time when no black man's picture or name appeared in a newspaper of Europe or America for having done anything —good or bad—there was Eboué with all the medals, earned in his chosen profession, pinned to his chest, and, "indisputably Negro," acting to influence the course of events. Even an anti-colonialist and pan-Africanist like George Padmore objected when anyone did not give credit to Eboué as a black man who influenced history, though he had once referred to him as a "lackey."[40]

No matter what names other blacks might have used to call him because he worked in Africa, the land of his ancestors, as a colonial official, Eboué never rejected blackness and never forgot Cayenne, his own colonial homeland. He had escaped the hope-

40 Georges Padmore, "Way to Win Africans Against Nazism," *The New Leader* (London), 3 October 1940, p. 3; Letter to Daniel Guerin, cited by James R. Hooker, *Black Revolutionary: George Padmore's Path from Communism to Pan-Africanism* (New York: Praeger, 1967), p. 129.

lessness of Guyane to make something of himself, and h ceeded under very difficult conditions with his own intelli a personal ideology, and a self-control which protected him some of the tensions of a man in his position living in his Always thinking of himself as a black person within the nation, he would have liked to work for the developm Guyane within the French nation. He had become assi and wished to see his country fully developed and inte but his premature death prevented him from exercising an influence over the affairs of Guyane after the war.

The most important part of Eboué's view of his own the belief in the need to participate fully in the affair French nation. Although he recognized the racism of ma Frenchmen, the existence of discrimination, and he k cutting pain of humiliation, he refused to withdraw system like Jean Veneuse, the central character in René *Un Homme pareil aux autres,* who says:

> I know now that neither education nor training can prev race prejudice. I know that most of my superiors never cor more than a Negro, more than a "dirty nigger." . . . Well, what is there to do if not to isolate one's self from a rejects you, and to analyze it? Such has been my conduct And such no doubt will continue to be my conduct unt rives to deliver me from the complex that is suffocating me

Eboué decided, rather, to participate in the game thought he could only realize his potential (helpe friends) within the French nation.

It is, of course, true that France used Eboué for he Every nation uses its participants, for it wants to distinct actor in the world. To succeed it needs men willing to act in such a way that it remains strong; needs men and women willing to give their lives nation—the "supreme loyalty group"—prevails. By accept the participation of groups of people on the religion, or sex the nation stupidly weakens itself.

Participation also permits the individual to us

41 René Maran, *Un Homme pareil aux autres* (Paris: Arc 25.

BIBLIOGRAPHY

I. ARCHIVES

Public

Archives Nationales de France, Annexe des Archives d'Outre-Mer, 1900-1920, Aix-en-Provence.
Archives Nationales de France, Fonds du Général de Gaulle, 1940-1944, Paris.
Archives Nationales de France, Section d'Outre-Mer, 1890-1920, Paris.
Archives Nationales de France—Cayenne, 1850-1910, Cayenne.
Archives Nationales de la République Centrafricaine, 1910-1945, Bangui, Kouango, Bambari, Rafai, Ippy.
Archives Nationales du Mali, Bamako.
Archives Nationales du Tchad, Fort Lamy.
National Archives, United States of America, State Department Files for Brazzaville, Lagos, Leopoldville, 1939-1944, Washington.

Private

E. L. Boutin, Paris.
Eboué Family, Paris-Asnières.
C. Lhuerre, Cayenne.
A. L. Locke, Howard University, Washington.
René Maran, Paris.

II. GUYANE

Abonnenc, E., J. Hurault, R. Saban, *et al., Bibliographie de la Guyane française,* Vol. I (Paris: Larose, 1957).
    Large and good.

Barrère, Pierre, *Nouvelle Relation de la France équinoxiale* (Paris: Piget, 1743).

> History before arrival of Africans; much about Indians.

Castonnet des Fosses, H., *La Colonisation de la Guyane française* (Angers: Lachèse et Dolbeau, 1888).

> Early history.

"Ce que sont, pensent, veulent les étudiants, antillo-guyanais en France: enquête sociologique 1964-1965," in *Alizés*, Special Number, December 1965.

> Opinions about future of Antilles and Guyane.

Compagnie de Jésus, *Mission de Cayenne et de la Guyane française* (Paris: Julien, Lanier, Cosnard et Cie., 1857).

> Letters and reports from early missionaries working among Indians.

Coudreau, Henri A., *La France équinoxiale: tome premier, études sur les Guyanes et l'Amazonie* (Paris: Challamel Ainé, 1886).

> Call for French colonization.

Curtin, Philip D., *The Atlantic Slave Trade: A Census* (Madison: University of Wisconsin, 1969).

> Important study. Information on Guyane and French West Indies.

Damas, L.-G., *Retour de Guyane* (Paris: Librairie Jose Corti, 1938?).

> Sharp criticism of Guyane society and French colonial rule.

———, *Veillées noires* (Paris: Stock, 1943).

> Guyanese stories and *dolos*.

Debien, G., "Les Travaux d'histoire sur les Antilles françaises, chronique bibliographique (1959 et 1960)," *Revue Française d'Histoire d'Outre-Mer*, Vol. XLVIII, No. 171, 1961, pp. 267-308.

De Nouvion, Victor, *Extraits des auteurs et voyageurs qui ont écrit sur la Guyane* (Paris: Société d'Etudes pour la Colonisation de la Guyane Française, Béthune, 1844).

> Appeal to end slavery and for French immigration and investment.

Haurigot, Georges, "Literature orale de la Guyane française," *Revue des Traditions Populaires*, Vol. VIII, No. 1, January 1893, pp. 1-17, 116-20, 164-73.

Henry, A., *La Guyane française—son histoire 1604-1946* (Cayenne: Laporte, 1950).

> Only general history about country, but details disputed by some Guyanese.

Hurault, Jean, *Les Noirs Refugiés boni de la Guyane française* (Dakar: IFAN, Mémoire de l'Institut Français d'Afrique Noire, No. 63).

> Important for African cultural survivals.

Jadfard, René, *Nuits de Chachiri—récit guyanais* (Paris: Fasquelle, 1946).

Jean-Louis, Paul, and Jean Hauger, *La Guyane française—présentation géographique* (Besançon: Imprimerie Jacques, n.d.).

Juminer, Bertène, *Les Bâtards* (Paris: Présence Africaine, 1961).
> "Marginal men": Should we return to Guyane or remain in France?

Lacroix, Louis, *Les Derniers Négriers* (Paris: Amiot-Dumont, 1952).
> Popular version. Information about the "cooly" trade in late 1880's.

Le Citoyen, Jacquemin, *Mémoire sur la Guyane française* (Paris: Baudelot et Eberhart, An II).
> Plea for development funds.

Le Fèvre, Georges, *Bagnards et chercheurs d'or* (Paris: J. Ferenczi, 1925).
> Defense of prison system.

Levat, David, *La Guyane française en 1902*, 2nd edition (Paris: Dunod, 1902).

Levat, E. D., "La Guyane française," *La Quinzaine Coloniale,* Vol. VIII, No. 87, 10 August 1900, pp. 469-72.

Lohier, Michel, *Les Grandes Étapes de l'histoire de la Guyane française (1498-1968)* (Clamecy: Imprimerie Laballery, 1969).
> Most recent general history.

Londres, Albert, *Au Bagne* (Paris: Albin Michel, 1923).
> Guyane as a prison colony. A book disliked by Eboué.

Maugat, E., "La Traite clandestine à Nantes au XIX siecle," *Bulletin de la Société Archéologique et Historique de Nantes,* Vol. 93, 1954, pp. 162-69.

Monnerville, Gaston, Léopold Sédar-Senghor, and Aimé Césaire, *L'Abolition de l'esclavage, discours prononcés, à la Sorbonne le 27 avril 1948,* (Paris: Presses Universitaires de France, 1948).

Mourié, J.-F.-H., *La Guyane française* (Paris: Paul Dupont, 1874).
> Good historical information up to ten years before birth of Eboué.

Owona, Adalbert, "A l'Aube du nationalisme camerounais: la curieuse figure de Vincent Ganty," *Revue Française d'Histoire d'Outre-Mer,* Vol. LVI, No. 204, 1969, pp. 199-235.
> Influence of a Guyanese on Camerounese nationalism.

Peytraud, Lucien, *L'Esclavage aux antilles françaises avant 1789* (Paris: Hachette, 1897).
> Definitions.

Rébufat, Paul, "La Guyane—province française," in *Les Quatre Samedis des Antilles* (Paris: Albert Prévaudeau *et al.*, 1946).
> Solidarity with France and plea for aid.

Resse, Alix, *Guyane française: terre de l'espace* (Paris: Berger-Levrault, 1964).
> Travel book.

Rivière, B., *Observations générales sur la Guyane française* (Bordeaux: Pierre Beaume, 1827).
> Written to encourage investment.

Scelle, Georges, *La Traite négrière aux Indes de Castille—contrats et traités d'assiento* (Paris: Larose et Tenin, 1906).
> Scholarly thesis. Good sources.
Schoelcher, Victor, "Des colonies françaises: abolition immédiate de l'esclavage," extract in Library of Congress, HT 1107.54.
> Statement against slavery by great abolitionist.
Sophie, Ulrich, *Le Cultivateur guyanais* (Cayenne: Paul Laporte, 1958).
> Some information on rural Guyane.
——, *Le Ralliement de la Guyane à la France Libre (16-17 mars 1943)* (Paris: Louis Soulanges, 1964).
> Chapter on Eboué as inspiration for switch to de Gaulle.
H. M. Stationery Office, *French Guiana* (London: Foreign Office, No., 137, 1920).
> Largely derived from Coudreau.
Tarrade, J., "Affranchis et gens de couleur libres à la Guyane à la fin du XVIII siècle, d'après les minutes des notaires," *Revue Française d'Histoire d'Outre-Mer*, Vol. XLIX, 1962, pp. 80-116.
> Data on slaves freed 1777-1798 and status after freedom.
Whily-Tell, A. E., *Je suis un civilisé* (Paris: Société d'Impression de Lancry, 1953).
> Assimilation.

Newspapers—Guyane

L'Avenir de la Guyane, 1919
L'Avenir Guyanais, 1929
Le Cri d'Alarme, 1893
Feuille de la Guyane Française, n.d.
La Feuille Guyanaise, 1935
La Guyane, 1896
La Jeune Garde, 1935
La Nouvelle Guyane, 1931
L'Oeil, 1902-1911
Les Opprimés, irregular
Parallèle 5, 1950's
Le Petit Guyanais, 1914-1916
Le Peuple, 1908
Le Réveil, 1923
Le Travail, n.d.
L'Union Guyanaise, 1914
La Voix de la Guyane, n.d.
La Voix du Peuple, n.d.

III. ANTILLES

Anonymous, "Origines et causes du mouvement gréviste du mois de février 1910 par les petits planteurs" (Basse-Terre: Imprimerie du Gouvernement, 1910).

Bastide, Roger, *Les Amériques noires: les civilisations africaines dans le nouveau monde* (Paris: Payot, 1967).

African survivals and new civilizations.

Boussenot, Georges, *Un Crime politico-judiciaire: l'affaire Légitimus et la race noire,* preface by Henry Bérenger (Paris: Maison des Publications Littéraires et Politiques, 1912).

Candace, Gratien, *La Guadeloupe française 1635-1935* (Paris: Collection de la France Active, 1935).

For the tourist.

Debien, G., "Les Antilles françaises (1968 et 1969)," *Revue Française d'Histoire d'Outre-Mer,* Vol. LVII, No. 208, 1970, pp. 299-354.

Valuable bibliographic essay.

Debien, G., J. Houdaille, *et al.,* "Les Origines des esclaves des Antilles," *Bulletin de l'Institut Français d'Afrique Noire,* Vol. XXIII, Series B, Nos. 3-4, 1961, pp. 363-87; Vol. XXV, Nos. 1-2, 1963, pp. 1-38; Vol. XXV, Nos. 3-4, 1963, pp. 215-65; Vol. XXVII, Nos. 1-2, 1965, pp. 319-71.

Du Bois, W. E. B., "The Negro Mind Reaches Out," in Alain Locke, (editor), *The New Negro: An Interpretation* (New York: Albert and Charles Boni, 1925), pp. 385-414.

Comments on Candace and Achille René-Boisneuf.

Guérin, Daniel, *Les Antilles decolonisées,* introduction by Aimé Césaire (Paris: Présence Africaine, 1956).

Denunciation of colonialism.

Haliar, André, *Dans les Départements d'outre-mer: du Colbertisme au Gaullisme* (Paris: Soulanges, 1965).

Integration of old colonies.

Lasserre, Guy, *La Guadeloupe: étude géographique* (Bordeaux: Union Française d'Impression, 1961).

Important background.

McCloy, Shelby T., *The Negro in the French West Indies* (Lexington: University of Kentucky, 1967).

René-Boisneuf, A., *Les Événements de la Guadeloupe—jours de bataille —mes procès* (Paris: Imprimerie d'Ouvriers Sourds et Muets, 1907).

Testimony on politics in Gaudeloupe.

———, "Comment on traite nos colonies: candidature officielle et moeurs électorales" (chez l'auteur, 1924).

Criticism of Guadeloupe politics and colonial policy.

———, *Manuel du conseiller général des colonies* (Paris: Émile Larose, 1922).

Important for description of workings of institutions in colonies.

Robert, G., *Les Travaux publics de la Guadeloupe,* preface by Gratien Candace (Paris: Librairie Militaire L. Fournier, 1935).

Sainte Croix de la Roncière, *L'Île d'émeraude—dans le sillage des caravelles de Colomb* (Paris: chez l'auteur, 1930).

Criticism of French policies and local corruption.

Newspapers—Guadeloupe (1936-1938)

La Démocratie Sociale (Candace)
La Dépêche Coloniale
L'Echo des Antilles et de la Guyane
L'Economiste
L'Empire Français et la Gazette Coloniale (Paris)
La Gazette Coloniale
L'Homme Enchaîné
L'Informateur
Le Midi Colonial
Le Miroir de la Guadeloupe
Le Nouvelliste (Adolphe Lara)
La Voix du Peuple (Satineau)

Newspapers—Martinique (1932-1934)

L'Action Nouvelle (Delmont)
Le Courier des Antilles
L'Echo
L'Effort
Justice (Aliker—Communist)
La Paix (Roman Catholic)
Le Ralliement
La Résistance (Lagrosillière, SFIO)

IV. FRENCH COLONIAL HISTORY

L'Armée Coloniale, 1891-1910.

Betts, Raymond F., *Assimilation and Association in French Colonial Theory (1890-1914)* (New York: Columbia 1961).
     Very useful book.
Blanchard, Marcel, "Administrateurs d'Afrique noire," *Revue d'Histoire des Colonies,* Vol. XXXIX, 1953, pp. 377-430.
Cohen, William Benjamin, *Rulers of Empire: The French Colonial Service in Africa 1880-1960,* unpublished Ph.D. Dissertation, Stanford University, 1968.
     Very important study.
Les Continents, Paris, 1920's.
     Very important newspaper, considered radical at the time.
Coston, Henry, *Dans les Coulisses de la république* (Paris: C.A.D., 1944).
     Anti-masonic.
———, editor, *La République du Grand Orient* (*Lectures Françaises,* Special Number, January 1964).
Delafosse, Maurice, "Sur l'orientation nouvelle de la politique indigène

dans l'Afrique noire," *Renseignements Coloniaux,* supplement to *Afrique Française,* July 1921, pp. 145-53.

    Call to study African society. Importance of local leadership.

Delavignette, Robert, "La Formation professionnelle de l'administrateur colonial," *L'Empire français et ses ressources (conférences)* (Paris: Presses Universitaires de France, n.d.).

———, *Freedom and Authority in French West Africa* (London: Cass, 1968, new impression, first published 1950).

    Classic liberal French colonial point of view.

———, *Les Paysans noirs* (Paris: Stock, 1947, new edition).

———, "La Politique et l'administration indigène en A.O.F.," *L'Afrique Française,* Vol. 43, No. 1, 1933, pp. 7-11.

    Says French must study African societies and use traditional methods to find chiefs.

———, "Propos sur la décolonisation," extract, *Bulletin des Séances 1967-2,* Académie Royale des Sciences d'Outre-Mer, Brussels.

    Colonial history seen as part of African history.

———, *Les Vrais Chefs de l'empire* (Paris: Gallimard, 1939).

    Important although censured.

La Dépêche Africaine (Paris).

    Newspaper, critical of some colonial abuses.

Des Forges, Roger V., *The Myths of Brazzaville: The War-Time Origins of the French Union 1939-1944,* senior thesis, unpublished, Princeton University, 15 April 1964.

    French currents of thought about empire during World War II.

Fanon, Frantz, *Black Skin White Masks: The Experiences of a Black Man in a White World,* translated by C. L. Markmann (New York: Grove Press, 1967).

    Praise for Eboué in passing.

———, "West Indians and Africans," in Fanon, *Toward the African Revolution,* translated by H. Chevalier (New York: Grove, 1967), pp. 17-27.

    West Indian attitudes, references to Eboué.

Fraisse, André, "Le Journal de poste," *France Eurafrique,* No. 185, June 1967, pp. 28-34.

    Stories taken from early administrative records.

Gann, L. H., and Peter Duignan, *Burden of Empire* (New York: Praeger, 1967).

    Conservative.

Le Grand Orient de France: liste des Francs-Macons du G.'.O.'., Vol. I, A-L (Paris: F.N.C., 1935?)

    Anti-masonic.

Guérin, Daniel, *Front populaire: revolution manquée* (Paris: Julliard, 1963).

    Personal and detailed.

————, "Le Front populaire et la 'décolonisation'," *La France Observateur*, 30 May 1963.

Guichard, Alain, *Les Francs-Maçons* (Paris: Grasset, 1969).
> Objective analysis and history.

Headings, Mildred J., *French Freemasonry Under the Third Republic*, Johns Hopkins University Studies in Historical and Political Science, Series LXVI, Vol. 66, No. 1, 1949 (Baltimore: Johns Hopkins University Press, 1948).
> Excellent but very little on colonies.

Iliffe, John, *Tanganyika Under German Rule 1905-1912* (Cambridge: Cambridge University Press, 1969).
> African response to colonial rule examined. Important point of view.

Janvion, Emile, *La Franc-Maçonnerie et la classe ouvrière—conférence, 3 April 1910* (Paris: Terre Libre, 1912).
> Anti-masonic.

Kanya-Forstner, A. S., *The Conquest of the Western Sudan: A Study in French Military Imperialism* (Cambridge: Cambridge University Press, 1969).
> Detailed and scholarly. Some discussion of Tchad.

Labouret, Henri, "La Politique indigène en Afrique" and "A la recherche d'une politique indigène dans l'Ouest Africain," series in *l'Afrique Française*, June 1930 through February 1931.
> Favors association rather than assimilation, training of chiefs.

Ledi, Alexandre, "De l'action maçonnique à la Guyane française," Cayenne, 26 December 1918.
> Pamphlet. Anti-clerical.

Lefranc, Georges, *Histoire du Front Populaire (1934-1938)* (Paris: Payot, 1965).

Léon Blum: chef de gouvernement 1936-1937 (Paris: Colin, Cahiers de la Fondation Nationales des Sciences Politiques, 1967).

Ly, Abdoulaye, *La Compagnie du Senegal* (Paris: Présence Africaine, 1958).

Mees, Robert, *Vade-mecum du planteur du coton au Congo belge* (Brussels: L'Afrique Belge, 1926).
> History of Belgian interest in cotton in first part of book.

Mortimer, Edward, *France and the Africans 1944-1960* (New York: Walker, 1969).
> Brazzaville Conference and period to independence.

Nardal, Paulette, "Eveil de la conscience de race," *La Revue du Monde Noir*, Paris, Vol. II, No. 6, April 1932, pp. 25-31.
> About Antillean *prise de conscience*. Mentions Eboué.

Newbury, C. W., "The Formation of the Government General of French West Africa," *Journal of African History*, Vol. I, No. 1, 1960, pp. 111-28.

Newbury, C. W., and A. S. Kanya-Forstner, "French Policy and the Origins of the Scramble for West Africa," *Journal of African History,* Vol. X, No. 2, 1969, pp. 253-76.

Roberts, Stephen, *The History of French Colonial Policy 1870-1925* (London: Frank Cass, new impression, 1963).

Saint-Charles, Pierre, *La Franc-Maçonnerie au Parlement* (Paris: Librairie Française, 1956).
> Names and "plots."

Sherwood, John M., *Georges Mandel and the Third Republic* (Stanford: Stanford University Press, 1970).
> Little on Mandel as Minister of Colonies.

Suret-Canale, Jean, *Afrique noire occidentale et centrale: l'ère coloniale 1900-1945* (Paris: Editions Sociales, 1964).
> Valuable information about concessionary regime, administrative organization of French colonies.

Thomas, R., "La Politique socialiste et le problème colonial de 1905 à 1920," *Revue Française d'Histoire d'Outre-Mer,* Paris, Vol. XLVII, 1960, pp. 213-45.
> Very interesting. "Marxist version of Colonial Pact."

Vanhove, Julien, *Histoire du Ministère des Colonies* (Brussels: Academie Royale des Sciences d'Outre-Mer, 1968).
> Comparison of Belgian ministry with French ministry. A little on Africa during World War II.

La Voix des Nègres (Paris).
> Newspaper.

V. OUBANGUI-CHARI AND FRENCH EQUATORIAL AFRICA

Alexandre, P., and G. Andrain, "Cour d'organisation politique et administrative des territoires relevant du Ministère de la France d'Outre-Mer" (Ministère des Finances: Centre de Formation Professionnelle, Paris, n.d.).

Anonymous, "L'Origine et les premières années d'un poste de l'Oubangui-Chari-Fort Crampel" (Bangui, unpublished manuscript, Archives of École Nationale d'Administration).

Augagneur, Victor, "L'Afrique Equatoriale Française," *Lyon Colonial,* Nos. 30 and 31, 1922.
> Economic development stressed.

———, *Erreurs et brutalités coloniales* (Paris: Montaigne, 1927).
> Well-known book at the time of publication. Critical but mainly of colonialism in Madagascar.

Augouard, Monseigneur, *44 Années au Congo: lettres de Mgr. Augouard, 1905-1921* (Evreux: Poussin, 1934).
> Racist.

Ballard, John A., *The Development of Political Parties in French Equatorial Africa,* unpublished thesis, Fletcher School of Law and Diplomacy, December 1963.
> Very detailed political history.

Bobichon, Henry, "Les Peuplades de l'Oubangui—M'Bomou à l'époque des missions Liotard et Marchand 1891-1901," *Renseignements Coloniaux, l'Afrique Française,* No. 9, 1931, pp. 500-505.

Boussenot, Georges, "Une Grande Oeuvre française: la construction du 'Congo-Océan,'" *Revue Politique et Parlementaire,* 9 October 1929, pp. 104-27.
> Apologist for railroad and Governor General Antonetti.

Britsch, Amedée, *Histoire de la dernière mission Brazza* (Paris: A. Davy, n.d.).

Bruel, Georges, *La France équatoriale africaine* (Paris: Larose, 1935).
> Source book.

———, "Noms donnés par des populations de l'Oubangui et du Chari à des planètes à des étoiles et à des constellations," *Journal de la Société des Africanistes,* Paris, Vol. II, Fasc. 1, 1932, pp. 49-53.
> Mentions Eboué's work.

Brunschwig, Henri, *L'Avènement de l'Afrique noire du XIXe siècle à nos jours* (Paris: Armand Colin, 1963).
> Important work.

———, *Mythes et réalités de l'impérialisme colonial français 1871-1914* (Paris: Colin, 1960).
> Basic work.

Challaye, Félicien, *Le Congo français: la question internationale du Congo* (Paris: Félix Alcan, 1909.
> Important. Challaye accompanied de Brazza in 1905 on mission of inspection to Equatorial Africa.

Chauvet, Stephen, *Musique nègre* (Paris: Société d'Editions Géographiques Maritimes et Coloniales, 1921).
> Eboué found this book interesting.

Coquery-Vidrovitch, Catherine, *Le Congo français au temps des grandes compagnies concessionnaires (1898-1930)* (Paris: Sorbonne, April 1970).
> Important study.

Daigre, P., *Oubangui-Chari: témoignage sur son évolution: 1900-1940* (Issoudin: Dillen et Cie., 1947).
> Missionary view.

de Dampierre, Eric, *Un Ancien Royaume bandia du Haut-Oubangui* (Paris: Plon, 1967).
> Section on colonial history very interesting. Important Sociological study.

de la Kéthulle de Ryhove, Lt. Charles, "Deux années de résidence chez le Sultan Rafai," extract from *Bulletin de la Société Royale Belge de Géographie,* Brussels, 1895.

Denis, M., *Histoire militaire de l'Afrique Equatoriale Française* (Paris: Exposition Coloniale Internationale, 1931), pp. 181-237.
> Section on Oubangui-Chari.

Even, "Quelques Coutumes des populations de la Haute-Sangha," *Bulletin de la Société des Recherches Congolaises,* No. 11, 1930, pp. 23-32.

Fontaine, Pierre, *La Mort mystérieuse du Gouverneur Général Renard* (Paris: Editions Jean-Renard, 1943).
> Curious book. Against "foreign trusts."

Georges, Michel, "Pouyamba—village banda en savane centrafricaine" (Paris: BDPA, 1960?).

Gide, André, *Le Retour du Tchad: suite du voyage au Congo* (Paris: Gallimard, 1928).
> Appendices have information on big companies' activities.

——, *Voyage au Congo: carnets de route* (Paris: Gallimard, 1927).
> Saw Eboué.

Gouet, G., "Monographie du village banda de Madmomale (Bambari)," mimeographed, Paris, BDPA, 1959?

Grall, Madame J., "Le Langage tambouriné des peuples d'Afrique," *La Revue du Monde Noir,* Paris, Vol. II, No. 6, April 1932, pp. 35-37.

Kalck, Pierre, *Histoire centrafricaine des origines à nos jours,* unpublished Thesis for Doctorat ès Lettres, University of Paris, June 1970.
> Much useful information about colonial period and beginnings of contemporary politics.

——, *Réalités oubanguiennes* (Paris: Berger-Levrault, 1959).
> General, but superseded by above.

——, *La République centrafricaine,* Encyclopédie Politique et Constitutionnelle, Series Afrique (Paris: Berger-Levrault, 1971).

Lapie, P.-O., *Mes tournées au Tchad* (Algiers: L'Office Français d'Edition, second edition, 1945).
> Eboué's successor in Tchad.

Lebeuf, Jean-Paul, "Le Dépôt national d'archives du Tchad," *Revue Française d'Histoire d'Outre-Mer,* Vol. LVII, No. 208, 1970, pp. 297-98.
> Inventory without too much detail, but helpful.

Le Cornec, Jacques, *Histoire Politique du Tchad de 1900 à 1962* (Paris: Pichon et Durand-Auzias, 1963).
> The only general history of Tchad.

Londres, Albert, *Terre d'ébène: la traite des noirs* (Paris: Albin Michel, 1929).
> First-hand view of horrors of construction of Congo-Océan Railroad.

Maran, René, *Batouala* (Paris: Albin Michel, 1921).

——, *Djouma chien de brousse* (Paris: Albin, Michel, 1927).

——, "Légendes et coutumes nègres de l'Oubangui-Chari: choses vues," in *Les oeuvres libres,* Andre Lichtenberger, editor (Paris: Fayard, No. 147, September 1933), pp. 325-81.

————, *Le Livre de la brousse* (Paris: Albin Michel, 1934).

Martin, R., "Le Paysannat de Ouango" (Bangui: mimeo, n.d.). Technical.

————, "Les Paysannats en Afrique centrale," *L'Agronomie Tropicale,* Vol. XI, No. 3, May-June 1956, pp. 361-77.

Ministère de la Cooperation and République Centrafricaine, "L'Emploi du temps du paysan dans une zone de l'Oubangui central 1959-1960" (Paris: Mission Socio-Economique Centre Oubangui, BDPA, November 1961).
Description of Banda society.

Nême, "Situation actualle de la culture du cotonnier et celle du caféier dans l'Oubangui-Chari," *Revue de Botanique Appliquée et d'Agriculture Coloniale,* Études et Dossiers, No. 73, September 1927.
Attack on Eboué and cotton.

Pepper, Herbert, "Musique centre africaine," in Eugène Guernier, editor, *Afrique Equatoriale Française* (Paris: Encyclopédie Coloniale et Maritime, 1950) pp. 553-72.
Pepper worked with Eboué.

Reste, Governor General, *Action politique économique et sociale en Afrique Equatoriale Française, 1936-1938* (Brazzaville: Imprimerie du Gouvernement Générale, 1938).
Useful data on development.

Rousset, A., "Rapport sur la situation générale pendant le 2e semestre 1900," *Revue Coloniale,* Paris, 1901-1902, pp. 302-18.
Discussion of porters and tax collection.

Sautter, Giles, "Notes sur la construction du chemin de fer Congo-Océan (1921-1934)," *Cahiers d'Études Africaines,* Vol. VII, No. 26, pp. 219-99.
Important study of history, recruitment, resistance, results. Compare with Boussenot.

Savorgnan de Brazza, Pierre, "Lettre à M. Paul Bourde 24 août 1905" (Paris: L. de Soye, 1906).
References to abuses in Africa.

Serre, J., "Histoire economique et sociale du district de Grimari, 1907-1958," mimeographed.
Based on administrative documents and a long sojourn in country.

Sousatte, René Paul, *L'A.E.F.—berceau de l'Union Française* (Paris: Collection, La Voix de l'A.E.F., 1953).
African civil servant's comments on days in Brazzaville with Eboué during the war.

Thompson, Virginia, and Richard Adloff, *The Emerging States of French Equatorial Africa* (Stanford: Stanford University Press, 1960).
Comprehensive and general.

Tisserand, R. P., "Constitution du peuple banda," manuscript in archives of École Nationale d'Administration, Bangui.

Toqué, Georges, "Essai sur le peuple et la langue Banda (region du Tchad)," unpublished.

Vergiat, A. M., *Les Rites secrets des primitifs de l'Oubangui* (Paris: Payot, 1936).
> Disliked by Eboué.

Weinstein, Brian, *Gabon: Nation-Building on the Ogooué* (Cambridge: MIT, 1967).

Zieglé, Henri, *Afrique Equatoriale Française* (Paris: Berger-Levrault, 1952).
> Short, general, free of most biases.

VI. ÉBOUÉ

Articles and Books by Eboué

"Atlantide, continent disparu," unpublished speech, Archives Eboué.

"La Clef musicale des langages tambourinés et sifflés," extract in Archives Nationales de France, Section d'Outre-Mer, Br 4093.

"Le Coton en Oubangui-Chari," *Le Monde Colonial Illustré*, October 1926, pp. 225-27.

Langues sango, banda, baya, mandjia: notes grammaticales, mots groupés d'après le sens, phrase usualles, vocabulaire (Paris: Larose, 1918).

"La Musique et le langage des Banda," *La Revue du Monde Noir*, Paris, Vol. II, No. 6, April 1932, pp. 32-34.
> Extract from résumé of mémoire presented at Exposition Coloniale, 1931.

Les Peuples de l'Oubangui-Chari: essai d'ethnographie, de linguistique et d'économie sociale (Paris: Comité de l'Afrique Française, 1933). Also printed as articles in *Bulletin de la Société des Recherches Congolaises*, No. 17, 1932, pp. 31-51; No. 18, 1933, pp. 57-86. Also in *Renseignements Coloniaux of l'Afrique Française*, No. 11, 1932, pp. 401-14; No. 12, 1932, pp. 452-62; No. 1, 1933, pp. 14-24.

Politique indigène de l'Afrique Equatoriale Française (Brazzaville: Afrique Française Libre, 1942?).

"Les Rites des sociétes de l'Afrique noire comparés aux pratiques de la Franc-Maçonnerie moderne," unpublished manuscript, Archives Eboué.

"Le Sport en Afrique Equatoriale," *Le Monde Colonial Illustré*, No. 103, March 1932, pp. 60-61.

"Les sociétés d'initiés en pays banda (à l'occasion d'un jugement récent)," *Bulletin de la Société des Recherches Congolaises*, No. 13, 1931, pp. 3-15.

With Simonin, N., "Les Bayas de l'Ouham Pendé: organisation familiale
—fiançailles et mariage," *Bulletin de la Société des Recherches Congolaises,* No. 9, 1928, pp. 32-38.

Principle speeches by Eboué

"L'A.E.F. et la Guerre: Discours prononcé devant le Conseil d'Adminis-
tration de la Colonie, le 1er Décembre 1943" (Brazzaville: Editions
du Baobab, 1943).
"A l'Audience Solennelle de la Cour d'Appel de la Guadeloupe et Dé-
pendances pour le Rentrée des Cours et Tribunaux," 4 October
1937, Guadeloupe, Basse-Terre.
"Au Banquet du Front Populaire à Pointe-à-Pitre," Guadeloupe, Basse-
Terre, 6 June 1937.
"Circulaire Générale du 21 mai 1941" (Brazzaville: Imprimerie du Gou-
vernement Général, 1941).
"Au Congrès Annuel des Anciens Combattants de la Guadeloupe,"
Guadeloupe, Point-à-Pitre, 6 February 1938.
"Discours en Conseil d'Administration," Afrique Equatoriale Française,
Afrique Française Libre, Brazzaville, 10 November 1941.
"Discours en Conseil d'Administration," Afrique Equatoriale Française,
Afrique Française Libre, Brazzaville, 19 November 1942.
"Discours prononcés le 1er juillet 1937 à la distribution des prix du
Lycée Carnot" (Jouez-le-jeu), Guadeloupe, Basse-Terre.
"Ouverture, Deuxième Session Ordinaire du Conseil Général," Marti-
nique, Fort-de-France, 28 October 1933.
"Ouverture du Congrés des Fonctionnaires de la Guadeloupe," Guade-
loupe, Basse-Terre, 12 September 1937.
"Ouverture de la Deuxième Session Ordinaire du Conseil Général,"
Guadeloupe, Basse-Terre, 31 October 1936.
"Ouverture de la Deuxième Session Ordinaire du Conseil Général,"
Guadeloupe, Basse-Terre, 30 October 1937.
"Ouverture de la Première Session Ordinaire du Conseil Général,"
Guadeloupe, Basse-Terre, 29 May 1937.
"Ouverture de la Première Session Ordinaire de 1938 du Conseil Géné-
ral," Guadeloupe, Basse-Terre, 28 May 1938.
"Ouverture des Travaux de l'Assemblée Générale de l'Union des An-
ciens Combattants de la Guadeloupe," Guadeloupe, Basse-Terre, 7
February 1937.
Preface to book by Jacques Rogué, *Présence de la France* (Cairo: Edi-
tions de la Revue du Caire, 1943).

Biographies

De La Roche, Jean, *Le Gouverneur Général Félix Eboué 1884-1944*
(Paris: Hachette, 1957).

Memories of Eboué's close collaborator and friend. The best biography in French with more information about Eboué's administrative career than the others.

Eboué, Ginette, "18 Juin 1940—au coeur de l'Afrique Noire avec Félix Eboué," *Voix et Visages—Bulletin Mensuel de l'Association Nationale des Anciens Deportées et Internées de la Résistance,* No. 2, May-June 1958, pp. 1, 2, 4.

Félix Eboué 1884-1944: album imprimé à l'occasion de l'inauguration officielle du monument Eboué, le 21 janvier 1957 (Guadeloupe, n.d.).

Félix Eboué—Compagnon de la libération, L'Hommage du Gouvernement de la France Libre (Basse-Terre: Imprimerie Officielle, 1945).

Les Fêtes funèbres, organisées par les loges maçonniques de Fort-de-France, les dimanches 18 juin 1944 et 17 juin 1945, à la mémoire du regretté et éminent Félix Eboué (Fort-de-France: Imprimerie Officielle, 1945).

Graëve, Eugène, "Georges Mandel et le Gouverneur Félix Eboué," *Union Française et Parlement,* March 1953, No. 36, p. 14.

Kaskeline, Egon, "Félix Eboué and the Fighting French," *Survey Graphic: Color—Unfinished Business of Democracy,* Special Number, Vol. XXXI, No. 11, November 1942, pp. 522-23, 548-50.

Lhuerre, Camille, "10e Anniversaire de la mort du Gouverneur Général Félix Eboué—Souvenirs," *Parallèle 5,* Cayenne, No. 7, 1 June 1954, p. 5.

Maran, René, *Félix, Eboué: grand commis et loyal serviteur 1885-1944* [sic] (Paris: Les Editions Parisiennes, 1957).

Memories of Eboué's intimate friend. Good for younger Eboué and citations from personal letters. Hints of untold events. Valuable but rapidly written and on commission.

Maurice, Albert, *Félix Eboué: sa vie et son oeuvre* (Brussels: Institut Royal Colonial Belge, 1954).

Written with assistance of René Maran and René Isambert. Short but letters and documents cited. The "lesson" of Eboué emphasized.

———, "René Maran et Félix Eboué, une amitié," in *Hommage à René Maran* (Paris: Présence Africaine, 1965), pp. 209-20.

Sketch of their friendship. Based on letters from Eboué to Maran, testimony of Maran.

Monnerville, President, Paul Coste-Floret, and M. Roussel, *Hommage à Victor Schoelcher et Félix Eboué à l'occasion du transfert de leurs cendres au Panthéon le 20 mai 1949* (Cayenne, 1949).

Pinhède, Robert, *Contribution à l'étude de la vie de Félix Eboué, premier gouverneur noir des colonies françaises,* unpublished study (Paris: École Nationale de la France d'Outre-Mer, 1945-1946).

Important because of information taken from Eboué's personnel dossier and reprinted here.

Sophie, Ulrich, *Le Gouverneur Général Félix Eboué*, preface by M. G. Monnerville, Président du Conseil de la République, 2nd edition (Paris: Larose, 1950).
> Personal anecdotes, long citations, information on Guyane by a Guyanese who knew Eboué but who did not know him well.

VII. FREE FRENCH MOVEMENT

Aglion, Raoul, *L'Épopée de la France Combattante* (New York: Editions de la Maison Française, 1943).

Aron, Robert, *Histoire de l'épuration: de l'indulgence aux massacres novembre 1942–septembre 1944* (Paris: Fayard, 1967).

———, *Histoire de Vichy* (Paris, Arthème Fayard, 1954).
> Excellent study.

Comité National Français, "Le Mouvement de la France Libre tel qu'il apparaît aujourd'hui," *Le Caire*, October 1940.
> Why movement formed, role of de Gaulle.

Coulet, Francois, *Vertu des temps difficiles* (Paris: Plon, 1967).

de Gaulle, Charles, *Mémoires de guerre*, three volumes (Paris: Plon, 1954, 1956, 1959).

de Larminat, Edgard, *Chroniques irrévérencieuses* (Paris: Plon, 1962), pp. 1-222, Laurentie Appendix III, pp. 380-90, and Appendix IV, pp. 391-404.
> Ralliement from de Larminat's point of view. A few comments on Eboué's role.

Horne, Alistair, *To Lose a Battle: France 1940* (Boston: Little, Brown, 1969).

Jouve, Gérard, "Les Trois Glorieuses (26, 27, 28 août 1940)," *Renaissances*, No. 15, 25 October 1945, pp. 39-43.

Laurentie, Henri, "Les Colonies françaises devant le monde nouveau," *Renaissances*, No. 15, 25 October 1945, pp. 3-13.

———, "L'Empire au secours de la métropole," Conférence at Palais de Chaillot, 26 January 1945, Office Français d'Edition.

Lémery, Henry, *D'Une République à l'autre: souvenirs de la mêlée politique 1894-1944* (Paris: La Table Ronde, 1964).
> Anti-Gaullist; follower of Pétain and Vichy.

Maule, Henry, *Out of the Sand: The Epic Story of General Leclerc and the Fighting Free French* (London: Odhams, 1966).
> Almost totally about Leclerc. Author dislikes de Gaulle. Some praise for Eboué.

Peyrouton, Marcel, *Du Service public à la prison commune: souvenirs* (Paris: Plon, 1950).
> Vichy point of view.

Préclin, Louis, *Pointe-Noire sous la Croix de Lorraine: vaudeville équatoriale* (Paris: Promotion et Edition, 1967).

Some first-hand accounts of events in A.E.F., 1940-1942.

Siriex-Hertrich, *L'Empire au combat* (Paris: Office Français d'Edition, 1945).

VIII. ASSORTED DOCUMENTS

Annuaire de la Guyane Française.

"Annuaire des Antilles et de la Guyane: indiquant les adresses des amis et des originaires de ces colonies en résidence hors du pays natal," Première Année, 1933 (Paris: Domivar, 1933?).

L'Association des Anciens Elèves de l'Ecole Nationale de la France d'Outre-Mer, *Annuaire* (Paris: 1964).

Guadeloupe et Dépendances, Conseil Général, *Sessions ordinaires,* First and Second for 1936, 1937, 1938.

Guyane Française, *Etats civils, tables décennales.*

Journal Officiel de l'Afrique Equatoriale Française.

Journal Officiel de l'Afrique Occidentale Française.

Journal Officiel de la Guadeloupe.

Lagrosillière, Joseph, "Rapport présenté à la Commission de l'Algérie, des colonies et pays de protectorat, au nom de la Sous-Commission d'enquête en Algérie, sur les résultats des investigations de la Sous-Commission relativement aux divers moyens préconisés pour étendre les droits politiques des indigènes algériens" (Chambre des Députés: Sous-Commission d'Enquête Parlementaire, March-April, 1937).

Martinique, *Bulletin Officiel de la Martinique,* 1932-1934.

————, *Conseil Privé,* 18 October 1929–30 March 1933, Volume 29.

Ministère des Colonies, *Bulletin Officiel,* 1909-1939.

————, *Compte Définitif des Dépenses de l'Exercice 1910.*

Ministère des Colonies, *Le Petit Bulletin de l'Office Colonial (1912).*

Ministère de la France d'Outre-Mer, *Annuaire,* 1909-1939.

République Française, *Journal Officiel,* various years, 1910 to 1945.

Société des Anciens Elèves de l'Ecole Coloniale, *Annuaire,* 1928 (Paris: Société des Anciens Elèves, 1928).

INDEX